Dwight L. Moody

GREAT JOY

Register This New Book

Benefits of Registering*

- ✓ FREE **replacements** of lost or damaged books
- ✓ FREE **audiobook** – *Pilgrim's Progress*, audiobook edition
- ✓ FREE information about new titles and other **freebies**

www.anekopress.com/new-book-registration

*See our website for requirements and limitations.

GREAT JOY

Comprising of Sermons and
Prayer-Meeting Talks Delivered
at the Chicago Tabernacle

"Behold, I bring you good tidings of <u>great joy</u>, which shall be to all people." – Luke 2:10

We love hearing from our readers. Please contact us
at www.anekopress.com/questions-comments with
any questions, comments, or suggestions.

Great Joy
© 2021 by Aneko Press
All rights reserved. First edition 1876.
Updated edition copyright 2021.

Please do not reproduce, store in a retrieval system, or transmit in any form
or by any means – electronic, mechanical, photocopying, recording, or
otherwise, without written permission from the publisher. Please contact us
via www.AnekoPress.com for reprint and translation permissions.

Scripture quotations from The Authorized (King James) Version. Rights in the
Authorized Version in the United Kingdom are vested in the Crown. Reproduced
by permission of the Crown's patentee, Cambridge University Press.

Cover Design: J. Martin

Aneko Press
www.anekopress.com
Aneko Press, Life Sentence Publishing, and our logos are trademarks of
Life Sentence Publishing, Inc.
203 E. Birch Street
P.O. Box 652
Abbotsford, WI 54405

RELIGION / Christian Living / Spiritual Growth
Paperback ISBN: 978-1-62245-559-1
eBook ISBN: 978-1-62245-560-7
10 9 8 7 6 5 4 3 2 1
Available where books are sold

Contents

Notice ix
A Biographical Sketch xi
Ch. 1: Hindrances 1
Ch. 2: The Reward of the Faithful 7
Ch. 3: Charity 17
Ch. 4: The Good Samaritan 27
Ch. 5: His Own Brother 35
Ch. 6: Where Are You? 41
Ch. 7: Heaven, First Address 53
Ch. 8: Heaven, Second Address 63
Ch. 9: The Precious Blood, First Address 73
Ch. 10: The Precious Blood, Second Address 85
Ch. 11: Excuses, First Address 95
Ch. 12: Excuses, Second Address 101
Ch. 13: The Prophet Daniel, First Address 111
Ch. 14: The Prophet Daniel, Second Address 117
Ch. 15: The Prophet Daniel, Third Address 125
Ch. 16: To the Afflicted 131
Ch. 17: Spiritual Blindness 141
Ch. 18: Repentance 151
Ch. 19: What Christ Is to Us 161
Ch. 20: Christ the Good Shepherd 171

Ch. 21: What Shall I Do to Be Saved? 175
Ch. 22: Christ's Command 177
Ch. 23: The Conversion of Saul 183
Ch. 24: Naaman 191
Ch. 25: How to Study the Bible, First Address 199
Ch. 26: How to Study the Bible, Second Address 211
Ch. 27: Trust 215
Ch. 28: Sudden Conversion 219
Ch. 29: Behold! 227
Ch. 30: How to Conduct Inquiry Meetings 237
Ch. 31: The Penitent Thief 247
Ch. 32: Address to Parents, First Address 255
Ch. 33: Address to Young Men, First Address 265
Ch. 34: Praise 275
Ch. 35: Weighed in the Balance 283
Ch. 36: The "I Wills" of Christ 293
Ch. 37: Mission of Christ 303
Ch. 38: The Life of Lot 311
Ch. 39: Their Rock Is Not as Our Rock 319
Ch. 40: The Pharisee and the Publican 331
Ch. 41: Address to Businessmen 341
Ch. 42: The Life and Character of Jacob 351
Ch. 43: Address to Parents, Second Address 355
Ch. 44: The Life of Peter 367
Ch. 45: Address to Young Men, Second Address 371
Ch. 46: The Sacrifice of Christ 385
Ch. 47: Sinners Called to Repentance 399
Ch. 48: Come 413
Ch. 49: Work 425
Ch. 50: Prayer Meeting Talks 437
Dwight L. Moody – A Brief Biography 455
Similar Updated Classics 457

Notice

When Mr. Moody began his series of meetings at the Tabernacle, *The Inter-Ocean* undertook to give accurate phonographic reports of his sermons. The undertaking was a success, and from many admiring friends of Mr. Moody, we have been requested to have the sermons reproduced in book form. In response to such requests, this volume is issued. The sermons have been carefully revised and corrected with the reporter's notes. Omissions made in the daily reports, for want of time or space, have been made good, and some entire sermons reported but crowded out of the paper, will be found in these pages. On the whole, it is believed to be the largest and most correct publication of Mr. Moody's sermons that has been offered to the public.

The Inter-Ocean.
Chicago, Dec. 19th, 1876.

Ira D. Sankey

A Biographical Sketch

The name most prominently associated with Mr. Moody's in evangelistic work is that of Ira David Sankey.

He is the acknowledged Asaph, the sweet singer, "Set over the service of song in the house of Israel."

Ira Sankey was born in Edinburgh, Lawrence County, Pennsylvania, August 28th, 1840.

His parents were highly esteemed in the community for their social qualities and noble traits of character. His father, a man of social and political prominence, was often honored with offices of political trust and responsibility. Young Ira was noted for his vivacious and sprightly spirit and was a universal favorite with his young companions. His pleasant, winning ways and his playful humor, combined with a high sense of honor and manly self-reliance, attracted others to him and enabled him to wield a strong influence over them. His early years at school were not idled away but spent in close and patient application to study. Inspired by a purpose to succeed, he became an excellent student, and soon acquired the elements of a practical and useful education. He was converted in his early life and joined the Methodist Episcopal Church. Here he found an excellent opportunity for the employment of his musical powers, as no Church is more devoted to sacred song and more appreciative of its beauty and power. He at once entered the

Sunday School, and teachers and scholars alike were charmed by the sweet strains of his captivating song.

He sang with so much naturalness, fervor, and sweetness, that all hearts seemed to thrill with a new inspiration and felt that a brighter era had dawned upon the school. During our civil war, he was in the army for a brief period, and on many occasions, inspired the desponding and cheered the sorrowing and dying soldier with the soft, sweet strains of some new song, or of some precious melody of other days. From 1862 to 1871, Mr. Sankey was connected with the Internal Revenue Service and was noted for his careful attention to his duties and enjoyed the entire confidence of his superior officers and also of the people.

Mr. Sankey's first interview with Mr. Moody occurred in June 1870, at the International Convention of the Young Men's Christian Association in Indianapolis. Mr. Moody had heard the sweet singer's voice in the convention, and impressed with its marvelous power, at once resolved to enlist it in his great work. After a formal introduction, Mr. Moody said to him, "I want you." "What for?" said Mr. Sankey. "To help me in my work," was the reply. "But I cannot leave my business," was the response. "You must," said Mr. Moody. "You must give up your business and come with me. I have been looking for you these eight years."

Thus, suddenly was this world-renowned singer called to join the most efficient evangelist of modern times. The history of his work with Mr. Moody in Europe, in Brooklyn, in Philadelphia, in New York, and Chicago, is too recent to need extended notice in this brief sketch. Suffice it to say, the almost universal conviction is that Mr. Sankey is as necessary to the great evangelistic work as Mr. Moody himself.

Both are divinely accredited heralds of the cross – one heralding in simple, lucid language the gospel of great joy, and the other enunciating the glad tidings in sweet, triumphant strains of Christian song.

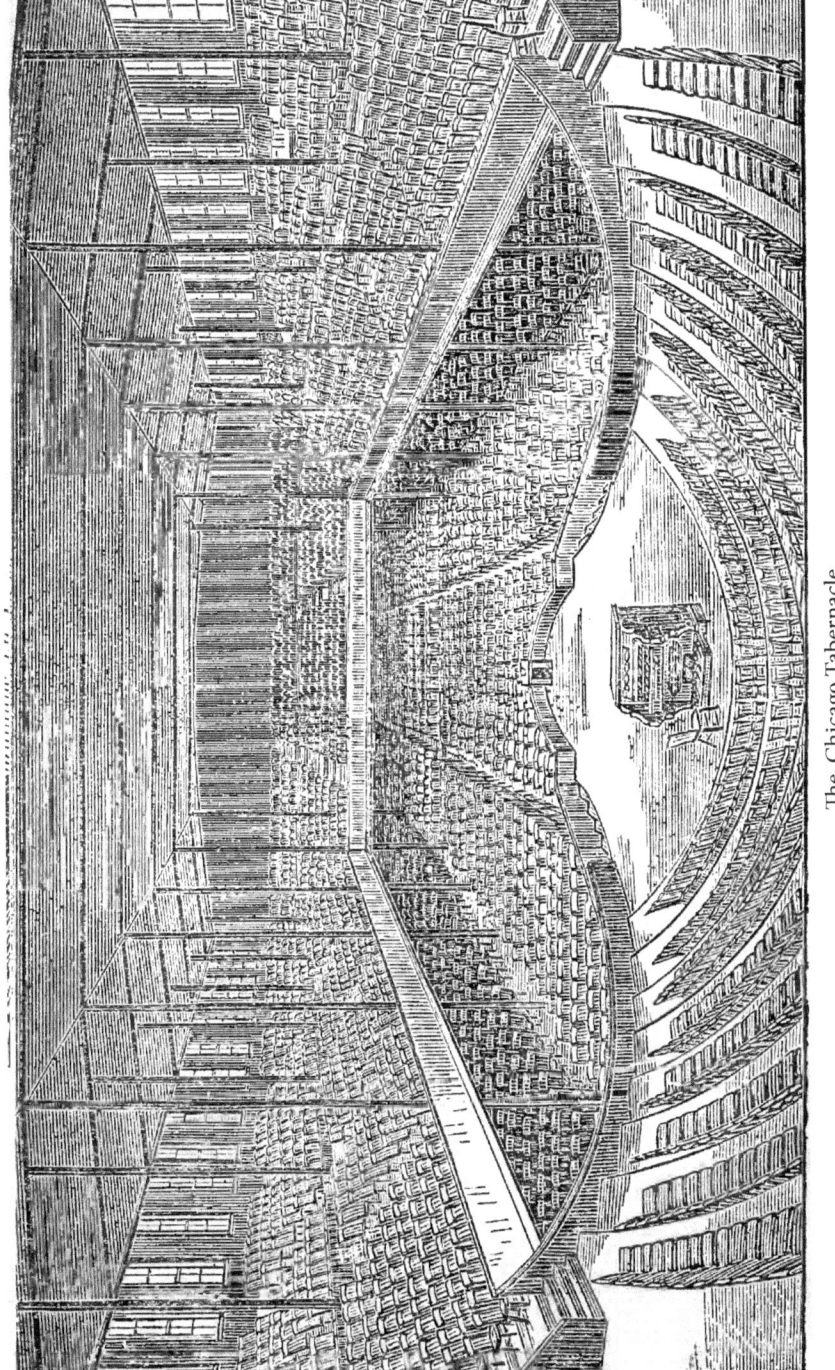

The Chicago Tabernacle

Hindrances

I want to call your attention for a few minutes this morning to a verse you have heard read in the 11th chapter of the gospel according to John – a part of the 39th verse: *"Jesus said, Take away the stone."* Now I have not any doubt but that nearly everyone in this congregation is looking for a blessing in Chicago. I've no doubt that hundreds of you are expecting a great work here. If you are not so expecting, you ought to be, and if God does not do a great and mighty work here it will not be His fault, but it will be our own. I find a class of people who say, "Well, we must wait until God works, and when God is ready, we will see a great work." Now, if I read my Bible and understand Scripture, God is always ready. We talk about the "set time" for God to favor us. The set time is when you and I get ready to let God work for us, just when we choose to roll away the stones that prevent His coming to our souls. Someone must take away these stones, someone must roll them off, so the Lord, Redeemer, and Savior can get at us. There is no doubt but that He himself could send down legions of angels to clear away every single stone. If even the word of His mouth should go out, every stone-like obstacle in His path would suddenly disappear, just as Satan did from His presence in the wilderness.

But God does not work in that way. He works through others. He did not Himself roll away the stone from Lazarus' grave; He said to His disciples surrounding Him, and to His disciples in all times, "Take away the stone." Now I find a great many men, and a great many wives, and a great many Christians, too, who ask God to roll away the stone, and because He does not answer their prayer, they throw the blame on God. Why, the blame is not His; it is theirs. God always works in partnership. When He is asked to do a thing, He can only do it when He first sees an active disposition in the asker to help to get the blessing. This failure to second God's work for us comes from unbelief. Such a halfhearted man does not believe God will grant his prayer and so fails to carry out his own part of the program. The mother that prays for the reclaiming of a drunken son or a dissolute husband must faithfully do her part to this end and then must have full belief that God will do the rest.

There is something for us all to do for our fellow creatures, and it is the stone of unbelief that blocks up the way and keeps us from doing it. It is just this great stone that must first be rolled out of the way in this city. Let us believe that God can do a great work here, and that practical belief will make us work as we ought to. It will be a hard work, but with this lever of faith it can be done, and in short order. There must be honest work, a lifting up of one's self first as far as may be and then a leaving of the rest to God, Whose word will completely roll the stone away and raise the dead. And what a need there is for this resurrection in all our souls! How dead our sense of sin! How we forget that iniquity cannot live in our heart, in our word, and in our act! How careless and indifferent even, to have things anywise different than they are! Is the fault God's? No, the only trouble is with ourselves; we will not ask Him that He will help us to do better things. We do not want to do them.

How lukewarm the love of God in our hearts and how selfish and cold in consequence, our thoughts towards our neighbor! It is a wonder to me how low our standard can fly, and yet we can profess to be Christians. Do we not need to cry that God will revive us? Yes, it is we ourselves that must first be quickened. Those of us who profess to be Christians must feel anew in our own hearts the joys of sins forgiven and a rekindling of the early fires of faith and holy living. Only thus can good influences be made effectual on those outside.

I have heard many complain of the answer of prayer being withheld when the secret lay just here. A woman, though a professing Christian, need not pray for her husband's conversion if she be governed by an evil temper. She need not talk even to God about her husband until she gets command of her railing tongue and wicked looks. If you are not Christ-like in your behavior, you need not expect to be taken for an example by your godless neighbor. He will not imitate you, even if he does not despise you for your hollow professions.

I recall an illustration used by my dear friend Morehouse when he was in this city. The Apostle Paul stood with the gathering crowd about the fire, warming himself after the shipwreck, when, as they piled the wood on the fire, a viper sprang from the flame and fastened itself on his hand. Immediately, the gaping crowd cried out that he was a reprobate, whom, though he had escaped the waves, vengeance would not let live. But presently, Paul shook the viper from his hand into the fire. The people, seeing he did not die, changed their opinion entirely, and Paul then preached to them the saving word of life. The apostle shook off the viper, and the confidence of men flowed out to him. Let us Christians all imitate this grand example; let us shake off, with God's help, the vipers of evil temper and all the evil things that make our Christianity a nullity, and too often, a reproach in the eyes of those we would call to a like name and inheritance with ourselves. And, as a community, as well, we must shake off the venomous beast, whose poison not only repels others, but kills and enfeebles ourselves.

The vipers of London are different from those of New York; and, again, our own are unlike either of these. Covetousness, the inordinate greed for gain, has fastened on the hand of Chicago, along with many another Western city, and the sting will be worse and worse unless a remedy is found for us. We talk with an appetite much too keen about getting gain and the chances for moneymaking. Yet this very trait, confessedly an evil, is an argument to our hand. There is a cry in commercial circles, loud and prolonged, for a revival in business – all classes of business. In this country, during the past twenty years, I never heard anyone crying out against it. But if you talk about getting a revival in God's business, there is a class of people who at once shake their heads. They do not know about it; they are afraid it won't work. A strange inconsistency, a thing is all right in their own concerns, but all wrong in God's. For the purposes of this comparison, the two things are not different at all.

God's work, like man's work, may have stages of activity, and the

Christian, just as much as the merchant, should seek earnestly for a revival in trade. Oh, let us roll away this stone of unbelief and indifference, and we will soon hear a voice from the place of the stone crying, "Lazarus, come forth." Let us only cry as earnestly and loud for a revival as our businessmen have done and are now doing, and the powers and affections of our souls will spring up and bloom to eternal life. Our quickened souls and those of our friends will be made glad, and rejoice together in time and eternity. Should no right time come in God's fields, when can the farmer have his harvest time? How active the farmers are in getting hands to help them through the rush. The right time also comes periodically in the kingdom of heaven on earth – a ripening time when God calls His reapers to put in their sickles.

Three stones I will especially refer to this morning, or mountains if you prefer – for that is what they are – to be rolled from our caves before the dead Lazarus, quickened to life, can come forth. A great stone to be rolled away is unbelief, already spoken of. If I ask the Christian man in Chicago, "Do you believe God can revive this work?" I do not want him to say, "I do not believe He can. I have been here about fifteen years, and during all that time there has not been a successful attempt at reviving His work." Well, it may be so that the work has not gone well. What was the trouble? I believe it was simply because people did not believe the work could really be done. But surely there is a person in the town that knows that everything is possible with God. Let us take this stand, to believe that God is actually going to do something. There is no drunkard who should despair, for I believe that God is going to save hundreds of them. He can and He will destroy their love of strong drink completely, and I believe there will soon be a cleansing thunderstorm in His atmosphere here.

When I was in Glasgow, a skeptic insisted that all my converts were women and old men verging on the grave. At the next meeting in that city, there were present in the hall thirty-three hundred men, and of these, twenty-seven hundred were young men. The skeptic next insisted that not a wild or reckless or drunken man came under God's reviving influence. At the very next meeting a gambler, and a short time afterwards, a most notorious drunkard in town experienced saving grace. And so let it be here. We want to see thieves, gamblers, and harlots saved. Let us have faith, for according to our faith shall it be done to us, just as Martha saw Lazarus alive through trust in Jesus's words. If we believe, we are told that we may order mountains to be removed and they will be cast into the sea. Oh, may God strike down our unbelief to the resurrection to life of even the vilest sinners in this city.

The next terrible stone to be rolled away is prejudice. Oh, how it came in among the churches against revivals. How many men you hear say: "Well, I am prejudiced against revivals; I do not believe in them." They believe in revivals in everything else. They say, "Agitate politics and trade, and let us have a revival in everything else – but religion." So many whom I have addressed here on this subject have inveighed against revivals in religion, shaking their heads and saying no good can come out of revivals. Well, my dear friends, when Philip, the sage deacon, went to Nathaniel to tell him about Jesus, and Nathaniel objected, "Could any good come out of Nazareth?" he just answered, "Come and see." So I answer you, come and see.

Spend a week waiting on God to see if the work is not to be a power of God to the saving of many. "Oh," but someone may say, "I know too many bad things about these unhealthy emotional outbreaks to approve of them." My friend, I know far more of the possible evils you would shun and know them to be sometimes real ones, but what of it? Because some revivals turn out to be useless or in some developments positively bad, must the system be thrown aside? No. The Democrat does not desert his politics for some minor flaw about them and neither does the Republican if some of his standard bearers have done corruptly. Professional and business men are not degraded by the shortcomings of individuals, and all through and through there is seen to be no limit to this principle. God's mighty engine in revivals is not to be thrown aside for even considerable defects. Under its operations time was when three thousand men were added to the Church in one day. Finally, we cannot speak against these special meetings for they are planned in Scripture. The Bible is full of chronicles of their workings. They are developments of Christianity, no manmade innovation whatever, and the best possible agencies for the redemption of sinners.

And then there is this miserable sectarian spirit that once had a despotic hold on men. There was a time when its grasp was that of iron, but blessed be God, that time is past. I remember fifteen years ago the Methodist insisted that he was a Methodist, although lending a hand to the revival in progress. The Congregationalist was a Congregationalist, though he too cooperated in the good work. The Presbyterian and the Baptist and others were first their denominational selves though condescending for a few days to work in yoke in a common cause. Yet it was really and necessarily condescension, and there was enough of it in those meetings to kill them, and it nearly did. This sectarian stone is a real stone though nothing like the boulder it used to be.

The rolling-away process must be pushed vigorously; let us heave it away altogether out of sight. Let us have none of that spirit in this meeting. Talk not of this sect and that sect, this party and that party, but solely and exclusively of the great, comprehensive cause of Jesus Christ. When Christ came into the world had He allied Himself with the Sadducees, they would have warmly upheld Him; if He had joined the Pharisees, they would not have let Him be crucified. But He kept clear of them, and just so we should do in this glorious work opening before us. In this ideal brotherhood there should be one faith, one mind, one spirit; in this city let us starve it out for a season to actualize this glorious truth.

You remember in the Old Testament Eldad and Medad took upon themselves priestly duties, and Joshua, agitated because of the irregularity, ran and told the scandal to Moses. But you also remember how Moses reproved his informant, who was engaged in perhaps the only small business of his life, and told him to rebuke them not; they prophesied well, however irregularly. It was just so with Christ. When word was carried by overly helpful followers that men who "were not of us" were casting out devils, He rebuked not those who were thus benefiting their kind but the talebearers. Oh yes, let us surrender partisanship and contend for Christ only. Oh, that God may so fill us with His love and the love of souls that no thought of minor sectarian parties can come in, that there may be no room for them in our atmosphere whatever, and that the Spirit of God may give us one mind and one spirit here to glorify His holy name. Let us pray.

The Reward of the Faithful

I want to call your attention to the 4th chapter of the gospel of St. John and to part of the 36th verse: *"And he that reaps receives wages and gathers fruit unto life eternal."* I want you to get the text into your hearts. We have a thousand texts to every sermon, but they slip past the hearts of men and women. If I can get this text into your hearts today with the Spirit of God, these meetings will be the brightest and most glorious ever held in Chicago, for it is the word of the Lord and His word is worth more than ten thousand sermons. "He that reaps receives wages." I can speak from experience. I have been in the Lord's service for twenty-one years, and I want to testify that He is a good paymaster, that He pays promptly. Oh, I think I see faces before me light up at these words. You have been out in the harvest fields of the Lord and you know this to be true. To go out and labor for Him is a thing to be proud of, to guide a poor, weary soul to the way of life and turn his face towards the golden gates of Zion.

The Lord's wages are better than silver and gold because He says that the loyal soul shall receive a crown of glory. If the mayor of Chicago proclaimed that he had work for the men, women, and children of the city and that he would give them a dollar a day, people would say this was very good of the mayor. This money, however, would fade away in a short time. But here is a proclamation coming directly from the throne of grace to every man, woman, and child in the wide world to gather into God's vineyard where they will find treasures that will never fade and will be crowns of everlasting life. The laborer will find treasures laid up in his Father's house and after serving faithfully here will be greeted by friends assembled there. Work for tens of thousands of men, women, and children! Think of the reward! These little children, my friends, are apt to be overlooked, but they must be led to Christ. Children have done a great deal in the vineyard. They have led parents to Jesus. It was a little girl that led Naaman to his Healer. Christ can find useful work for these little ones. He can see little things, and we ought to pay great attention to them.

As I was coming along the street today I thought that if I could only impress upon you all that we have come here as to a vineyard to reap and to gather, we shall have a glorious harvest and we will want every class to assist us. The first class we want is the ministers. There was one thing that pleased me this morning and that was the eight thousand people who came to this building and the large number of ministers, tears trickling down their cheeks, who seized me by the hand and gave me a "God bless you!" It gave me a light heart.

There are some ministers who get behind the posts as if they were ashamed of being seen in our company and of our meetings. They come to criticize the sermon and to pick it to pieces. No effort is required to do this. We don't want the ministers to criticize but to help us and tell us when we are wrong. There was one minister in this city who did me a great deal of good when I first started out. When I commenced to teach the Word of God I made many blunders. I have learned that in acquiring anything a man must make many blunders. If a man is going to learn any kind of trade – carpenter's, plumber's, painter's – he will make any number of mistakes. Well, this minister, an old man, used to take me aside and tell me my errors. So we want the ministers to come to us and tell us of our blunders. If we get them to do this and join hands with us, a spiritual fountain will break over every church in the city.

Many ministers have said to me, "What do you want us to do?" The Lord must teach us what our work shall be. Let every child of God come up to these meetings and say, "Teach me, O God, what I can do to help these men and women who are inquiring the way to be saved," and at the close of the meetings draw near to them and point out the way. If men and women are to be converted in great meetings, it will be by personal dealings with them. What we want is personal contact with them. If a number of people were sick, and a doctor prescribed one kind of medicine for them all you would think this was wrong. This audience is spiritually diseased, and what we want is that Christian workers will go to them and find out their trouble. Five minutes' private consultation will teach them. What we want is to get at the people. Every person has his own burden; every family has a different story to tell. Take the gospel of the Lord to them and show its application. Tell them what to do with it to answer their own cases; let the minister come into the inquiry room.

An old man, a minister in Glasgow, Scotland, was one of the most active in our meetings over there. When he would be preaching elsewhere, he would drive up in a cab with his Bible in his hand. It made no difference where in Glasgow he was preaching - he managed to attend nearly every one of our services. This old man would come in and tenderly speak to those assembled and let one soul after another see the light. When we arrived in Scotland, this man's congregation was comparatively small, but through his painstaking efforts to minister to those in search of the word, by the time we left Glasgow, his church could not hold all the people who sought admission. I do not know of any man who helped us like Dr. Andrew Bonar. He was always ready to give the weak counsel and point the way out to the soul seeking Christ. If we have not ministers enough, let those we have come forward and their elders and deacons will follow.

The next class we want to help us reach the people is the Sunday school teachers; I value their experience next to that of the ministers. In the cities where we have been, teachers have come to me and said, "Mr. Moody, pray for my Sunday school scholars," and I took them aside and pointed out their duties and showed them that they ought to be able to pray for their pupils. Very often they would come to the next meeting, and the prayer would go up from them, "God bless my scholars."

In one city we went to, a Sunday school superintendent came to his minister and said, "I am not fit to gather sinners to life eternal; I cannot be superintendent any longer." The minister asked, "What is the reason?" and the man said, "I am not right with God." Then the minister advised him that the best thing, instead of resigning, was to get right with God. So he prayed with the teacher that the truth would shine upon him, and God lit up his soul with the word. Before I left that town, the minister told me all doubt had fled from that superintendent's mind, and he had gone earnestly to work and gathered over six hundred scholars into the school of his church.

The Lord can bless, of course, despite schools and teachers, but they are the channels of salvation. Bring your classes together and pray for God to convert them. We have from three thousand to five thousand teachers here. Suppose they all said, "I will try to bring my children to Christ." What a reformation we should have! Don't say that boy is too small or that girl is too puny or insignificant. Everyone is valuable to the Lord. I once found a teacher at our services who ought to have been attending to her class. When I asked why she was at our meeting, she replied, "Well, I have a very small class – only five little boys. "What," said I, "you have come here and neglected these little ones? Why, in that little towhead may be the seeds of a reformation. There may be a Luther, a Wheaton, a Wesley, or a Bunyan among them. You may be neglecting a chance for them, the effects of which will follow them through life." If you do not look to those things, teachers, someone will step into your vineyard and gather the riches you would have.

Look what that teacher did in southern Illinois. She had taught a little girl to love the Savior, and the teacher said to her, "Can't you get your father to come to the Sunday school?" This father was a swearing, drinking man, and the love of God was not in his heart. But under the tutoring of that teacher, the little girl went to her father, told him of Jesus's love and led him to that Sunday school. What was the result? I heard before leaving for Europe that he had been instrumental in founding over seven hundred and eighty Sunday schools in southern Illinois. What a privilege a teacher has – a privilege of leading souls to Christ. Let every Sunday school teacher say, "By the help of God I will try to lead my scholars to Christ."

It seems to me that except for mothers, we have more help in our revivals from young men than from any other class. The young men are pushing, energetic workers. Old men are good for counsel and they should help, by their good words, the young men in making Christianity aggressive. These billiard halls have been open long enough. There is many a gem in those places that only needs the way pointed out to fill their souls with love of Him. Let the young men go plead with them, bring them to the Tabernacle, and do not let them go out without presenting the claims of Christ and His never-dying love. Take them by the hand and say, "I want you to become a Christian." What we want is hand-to-hand conflict with the billiard saloons and drinking halls. Do not fear but enter them and ask the young men to come. I know that some of you say in a scornful way, "We will never be allowed to enter; the people who go there will cast us out." This is a mistake. I know that I have gone to them and remonstrated and have never been unkindly treated. Some of the best workers have been men who have been proprietors of these places and men who have been constant frequenters.

There are young men there breaking their mothers' hearts and losing themselves for all eternity. The Spirit of the Lord Jesus Christ asks you to seek them out. If we cannot get them to come here, let the building be thrown aside and let us go down and hunt them up and tell them of Christ and heaven. If we cannot get a multitude to preach to, let us preach, even if it be to one person. Christ preached one of His most wonderful sermons to that woman at the well. Shall we not be willing to go to one, as He did, and tell that one of salvation?

And let us preach to men, even if they are under the influence of liquor. I may relate a little experience. In Philadelphia, at one of our meetings, a drunken man stood up. Till that time, I had no faith that a drunken man could be converted. But this man got up and shouted, "I want to be prayed for!" The friends who were with him tried to draw him away, but he shouted only louder. Three times he repeated his request. His call was attended to and he was converted. God has power to convert a man, even if he is drunk.

I have still another lesson. I met a man in New York who was an earnest worker, and I asked him to tell me his experiences. He said he had been a drunkard for over twenty years. His parents had forsaken him and his wife had cast him off and married someone else. Once, while he was drunk, he walked into a lawyer's office in Poughkeepsie. This lawyer proved a good Samaritan; he reasoned with him and told him he could be saved. The man rejected the idea. He said, "I must be pretty low when my father, my mother, my wife, and kindred cast me off, and there is no hope for me here or hereafter." But this good Samaritan showed him how it was possible to secure salvation. He got him on his feet, got him on his beast, like the good Samaritan of old, and guided his face toward Zion. And this man said to me, "I have not drunk a glass of liquor since." He is now leader of a young men's meeting in New York. I asked him to come up last Saturday night to Northfield, my native town, where there are a good many drunkards, thinking he might encourage them to seek salvation. He came and brought a young man with him.

They held a meeting and it seemed as if the power of God rested upon that meeting when these two men told what God had done for them – how He had destroyed the works of the devil in their hearts and brought peace and complete happiness to their souls. These grog shops here are the works of the devil; they are ruining men's souls every hour. Let us fight against them, and let our prayers go up in our battle, "Lord, manifest Your power in Chicago this coming month." Converting rum sellers may seem a difficult thing for us, but it is an easy thing for God.

A young man in New York got up and thrilled the meeting with his experience. "I want to tell you," he said, "that nine months ago a Christian came to my house and said he wanted me to become a Christian. He talked to me kindly and encouragingly, pointing out the error of my ways, and I became converted. I had been a hard drinker, but since that time I have not touched a drop of liquor. If anyone had asked who the most hopeless man in that town was, they would have pointed to me." Today this young man is the superintendent of a Sunday school. Eleven years ago, when I went to Boston, I had a cousin who wanted a little of my experience. I gave him all the help I could, and he became a Christian. He did not know how near death was to him. He wrote to his brother and said, "I am very anxious to get your soul to Jesus." The letter somehow went to another city and lay from the 28th of February to the 28th of March – just one month. He saw it was in his brother's handwriting and tore it open and read the above words. It struck a chord in his heart and was the means of converting him. And this was the Christian who led this drunken young man to Christ.

This young man had a neighbor who had drunk for forty years. He went to that neighbor and told him what God had done for him and the result was another conversion.

I tell you these things to encourage you to believe that the drunkards and saloonkeepers can be saved. There is work for you to do. The harvest shall be gathered and what a scene will be on the shore when we hear the Master on the throne shout, "Well done! Well done!"

Let me say a word to you, mothers. We depend a good deal upon you. It seems to me that there is not a father or mother in all Chicago who should not be in sympathy with this work. You have daughters and sons, and if work is done now, they will be able to steer clear of many temptations and will be able to lead better lives. It seems to me selfishness if they sit down inactive and say, "There is no use in this. We are safe ourselves, what is the use of troubling?" If the mothers and fathers of the whole community would unite their prayers and send up appeals to God to manifest His power, He would answer with a mighty work.

I remember in Philadelphia we wanted to see certain results, and we called a meeting of mothers. There were five to eight thousand mothers present, and each of them had a particular burden upon her heart. There was a mother who had a wayward daughter, another a reckless son, another a bad husband. We spoke to them confidently, and we bared our hearts to one another. They prayed for aid from the Lord and that grace might be shown to these sons and daughters and husbands, and the result was that our inquiry rooms were soon filled with anxious and earnest inquirers.

Let me tell you about a mother in Philadelphia. She had two wayward sons. They were wild, self-indulgent youths. They were to meet on a certain night and join in immorality. The rendezvous was at the corner of Market and Thirteenth streets where our meetings were held. One of the men entered the large meeting, and when it was over went to the young men's meeting nearby, was quickened, and there prayed that the Lord might save him. His mother had gone to the meeting that night and, arriving too late, she found the door closed. When that young man went home, he found his mother praying for him, and the two mingled their prayers together. While they were praying, the other brother came from the other meeting and brought tidings of being converted. At the next meeting, the three got up and told their experience, and I never heard an audience so thrilled before or since.

Another incident. A wayward boy in London whose mother was very anxious for his salvation said to her, "I am not going to be bothered with your prayers any longer. I will go to America and be rid of them." "But, my boy," she said, "God is on the sea, and in America, and He hears my prayers for you." Well, he came to this country, and as they sailed into the port of New York, some of the sailors told him that Moody and Sankey were holding meetings in the Hippodrome. The moment he landed he started for our place of meeting, and there he found Christ. He became a most earnest worker, and he wrote to his mother to tell her that her prayers had been answered; that he had been saved and had found his mother's God.

Mothers and fathers, lift up your hearts in prayer that there may be hundreds of thousands saved in this city.

When I was in London, there was a lady dressed in black up in the gallery. All the rest were ministers. I wondered who that lady could be. At the close of the meeting, I stepped up to her, and she asked me if I did not remember her. I did not, but she told me who she was, and her story came to my mind.

When we were preaching in Dundee, Scotland, a mother came up with her two sons, 16 and 17 years old. She said to me, "Will you talk to my boys?" I asked her if she would talk to the inquirers because there were more inquirers than workers. She said she was not a good enough Christian, was not prepared enough. I told her I could not talk to her then. Next night she came to me and asked me again, and the following night she repeated her request. Five hundred miles she journeyed to get God's blessing for her boys. Would to God we had more mothers like her. She came to London, and the first night I was there I saw her in the Agricultural Hall. She was accompanied by only one of her boys – the other had died. Towards the close of the meetings, I received this letter from her:

"Dear Mr. Moody, For months I have never considered the day's work ended unless you and your work had been specially prayed for. Now it appears before us more and more. What in our little measure we have found has no doubt been the happy experience of many others in London. My husband and I have sought as our greatest privilege to take unconverted friends one by one to the Agricultural Hall, and I thank God that, with a single exception, those brought under the preaching from your lips have accepted Christ as their Savior and are rejoicing in His love."

That lady was a lady of wealth and position. She lived a little way out of London; gave up her beautiful home and took lodgings near the Agricultural Hall, so as to be useful in the inquiry room. When we went down to the Opera House, she was there. When we went down to the east end, there she was again, and when I left London she had the names of 150 who had accepted Christ from her. Some said that our work in London was a failure. Ask her if the work was a failure, and she will tell you. If we had a thousand such mothers in Chicago, we would lift it.

Go bring your friends here to the meetings. Think of the privilege, my friends, of saving a soul. If we are going to work for good, we must be up and about it. Men say, "I have not the time." Take it. Ten minutes every day for Christ will give you good wages. There is many a man who is working for you. Take them by the hand. Some of you with silver locks, I think I hear you saying, "I wish I were young, how I would rush into the battle!" Well, if you cannot be a fighter, you can pray and lead on the others. There are two kinds of old people in the world. One grows chilled and sour, and other lights up every meeting with their genial presence and cheers on the workers. Draw near, old age, and cheer on the others. Take them by the hand and encourage them.

There was a building on fire. The flames leaped around the staircase, and from a three-story window a little child was seen who cried for help. The only way to reach it was by a ladder. One was obtained and a fireman ascended, but when he had almost reached the child, the flames broke from the window and leaped around him. He faltered and seemed afraid to go further. Suddenly someone in the crowd shouted, "Give him a cheer!" and cheer after cheer went up. The fireman was nerved with new energy and rescued the child. Just so with our young men. Whenever you see them wavering, cheer them on. If you cannot work yourself, give them cheers to nerve them on in their glorious work. May the blessing of God fall upon us this afternoon, and let every man and woman be up and doing.

Charity

You will find the text in the first verse of the chapter I read this evening, 1st Corinthians 13: "*Though I speak with the tongues of men and of angels, and have not charity, I am become as sounding brass or a tinkling cymbal.*" You, I have no doubt, wondered how it is that they have not met with more success. I think if I have asked myself this question once, I have a thousand times: "Why is it that I have not had greater success?" But I never read this chapter without finding out. I think it would profit every Christian to read it at least once a week. A man may be a preacher and have all the eloquence of a Demosthenes; he may be the greatest pulpit orator that ever lived, but if love is not the motive power "it is as sounding brass or tinkling cymbal." A good many churches have eloquent ministers. The people go there and listen critically and closely, but there are no converts. They wonder why. The cause has been the lack of love. If a minister has not got love deep in his heart, you may as well put a boy in the pulpit and make him beat a big drum. His talking is like the "sounding of brass."

Failures to make converts in those churches are common, and the reason so many preachers have failed is because love has not been the motivating power. The prophet may understand, prophesy, and interpret it in such a clear way as to astonish you. I have met men and sat down beside them, and they would dig out the most wonderful truths of prophecy which I could not see. I have sat at their feet and wondered at their power in this respect and wondered also why it was that they were not blessed with more converts. I have sought the cause and invariably found it was want of love. Though he is deep in learning and in theology, if a man has no love in his heart he will do no good. A man may understand all the mysteries of life, may be wonderful in seeking out truths, yet may not be blessed by winning men.

Paul says that though a man understands all mysteries but has no love, his understanding goes for nothing. He goes a step further and says that a man may give large sums to feed the poor, but if love does not accompany the gift, it goes for naught in the sight of God. The only fruit on the tree of life worth having is love. Love must be the motivating power. A good, philanthropic man may give his thousands to the poor and be praised in the newspaper, yet if love does not prompt the deed, it goes for nothing in God's sight. Many a man here is very liberal to the poor. If you ask him for a donation to a charitable purpose, he draws his purse and puts down $1,000; if you come to him for a subscription for this or that theological seminary, he will draw his check instantly. But God looks down into that man's heart, and if he has no love, it goes for nothing. Some men would give everything they have; they would even give their body for a good cause or truth they value, yet there is no love in the act.

The main teaching of this chapter is that love must be the motivating power in all our actions. If our actions are performed merely out of a sense of duty, God will not accept us. I've heard this word *duty* in connection with Christian work till I am tired of it. I have come down to a meeting and someone has asked a brother to get up and speak. After considerable persuasion he has got upon his feet and said, "Well, I did not intend to speak when I came down tonight, but I suppose it is my duty to say something." And it is the same with the Sunday school; many teachers take up classes from a sense of duty. There is no love in them, and their services go for nothing. Let us strike for a higher plane – let us throw a little love into our actions, and then our services will be accepted by God if love will be the motivating power.

I have an old mother away down in the Connecticut mountains, and I have been in the habit of going to see her every year for twenty years. Suppose I go there and say, "Mother, you were very kind to me when I was young, you were very good to me. When father died, you worked hard to keep us together, and so I have come to see you because it is my duty." I went then only because it was my duty. Then she should say to me, "Well, my son, if you only come to see me because it is your duty, you need not come again." And that is the way with a great many of the servants of God. They work for Him because it is their duty, not for love. Let us abolish this word *duty*, and feel that it is only a privilege to work for God. Let us try to remember that what is done merely from a sense of duty is not acceptable to God.

One night when I had been speaking in this way in London, a minister said to me after services, "Now, Moody, you are all wrong. If you take this word *duty* out from its connection with our works, you will soon have all the churches and Sunday schools empty." "Well," said I, "I will try to convince you that I am all right. You are married?" "Yes." "Well, suppose this was your wife's birthday, you bought a book for her, and you went home and said, 'Now, my wife, this is your birthday, so I have felt it my duty to buy something for you. Here's a book; take it.' Would your wife not be justified in refusing it?" "Well," said he, "I think you are correct; she would be right in refusing it." That wife would want a present given her through love, not duty. What Christ wants is that we will work for Him because we love Him.

The first impulse of a young convert is to love, and if a young man attempts to talk to people without having been won to Christ by love – without having been converted by the true spirit of the Holy Spirit – his efforts fall short of their mark. If he has been touched to the heart with the love of Jesus, the first thing he does is shout out that love which is waiting for all hearts. Paul, in the fifth chapter of Galatians, tells you that the fruit of the Spirit is "love, joy, peace, long-suffering." That is the fruit of the Spirit. He commences this line with love at the head of the list, and if love is not the motive, we have not been born of the Spirit.

Let us ask ourselves the question, "Is love the motivating power that urges us to go out and work for God?" This is the first question we ought to ask ourselves. Without it a great deal of work will go for naught. Without it the work will be swept away like chaff. Christ looks down and examines our hearts and actions, and although our deeds may be great in the eyes of the world, they may not be in His eyes.

Look at that woman in Jerusalem. All the rich people were casting in their treasures to the Lord. I can see the women and men come into the temple, some giving $100, others giving $300, and others putting in $500. If there had been newspapers in Jerusalem in those days, there would have been notices of these contributions. It would have sounded very well in print. But by and by a poor, widow woman comes along and puts in a humble two mites. I can see the Lord sitting at the treasury when that woman comes with her all, and I can hear Him saying, "That woman has given more than all of them." Why? Not owing to the large amount. No; simply because it was love that prompted that woman.

The one great thing that the church lacks at the present day, and if you ask me to put it into as small a space as possible, I can put it into a word of four letters. That is, "Love." Show me a church in which the members love one another, and I will show you a church that is alive for the cause of Christ. In it there is a revival every day for the twelve months of the year; the 365 days of the year are filled with continual manifestations of Christ's love. That is the lack today. There is lukewarmness, coldness one towards another. In Titus 2, Paul tells what Christians' lives should be – sound in faith, sound in love, and sound in patience. If a man is not sound in faith, we would draw his head right off; if he is not sound in faith, put him out. But let him be ever so unsound in love, he will be kept in. How many church-going men here in Chicago are continually picking to pieces and slandering their brothers? They are continually going about finding fault with someone. They have no love. Those who do not love in the way stated in this chapter, ponder well its meaning.

Let the question go home to every heart here tonight, "Is there any one I do not love?" If you are treasuring up in your heart any feeling of hatred toward any man or woman, God will not love you. You must be ready to forgive and to love. I do not know that we could put up anything better on the platform than that motto, "God is love," and may it be burned into your heart. You say you love them who love you. Any black-hearted hypocrite can love those who love him. But what Christ wants to teach us is to love those that hate us and slight us. If you can convince men that you love them, you can influence them. That is what we want to do in order to touch the hearts of those we encounter in the coming month. If one of us went to a bad man and said to him, "You are the worst man in Chicago," that would probably not touch him, and it would likely only harden his heart even more. We want to lovingly show him the love that Christ offers. When the Son of Man came into the world it was love that moved Him, and we will never do any good with anybody till our own hearts are touched with that same love. If we are not loving toward others, they will not like us, and instead of trying to talk for Christ we had better keep away. A worker must win the hearts and affections of the people before he can do any effective work.

Dr. Arnott came down from Edinburgh to one of our meetings in London, and he told those people something. I don't think the Londoners understood him, but if they knew of farm life as I did, they would have known what he meant. He said, "On my father's farm, when they wanted to teach a calf to drink, they would bring it to the pail. A man would dip his finger into the milk, put it into the calf's mouth, then slowly draw away his hand. Before you knew it the calf was drinking. "And so," he said, "if you want to win people to Christ you have to go lovingly to them and lead them gradually to Him." If you do not make people love you, you need not talk to them. Oh, that God may show you this truth tonight, that the great lever of the Christian is love! If a Sunday school teacher does not love his scholars – if he goes to them as if it were a lesson he wished to get over, it will not be long before they find it out. They will see it in his eyes, in his face, in his actions. And so, let us see tonight the necessity of having the love of God in our hearts, so that when we approach that drunkard or that gambler, we can win him to Christ; so that when you show him the gospel and tell him you want him to be saved, he will receive you with a welcome. If you go to him from a sense of duty, you will make no progress with him, but if you go to him and talk of the love of Christ and show kindness in your actions, he will hear you.

A minister in London said to me one night, "Mr. Moody, I want you to pray for a lot of people who will be at the meeting tonight." When I went there, I saw in one corner a father, mother, and four or five children. I prayed for them. When I got home, I asked the minister about that family, and he said they had been won to Jesus by a smile. He said one day he was passing by a house at the window of which a little child was standing. He liked children, and he smiled to it and bowed.

This minister was in the habit of passing the house every day, and the second time he noticed the child again, and he again smiled. The next time there were several children there, and he smiled and bowed again.

When he came again, he saw the same children standing there, but this time a lady was standing with them. He thought it would not be right to bow to the lady, but he smiled at the children, and the lady said when she saw him looking so pleasant, "That man must be a minister." My friends, it would be a good thing if all ministers had a smile on their faces. There are more men driven away from churches by sour looks than by anything else. A minister ought to have a clear conscience and should wear a pleasant smile. Some of you will say, "Well, Christ was melancholy and wept over sinners." Ah, but it was love.

There is such a thing as a man weeping in his love. Well, the lady said to her little ones, "I want you to follow that gentleman, for I am sure he is a minister." When he came around again, the children went after him, shadowing him through several streets, until by and by he turned into an Independent church. The children followed him right in, and they brought home a good report. They said they never had such a preacher, although they probably did not understand a word he said. But you know a little pat on the head and a kindly look goes a long way with children. Well, the result was that the mother came, and she brought the father. They became converted, and thus a whole family was brought to Christ by a smile.

We want to believe that the love of Christ is the best thing we can have. If a man wants to buy a horse, he goes around till he finds the best horse for his money. You women, if you want to buy a dress, go from one store to another and search till you find the best dress. And it is the universal law of the world over. So if we can show the sinners, by love, that the religion of Jesus Christ is the best thing to have, we can win the world to us. If we can show that we are full of love and not full of envy and malice and bitterness, everyone can be won to Christ. If the spirit of love can come upon all of us, so that we can talk to everyone kindly, it will not be long before salvation shall break over us through Christ.

You go into a church that is all aglow with love and into another where there is a lack and mark the difference. In the latter the people get as far away from the pulpit as possible, mark the coldness, then see how quick they get out of the church. Their hearts are cold to one another, and they have no sympathy. But when their hearts are all aglow, they crowd round and are genial toward one another, and "God bless the sermon," however poor the minister who preaches. The reason that we have so many poor ministers is because we have so few praying people. Look at Joshua - while he was fighting for the Lord, Moses was up on the mountain praying. So we want everyone to pray for their ministers while they are fighting for the Lord.

When a man comes to me and grumbles and complains about his minister, I ask him, "Do you ever pray for your minister?" He runs away. It thwarts his plans. They do not work with the minister and never think of praying for him. We want to see every man red-hot for the Savior, and he will wake up the church. If his heart is red-hot, sparks will kindle in the little circle, and the whole church will be ablaze. Every soul will be filled with the glory of Christ. There is not a man in all Chicago - I do not care what he is; he may be an Atheist, a Pantheist, a drunkard, or a gambler - I do not believe that a man's heart is so hard but that God can break it.

Mr. Warner, superintendent of probably one of the largest Sunday schools in the world, had a theory that he would never put a boy out of his school for bad conduct. He argued that if a boy misbehaved himself it was because of bad training at home, and that if he put him out of the school no one would take care of him. Well, this theory was put to the test one day. A teacher came to him and said, "I have a boy in my class that must be taken out; he breaks the rules continually, he swears and uses obscene language, and I cannot do anything with him."

Mr. Warner did not care to put the boy out, so he sent the teacher back to his class. But he came again and said that unless the boy was taken from his class, he must leave it. Well, he left, and a second teacher was appointed. The second teacher came with the same story and met with the same reply from Mr. Warner. And he resigned. A third teacher was appointed, and he came with the same story as the others. Mr. Warner then thought he would be compelled to turn the boy out at last. One day a few teachers were standing about and Mr. Warner said, "I will bring this boy up and read his name out in the school and publicly excommunicate him." Well, a young lady came up and said to him, "I am not doing what I might for Christ; let me have the boy. I will try to save him." Mr. Warner said, "If these young men cannot do it, you will not." But she begged to have him, and Mr. Warner consented.

She was a wealthy young lady, surrounded with all the luxuries of life. The boy went to her class, and for several Sundays he behaved himself and broke no rule. But one Sunday he broke loose, and in reply to something she said, spat in her face. She took out her pocket-handkerchief and wiped her face but said nothing. Well, she thought upon a plan, and she said to him, "John" – we will call him John – "John, come home with me." "No," says he, "I won't; I won't be seen on the streets with you." She was fearful of losing him altogether if he went out of the school that day, so she said to him, "Will you let me walk home with you?" "No, I won't," said he. "I won't be seen on the street with you." Then she thought upon another plan. She thought on the "Old Curiosity Shop," and she said, "I won't be at home tomorrow or Tuesday, but if you will come round to the front door on Wednesday morning, there will be a little bundle for you." "I don't want it, you may keep your old bundle." She went home but made the bundle up. She thought that curiosity might make him come.

Wednesday morning arrived, and he got over his mad fit, and he thought he would just like to see what was in this bundle. The little fellow knocked at the door, which was opened, and he told his story. The woman who answered the door said, "Yes, here is the bundle." The boy opened it, and found a vest and a coat and other clothing, and a little note written by the young lady, which read something like this:

"Dear Johnnie, Ever since you have been in my class, I have prayed for you every morning and evening that you might be a good boy, and I want you to stop in my class. Do not leave me."

The next morning before she was up, the servant came to her and said there was a little boy below who wished to see her. She dressed hastily, went downstairs, and found Johnnie on the sofa weeping. She put her arms around his neck, and he said to her, "My dear teacher, I have not had any peace since I got this note from you. I want you to forgive me." "Won't you let me pray for you to come to Jesus?" And she went down on her knees and prayed. And now, Mr. Warner said, that boy was the best boy in the Sunday school.

And so it was love that broke that boy's heart. May the Lord give us that love in abundance! May we be so full of love that everyone may see that it only prompts us to bring them to heaven!

The Good Samaritan

You will find my text in part of the 29th verse of the 10th chapter of Luke, *"And who is my neighbor?"* We are told that as Christ stood with His disciples, a lawyer stood up and tempted Him and said, "Master, what shall I do to inherit eternal life?" He asked what he could do to inherit eternal life, what he could do to buy salvation. And the Lord answered his question. "What is written in the law? How do you read it?" To which the lawyer answered, "Thou shalt love the Lord God with all thy heart, and with all thy soul, and with all thy strength, and with all thy mind; and thy neighbor as thyself." "Thou hast answered right." "Who is my neighbor?" And Jesus drew a vivid picture, which has been told for the last 1,800 years, and I do not know anything that brings out more truthfully the wonderful power of the gospel than this story – the story of the man who went down from Jerusalem to Jericho and who fell among thieves.

Jerusalem was called the "city of peace." Jericho and the road leading to it were infested with thieves. Probably it had been taken possession of by the worst of Adam's sons. I do not know how far the man got from Jerusalem to Jericho, but the thieves had come out and fallen upon him, taken all his money, stripped him of his clothes, and left him wounded – left him, I suppose, for dead. By and by a priest came down the road from Jerusalem. We are told that he came by chance. Perhaps he was going down to dedicate some synagogue or preach a sermon on some important subject and had the manuscript in his pocket.

As he was going along on the other side, he heard a groan. He turned around and saw the poor fellow lying bleeding on the ground and pitied him. He went up close, looked at him, and said, "Why, that man's a Jew. He belongs to the seed of Abraham. If I remember aright, I saw him in the synagogue last Sunday. I pity him, but I have too much business and cannot attend to him." He felt a pity for him and looked on him and probably wondered why God allowed such men as those thieves to come into the world - yet passed by. There are a good many men just like him. They stop to discuss and wonder why sin came into the world. They look upon a wounded man but do not stop to pick up the poor sinner, forgetting the fact that sin is in the world already and it has to be rooted out. But another man came along, a Levite, and he heard the groans. He, too, turned and looked on him with pity. He felt compassion for him. He was one of those men that if he were here we should probably make him an elder or a deacon. He looked at him and said, "Poor fellow! He's all covered with blood, and he has been badly hurt. He is nearly dead, and they have taken all his money and stripped him naked. Ah, well, I pity him!" He would like to help him, but he, too, had pressing business, and passed by on the other side. But he's scarcely out of sight when another came along riding on a beast.

He heard the groans of the man and went over and took a good look at him. The traveler was a Samaritan, but the wounded man was a Jew. Ah, how the Jews looked down upon the Samaritans. There was a great, high partition wall between the Jews and the Samaritans. The Jews would not allow them into the temple. They would not have any dealings with them. They would not associate with them. I can see him coming along that road with his good, benevolent face, and as he passes, he hears a groan from this poor fellow. He draws in his beast and pauses to listen. "And he came to where he was." This is the sweetest thing to my mind in the whole story.

A good many people would like to help a poor man if he were on the platform, if it cost them no trouble. They want him to come to them. They are afraid to touch the wounded man; he is all bloody, and they will get their hands soiled. And that was just the way with the priest and the Levite. This poor man, perhaps, had paid half of all his means to help the service of the Temple, and might have been a constant worshipper, but they only felt pity for him. This good Samaritan "came to where he was," and when he saw him, he had compassion on him. That word "compassion" – how sweet it sounds!

The first thing he did on hearing him cry for water – the hot sun had been pouring down upon his head – was to go and get it from a brook. Then he gets a bag that he has with him – what we might call a carpetbag or a saddlebag in the West – and pours oil on his wounds. Then he thinks, "the poor fellow is weak," so he gets a little wine. He has been lying so long in the burning sun that he is nearly dead now – he was left half dead – and the wine revives him. He looks him over and sees his wounds need to be bound up. But he has nothing to do this with. I can see him now tearing the lining out of his coat, and with it binding up his wounds. Then he takes him up and lays him on his bosom till he revives, and when the poor fellow gets strength enough, the good Samaritan puts him on his own beast. If the Jew had not been half dead, he would never have allowed him to put his hands on him. He would have treated him with scorn. But he is half dead, and he cannot prevent the good Samaritan treating him kindly and putting him on his beast.

Did you ever stop to think what a strong picture it would have been if the Samaritan had not been able himself to get the man on the beast – if he had had to call for assistance? Perhaps a man would have come along, and he would have asked him to help him with the wounded man. "What are you?" he might have said. "I am a Samaritan." "You are a Samaritan, are you? I cannot help you. I am a Jew." There is a good deal of that spirit now, just as strong as it was then. When we are trying to get a poor man on the right way, when we are tugging at him to get his face towards Zion, we ask someone to help us, and he says, "I am a Roman Catholic." "Well," you say, "I am a Protestant." So they give no assistance to one another.

The same party spirit of old is present today. The Protestants will have nothing to do with the Catholics, the Jews will have nothing to do with the Gentiles. And there was a time, but thank God we are getting over it, when a Methodist would not touch a Baptist or a Presbyterian a Congregationalist; and if we saw a Methodist taking a man out of the ditch, a Baptist would say, "Well, what are you going to do with him?" "Take him to a Methodist church." "Well, I'll have nothing to do with him." But the time is coming when, if others see us tugging at a man trying to get him out of the ditch, but we are so weak that we cannot get him on the beast, then they will help him. And that is what Christ wants.

Well, the Samaritan gets him on his beast and says to him, "You are very weak; my beast is sure-footed. He will take you to the inn, and I will hold you." He held him firmly, just as God is able to hold every one he takes out of the pit. I see them going along that road, he holding him on and gets him to the inn. He says to the innkeeper, "Here is a wounded man; the thieves have been after him. Give him the best attention you can, nothing is too good for him." And I can imagine the good Samaritan stopping there all night, sitting up with him, and attending to his needs. The next morning he gets up and says to the landlord, "I must be off," leaving a little money to pay for what the man has had; "and if that is not enough, I will pay what is necessary when I return from my business in Jericho."

This good Samaritan not only gave the landlord two pence to pay for what he already owed and a promise to come again and repay whatever had been spent to take care of the man, but he had also given him all his sympathy and compassion. And Christ tells this story in answer to the lawyer who came to tempt Him and shows him that the Samaritan was the neighbor. Now this story is brought out here to teach the churchgoers this thing: that it is not creeds or doctrines that we lack, so much as compassion and sympathy. I have been talking about the qualifications which we require in working for Christ. First night I took "Courage," then "Love," last night "Faith," and now it is "Compassion and Sympathy."

If we have not compassion and sympathy our efforts will go for naught. There are hundreds of Christians who work here who accomplish very little because they have not sympathy. If they go to lift up a man, they must put themselves into his place. If you place yourself in sympathy with a man you are trying to do good to, you will soon lift him up.

When at the Hippodrome in New York, a young man came up to me; he looked very sad, his face was troubled. I asked him what the matter was, and he said, "I am a fugitive from justice. In England, when I was young, my father used to take me into the public-house with him. I learned the habit of drinking, and liquor has become to me like water. A few months ago, I was in England, where I was head clerk in a large firm. I was doing well, making $50 a week.

Well, one night I was out, and I had some money of my employers with me; I got to gambling and lost it. I ran away from England and left a wife and two lovely children. Here I am. I cannot get anything to do; I have no letters of recommendation. What shall I do?" "Believe in the Lord Jesus Christ," said I. "I cannot become a Christian with that record behind me. There is no hope for me," he replied. "There is hope; seek Jesus, and leave everything behind," I told him. "Well," said he, "I cannot do that until I make restitution." But I kept him to that one thing. He wrote me a letter and said that the sermon, "He Must be Born Again," had made a great impression on him.

He could not sleep that night, and he finally passed from darkness into light. He came to me and said, "I am willing to go back to England and surrender myself and go into prison if Christ wants it." I said to him, "Don't do that, but write to your employers and say that if Christ helps you, you will make restitution. Live as economically as you can and be industrious, and you will soon find all well." The man wrote to his employers, and I got a letter from him shortly afterward and he told me that his wife was coming out to New York. When I was last there, I made inquiry about him and found that he was doing well. He only wanted sympathy – someone to take him by the hand and help him.

I believe that there are not less than ten thousand young men in Chicago who are just waiting for someone to come to them with sympathy. You do not know how far a loving word will go. When I came to this city twenty years ago, I remember I walked up and down the streets trying to find a situation. I recollect how, when someone roughly answered me, it would chill my soul. But when someone would say, "I feel for you. I would like to help you. I can't, but you will be all right soon," I went away happy and lighthearted. That man's sympathy did me good.

When I first went away from home to a place some thirteen miles away, it seemed as if I could never be any further away. My brother had gone to live at that town a year and a half before. I recollect as I walked down the street with him that I was very homesick and could hardly keep down the tears. My brother said to me, "There's a man here who will give you a cent; he gives a cent to every new boy that comes here." I thought that he would be the best man I had ever met. By and by he came along, and I thought he was going to pass me. My brother stopped him, thinking I suppose, I was going to lose the cent, and the old gentleman – he was an old gentleman – looked at me and said, "Why, I have never seen you before. You must be a new boy." "Yes," said my brother, "he has just come." The old man put his trembling hand upon my head and patted it and told me that I had a Father in heaven, although my earthly father was dead, and he gave me a new cent. I don't know where that cent went to, but the kindly touch of that old man's hand upon my head has been felt by me all these years.

What we want is sympathy from men. There are hundreds of men with hearts full of love whose hearts would be won to a higher life if they received but words of sympathy. But I can imagine men saying, "How are you going to reach them? How are you going to do it? How are you going to get into sympathy with these people?" It is very easily done. Put yourself into their places. There is a young man, a great drunkard; perhaps his father was a drunkard. If you had been surrounded with influences like his, perhaps you would have been a worse drunkard than he is. Well, just put yourself into his place, and go and speak to him lovingly and kindly.

I want to tell you a lesson taught me in Chicago a few years ago. In the months of July and August, as you all know, a great many deaths occurred among children. I remember I attended a great many funerals, sometimes I would go to two or three funerals a day. I got so used to it that it did not trouble me to see a mother take the last kiss and the last look at her child and see the coffin lid closed. I got accustomed to it, as in the war we got accustomed to the great battles, and to see the wounded and the dead never troubled us.

When I got home one night, I heard that one of my Sunday school pupils was dead, and her mother wanted me to come to the house. I went to the poor home and saw the father drunk. Adelaide had been brought from the river. The mother told me she washed for a living. The father earned no money and poor Adelaide's work was to get wood for the fire. She had gone to the river that day and seen a piece floating on the water, stretched out for it, lost her balance, and fallen in. The poor woman was very much distressed. "I would like you to help me, Mr. Moody," she said, "to bury my child. I have no lot. I have no money."

Well, I took the measure for the coffin and came away. I had my little girl with me, and she said, "Papa, suppose we were very, very poor, and mamma had to work for a living, and I had to get sticks for the fire, and was to fall into the river, would you be very sorry?" This question reached my heart. "Why, my child, it would break my heart to lose you," I said, and I drew her to my bosom. "Papa, do you feel bad for that mother?" she asked. This word woke my sympathy for the woman, and I went back to the house and prayed that the Lord might bind up that wounded heart.

When the day came for the funeral I went to Graceland. I had always thought my time too precious to go out there, but I went. The drunken father was there and the poor mother. I bought a lot, the grave was dug, and the child laid among strangers. There was another funeral coming up, and the corpse was laid near the grave of little Adelaide. And I thought how I would feel if it had been my little girl that I had been laying there among strangers. I went to my Sunday school thinking this and suggested that the children should contribute and buy a lot in which we might bury a hundred poor little children.

We soon got it, and the papers had scarcely been made out when a lady came and said, "Mr. Moody, my little girl died this morning. Let me bury her in the lot you have got for the Sunday school children." The request was granted, and she asked me to go to the lot and say prayers over her child. I went to the grave – it was a beautiful day in June, and I remember asking her what the name of her child was. She said Emma. That was the name of my little girl, and I thought what if it had been my own child. We should put ourselves in the places of others. I could not help shedding a tear. Another woman came shortly after and wanted to put another one into the grave. I asked his name. It was Willie, and it happened to be the name of my little boy – the first two laid there were called by the same names as my two children, and I felt sympathy and compassion for those two women.

If you want to get into sympathy, put yourself into a man's place. Chicago needs Christians whose hearts are full of compassion and sympathy. If we haven't got it, pray that we may have it, so that we may be able to reach those men and woman that need kindly words and kindly actions far more than sermons. The mistake is that we have been preaching too much and sympathizing too little. The gospel of Jesus Christ is a gospel of deeds and not of words. May the Spirit of the Lord come upon us this night. May we remember that Christ was moved in compassion for us, and may we, if we find some poor man going down among thieves or lying wounded and bleeding, look upon him with sympathy, get below him, and raise him up. Let us pray.

His Own Brother

I want to call your attention this morning to a text you will find in the 1st chapter according to John, part of the 41st verse: *"He first found his own brother and brought him to Jesus."*

I thought this morning I would like to just take a leaf out of my own life, that it may help some of those present in this hall who have brothers that are very dear to them, but who are out of Christ. Twenty-one years ago last March, when God converted me, the very first thing that came into my mind was my six brothers. Then and there I began to pray for them. I had never prayed for them before, and I began to cry to God that these six brothers and two sisters might be led home to peace. And for twenty-one years that has been my prayer: that has been my cry to God.

I remember the first time I went home after my conversion. I thought I could tell them what God had done for me. I thought I had only to explain it to have them all see the light. How disappointed I was when I left home that first time, after remaining for a few days, to find that they did not see it. I was not very experienced in pleading for souls then. Perhaps I did not go at it in the right way. But I kept on as best I could. And a few years after, when I was in this city – three years after, I was in a store on Lake Street. A postman came one day and brought a letter that told me my youngest brother was given up by the physician to die. That day he was dying. I went into the fifth story of that building, and if ever I prayed earnestly in my life I did then that my brother might be spared. He was the Benjamin of the family; he was born after my father died. I thought I could give him up then if he only was a Christian. But I had not any hope. The thought that my brother, who was very dear to me, dearer to me than my life it seemed, should die thus in his sins, was too much for me to stand, and I wrestled with God in prayer.

It seemed God answered my prayer. The next letter said he was better. He had a run of typhoid fever that lasted forty-two days. And when he got off that bed I felt, in answer to prayer, the boy was much dearer to me than ever before. But he never was well during sixteen or eighteen years. I remember fourteen years ago he came to me to this city. I have that dear boy in my heart now. I thought then my opportunity had surely come, and I could lead him to Christ. But he was taken sick again. I could not keep him here. The doctor said he might live several years but could not be cured. Naturally ambitious and proud-spirited, he did not want to go back home. But the doctor said it was the best I could do, and I took him back to Massachusetts.

I took him home from Chicago to Northfield, all the way preaching Christ to him. But he took no interest in my speech. Everything I said failed to influence him, although he seemed to love me very much. And for fourteen years I kept that dear boy on my heart. I just kept on praying for him. Year after year I went back to the old home just to spend a few days with him that I might win him to Christ. He knew I wanted him to be a Christian, but it seemed he would not comply. He took no interest in the Bible, no interest in Christianity. He would talk politics, he would talk everything else, but you could not get him to talk of Christ or Christianity.

I went back home a year ago with a heart just burdened for the salvation of my family. My heart burned to draw them to Christ. I went to preaching in that town. In the last month, my heart going out to that dear boy, I asked all those present in the church willing to become Christians to rise, and he, my long-sought brother, rose for prayers. What a precious relief for my heart! He turned his face toward Heaven that very night. He became an earnest and active Christian. And when they soon after decided to have a Young Men's Christian Association for that town, the young men wanted a president, and they elected him.

Oh, that was a blessed day for me, when my brother, converted to God after twenty years of prayer, took charge of that little band. I heard him make his first speech, and that seemed the happiest day of my life. He was a young man of great talents. He was the star of the family, the most promising one of the family. No one of us could have done as much for Christ had He gone to him in his earliest manhood. And he went to work. He took a leading part in religious meetings. He went and talked with weak brothers and set them on their feet again. He searched for souls on both sides of the Connecticut River, in both sides of the valley.

More conversions took place after I left than when I was there. Every Sunday afternoon he would go out into the country and take charge of meetings. As I used to stand in the pulpit at times and look down on that young brother in his zealous work, no one but God knows how I loved him and rejoiced with great joy. And when God took him, he was in the midst of His work, bringing others to Christ. Oh, I want to tell you my thoughts after I left you suddenly. The first thought as I went toward my home. Oh, how deep the sorrow! The dear boy was gone forever, and in the first moments grief will have its way.

That text in Scripture, the expression that David used when he lost Jonathan, kept coming into my mind: "I am very much distressed for you, my brother Jonathan; very pleasant have you been unto me; your soul to me was wonderful." Yes, your soul to me was wonderful.

And that sadly beautiful hymn also keeps coming into my mind: "We shall meet but we shall miss him. There will be one vacant chair." But over and above all these the voice from heaven at last made itself heard to my heart, "Thy brother shall rise again." The cloud was lifted, and for about five hundred miles on my way to my home that verse rung in my ears. It seemed to echo and re-echo throughout all the journey, "Thy brother shall rise again."

Oh, the precious Bible! It never seemed to me so precious as it did that day. My call to mourning was the deepest I have ever known, for next, perhaps, to my wife, my two children, and my aged mother, I loved none so dearly as this youngest brother. But that precious promise gives the heart cause to rejoice even in the sorrow of death. And again, from the 15th chapter of Corinthians, what divine sustaining words I took to my soul.

"But some men will say, 'How are the dead raised up? And with what body do they come?'" Thou fool, what you sow is not made alive unless it dies. And what you sow, you do not sow the body that shall be, but bare grain; perhaps wheat or some other grain. But God gives it a body as it has pleased Him and to every seed his own body. "So also is the resurrection of the dead. It is sown in corruption, it is raised in incorruption. "It is sown in dishonor, it is raised in glory. It is sown in weakness, it is raised in power."

Dishonor. Oh, as we laid him down in the cold grave, I thought of the worms that would come to his body and of the dishonor. But with what power the Word of God came to my soul then in these words, "It is raised in glory." We sowed it in weakness, but it shall be raised in power. It seemed there was victory even in that trying hour. It was sown in corruption, but it shall be raised incorruptible. It was sown mortal, but it shall be raised immortal. It was sown a natural body, but it shall be raised a spiritual body. And, as it had borne the image of the earthly, it shall also bear the image of the heavenly. I shall see that brother by and by; then shall he be glorified.

Yes, my friends, I could even rejoice as I read these blessed assurances of Scripture. The Word of God came to my soul as never before. Blessed Bible, how dark it would have been but for that blessed Book. But by its beams all darkness was driven away. It seemed I could even thank God for the triumphant death of my dear brother and almost envy him. No, I would not have God call him back from heaven into this dark world. Yon happy home beyond the grave is far better. What joy to tell of good deeds done!

A minister down home told me that he did not know, a short time back, of a solitary young man in his neighborhood who would offer prayer, but now a numerous and zealous band of praying Christians were the fruits of my brother's life. And that text came forcibly to my mind: "Blessed are the dead that die in the Lord; even so, saith the Spirit, and their works do follow them." There were these dear, young, Christian converts following him to his grave; his works did follow him. In the graveyard of the church that funeral day I saw 50 of these young men, converted mostly in the past year. I shouted even there by the grave, I could not help it. "Oh, death, where is thy sting? Oh grave, where is thy victory?" And I seemed to hear a voice as from the bosom of the Son of God, "Because I live you shall live also."

And on my way back from Northfield to Chicago this has been my thought: If you, my dear, Christian friend, have a brother out of Christ, go bring him in. You will by and by have to stand by the open grave of some dear brother, and if he is without Christ, how can you bear it? And so, my friends, let me urge upon you first, go find your own brother. If you have a brother out of Christ, go to him today. Tell him how you love him, how you want him to be a Christian, how you are burdened and weighed down for his salvation. And then go to your sister, to your cousin, to your friend. Oh! Each one of you write to some absent friend today beseeching that Christ may be accepted just now! I thank God from the bottom of my heart that my dear brother took a stand for Christ and went to work. I thank God that now his works do follow him.

The young Christian men met immediately after he died; a hundred of them came together to choose someone to take his place. And how it rejoiced my heart that George Moody took the place of Samuel and has set himself earnestly to the work. He said, "From now I will try to follow more faithfully after Christ." And when we met Wednesday night – it was Tuesday we laid him away – another brother was harnessed to the work in place of the dear buried one. Oh, dear friend, if souls weigh on our hearts, let us go bring them to Jesus. Let us write to them beseeching letters if our lips cannot reach them. Let us not rest day or night. Let us this morning go out and bring our friends to Christ. Let us commence with our own families; let us find our brothers. If our brothers have yielded, let us go to our friends. If they are strangers to Christ, oh, go bring them now while you may. Exhort by word of mouth, exhort by fervent and repeated letters. Begin at once your mission, lest it be too late forever, and praise God for the dear privilege of bringing others to Him.

Where Are You?

I want to direct your attention to the 3rd chapter of Genesis, part of the 9th verse: *"Where are you?"* You see I have got a very personal text this afternoon. All those ministers in this audience will bear me out in this statement that it is the hardest kind of work to get their congregations to apply this text to themselves. When they hear it, one man passes it on to another, and away it goes, text and sermon. This afternoon I want you to understand that it means me, you, and every one of us – that it points to us; that it applies to us personally – that it ought to come home to every soul here – to these merchants, to these ministers, to these reporters, to these great-hearted men, to these women, to these little boys and girls as a personal question. It was the first question God put to man after his fall, and in the 6,000 years that have rolled away all of Adam's children have heard it. It has come to them all. In the silent watches of the night, in the busy hours of the day, it has come upon us many a time – the question "Where am I, where am I going?" and I want you to look at it now as a personal question.

So let us be solemn for a few minutes while we try to answer it. Some men look with great anxiety as to how they appear in the sight of their fellow men. It is of little account what the world thinks of us. The world is not worth heeding; public opinion is of really little account. We should not pay any attention to its opinion. "Where are you going?" is the question that ought to trouble – "what is to be your hereafter?"

May the question strike home to us, and may a heart-searching take place in us. May the Holy Spirit search us so that we may know before we sleep tonight where we are now in the sight of God and where we are going in eternity.

I remember when preaching in New York City, at the Hippodrome, a man coming up to me and telling me a story that thrilled my soul. One night, he said, he had been gambling, had gambled away all the money he had. When he went home to the hotel that night, he did not sleep much – half drunk, and with a sort of remorse for what he had done. The next morning happened to be Sunday. He got up, felt bad, couldn't eat anything, didn't touch his breakfast, was miserable, and thought about putting an end to his existence. That afternoon he took a walk up Broadway, and when he came to the Hippodrome he saw great crowds going in and thought of entering too. But a policeman at the door told him he couldn't come in, as it was a women's meeting. He turned from it and strolled on. He went back to his hotel and had dinner.

At night he walked up the street until he reached the Hippodrome again, and this time he saw a lot of men going in. When inside, he listened to the singing and heard the text, "Where are you?" and he thought he would go out. He rose to go, and the text came upon his ears again, "Where are you?" This was too personal, he thought, too disagreeable, so he made for the door. But as he got to the third row from the entrance, the words came to him again, "Where are you?" He stood still, for the question had come to him with irresistible force, and God had found him right there. He went to his hotel and prayed all that night, and now he is a bright and shining light. This young man, who was a commercial traveler, went back to the village in which he had been reared and in which he had been one of the most rakish young men – went back there, and went around among his friends and acquaintances and testified for Christ as earnestly and beneficially for Him as his conduct had been against him.

I hope the text will find out some young man here who has strayed away from God and come upon him with such force personally as will turn him from his present course to take the offers of salvation. Won't you believe we are here for you, won't you believe we are preaching for you, won't you believe that this enterprise has been carried out for you, and that this assembly has been drawn together for you, and may you ask your heart solemnly and candidly this question, "Where are you?"

I am going to divide this audience into three classes. Don't let this startle you, I am not going to make three divisions among you. The first class is the class who profess to be Christians. I don't know who you are or whether you are sincere. It rests between you and God. The other class are the backsliders – those who have been good children, but who have turned their backs on Him and have gone into the regions of sin. And the other class are those who have never been saved, who have never been born of the Spirit, who have never sought to reach Christ.

And now, my friends, you who profess to be Christians. We who profess to be Christians, are we living up to what we preach? God forgive me, I feel I am not doing as much as I should for Him. I don't except myself. You who profess to be Christians, this question is personal to you: "Where are you?" Do you believe what you are preaching; do you live the life you ought to be living as professed Christians? If you were doing this, tens of thousands of people would be converted in Chicago within thirty days. By your neglect to practice what you preach, men have gotten sick of you, the world has become tired of you. They say if we really feel what we talk about and profess we would be more earnest about their salvation. And I say they are right. If Christians felt as they should, every church in Chicago, every church in the Northwest, would be active for the salvation of souls. They are lukewarm. Is the church today in its right position? Is it true to its teachings? Are we not mingling with the world in our professed Christian lives so that the world has become tired of our shamming professions? If the world does not see us act according to our professions, they say Christianity is not real.

Some time ago, a young man, a professed Christian, spoke to another young man upon the subject and the Christian was answered with the words: "I don't believe a word of your Christianity. I don't believe a word of what you talk about. I don't believe your Bible." "You don't mean that?" asked the Christian. "Yes, I do," said the young man. "It's all a sham; you are all hypocrites." The Christian said to him, knowing he had a mother who was a professed Christian, "you don't mean to say that your mother is a hypocrite?" "Well, no," said the young fellow, not willing to admit his mother was one, "she is not exactly a hypocrite, but she doesn't believe what she professes. If she did, she would have talked to me about my soul long ago."

That young man, my friend, had the best of it. And this is the condition of nine-tenths of us – we don't practice what we profess to believe. We have not really taken the cross of Christ, we have not put off the old man and taken on the new. We are not living truly in Christ Jesus, and the world is sick of us and goes stumbling over us. If we don't practice in every particular the professions we make, if we don't try to influence the lives of others and lead the lives of Christians according to Christian precept, the world will go on stumbling over us.

A few years ago, in a town somewhere in this state, a merchant died, and while he was lying a corpse I was told a story I will never forget. When the physician that attended him saw there was no chance for him here, he thought it would be time to talk about Christ to the dying man. And there are a great many Christians just like this physician. They wait till a man is just entering the other world, till he is just about nearing the throne, till the sands of life are about run out, till the death rattle is in his throat, before they commence to speak of Christ. The physician stepped up to the dying merchant and began to speak of Jesus, the beauties of Christianity, and the salvation He had offered to all the world. The merchant listened quietly to him and then asked him, "How long have you known of these things?" "I have been a Christian since I came from the East," he replied. "You have been a Christian so long and have known all this. You have been in my store every day. You have been in my home, have associated with me. You knew all these things; why didn't you tell me before?"

The doctor went home and retired to rest but could not sleep. The question of the dying man rang in his ears. He could not explain why he had not spoken before, but he saw he had neglected his duty to his principles. He went back to his dying friend, intending to urge upon him acceptance of Christ's salvation, but when he began to speak to him the merchant only replied in a sad whisper, "Oh, why didn't you tell me before?" Oh, my friends, how many of us act like this physician. You must go to your neighbor and tell him who does not know Christ, of what He has done for us. If you do not tell the glad tidings, they are listening to the promptings of the devil, and we make people believe that Christianity is hypocrisy, and that Christ is not the Savior of the world. If we believe it shall we not publish it and speak out the glorious truth to all for Christ – that He is the Redeemer of the world.

Some time ago I read a little account that went through the press, and it burned into my soul. A father took his little child into the fields one day. He lay down while the child was amusing itself picking up little blades of grass and flowers. While the child was thus engaged the father fell asleep, and when he awoke the first thought that occurred to him was, "Where is my child?" He looked around everywhere, but nowhere could he see the child. He looked all around the fields, over the mountains, but could not see her, and finally he came to a precipice and looked down among the stones and rocks, and there he saw his little child lying down at the bottom. He ran down, took the child up, and kissed it tenderly, but it was dead. He was filled with remorse and accused himself of being the murderer of his child. This story applies to Christians in their watchful care of their fellow creatures.

It was not long ago that I heard of a mother making all sorts of fun and jeering at our preaching, not in Chicago, but in another town. She was laughing and scoffing at the meetings. She was scorning the preachers and yet she had a drunken son. It might have been if she had helped to support the meetings, the meetings would have been the means of saving that son from a drunkard's grave. Mothers and fathers here today, you have the responsibility upon you of turning the faces of your children toward Zion. Ah, my friends, it is a solemn question to you today, and may you ask yourself where you are in the sight of God.

The next class I want to speak to for a few moments, for I cannot help believing that in this assembly there must be a number of backsliders who have gone away from the wayside. You have probably come from an Eastern town to this one, and you have come to some church with a letter – to some Presbyterian, or Methodist, or Episcopalian church. And when you came to that church you did not find the love you expected, you didn't find the cordiality you looked for, and you did not go near it again. So you kept the letter in your pocket for weeks, for years; might have been thrown in your trunk, might have been burned up in the Chicago fire. You have forgot all about your church life and the letter has disappeared. You lead an ungodly life, but you are not happy. I have travelled about a good deal in the last five years, and I never knew a man who had turned away from religion to be a happy man. That man's conscience is always troubling him. He may come to Chicago and become prosperous and wealthy, but his wealth and position in the world cannot fill his heart.

If there is a poor backslider in this building today let him come back. Hear the voice that calls you to come back. There is nothing you have done which God is not ready and able to forgive. If there is a poor wanderer on the mountains of sin turn right round and face Him. He will hear your transgressions, forgive your backsliding, and take you to His loving bosom. This will be a happy night to you. Look at the home of the backslider. No prayers, no family altar there. As in the days of Elijah they have put up the image of Baal in the place of their God. They have no peace, their conscience troubles them. They know they are not bringing up their family as they should. Is not that the condition of a good many here today? Oh, backslider, you know what your life is, but what will be your eternity if you fight against the Lord, who is only waiting to do you good?

I heard of a young man who came to Chicago to sell his father's grain. His father was a minister somewhere down here. The boy arrived in Chicago and sold the grain, but when the time came for him to return home, the boy did not come. The father and mother were up all night, expecting to hear the sound of the wagon every minute. They waited and waited, but still he did not come. The father became so uneasy that he went into the stable and saddled his horse and came to Chicago.

When he reached here, he found that his son had sold the grain, but had not been seen since the sale and concluded that he had been murdered. After making investigation, however, he found that the boy had gone into a gambling house and lost all his money. After they had taken all his money from him, they told him to sell his horse and wagon, and he would recover his money, which he did. He was like the poor man who came down from Jericho to Jerusalem, who fell among thieves who stripped him of everything and cast him off. A great many of you think as this young man thought. You think that rum sellers and gamblers are your best friends, when they will take from you your peace, your health, your soul, your money – everything you have, and then run away.

Well, the father, after fruitlessly looking about for him, went home and told his wife what he had learned. But he did not settle down. He just took his carpetbag in his hand and went from one place to another, getting ministers to let him preach for them. He always told the congregation that he had a boy dearer to him than life, left his address with them, and urged them if ever they heard anything about his boy to let him know. At last, after going around a good deal, he got on his track and learned that he had gone to California. He went home but did not write a letter to him. No, he just arranged his business affairs and started for the Pacific coast to find his boy. This is but an illustration of what God has been doing for you. There has not been a day, an hour, a moment, but God has been searching for you. When the father got to San Francisco he got permission to preach, and he had a notice put in the papers in the hope that it might reach the mining districts, trusting that if his son were there it might reach him. He preached a sermon on the Sunday, and when he pronounced the benediction the audience went away. But he saw in a corner one who remained.

He went up to him and found that it was his boy. He did not reprimand him, he did not deliver judgment upon him, but put his loving arms around him, drew him to his bosom, and took him back to his home. This is an illustration of what God wants to do to us, what He wants to do today. He offers us His love and His forgiveness.

There is one peculiarity about being a backslider; you must get back to Christ the same as you went away. It is you who have gone away by turning, by leaving Him, not He by leaving you. And the way to get back to Him is to turn your face toward Him, and He will receive you with joy and forgiveness. There will be joy in your heart and there will be joy in heaven this afternoon if you return to Him. If you treated God as a friend, there would not be a backslider. A rule I have had for years is to treat the Lord Jesus Christ as a personal friend. His is not a creed, a mere empty doctrine, but it is He Himself we have. The moment we have received Christ we should receive Him as a friend. When I go away from home, I bid my wife and children goodbye. I bid my friends and acquaintances goodbye, but I never heard of a poor backslider going down on his knees and saying: "I have been near You for ten years; Your service has become tedious and monotonous. I have come to bid You farewell. Goodbye, Lord Jesus Christ." I never heard of one doing this. I will tell you how they go away. They just run away. Where are you, you backslider? Just look upon your condition during the past ten years. Have they been years of happiness? Have they been years of peace? Echo answers ten thousand times, "No." Return to Him at once. Never mind what your past has been, He will give you salvation.

But I must hasten on to the next class – the unsaved. I will admit that professed Christians have their failings; we are far from being what we ought to be. But is that any reason you should not come to Him? We do not preach ourselves – we do not set ourselves up as the Savior; if we did, you might make this an excuse. But we preach Christ. Now, you who are unsaved, won't you come? I do not know who you are in this audience, but if the Spirit of God is not born in you and does not tell you that you are the children of God, this is an evidence that you have not been born of God. Do you love your enemies? Do you love those who slander you? Do you love those who hate you? Have you joy, peace, long-suffering, courage, charity? If you have the fruit of the Spirit, you have those qualities; if you have not, you have not been born of the Spirit. Now, friends, just ask yourself this question, "Where am I?" Here I am in this hall today, surrounded with praying friends. It seemed to me sometimes as if the words came to me and fell to the floor, and at other times the words fell on the heart.

We can feel it in this hall today, in the atmosphere; we feel its influence all around. It may be that that mother is praying for the return of an erring son; it may be that that brother has been praying all afternoon, "O, my God, may the Spirit come to my brother." Dear friends, let us ask each other today, "Where are you?" Resisting the earnest, trembling prayers of some loving mother, of some loving wife – trampling them underfoot? Now, be honest. Have I not been talking to many in this audience who made promises five, ten, fifteen, twenty years ago – who made a promise to serve Him? Those promises have faded away, and those five, ten, fifteen, twenty years have rolled on and you are no nearer. Oh, sinner, where are you? Are you making light of all offers of mercy? Are you turning your back and ridiculing Him and laughing at

Him? If you are, may He, the God of mercy, arrest you and have mercy on your soul and save you.

A man's life is just like going up and down a hill. If I live the allotted time, I am going down the hill. Many of you are on the top of the hill and are not saved. Suppose you pause a moment and look down the hill on the road from whence you came – look back toward the cradle. Don't you remember that the sermons you heard ten or fifteen years ago moved you? You say, "When you look back at those times, we used to have good sermons, better and more earnest ministers than now." Don't you make any mistake. The gospel is the same as it was then, as powerful today as ever. The fault is not with the ministers of the gospel; it is with yourself. Your heart has become hard. Then, as you look down into the valley, don't you see a little mound and a tombstone? It marks the resting place of a loving father or a loving mother.

Ten years ago, you had a praying mother. Every morning and evening she went down on her knees in her closet and prayed for you. Her prayers are ended now, yet you are not saved. It may be, as you look down the stream of time, you see a little grave that marks the resting place of your child. It may be that child took you by the hand and asked you, "Will you meet me in that land?" And you promised her that you would meet her there. As you looked down into that little grave and heard the damp, cold earth falling down, you repeated that promise. Five, ten, fifteen years ago you promised this; have you kept it? Some of you are far down the hill and hastening to judgment. May God open your eyes today as you look back upon your lives and look to the future. It may be that you will live the allotted time, but the end is soon to come. The average age now is thirty-three years. There are a number of you in this hall this afternoon who will be in eternity inside of thirty days. Ask yourselves where you are – resisting the offer of mercy, turning back the offer of God. May the loving God show you the Savior standing at the door of your heart, knocking, and telling you He wants to come in and save you.

When I was in London in 1867, I was told a story which made a very deep impression upon me. A young, French nobleman came there to see a doctor, bringing letters from the French Emperor. The Emperor Napoleon III had a great regard for this young man, and the doctor wanted to save him. He examined the young man and saw there was something upon his mind. "Have you lost any property? What is troubling you? You have something weighing upon your mind," said the doctor. "Oh, there is nothing particular." "I know better; have you lost any relations?" asked the doctor. "No, none within the last three years." "Have you lost any reputation in your country?" "No."

The doctor studied for a few minutes and then said, "I must know what is on your mind – I must know what is troubling you." And the young man said, "My father was an infidel, my grandfather was an infidel, and I was brought up an infidel. For the last three years these words have haunted me, 'Eternity, and where shall it find me?'" "Ah," said the doctor, "you have come to the wrong physician." "Is there no hope for me?" cried the young man. "I walk about in the daytime; I lie down at night, and it comes upon me continually – 'Eternity, and where shall I spend it?' Tell me, is there any hope for me?" The doctor said, "Now, just sit down and be quiet. A few years ago, I was an infidel. I did not believe in God and was in the same condition in which you now are." The doctor took down his Bible and turned to the 53rd chapter of Isaiah and read: "He was wounded for our transgressions, He was bruised for our iniquities; the chastisement of our peace was upon Him, and with His stripes we are healed." And he read on through this chapter.

When he had finished, the young man said, "Do you believe this, that He voluntarily left heaven, came down to this earth, and suffered and died that we might be saved?" "Yes, I believe it. That brought me out of infidelity, out of darkness into light." And he preached Christ and His salvation and told him of heaven, and then suggested that they get down on their knees and pray. And when I went there in 1867, a letter had been received from that young nobleman, who wrote to Dr. Whinston in London, telling him that the question of "Eternity, and where he should spend it," was settled and troubling him no more.

My friends, this question of eternity and where we are going to spend it, forces itself upon every one of us. We are staying here for a little day. Our life is but a fiber, and it will soon be snapped. I may be preaching my last sermon. Tonight may find me in eternity. By the grace of God say that you will spend it in heaven. If you make up your mind to come to heaven all the hosts of hell cannot hinder you, because if God says,

"Let him come," who can resist you? If that little child sitting yonder says it will enter heaven, all the hosts of hell cannot keep it out. May God help you to spend your eternity in heaven, and may you say: "By the grace of God, I accept Jesus as my Redeemer."

Heaven

First Address

One night I was on my way to a meeting with a friend, and as we were drawing near the church he asked, "Mr. Moody, what are you going to preach about?" "I am going to preach about heaven," I said. I noticed a scowl passing over his face, and I said, "What makes you look so?" "Why, your subject of heaven. What's the use of talking upon a subject that's all speculation? It's only wasting time on a subject about which you can only speculate." My answer to that friend was, "If the Lord doesn't want us to speak about heaven, He would never have told us about such a place in the Scriptures, and as Timothy says, 'All the Scriptures are given by inspiration and all parts are profitable.'" There's no part of the Word of God that is not profitable, and I believe if men would read more carefully these Scriptures they would think more of heaven. If we want to get men to fix their hearts and attention upon heaven, we must get them to read more about it. Men who say that heaven is a speculation have not read their Bibles. In the blessed Bible there are allusions scattered all through it. If I were to read to you all the passages upon heaven from Genesis to Revelation, it would take me all night and tomorrow to do it.

When I took some of the passages lately and showed them to a lady,

"Why," said she, "I didn't think there was so much about heaven in the Bible." If I were to go into a foreign land and spend my days there, I would like to know all about it; I would like to read all about it. I would want to know all about its climate, its inhabitants, their customs, their privileges, their government. I would find nothing about that land that would not interest me. Suppose you all were going away to Africa, to Germany, to China, and were going to make one of those places your home, and suppose that I had just come from some of those countries, how eagerly you would listen. I can imagine how the old, grey-haired men and the young men and the deaf would crowd around and put up their hands to learn anything about it.

My friends, where are you going to spend eternity? Your life here is very brief. Life is but an inch of time; it is but a span; but a fiber which will soon be snapped, and you will be ushered into eternity. Where are you going to spend it? If I were to ask you who were going to spend your eternity in heaven to stand up, nearly every one of you would rise. There is not a man here, not one in Chicago, who has not some hope of reaching heaven. Now, if we are going to spend our future there it becomes us to go to work and find out all about it. I call your attention to this truth that heaven is just as much a place as Chicago. It is a destination, it is a locality. Some people say there is no heaven. Some men will tell you this earth is all the heaven we have. Queer kind of heaven this. Look at the poverty, the disease in the city; look at the men out of employment walking around our streets, and they say this is heaven. How low a man has got when he comes to think in this way. There is a land where the weary are at rest. There is a land where there is peace and joy, where no sorrow dwells, and as we think and speak about it, how sweet it looms up before us.

I remember soon after I was converted a pantheist got hold of me and tried to draw me back to the world. Those men who try to get hold of a young convert are the worst set of men. I don't know a worse man than he who tries to pull young Christians down. He is nearer the borders of hell than any man I know. When this man knew I had found Jesus, he just tried to pull me down. He tried to argue with me, and I did not know the Bible very well then, and he got the best of me. The only thing to get the best of these atheists, pantheists, or infidels is to have a good knowledge of the Bible. Well, this pantheist told me God was everywhere – in the air, in the sun, in the moon, in the earth, in the stars, but really, he meant nowhere. And the next time I went to pray it seemed as if I was not praying anywhere or to anyone.

We have ample evidence in the Bible that there is such a place as heaven, and we have abundant manifestation that His influence from heaven is felt among us. He is not in person among us, only in spirit. The sun is ninety-five million miles from the earth, yet we feel its rays. In 2nd Chronicles we read, "If my people, which are called by my name, shall humble themselves, and pray, and seek my face, and turn from their wicked ways; then will I hear from heaven, and will forgive their sin, and will heal their land." Here is one reference, and when it is read a great many people might ask, "How far is heaven away? Can you tell us that?" I don't know how far it is away, but there is one thing I can tell you. He can hear prayer as soon as the words are uttered.

There has not been a prayer said that He has not heard; not a tear shed that He has not seen. We don't want to learn the distance. What we want to know is that God is there, and Scripture tells us that. Turn to 1st Kings and we read, "And may you hear the supplication of Your servant and of Your people Israel, when they pray toward this place. Hear in heaven, Your dwelling place, and when You hear, forgive." Now, it is clearly taught in the Word of God that the Father dwells there. It is His dwelling place, and in Acts we see that Jesus is there too. "But he being full of the Holy Spirit looked up steadfastly into heaven and saw the glory of God, and Jesus standing on the right hand of God," and by the eye of faith we can see them there tonight too. And by faith we shall be brought into His presence, and we shall be satisfied when we gaze upon Him.

Stephen, when he was surrounded by the howling multitude, saw the Son of Man there. Jesus, looking down upon earth, saw this first martyr in the midst of his persecution and gave him a welcome. We'll see him by and by. It is not the jasper streets and golden gates that attract us to heaven. What are your golden palaces on earth – what is that that makes them so sweet? It is the presence of some loving wife or fond children. Let them be taken away and the charm of your home is gone. And so it is Christ that is the charm of heaven to the Christians.

Yes, we shall see Him there. How sweet the thought that we shall dwell with Him forever and shall see the nails in His hands and in His feet which He received for us.

I read a little story not long since which went to my heart. A mother was on the point of death, and the child was taken away from her in case it would annoy her. It was crying continually to be taken to its mother and annoyed the neighbors. By and by the mother died, and the neighbors thought it was better to bury the mother without letting the child see her dead face. They thought the sight of the dead mother would not do the child any good, so they kept her away. When the mother was buried and the child was taken back to the house, the first thing she did was to run into her mother's sitting room and look all round it, and from there to the bedroom, but no mother was there. She went all over the house crying, "Mother, mother!" but the child could not find her. She then said to the neighbor, "Take me back, I don't want to stay here if I cannot see my mother." It wasn't the home that made it so sweet to the child. It was the presence of the mother. And so it is not heaven that is alone attractive to us; it is the knowledge that Jesus, our leader, our brother, and our Lord is there.

And the spirits of loved ones, whose bodies we have laid in the earth will be there. We shall be in good company there. When we reach that land, we shall meet all the Christians who have gone before us. We are told in Matthew, too, that we shall meet angels there: "Take heed that you do not despise one of these little ones, for I say unto you that in heaven their angels always behold the face of my Father which is in heaven." Yes, the angels are there, and we shall see them when we get home.

He is there, and where He is His disciples shall be, for He has said, "I go and prepare a mansion for you, that where I am, there you may be also." I believe that when we die the spirit leaves the body and goes to the mansion above, and by and by the body will be resurrected and it shall see Jesus. Very often people come to me and say, "Mr. Moody, do you think we shall know each other in heaven?" Very often it is a mother who has lost a dear child and who wishes to see it again. Sometimes it is a child who has lost a mother or a father, and who wants to recognize them in heaven. There is just one verse in Scripture in answer to this, and that is: "We shall be satisfied." It is all I want to know. My brother, who went up there the other day, I shall see, because I will be satisfied. Up there, we will see all those we loved on earth, and if we loved them here, we will love them ten thousand times more when we meet them there.

Another thought. In the tenth chapter of Luke, we are told our names are written there if we are Christians. Christ just called His disciples up and paired them off and sent them out to preach the gospel. Two of us, Mr. Sankey and myself, going about and preaching the gospel is nothing new. You will find them away back 1,800 years ago going off two by two, like Brothers Bliss and Whittle and Brothers Needham and Morehouse to different towns and villages. They had gone out, and there had been great revivals in all the cities, towns, and villages they had entered. Everywhere they had met with the greatest success. Even the demons were subject to them and disease fled before them.

When they met a lame man, they said to him, "You don't want to be lame any longer," and he walked. When they met a blind man, they told him to open his eyes and behold, he could see. And they came to Christ and rejoiced over their great success, and He just said to them, "I will give you something to rejoice over. Rejoice that your names are written in heaven." Now, there are a great many people who do not believe in such an assurance as this. "Rejoice, because your names are written in heaven." How are you going to rejoice if your names are not written there? While speaking about this some time ago, a man told me we were preaching a very ridiculous doctrine when we preached this doctrine of assurance. I ask you in all candor, what are you going to do with this assurance if we don't preach it? It is stated that our names are written there; blotted out of the Book of Death and transferred to the Book of Life.

I was with a friend while in Europe. On one occasion we were traveling from London to Liverpool, and the question was put as to where we would stop. We said we would go to the North Western at Lime Street, as that was the hotel where Americans generally stopped at. When we got there, the house was full. They could not let us in. Every room was engaged. But this friend said, "I am going to stay here. I engaged a room for myself ahead of time." My friends, that is just what the Christians are doing – sending their names in ahead. They are sending a message up saying, "Lord Jesus, I want one of those mansions you are preparing; I want to be there." That's what they're doing. And every man and woman here who wants one, if you have not already got one, had better make up their mind. Send your names up now. I would rather a thousand times have my name written in the Lamb's Book than have all the wealth of the world rolling at my feet.

A man may get station in this world, it will fade away; he may get wealth, but it will prove a bauble. "What shall it profit a man if he gain the whole world and lose his own soul." It is a solemn question. Let it go around the hall tonight, "Is my name written in the book of life?" I can imagine that man down there saying, "Yes. I belong to the Presbyterian Church; my name's on the church's books." It may be, but God keeps His books in a different fashion than that in which the church records of this city are kept. You may belong to a good many churches; you may be an elder or a deacon and be a bright light in your church, and yet you may not have your name written in the Book of Life.

Judas was one of the twelve, and yet he hadn't his name written in the Book of Life. Satan was among the elect – he dwelt among the angels, and yet he was cast from the high hallelujahs. Is your name written in the Book of Life? A man told me while speaking upon this subject, "That is all nonsense you are speaking." And a good many men here are of the same opinion; but I would like them to turn to Daniel, 12th chapter, "And there shall be a time of trouble, such as never was since there was a nation, even to that same time, and at that time thy people shall be delivered, every one that shall be found written in the book." Everyone shall be delivered whose names shall be found written in the book.

And we find Paul, in the letters which he wrote to the Philippians, addressing them as those "dear yokefellows, whose names were written in the Book of Life." If it is not our privilege to know that our names are written in the Book of Life, here is Paul sending greeting to his companions whose names were written in the Book. Let us not be deceived in this. We see it too plainly throughout the Holy Word. In the chapter of Revelations which we have just read, we have three different passages referring to it, and in the 27th verse, almost the last words in the Scriptures, we read: "And there shall in nowise enter into it anything which defiles, neither whatsoever works abomination or makes a lie, but they which are written in the Lamb's Book of Life."

My friends, you will never see the city unless your name is written in that Book of Life. It is a solemn truth. Let it go home to everyone and sink into the hearts of all here tonight. Don't build your hopes on a false foundation; don't build your hopes on an empty profession. Be sure your name is written there. And the next thing after your own names are written there is to see that the names of the children God has given you are recorded there. Let the fathers and mothers assembled tonight hear this and take it to their hearts. See that your children's names are there. Ask your conscience if the name of your John, your Willie, your Mary, your Alice – ask yourselves whether their names are recorded in the Book of Life. If not, make it the business of your life. Rather than to pile up wealth for them, make it the one object of your existence to secure for them eternal life rather than to pave the way to their death and ruin.

I read some time ago of a mother in an Eastern city who was stricken with consumption. At her dying hour she requested her husband to bring the children to her. The oldest one was brought first to her, and she laid her hand on his head and gave him her blessing and dying message. The next one was brought, and she gave him the same; and one after another came to her bedside until the little infant was brought in. She took it and pressed it to her bosom, and the people in the room, fearing that she was straining her strength, took the child away from her. As this was done, she turned to the husband and said, "I charge you, sir, bring all those children home with you." And so God charges us. The promise is to us and to our children. We can have our names written there, and then by the grace of God we can call our children to us and know that their names are also recorded there. That great roll is being called, and those bearing the names are summoned every day – every hour; that great roll is being called tonight, and if your name were shouted, could you answer with joy?

You have heard of a soldier who fell in our war. While he lay dying, he was heard to cry, "Here! here!" Some of his comrades went up to him thinking he wanted water, but he said, "They are calling the roll of heaven, and I am answering," and in a faint voice he whispered, "Here!"

and passed away to heaven. If that roll were called tonight, would you be ready to answer "Here!" I am afraid not. Let us wake up: may every child of God wake up tonight. There is work to do. Fathers and mothers, look to your children. If I could only speak to one class, I would preach to parents, and try to show them the great responsibility that rests upon them.

There is a man living on the bank of the Mississippi River. The world calls him rich, but if he could call back his first-born son he would give up all his wealth. The boy was brought home one day unconscious. When the doctor examined him, he turned to the father, who stood at the bedside, and said: "There is no hope." "What!" exclaimed the father, "is it possible my boy has got to die." "There is no hope," replied the doctor. "Will he not come to?" asked the father. "He may resume consciousness, but he cannot live." "Try all your skill, doctor. I don't want my boy to die." By and by the boy regained a glimmering of consciousness, and when he was told that his death was approaching, he said to his father, "Won't you pray for my lost soul, father? You have never prayed for me." The old man only wept. It was true. During the seventeen years that God had given him his boy he had never spent an hour in prayer for his soul. The object of his life had been to accumulate wealth for that firstborn. Am I speaking to a prayerless father or mother tonight? Settle the question of your soul's salvation and pray for the son or daughter God has given you.

But I have another anecdote to tell. It was Ralph Wallace who told me of this one. A certain gentleman had been a member of the Presbyterian Church. His little boy was sick. When he went home, his wife was weeping, and she said, "Our boy is dying. He has had a change for the worse. I wish you would go in and see him." The father went into the room and placed his hand on the brow of his dying boy and could feel that the cold, damp sweat was gathering there, that the cold, icy hand of death was feeling for the chords of life. "Do you know, my boy, that you are dying?" asked the father. "Am I? Is this death? Do you really think I am dying?" "Yes, my son, your end on earth is near." "And will I be with Jesus tonight, father?" "Yes, you will be with the Savior." "Father, don't you weep, for when I get there I will go right straight to Jesus and tell Him that you have been trying all my life to lead me to Him."

God has given me two little children, and ever since I can remember I have directed them to Christ, and I would rather lead them to Jesus than give them the wealth of the world. If you have got a child, go and point the way. I challenge any man to speak of heaven without speaking of children. "For of such is the kingdom of heaven." Fathers and mothers and professed Christians ignore this sometimes. They go along themselves and never try to get any to heaven with them. Let us see to this at once. Let us pray that there may be many names written in the Lamb's Book of Life tonight.

Heaven

Second Address

You who were here last night remember that the subject upon which I spoke was Heaven and who is there. We tried to prove from Scripture that God the Father, Christ the Son, and angels and redeemed saints who have gone up from earth are there, and that if we have been born of God, our names are recorded there. Now I will commence tonight right where I left off last night. The next thought upon the subject that presents itself is, "Are we laying our treasures there?" If we are living as God would have us live, we are doing this.

There are a great many people who forget that there are eleven commandments. They think there are only ten. The eleventh commandment is: "Lay up for yourselves treasures in heaven." How many of us remember – ah! How people in Chicago forget the words of the Lord now in His wonderful sermon on the mount: "Lay not up for yourselves treasures upon earth, where moth and rust doth corrupt, and where thieves break through and steal; but lay up for yourselves treasures in heaven, where neither moth nor rust doth corrupt, and where thieves do not break through nor steal." How few of our people pay any heed to these words. That's why there are so many broken hearts among us; that's why so many men and women are disappointed and going through the streets with shattered hopes. It's because they have not been laying up treasures in heaven. They pile up treasures on earth, and some calamity comes upon them and sweeps all away.

The Chicago fire burned up a good many of these treasures. A great number of people put their treasures in banks, which dissolve, and away they go. Some have put their treasures in railway shares which have all disappeared like a vapor. That is why so many are brokenhearted today, and in great distress, and do not know what is before them. If they had taken heed of the words of this commandment, this thing would not have happened to them. "Lay up your treasures in heaven." It doesn't take long in conversation with a man to find out where his heart is. Wherever it is, there is his treasure.

Go to a political man and talk to him about Hayes and Wheeler, or Tilden and Hendricks on any political question and how his heart gets ablaze and his eye sparkles. His treasure is in politics. Go talk to a man who loves the theater about a new play and see how his eye glistens. His heart is set upon pleasure, upon the world. And yet another class whose heart is set on business. Go to him and talk to him about some new speculation, show him where he can make a few thousand dollars, and you will soon tell where his treasure lies. But talk about heaven and all interest is lost. I could not help that thought coming to me last night, when I saw before me some dozing – some almost asleep, as if they thought I was talking about a myth; and others were sitting with eyes aglow and all attention when I mentioned heaven. Ah! They expected to go there and were glad to hear about it.

Some men think it is too far away to lay up their treasures. I was talking to a businessman before the Chicago fire about laying up treasures in heaven, and he said, "I like to have my treasure where I can see it." And that is the way with a great many people – they like to have their treasures here so they can see them. It is a great mistake. People go on accumulating what they must leave behind. How many here do not devote five minutes to anything else than money-making. It is money, money, money, and if they get it, they are satisfied, or at least they think they are. You will see occasionally in the newspapers accounts of men dying who are worth so many millions. It is a great mistake. He cannot take it with him. If it is in business, it isn't his. If it is in banks, it isn't his. If in real estate, he cannot take it. It isn't his. Now, ask yourselves tonight, "Where is my treasure?" Is my heart set upon things down here?" If it is set upon wealth, it will by and by take to itself wings and fly away. Oh, think of this. If your heart is set upon pleasure, it will melt away. If your heart is set upon station or reputation, some tongue may blast it in a moment, and it is gone. If your hopes and heart are set upon some loved wife or dear children, whom you have set up in your hearts as an idol in place of your God, death may come and snatch your god from your life. It is wrong to set up anything, however dear to us, in the place of our God. And so it is wrong "to lay up treasures for yourselves upon earth."

Now, are you, are the people of Chicago heeding this commandment? Ask yourselves this as you are passing through the street tomorrow: "How many of the people of this city are obeying this commandment, 'Lay up for yourselves treasures in heaven?'"

I remember before the Chicago fire hearing of a minister coming up to see his son. He found him completely absorbed in real estate. You remember before the fire how everyone was mad about real estate. It was a mania with all of us. If we could get a corner lot, no matter whether we threw ourselves in debt, or smothered it with mortgages, we were confident that in time, when prices went up, we would make our fortune.

This minister came up, and when he saw his son he tried to talk about his soul, but it was no use. Real estate was there. He talked about real estate in the morning, in the afternoon, and night. No use of trying to talk of heaven to him. His only heaven was real estate. The son had a boy in his real estate office, but he being absent, the father was left to mind the business one day. When a customer came in and started upon the subject of real estate, it was not long before the minister was speaking to the customer about his soul, telling him he would rather have a corner lot in the New Jerusalem than all the corner lots in Chicago. And the people used to say that no real estate could be sold when the father was around. The trouble was that the son had real estate in his heart – that was his god – and his father had in his heart treasures in heaven. If we have anything in our hearts which we put up as our god, let us ask Him to come to us and take it away from us.

I remember when I went to California just to try to get a few souls saved on the Pacific coast. I went into a school there and asked, "Have you got someone who can write a plain hand?" "Yes." Well, we got up the blackboard, and the lesson upon it proved to be the very text we have tonight, "Lay up for yourselves treasures in heaven." And I said, "Suppose we write upon that board some of the earthly treasures. We will begin with 'gold.'" The teacher readily put down gold, and they all comprehended it, for all had run to that country in the hope of finding it. "Well, we will put down 'houses' next, and then 'land.' Next we will put down 'fast horses.'" They all understood what fast horses were – they knew a good deal more about fast horses than they knew about the kingdom of God. Some of them, I think, actually made fast horses serve as gods. "Next we will put down 'tobacco.'"

The teacher seemed to shrink at this. "Put it down," said I. "Many a man thinks more of tobacco than he does of God. Well, then, we will put down 'rum.'" He objected to this – didn't like to put it down at all. "Down with it. Many a man will sell his reputation, will sell his home, his wife, children, everything he has. It is the god of some men." Many here in Chicago will sell their present and their eternal welfare for it. "Now," said I, "suppose we put down some of the heavenly treasures. Put down 'Jesus' to head the list, then 'heaven,' then 'river of life,' then 'crown of glory,'" and went on till the column was filled, and just drew a line and showed the heavenly and the earthly things in contrast.

My friends, if a man just does that, he cannot but see the superiority of the heavenly over the earthly treasures. Well, it turned out that the teacher was not a Christian. He had gone to California on the usual hunt – gold; when he saw the two columns placed side by side, the excellence of the one over the other was irresistible, and he was the first soul God gave me on that Pacific coast. He accepted Christ, and that man came to the station when I was coming away and blessed me for coming to that place.

Those of you who do not lay your treasures up in heaven will be sure to be disappointed. You cannot find a man who has devoted his life to the treasures of this life – not one in the wide, wide world – but who has been disappointed. Something arises in life to sweep all away, or the amount of joy which they expect to obtain from their riches falls short of their anticipations. If men center their affections on heaven, they will have no disappointment. All is joy and comfort from that source, and the whole current of their lives will be drifting towards heaven.

Someone has heard of a farmer who, when an agent called upon him to give something for the Christian Commission, promptly drew a check for $10,000. He wanted the agent to have dinner with him, and after they had dined, the farmer took the man out on the veranda and pointed to the rich lands sweeping far away laden with rich products. "Look over these lands," said the farmer. "They are all mine." He took him to the pasture and showed the agent the choice stock, the fine horses he had; he then pointed to a little town, and then to a large hall where he lived, saying, "They are all mine. I came here when a poor boy and I have earned all that you see."

When he got through, my friend asked him, "Well, what have you got up yonder?" "Where?" replied the farmer, who evidently knew where my friend meant. "What have you got in heaven?" "Well," said the farmer, "I haven't anything there." "What!" replied my friend, "You, a man of your discretion, wisdom, and business ability have made no provision for your future!" He hadn't, and in a few weeks, he died – a rich man here and a beggar in eternity. A man may be wise in the eyes of the world to pursue this course, but he is a fool in the sight of God. Wealth to most men proves nothing more or less than a great rock upon which his eternity is wrecked.

A great many Christians wonder how it is they don't get on better – how it is that they don't get on. It is because you have got your heart on things down here. When they look towards heaven, they don't have a love for the world. We are then living for another world. We are pilgrims and strangers upon the earth. It is easy to have love for God when we have our treasures there. The reason, then, why so many of us do not grow in Christianity is because we have our treasures here.

Mr. Moorhouse told me he was looking down the harbor of Liverpool one day, when he saw a vessel coming up, being towed by a tug. The vessel was sunk in the water nearly to her edge, and he wondered it did not sink altogether. Upon inquiry, he found that it was loaded with lumber and that it was waterlogged. Another vessel came up, her sails set, no tug assisting her, and she soon darted past the waterlogged vessel. And so it is with some Christians. They are waterlogged. They may belong to a church, but if they find anything in the church disagreeing with them, they won't go back. They want the whole church to come out and look for them and tow them in; if the church doesn't, they think they are not getting the attention due them.

When men go up in balloons, they take bags of sand with them; when they want to rise higher, they throw them out. There are a great many Christians who have got too many bags of sand, and to rise they want to throw some out. Look at the poor men here in the city – the rich Christians can relieve themselves by giving some of their bags of sand to them. A great many Christians would feel much better it they relieved themselves of their bags of sand. "He that gives to the poor lends to the Lord." If you want to be rich in eternity, just give to the poor with your heart, and the Lord will bless not only you, but all connected with you.

The next thing is our rest in heaven. A great many people have got a false idea about the church. They have got an idea that the church is a place to rest in. Instead of thinking that it is a place of work, they turn it into a resting place. To get into a nicely cushioned pew, contribute to the charities, listen to the minister, and do their share to keep the church out of bankruptcy is all they want. The idea of work for them, actual work in the church, never enters their mind. In Hebrews we see the words: "There is a rest for the people of God." We have got all eternity to rest in. Here is the place for work; we must work till Jesus comes. This is the place of toil – eternity of repose. "Blessed are they that die in the Lord, for their works do follow them." Let us do the work that God gives us today. Don't think that you have to rest in the world where God sent His son who was murdered.

I remember hearing a man who had worked successfully for the Lord complaining that he didn't have the success he used to. One night he threw himself on his bed, sick of life and wanting to die. While in this state of mind, he dreamed that he was dead and that he had ascended to heaven. As he was walking down the crystal pavement of Paradise he saw all at once three friends in a chariot, and when the chariot came opposite to where he was, one of them stepped out and came to him. He noticed that His face was illuminated with a heavenly radiance, and He came to this man and took him to the battlements of heaven. "Look down," said He, "what do you see?" "I see the dark world," replied the dreamer. "Look down again and tell me what you see." "I see men walking blindfolded over bridges, and below them are bottomless pits," was the dreamer's reply. "Will you prepare to stay here or go back to earth and tell those men of their danger – tell them of the bottomless pits over which they walk." At this the man awoke from his sleep and said he didn't want to die any more. He just wanted to remain down here and warn his fellowmen from the dangers which surrounded them.

When we turn a soul to Christ, we do not know what will turn up – what will be the result of it. It may be the means of saving a million souls. The one man may convert another man, and those two may convert a hundred, and that hundred may convert a thousand, and the current keeps widening and widening and deepening and deepening, and as time rolls on, the fruit will be ripening which you have gathered for God. It is a great privilege, my friends, to work for God.

I want to call your attention to the 11th chapter of Hebrews. After Paul mentions Jacob, Isaac, and Enoch, he says: "They all died in faith, not having received the promises, but having seen them afar off, and were persuaded of them, and embraced them, and confessed that they were strangers and pilgrims on the earth." Are the Christians of Chicago living like pilgrims and strangers, and by their faith do they show "that they seek another country;" do they show by their fruits and their deeds that they are pilgrims and strangers here?

When I get into a man's mind the beauties of that country beyond the grave, it looks as if his only thought was for it. We are to be pilgrims and strangers passing through this world on our way to a better land. The moment Abraham by faith got sight of that land he declared himself a pilgrim and a stranger. This earth had no charm for him then. Lot might go down to that city of Sodom or Gomorrah, and that city might be burned up. We might fix our affections on this city. Chicago has been burned twice, and it will be burned again. This whole world shall pass away with all its boasted riches and glory, and where shall we be then? If we build our hopes here, we shall be disappointed; if we build our hopes upon that foundation whose builder and maker is God, we shall not be disappointed.

We are told in Matthew to set our affections on things above, and that "there shall be joy in heaven over one sinner that repents." There are rumors of war in Europe, and if war were declared, probably it would excite the whole civilized world. Trade would be affected and relations of all kinds. I don't know whether it would excite heaven at all. If the President of the United States issued a proclamation, I don't know whether it would be noticed in heaven or not, but the papers would speak of it, the people would be excited, and great changes might take place over it. If Queen Victoria died, telegrams would go all over the world, newspapers would speak of it, the whole world would be excited – I don't know if it would be noticed in heaven at all. But if that girl there should repent, there would be joy in heaven. Just think of it – think of a little girl, of a little girl being the cause of joy in heaven. I don't think the papers would record it – they would never notice it. There would be no head in the morning telling the people that there had been joy in heaven over the repentance of a little girl in the Tabernacle. "There is joy over one sinner that repents."

I have been wondering who it is that rejoiced in heaven when He brought back that lost sheep. We are told that there is joy in the presence of the angels, but who else is it that rejoices? It may be that I am going a little too far, but I'd like to think that I have a right to believe that the redeemed saints who have gone up from earth may be led to rejoice when they hear in heaven of the conversion of some living ones here.

Perhaps while I am speaking, some loving mother may be looking over the battlements of heaven on her boy in the gallery yonder, and it may be that while she was on earth she prayed earnestly and constantly, and when she got there she pleaded at the throne for mercy to her son. It may be that as she is watching, some angel will carry the news to her of that boy's conversion, and take his name there to be recorded in the Book of Life. Perhaps that mother and the Lord Jesus Christ will rejoice over that son, or it may be some daughter. Perhaps it is some child who is looking from that country down to her mother in this hall, and when the news of her acceptance of salvation reaches that little child, she will strike her golden harp and shout, "Mother! Mother is coming!" While I was touching on this topic in Manchester, I remember a man getting up and shouting, "Oh, Mother, I am coming!" The mother had been fruitless in her endeavors to convert that man while on earth, but her intercession there and the influence of her prayers here touched his heart and he decided.

I remember in the Exposition building in Dublin, while I was speaking about heaven, I said something to the effect that "perhaps at this moment a mother is looking down from heaven upon her daughter here tonight," and I pointed down to a young lady in the audience. Next morning, I received this letter: "On Wednesday when you were speaking of heaven, you said, 'It may be this moment there is a mother looking down from heaven expecting the salvation of her child who is here.' You were apparently looking at the very spot where my child was sitting. My heart said, 'that is *my* child. That is *her* mother.' Tears sprang to my eyes. I bowed my head and prayed, 'Lord, direct that word to my darling child's heart; Lord, save my child.' I was then anxious till the close of the meeting when I went to her. She was bathed in tears. She rose, put her arms round me, and kissed me. When walking down to you, she told me it was that same remark (about the mother looking down from heaven) that found the way home to her, and asked me, 'Papa, what can I do for Jesus?'"

May the Spirit of God bring hundreds to the cross of Christ tonight.

The Precious Blood

First Address

The subject tonight will be "The Precious Blood." I want to call your attention first to the 2nd chapter and 16th verse of Genesis, *"And the Lord God commanded the man, saying, Of every tree of the garden you may freely eat: But of the tree of the knowledge of good and evil, you shall not eat of it: for in the day that you eat thereof you shall surely die."* There cannot be a law without a penalty. There is not a law in our land that doesn't have a penalty attached to it. If our legislative representatives or members in Congress were to make a law and have no penalty appended to it, it would be worthless. We might make a law forbidding men to steal, but if we had no penalty to that law, I don't think we could go home without having our watches stolen from us. We could not live without law, and God put Adam into the garden under a law, attached to which was a penalty. Well, we know how he disobeyed and how he fell, and so the penalty of death came upon him. Many people stumble over this.

I used to wonder how it was that the penalty of death fell upon him when he lived, I think, some nine hundred and thirty years after he broke the law; but when I understood my Bible better, I learned that it was death to the soul – not physical death, but spiritual death. When

God came to seek him in the garden, we are told that Adam hid himself; he was ashamed of his iniquity – just like hundreds of his sons in Chicago. And then we find God dealing with Adam by showing him grace. This was the very first thing He did. A great many people think God was very severe in His treatment of Adam, but He, whenever the offence was committed, whenever the law was broken, showed mercy, showed grace; and by this grace a way of escape was presented to them. Ah, that little hymn expresses it: "Grace, friend, contrived a way," by which Adam could regain the life he had forfeited. And so we read that the Lord made "coats of skin" to clothe them before He drove them out of Paradise. They received grace before, as we see in the 24th verse: "He drove out the man, and He placed at the east end of the Garden of Eden cherubims and a flaming sword which turned every way to keep the way of the tree of life."

There's grace and government, and from that day till the present God has been dealing with us in that way. He rides, we may say, in a chariot with two wheels – one grace and the other government. We can see in this world how it would be if we had no government. There would be no living in it. Adam broke the divine law, and so he had to suffer the penalty; but He gave him grace to be redeemed by. He showed Adam and Eve grace by killing the animals and then covering their nakedness with coats made from the skins. I can imagine Adam turning to Eve and saying, "Well, in spite of what we've done, God loves us after all. He has clothed us; He has given us grace for our sin." And here we find the first glimpse of the doctrine of substitution – the substitution of the just for the unjust, the great doctrine of atonement and substitution foreshadowed in Genesis.

Then, as we go on, we find the story of Cain and Abel, and we are told that "in process of time it came to pass that Cain brought of the fruit of the ground an offering unto the Lord. And Abel, he also brought of the firstlings of his flock, and of the fat thereof; and the Lord had respect unto Abel and to his offering; but unto Cain and his offering He had not respect. And Cain was very angry and his countenance fell." Now we find that Cain brought a bloodless sacrifice – "he brought of the fruit of the ground" – and Abel brought a bleeding lamb. Right on the morning of grace we see here that God had marked a way for men to come to Him, and that way was the way that Abel took, and Cain came to God with a sacrifice of his own, in his own way.

So we find men and women in the churches of today coming to God with a sacrifice, not in God's way, but in their own – coming with their own good deeds, or their works, or their righteousness, and ignoring the Lamb altogether, ignoring the blood completely. They don't want to come that way; they want to come in their own fashion. Cain, perhaps, reasoned that he didn't see why the products of the earth, why the fruit, shouldn't be as acceptable to God as a bleeding lamb. He didn't like a bleeding lamb, and so he brought his fruit. Now we don't know how there was any difference between those two boys. Both must have been brought up in the same way; both came from the same parents, yet we find in the offering there was a difference between them. One came with the blood and the other without the blood, and the one with the blood had the acceptable sacrifice to God.

We pass over to the second dispensation – to the 8th chapter of Genesis – where we find Noah coming out of the ark and putting blood between him and his sins. "And Noah built an altar unto the Lord, and took of every clean beast and of every clean fowl and offered burnt offerings on the altar." God had Noah bring those animals clear through the flood so that he could offer them as a sacrifice when he came from the ark. He took a couple of each kind into the ark, and when he came out, we find him making a blood offering the very first thing. He was a man of God; he walked in the fear of the Lord, and so he made the offering of blood. The first thing in the first dispensation we see is blood, and the first thing in the second dispensation is blood.

In the 22nd chapter of Genesis, we find the story of Abraham and his only son, Isaac. Abraham was a follower of God, a man who loved and feared God, and He commanded him to make a blood sacrifice. We read in this chapter that He commanded Abraham to make the sacrifice of his only son. And we read that the next morning the old man saddled his ass and started. He didn't tell his wife anything about it. If he had, she would likely have persuaded him to remain where he was. But he has heard the voice of God, and he obeys the command; he has heard God's wish, and he is going to do it.

So, early in the morning – he didn't wait till ten or twelve o'clock but went early in the morning – he takes two of his young men with him and his son Isaac, and you can see him starting out on the three days' journey. They have the wood and the fire, for he is going to worship his God. As he goes on, he looks at his boy and says, "It is a strange commandment that God has given. I love this boy dearly. I don't understand it; but I know it's all right, for the Judge of all the earth makes no mistakes." An order from the Judge of Heaven is enough for him. The first night comes and their little camp is made, and Isaac is asleep.

But the old man doesn't sleep. He looks sadly into his face and says, "I will have no boy soon. I shall never see him on earth again, but I must obey God." I can see him marching on the next day, and you might have seen him drying his tears as he glanced upon that only son and thought upon what he had been called upon to do. The second night comes; tomorrow is the day for the sacrifice. What a night that must have been to Abraham. "Tomorrow," he says sadly, "I must take the life of that boy – my only son, dearer to me than my life – dearer to me than anything on earth." And the third day comes, and as they go along, they see the mountain in the distance. He says to the young men, "You stay here with the beasts." He takes the wood and the fire, and along with his boy prepares to ascend Mount Moriah, from which could be seen the spot where a few hundred years later the Son of man was offered up.

As they ascend the mountain Isaac says, "There's the wood and the fire, father, but where's the sacrifice?" – thus showing that the boy knew nothing of what was in store. How the question must have sunk down into the old man's heart. And he answers, "The Lord will provide a sacrifice." It was not time to tell him. They go on until they come to the place appointed by God; they build the altar and lay the wood upon it. Everything is ready, and I can just imagine the old man taking the boy by the hand, leading him to a rock, sitting down there, and telling him how God had called upon him to come out of his native land; how God had been in communion with him for fifty years; what God had done for him.

"And now," he says, "my boy, when I was in my bed three nights ago, God came to me with a strange message, in which He told me to offer my child as a sacrifice. I love you, my son, but God has told me to do this, and I must obey Him. So let us both go down on our knees and pray to Him." After they have sent up a petition to God, Abraham lays him on the altar and kisses him for the last time. He lifts the knife to drive it into his son's heart, when all at once he hears a voice: "Abraham, Abraham, spare your only son." Ah, there was no voice heard on Calvary to save the Son of man. God showed mercy to the son of Abraham.

You fathers and mothers, just picture to yourselves how you would suffer if you had to sacrifice your only son; think what it must have caused God to give up His only Son. We are told that Abraham was glad. The manifestations of Abraham's faith so pleased God that He showed him the grace of heaven and lifted the curtain of time to let him look down into the future to see the Son of God offered, bearing the sins of the world. From the peak of this very mountain might have been seen the very spot where died the Savior of the world.

We find Abel the first man who went to heaven, and he went by way of blood, and we find it in all the worship of God from the earliest times. Mr. Sankey sings solos upon the redeeming blood. I can imagine when Abel got there how he sang the song of redemption. How the angels gathered around him and listened to that song. It was the first time they had ever heard that song, but 6,000 years have gone and there's a great chorus of the saints redeemed by the atoning blood.

The first man that went to heaven went by the way of blood, and the last man who passes through those pearly gates must go the same way. We find not only Abel and Abraham and Isaac and Jacob, but all of them, went there through an atonement. Now, we find in the 12th chapter and 2nd verse of Exodus – the most important chapter in the Word of God: "This month shall be unto you the beginning of months; it shall be the first month of the year to you." And then in the fourth verse, "And if the household be too little for the lamb, let him and his neighbor next unto his house take it according to the number of the souls; every man according to his eating shall make your count for the lamb." Now it doesn't say "if the lamb be too small for the household," but "if the household be too little for the lamb." You may have some pretty large households; your houses may be too small for them, but Christ has plenty of room.

We don't start from the cradle to heaven but from the cross. That's where eternal life begins – when we come to Calvary; when we come to Christ and get grace. We don't come to heaven when we are born into the natural world, but into the spiritual world. That's where we date our spiritual lives from. Before that our lives are a blank so far as grace is concerned. Adam dated from the time of the flood, and Noah when he came from the ark dated from the blood offering, and so the children of Israel when they came out of Egypt. And even today when they take up their pens and date 1876 years – when do they date from? Why, from the blood of Christ. Everything dates from blood. In this chapter we see the command to sacrifice. They slew the lamb. God didn't say, "Put a lamb to your front door, and I will spare you," but on the houses.

Some classes of people say, "Preach anything but the death, preach the life of Christ." You may preach that and you'll never save a soul. It is not Christ's sympathy – His life – we preach, it is His sacrifice. That's what brings men out of darkness. I can imagine some proud Egyptians that day, who when they heard the bleating of the lambs – there must have been over 200,000 lambs – saying, "What an absurd performance. Every man has got a lamb, and they have got the best lambs out of the flock, too, and they are going to cover their houses with the blood." They looked upon this as an absurd proceeding – a flaw in their character. You may find a good many flaws in your character, but you cannot find a flaw in the Lamb of God. When the hour came you could see them all slaying their lamb, and not only that, but putting the blood on the doorposts.

To those Egyptians or to the men of the world how absurd it looked. They probably said, "Why are you disfiguring your houses in that way?" It was not upon the threshold. God didn't want that, but they were to put it upon the lintels and doorposts – where God could see it that night so that (13th verse) He might see it as a token. This blood was to be a substitution for death, and all who hadn't that token in the land of Egypt had their firstborn smitten at midnight. There was a wail from Egypt from one end to the other. But death didn't come near the homes where was the token. It was death that kept death out of the dwelling.

Many people say, "I wish I were as good as that woman who has been ministering to the sick for the last fifty years. I would feel sure of heaven." My friends, if you have the blood behind you, you are as safe as anybody on this earth. It is not because that woman has been living a life of sacrifices in her ministrations to the poor that she will enter the kingdom of God. It is not our life of good deeds or our righteousness that will take us to heaven, but the atonement. And the question ought to come to everyone tonight, "Are we sheltered behind the blood?" If not, death will come by and by and you will be separated from God for eternity. If you have not a substitute, you will die. Death is passed upon all of us. Why? Because of our sin. If we have not a substitute, we have no hope.

Not only were they to have a token, but they were to do something else. We read in the 11th verse: "And thus shall you eat it; with your loins girded, your shoes on your feet, and your staff in your hand; and you shall eat it in haste; it is the Lord's passover." Now a great many people wonder why they haven't got more spiritual power and have not the joy of the Lord with them all the time. It is because they haven't got the blood of the Lamb with them. These pilgrims had a long journey before them, and the Lord told them to eat the lamb. If we feed upon the Lamb, we will get strength in proportion. My friends, be sure before you commence on your pilgrimage that you are sheltered behind the blood, for when He sees the blood, death will pass over you. And let me ask this assemblage tonight if every one of you have the token. I was speaking to a man some time ago, who, when I asked him if he had the token said, "I have prayer," and when he got to heaven he would pray, and he thought that would admit him. I said to him, "You won't get in that way. You must be cleansed by the blood of Christ. That is the only power that will open the gates of heaven – the only countersign."

When I went East the other night the conductor came around and called for the tickets. I pulled out my ticket and he punched it. He didn't know whether it was a white or a black man who presented it, I believe. He didn't care who it was; all he wanted was the token. So all that God wants is the token of our salvation. It doesn't depend upon our deeds, our righteousness, or upon our lives; it depends upon whether or not we are sheltered behind the blood. That is the question. It didn't matter in that land of Goshen whether the child was six months or six years old if it was behind the blood. It was not their moral character, nor their connections, but the blood that saved them. It is the atonement that saves, and that is the teaching all through your Bible.

There is another verse in the 29th chapter of Exodus I want to call your attention to: "You shall slay the ram, and you shall take his blood and sprinkle it round about the altar." Now we see that Aaron the high priest could not come to God with his prayers alone. He had to sprinkle the blood upon the altar. There was a time when I didn't believe in the substitution and in the blood, and my prayers went no higher than my head; but when I came to God by Jesus Christ – by the way of blood – it was different. I never knew a man who came to God really but who came this way. That great high priest Aaron had to come this way, too.

Then, again in the 30th chapter, 10th verse, we see: "And Aaron shall make an atonement upon the horns of it once in a year, with the blood of the sin offering of atonements; once in the year shall he make atonement upon it throughout your generations; it is most holy unto the Lord." Now, an atonement is the only thing that makes a sinner and God one, the only thing that will bring God and the sinner together. I would like, if I had time, to give you all the passages touching upon atonement in the Old Testament, but it would take too long.

Turn again to the 8th chapter of Leviticus. This book of Leviticus is one of the most valuable, because it relates all about the worship of God. I remember when I used to read this book, I used to wonder what it was all about – a verse like this, for instance: "And he slew it; and Moses took of the blood of it and put it upon the tip of Aaron's right ear, and upon the thumb of his right hand, and upon the great toe of his right foot." I would say, "What does this mean: 'Put it upon the tip of Aaron's right ear?' What for?" I think I have got a little light upon the subject since those days. "Blood upon the ear?" So that a man could hear the voice of God, of course. And so a man who has accepted the atonement can hear the word rightly. Blood upon the hand of a man, so that he who works for God can work rightly.

Hundreds of men think they are working out their salvation, but they are only deceiving themselves. Bear in mind then, that a man cannot do anything until he is sheltered behind the blood. When a man is in this position then he can go and be acceptable to God. Then blood upon the feet, so that a man can walk with God. You know when God came to Adam, he hid himself. He hadn't the blood, and he couldn't walk with God. He put those people in question behind the blood, and He walked among them. When they came to the Red Sea, the mighty waters opened, and God walked with them. In the wilderness they wanted water, and a rod struck the rock, and a crystal stream gushed forth. Why? Because they had had the substitution.

Many people say this is a very mysterious thing. We don't understand why God wants blood as an atonement. A man said to me, "I detest your religion; I hate your God." "Why?" I asked. "I detest a God who demands blood," he replied. Now, God is not an unjust God. He doesn't demand it without giving us a reason. He tells us in His word that "the life of the flesh is in the blood." Take the blood out of me and I am a dead man. Life has been forfeited, the law has been broken, and the penalty must come upon us, and His blood He gives us is life; it is the life of our flesh. Three times we see "blood" mentioned in the 23rd and 24th verses, and the reason is that it is life. You and I have lost life by the fall, and what we want is to get back that life we lost, and we have it offered to us by the atonement of Christ.

I have often thought I would far rather be out of Eden and have the blood than be in Eden without it. Adam might have been there ten years and Satan might have been there ten years, and Satan might have come and got him. But some can't see why God permitted Adam to fall. They can't begin to discern the philosophy of it. They can't see why God ever permitted original sin to come into the world. The best answer to that was given by Andrew Bonar who said, "It was a great deal more wonderful that God should send His Son down to bear the brunt of it." Let us thank God we have a refuge, a substitute for the sin we are groaning under.

Turn to the 53rd chapter of Isaiah. You hear a good many people saying, "I don't believe in the Old Testament, I believe in the New." My friends, both are inseparable. A scarlet thread runs through the two and binds them together. We, like sheep, have gone astray, but "He was wounded for our transgressions. He was bruised for our iniquities; the chastisement of our peace was upon Him; and with His stripes we are healed." My friends, in the 53rd chapter of Isaiah we see it prophesied 700 years before it took place that He would die and be a substitute for you and me, that we might live. And now, my friends, let us accept Him. It seems base ingratitude not to praise God every hour of our lives that He has given such a Savior. Let us take time. Many a young man thinks it noble to scoff at this: I think it the basest ingratitude. This atonement is the only hope of my eternal life. Take the doctrine of substitution out of my Bible, and I would not take it home with me tonight. Let us praise God that He loved us so as to give us His only Son so that we might be saved.

I remember some years ago reading about a New York family. A young man, during the gold fever, went out to the Pacific and left his wife and little boy. Just as soon as he was successful, he was going to send money. A long time elapsed, but at last a letter came enclosing a draft and telling his wife to come on. The woman took a passage in one of the fine steamers of the Pacific line, full of hope and joy at the prospect of soon being united to her husband. They had not been out many days when a voice went ringing through the ship, "Fire! Fire!" The pumps were set to work, and the buckets were brought into operation, but the fire gained upon them. There was a powder magazine on board, and the captain ordered all the boats to be lowered. He knew whenever the fire reached the powder they would all be lost.

The people scrambled into the boats and the mother and boy were left on deck. As the last boat was being pushed off, the woman begged to be taken in. The majority insisted the boat was too full and wanted to push off, but one man put in a word for her, and they said they could allow one more on board, but no more. What did the mother do? Did she go on board and leave her son? No. She put her boy into that lifeboat and told him if he ever lived to see his father to tell him, "I died to save you." And the boat pulled away from that ship and left the mother standing there. The vessel went on burning. Presently an explosion was heard, and all was buried in the ocean. Suppose that young man was here tonight. Suppose you spoke to him about the act of his mother, and he turned around and scoffed at it. "Why," you would say, "that ungrateful wretch doesn't deserve to live." This is what you are doing. Jesus laid down His life for you. Now will you speak contemptuously about Him? Will you speak lightly of the blood laid down on Calvary for you? Let us rather all thank God we have such a Savior. Let us live for Him when He died for us. Let us pray.

The Precious Blood

Second Address

Y ou who were here last night remember that we spoke of the "Precious Blood," and that we looked at a few passages in the Old Testament bearing upon the subject. Tonight, I want to take up some passages referring to the subject in the New Testament. Soon after we came back from Europe to this country, I received a letter from a lady saying that she had looked forward to our coming back to this country with a great deal of interest, and that her interest remained after we had commenced our services, until I came to the lecture on the blood, when she gave up all hope of our doing any good. In closing that letter she said, "Where did Jesus ever teach the perilous and barbarous doctrine that men were to be redeemed by the shedding of His blood? Never, never did Jesus teach that monstrous idea."

Let us turn to the 14th chapter of Mark, 24th verse, and we will find: "And He said unto them, this is My blood of the New Testament, which is shed for many," and also, in Matthew, 26th chapter and 28th verse: "For this is My blood of the New Testament, which is shed for the remission of sin." There are a good many passages, but it is not necessary to refer to more. If Christ and the apostles did not teach it – if Christ did not preach it, then I have read my Bible wrong all these years. I haven't got the key to the Scriptures; it is a sealed book to me, and if I don't preach it – if I give it up, I've nothing left to preach. Take the blessed doctrine of the blood out of my Bible, and my capital is gone, and I've got to take to something else.

I remember when in the old country, a young man came to me – a minister came 'round to me and said he wanted to talk with me. He said to me, "Mr. Moody, you are either all right, and I am all wrong, or else I am right, and you are all wrong." "Well, sir," said I, "you have the advantage of me. You have heard me preach and know what doctrines I hold, whereas, I have not heard you and don't know what you preach." "Well," said he, "the difference between your preaching and mine is that you make out that salvation is got by Christ's death, and I make out that it is attained by His life." "Now, what do you do with the passages bearing upon the death?" and I quoted the passages, "Without the shedding of blood there is no remission," and "He Himself, bore our own sins by His own body on the tree," and asked him what he did with them, for instance. "Never preach on them at all."

I quoted a number of passages more, and he gave me the same answer. "Well, what do you preach?" I finally asked. "Moral essays," he replied. Said I, "Did you ever know anybody to be saved by that kind of thing – did you ever convert anybody by them?" "I never aimed at that kind of conversion; I mean to get men to heaven by culture, by refinement." "Well," said I, "if I didn't preach those texts and only preached culture, the whole thing would be a sham." "And it is a sham to me," was his reply. I tell you, the moment a man breaks away from this doctrine of blood, religion becomes a sham, because the whole teaching of this book is of one story, and this is that Christ came into the world and died for our sins.

I want to call your attention to the 19th chapter of John, and the 34th verse: "But one of the soldiers with a spear pierced His side, and forthwith came there out blood and water." Came there out blood and water. Now, it was prophesied years before that there should open a fountain, which should wash away sin and uncleanness, and it seems that this fountain was opened here by the spear of the soldier, and out of the fountain came blood and water. It was the breaking of the crown of hell, and the giving of the crown to heaven. When the Roman soldier drove out the blood, out came the water, and it touched that spear, and it was not long before Christ had that Roman government. It is a throne and a footstool now, and by and by it will sway the earth from pole to pole. This earth has been redeemed by the blessed blood of Christ.

Peter says in his first epistle 1:18 and 19: "Forasmuch as you know that we were not redeemed by corruptible things, as silver and gold, from your vain conversation received by tradition from your fathers; but with the precious blood of Christ, as of a lamb without blemish and without spot." You are not redeemed by such corruptible things as gold or silver, but by the precious blood of the Lamb – "the precious blood of Christ – as of a lamb without blemish." If silver and gold could have redeemed us, it would have been the easiest thing to have made a pile of gold ten thousand times larger than the bulk of the earth. Why, the poorest thing is gold in heaven. But gold couldn't do it. As I said last night, the law had been broken, and the penalty of death had come upon us; it required life to redeem us. Now, it says we shall be redeemed. My friends, redemption is to me one of the most precious treasures in the Word of God – to think that Christ has bought me by His blood. I am no longer my own, I am His. He has ransomed me.

A friend of mine once told me that he was going out from Dublin one day and met a boy who had one of those English sparrows in his hand. It was frightened and just seemed to sit as if it pined for liberty, but the boy held it so tight that it could not get away. The boy's strength was too much for the bird. My friend said, "Open your hand and let the bird go. You will never tame him, he is wild." But the boy replied, "Faith an' I'll not; I've been a whole hour trying to catch him, an' now I've got him, I'm going to keep him." So the man took out his purse and asked the boy if he would sell it. A bargain was made, and the sparrow was transferred to the man's hand.

He opened his hand, and at first it did not seem to realize it had liberty, but by and by it flew away, and as it went it chirped, as much as to say, "You have redeemed me." And so Christ has come down and offered to redeem us and give us liberty when we were bound with sin. Satan was stronger than we were. He has had 6,000 years' experience. He did not come to buy us from Satan, but from the penalty of our sin.

Another thought about the blood. It makes us all one. The blood brings us into one family, into the household of faith. I remember during the war Dr. Kirk, one of the most eloquent men I ever heard, was speaking in Boston. At that time, you recollect, there was a good deal said about the Irish and the black man, and what an amount of talk about the war of races. He said while preaching one night, "I saw a poor Irishman and a black man and an Englishman, and the blood of Christ came down and fell upon them and made them one." My friends, it brings nationalities together; it brings those scattered with the seeds of discord together and makes them one.

Let us turn to Acts 17:26 and we read: "And hath made of one blood all nations of men for to dwell on all the face of the earth, and hath determined the times before appointed and the bounds of their habitation." That's what the blood of Christ does. It just makes us one. I can tell a man that has been redeemed by the blood. They speak all the same language. I don't require to be in his company ten minutes before I can tell whether or not he has been redeemed. They have only one language, and you can tell when they speak whether they are outside the blood or sheltered by it. The blood has two voices – one is for salvation and the other is for condemnation. The blood tonight cries out for my salvation or for my condemnation. If we are sheltered behind the blood, it cries for our salvation; for we see in Galatians, "It cries for our peace." There is no peace till a man has been sheltered by that blood.

Again, I would like to call your attention to the 26th chapter of Matthew, 28th verse, where we find Christ speaking of His blood: "For this is My blood of the New Testament, which is shed for the remission of sins." This blood was "shed for the remission of sins." Then in Hebrews 9:22 where it says, "Without the shedding of blood is no remission of sins." Men don't realize that this is God's plan of salvation. Said a man to me last night after the meeting, "Why, God has got a plan to save us." Certainly, He has. You must be saved by God's plan. It was love that prompted God to send His Son to save us and shed His blood. That was the plan. And without the blood, what hope have you? There is not a sin from your childhood, from your cradle up till now that can be forgiven, unless by the blood. Let us take God at His word: "Without the shedding of blood there is no remission of sins." Without the blood, no remission whatever. I don't see how a man can fail to comprehend this. That's what Christ died for; that's what Christ died on Calvary for. If a man makes light of that blood, what hope has he?

How are you going to get into the kingdom of God? You cannot join in the song of the saints if you don't go into heaven that way. You cannot sing the song of redemption. If you did, I suppose you would be off in some corner with a harp of your own singing, "I saved myself; I saved myself." You can't get in that way. You must accept the plan of redemption and come in through it. "He that climbs up some other way, the same is a thief and a robber."

Then, in the 10th chapter of Hebrews, we find Paul, if he wrote this, just taking up the very thought: "He that despised Moses's law died without mercy under two or three witnesses." You know, when a man made light of the law under the Mosaic dispensation, whenever two witnesses came into court and swore that he hadn't kept the law, they just took him out and stoned him to death. Take up the next verse: "Of how much surer punishment suppose you shall be thought worthy who has trodden underfoot the Son of God and has counted the blood of the covenant wherewith He was sanctified an unholy thing and has done despite unto the spirit of grace." My friends, what hope is there if a man tramples the blood of Christ under his foot, if he says, "I will have nothing to do with that blood?" I ask in all candor what mercy is there? What hope has he if he "hath trodden underfoot the Son of God and hath counted the blood of the covenant wherewith He was sanctified an unholy thing?" This is the only way to get to heaven, no other way.

Turn again to the 12th verse of the same chapter and we see: "But the Man after He had offered one sacrifice for sin" – mark that, He had settled the question of sin – "forever, sat down on the right hand of God." The high priests could never sit down. Their work was never done, but our High Priest put sin away by one sacrifice and then ascended to God. And in this same chapter of Hebrews we see again: "Having therefore, brethren, boldness to enter into the holiest by the blood of Jesus, by a new and living way, which He has consecrated for us through the veil, that is to say, His flesh, and having a High Priest over the home of God, let us draw near with a true heart in full assurance of faith, having our hearts sprinkled from an evil conscience, and our bodies washed with pure water. Let us hold fast the profession of our faith without wavering, for He is faithful that promised."

I want to call your attention to the 20th verse more particularly – "by a new and living way." Now Christ has opened a new and a living way. We cannot get to heaven by our own deeds now. He has opened "a new and a living way." We don't need a high priest to go once a year and pray to God. Thank God we are all kings and all priests. We can go straight to the Father in the name of the Lord Jesus Christ. When Christ died, that temple was rent from the top to the bottom – not from the bottom to the top – and every poor son of Adam can walk right in and worship – right into the presence of God, if he only comes by the way of the blood. Yes, thank God, He has opened a new and a living way whereby we can come to Him. Let us thank God for the new and the living way. We don't need any bishop, we don't need any pope, we don't need any priest or prophet now; but everyone can be made kings and priests, and we can come through this living way to His presence and ask Him to take away our sins. There's not a man in this assemblage but can come to Him tonight.

There's a good deal about the blood in Hebrews that I would like to bring up; time passes, and I have just to fly through the subject. Now I don't know any doctrine I have preached that has been talked about more than the doctrine of blood. Why, the moment Satan gets a man to leave out this doctrine of blood, he has gained all he wants. It is the most pernicious idea to leave it out. A man may be a brilliant preacher, may have a brilliant intellect, and may have large crowds of people, but if he leaves this out, no one will be blest under his ministry, no one will be born in God's kingdom. If a man leaves out this blood he may as well go and whistle in the streets and try to convert people that way for all the good he will do in saving souls.

It is said that when a young student used to start out to preach, old Dr. Alexander of Princeton College always gave him a piece of advice. The old man would stand with his gray locks and his venerable face and say, "Young man, make much of the blood in your ministry." Now, I have travelled considerable during the past few years and never met a minister who made much of the blood and much of the atonement, but God had blessed his ministry and souls were born into the light by it. But a man who leaves it out, the moment he goes, his church falls to pieces like a rope of sand, and his preaching has been barren of good result. And so if you find a man preaching who has covered up this doctrine of blood, don't sit under his ministry. I don't care what denomination he belongs to, get out of it. Fly from it as those who flew from Sodom. Never mind how you get out of it – leave it. It is a whitened sepulcher. There is no life if they don't preach the blood. It is the only way we've got to conquer Satan; the only way we can enter heaven, and we cannot get there unless we have washed our robes in the blood of the Lamb. If we expect to conquer, we must be first washed by that blood.

A man who has not realized what the blood has done for him has not the token of salvation. It is told of Julian the apostate, that while he was fighting, he received an arrow in his side. He pulled it out and taking a handful of blood threw it into the air and cried, "Galilean, Galilean, you have conquered!" Yes, the Galilean is going to conquer, and you must bear in mind, if you don't accept the blood – don't submit to it and let it cleanse you – the rock will fall on you, because the decree of Heaven is that every knee will bow to the will of heaven. The blood is a call of mercy now. He wants you to come – He beseeches you to accept and be saved.

I heard of an old minister who had preached the gospel faithfully for fifty years. "Ah!" many here will say, "I wish I was as safe to go to heaven as he." When he was reaching his end, he asked that his Bible should be brought to him. His eyes were growing dim in death, and he said to one of those about him, "I wish you would turn to the first epistle of John, 1:7." When it was found, the old man put his dying finger on the passage where it says: "But if we walk in the light as He is in light we have fellowship one with another, and the blood of Jesus Christ His Son, cleanses us from all sin," and he said, "I die in the hope of that." It was the blood in his ministry that cleansed him. And so it is the only way by which our sins can be washed away. Why, there was a question once asked in heaven when a great crowd were gathering there, "Who are those?" and the answer was, "They are those who have come by great tribulation and have been washed by the blood of the Lamb."

Now, the question here tonight is, what are you going to do with that blood? We have had it for two nights, and before I close, I would like to ask you, what are you going to do about it? You must do either of two things – take it or reject it. Trample it under foot or cleanse your sins by it. I heard of a lady who told a servant to cook a lamb. She told him how to do it up and all about it, but she didn't tell him what to do with the blood. So he went to her and asked, "What are you going to do with the blood of the lamb?" She had been under conviction for some time, and such a question went like an arrow to her soul. She went to her room and felt uneasy, and the question kept continually coming to her, "What are you going to do with the blood of the Lamb," and before morning she was on her knees asking for the mercy of the blood of the Lamb.

Now the most solemn truth in the gospel is that the only thing He left down here is His blood. His body and bones He took away, but He left His blood on Calvary. There is either of two things we must do. One is to send back the message to heaven that we don't want the blood of Christ to cleanse us of our sin; the other is to accept it. Why, when we come to our dying hour, the blood will be worth more than all the kingdoms of the world to us. Can you afford to turn your back upon it and make light of it? Dr. King, when the war was going on, went down to the field with the Christian Commission. He used to go among the soldiers, and during one of his visits he heard a man cry, "Blood! Blood! Blood!" He thought that, as the man had just been taken off the battlefield, the scene of carnage and blood was still upon his mind. The doctor went to him and tried to talk to the man about Christ and to divert his mind from the scenes of the field. "Ah, Doctor," said the man, feebly, "I was not thinking of the battlefield, but of the blood of Christ," and he whispered the word "blood" once more and was gone.

Dear friends, do you want all your sins washed away from you? It was shed for the remission of sins, and without the shedding of blood there would be no remission. There is blood on the mercy seat tonight. "I am not looking to your sins now," God says, "but come and press in, press in and receive remission." Thank God, the blood is still on the mercy seat. It is there, and He implores you to accept it. What more can He do for your salvation? Now, my friends, don't go out of this Tabernacle laughing and scoffing at the precious offering made to you, but just bow your head now and lift up your voice, "O God of heaven, may the blood of Thy Son cleanse me from all sin." The blood is sufficient.

Some years ago, I was journeying to the Pacific coast, and nearly every stage driver I met was talking about a prominent stage driver who had just died. You know that in driving over these rocky roads they depend a good deal upon the brake. This poor man, when he was dying, was heard to say, "I am on the downgrade and cannot keep the brake." Just about that time one of the most faithful men of God, Alfred Coopman, passed away. His wife and friends gathered around his death bed, and when his last moments arrived, it seemed as if heaven had opened before him, as with a shout he cried, "I am sweeping through the gates, washed by the blood of the Lamb." What a comfort this must have been to his friends; what a comfort it must have been to him, the blood of the atonement in his last hours.

My friends, if you want a glorious end like the end of that sainted man, you must come to the blood of Christ. Let us bow our heads in prayer; let us have a few moments of silent prayer, and let us ask the Lord to let us see this great truth.

Excuses

First Address

The text today is found in Luke 14, the 19th verse: *"I pray thee have me excused."* Christ had been invited to dine with a rich Pharisee, and it seemed as though this man had gathered his friends together in a kind of conspiracy to catch Christ. They watched Him. A man who had had dropsy was placed before Jesus as though they wanted to see what He would do. Christ read their hearts, and so before He healed the man, He asked them if it was lawful to heal on the Sabbath day. But they didn't want to answer for fear they'd betray themselves, and so they held their peace.

Then Christ put the question to them in another way and asked if any of them had an ox or an ass fall into a pit on the Sabbath day, should he not straightway pull him out? Then He healed the man as the Pharisees and lawyers weren't able to answer Him. Then He told them about the feast and told them to be humble. When a man prepares a feast, men rush in, but when God prepares one, they all begin to make excuses and don't want to go. The first excuse was that made by Adam, "The woman You gave me, she gave me to eat." These men that excused themselves made manufactured excuses; they didn't really have any. The drunkard, the libertine, the businessman, the citizen, and the harlot all had their excuses. If God were to take men at their word about these excuses, and swept everyone into his grave who had an excuse, there would be a very small congregation in the Tabernacle next Sunday, there would be little business in Chicago, and in a few weeks the grass would be growing on these busy streets. Every man who was nursing a sin had an excuse, as though God had asked them to go into a plague-stricken city, or a hospital, or to hear a dry lecture, or something repelling and objectionable, something that wasn't for their greatest good.

Take the excuses. There wasn't one that wasn't a lie. The devil made them all and if the sinner hadn't one already, the devil was there at his elbow to suggest one about the truth of the Bible, or something of that sort. One of the excuses mentioned was that the man invited had bought a piece of ground and had to look at it. Real estate and corner lots were keeping a good many men out of God's kingdom. It was a lie to say that he had to go and see it then, for he ought to have looked at it before he bought it. Then the next man said he'd bought some oxen and must prove them. That was another lie; for if he hadn't proved them before he bought them, he ought to have done, and could have done it after the supper just as well as before it. But the third man had the silliest, the worst, excuse of all; he said he had married a wife and couldn't come. Why didn't he bring her with him? She'd have liked the supper just as well as he and would have enjoyed a supper, as almost any young bride would.

These seemed to be foolish excuses, but they were not any more so than the excuses of today. Indeed, the excuses of men are getting worse and worse all the time. They say they can't believe the Bible; it's so mysterious. Well, what of it? Infidels, skeptics, pantheists, deists said they didn't believe the Bible. Had they ever used it? Did they read it as carefully as they read any other book? This was their excuse. If everybody could understand everything the Bible said it wouldn't be God's book. If Christians, if theologians had studied it for forty, fifty, sixty years, and then only began to understand it, how could a man expect to understand it by one reading? A child the first day at school couldn't even know the alphabet, and yet it wasn't a sign that it was a poor school because he didn't learn the first day all about grammar, arithmetic, and geometry.

Another said God was a hard master. No, that was one of Satan's lies. The devil's the hard master. In the Tombs in New York, there is over the door the remark, "The way of the transgressor is hard." God's yoke is easy, His burden light. Ask prisoners, ask gamblers, ask sinners if Satan's yoke is easy. It's the hardest of all. Christians here tonight, is God a hard master? No! you reply. God's service a hard one! How will that sound in the judgment! Many said it wasn't that, but there is such a struggle. Wasn't all life a struggle?

Some said they were wicked. Those are just the kind Jesus came to save. They weren't too wicked to be saved. They were so worldly-minded, so hard-hearted; that was another falsehood. Look at what God did for Bunyan and John Newton and many others who were the wickedest, even the thief on the cross. God is already reconciled; He doesn't need the sinner to be reconciled to Him. The Lord prepares the sinner.

A touching story was told of an English father and son who had become estranged, but who were united over the deathbed of the wife and mother. The father was stern but was reconciled by the prayers of the dying parent. And this was so with God: the sinner had left Him, God was removed from him, but God and the sinner were brought near by the death of our Lord Jesus Christ.

This afternoon I chose for my text the 14th verse of the 14th chapter of Luke, and you will remember I took up certain of the excuses of the present day in regard to accepting Christ. One of these excuses I said was that Christ was a hard master; it was a very difficult thing to become a Christian. The other was that Christ would not receive them. Now, I just want to take up where I left off and notice the excuses we hear in the inquiry room, in the streets of Chicago – everywhere. I said this afternoon you were not invited when asked to come to Christ to a dry lecture on a disagreeable subject, but to a marriage feast. The Lord has said, "Blessed is he who shall be at the marriage supper of the Lord." I have missed a good many appointments in my life, but there is one I will not miss. I would rather be at the marriage feast than have the whole world rolled at my feet. I want to be there and sit down with Isaac and Jacob and Abraham at that supper.

It is an invitation for joy and gladness that comes from the King of Kings, from the Lord of Glory, to every man and woman in this assembly

– the invitation to be at the marriage supper of the Lamb. It is not a personal invitation, but a universal one – "Go out into the highways and hedges and compel them to come in, that my house may be filled." Bid them come, "the poor and the maimed and the halt and the blind," to the marriage feast, prepared at great expense by our blessed Redeemer.

I said in the afternoon that people began to make excuses very early in the history of Christianity, and they are still at it. Nineteen hundred years have rolled away and still there are excuses. One of the excuses that we very often hear people giving is that they don't want to become Christians because it will make them gloomy – they will have to put on long faces and button their coats up, cut off all joy and walk through the world till they get to heaven, where they will have pleasure for evermore. We look forward to that happy future, but thank God, we have some pleasure here. Indeed, no man in the world should be so happy as a man of God. It is one continual source of gladness. He can look up and say, "God is my Father, Christ is my Savior, and the Church is my mother." All who think otherwise than that a Christian's life is one of unceasing joy are deceiving themselves.

I was going by a saloon the other day and saw a sign, "Drink and be merry." Poor, blind, deluded fellows if they think this will make them merry. If you want to be merry you must come to the living fountain that bursts from the throne of God; then you will have true pleasure. A man away from God cannot have true pleasure. He is continually thirsting for something he cannot get – thirsting for something that can quench his thirst, and he cannot get it until he comes to the living fountain. My friends, that is just another wile of the devil to keep men from grace. It is false. The more a man is lifted up to heaven the more joy and peace and gladness he has. He is lifted away from gloom.

Look at a man on his way to execution. Suppose I run up to him, hold out my hand, and say, "Here is a pardon that has been signed by the governor," and I give it him. Would he be gloomy and joyless? That is Christ. He comes down with a pardon to us poor men and women on our way to execution. Yonder is a man starving. I go to him and give him bread. Is that going to make him gloomy? A poor man comes along crying with thirst, and I give him a glass of ice water; would that make him gloomy? That is what Christ is doing for us. He has a well of living water, and He asks every thirsty soul to drink freely. Don't you believe for a moment that Christianity is going to make you gloomy.

I remember when I was a boy, I thought I would wait till I died and then become a Christian. I thought if I had the consumption or some lingering disease, I would have plenty of time to become one, and in the mean time I would enjoy the best of the pleasures of the world. My friends, I was at that time under the power of the devil. The idea that a man has more pleasure away from church is one of the devil's lies. Do not believe it but accept of this universal invitation to the marriage feast.

Excuses

Second Address

I can imagine some men saying, "Mr. Moody has not touched my case at all. That is not the reason why I won't accept Christ. I don't know if I am one of the elect." How often am I met with this excuse – how often do I hear it in the inquiry room! How many men fold their arms and say, "If I am one of the elect, I will be saved, and if I ain't, I won't. No use of your bothering about it." Why don't some of those merchants say, "If God is going to make me a successful merchant in Chicago, I will be one whether I like it or not, and if He hasn't, I won't." If you are sick, and a doctor prescribes for you, don't take the medicine. Throw it out of the door; it doesn't matter, for if God has decreed you are going to die, you will, and if He hasn't, you will get better. If you use that argument you may as well not walk home from this Tabernacle. If God has said you'll get home, you'll get home – you'll fly through the air, if you have been elected to go home.

These illustrations are just the same as the excuse. You cannot go up there and give that excuse. The water of life is offered freely to everyone. No unconverted man in the wide, wide world has anything to do with the doctrine of election any more than I have to do with the government of China. That epistle of Paul was written to godly men.

Suppose I pick up a letter and open it, and it tells me about the death of my wife. Dear me – my wife dead. But I look on the other side of the letter and find that it is directed to another man. And so a great many people take Paul's letter to the churches and take it as a personal letter. This is what you have to take up: "Whosoever will, let him drink of the water of life freely."

He came down sixty years after his resurrection and said to John – put it so broad that no one will mistake it; put it so broad that no one in Chicago can be stumbling over it, so that all men may see it plainly – "Whosoever will, let him drink of the water of life freely." If you will, you will; if you won't, you won't. Do you think that God will come down here to give you salvation without giving you the power to take it, and then condemn you to eternity for not taking it? With the gift comes the power, and you can take it and live if you will. Don't stumble over election anymore. You have to deal with that broad proclamation: "Whosoever will, let him drink of the waters of life freely." I can imagine someone in the gallery clear up there saying, "I never have bothered my head about election, I don't believe men are gloomy when they become Christians. If I were alone, I would tell you my reason, but I do not like to get up in this large assemblage and talk here. The fact is there are hypocrites in the churches. I know a man, a prominent man in the church, who cheated me out of twenty-five dollars. I won't accept this invitation because of those hypocrites in the churches." My friend, you will find very few there if you get to heaven.

There won't be a hypocrite in the next world, and if you don't want to be associated with hypocrites in the next world, you will take this invitation. Why, you will find hypocrites everywhere. One of the apostles was himself the very prince of hypocrites, but he didn't get to heaven. You will find plenty of hypocrites in the church. They have been there for the last 1,800 years and will probably remain there. But what is that to you? This is an individual matter between you and your God. Is it because there are hypocrites that you are not going to accept the invitation?

"Ah, well, Mr. Moody, that is not my case. I am a businessman, and I have no time. Since the Chicago fire I have had as much as I could attend to in recovering what I lost." I believe if I stood at the door and asked anyone who went out to accept the invitation, I believe hundreds of you would say, "Mr. Moody, you will have to excuse me tonight; time is very precious with me, and you'll have to excuse me." What have you been doing the last twenty, thirty, forty, fifty years that you haven't had a moment to devote to the acceptance of the invitation? That is the cry of the world today: "Time is precious; business must be attended to, and we have no time to spare."

Some of you will say, "I cannot wait. I have to go home and put the children to bed; this is more important." My friends, to accept this invitation is more important than anything else in this world. There is nothing in the world that is so important as the question of accepting the invitation. How many mechanics in this building have spent five years learning their trade in order to support their families and support themselves a few years – forty or fifty years at the longest? How many professional men have toiled and worked hard for years to get such an education that they might go out to the world and cope with it, and during all these years have not had a minute to seek their salvation? Is that a legitimate excuse? Tell Jesus tonight that you haven't time or let this be the night – the hour – cost you what it will, when you shall say, "By the grace of God, I will accept the invitation and press up to the marriage supper of the Lamb."

"Oh, but that is not my case," says another, "I have time. If I thought I could become a Christian I would sit here all night and let business and everything else go and press into the kingdom of God. I am not fit to become a Christian, that's the trouble with me." He says, "Go into the highways and hedges," and "bring in hither the poor, and the maimed, and the halt and the blind," – just invite them all, without distinction of sect or creed, station or nationality; never mind whether they are rich or poor. If the Lord doesn't complain about your fitness, you shouldn't look to see if you have the right kind of clothes.

I had to notice during the war, when enlisting was going on, sometimes a man would come up with a nice silk hat on, patent leather boots, nice kid gloves, and a fine suit of clothes, which probably cost him one hundred dollars; perhaps the next man who came along would be a hod carrier dressed in the poorest kind of clothes. Both had to strip alike and put on the regimental uniform. So when you come and say you aren't fit, haven't got good clothes, haven't got righteousness enough remember that He will furnish you with the uniform of heaven, and you will be set down at the marriage feast of the Lamb.

I don't care how black and vile your heart may be, only accept the invitation of Jesus Christ and He will make you fit to sit down with the rest at that feast. How many are continually crying out, "I am too bad; no use of me trying to become a Christian." This is the way the devil works. Sometimes he will say to a man, "You don't want to be saved; you're good enough already," and he will point to some black-hearted hypocrite and say, "Look at him and see how you appear in comparison; you are far better than he is."

But by and by the man gets a glimpse of the blackness of his heart and his conscience troubles him. Then says the devil, "You are too bad to be saved; the Lord won't save such as you. You are too vile; *you* must get better before you try to get God to save you." And so men try to make themselves better and instead get worse all the time. The gospel bids you come as you are. Seek first the kingdom of heaven – make no delay; come just as you are.

I heard of an artist who wanted to get a man to sit for a painting of the prodigal son. He went down to the almshouses and the prisons but couldn't get one. Going through the streets one day he found a poor wretched man, a beggar, coming along, and he asked him if he would sit for the study. He said he would. A bargain was made, and the artist gave him his address. The time for the appointment arrived, and the beggar duly appeared and said to the artist, "I have come to keep that appointment which I made with you." "An appointment with me?" replied the artist; "you are mistaken. I have an appointment with a beggar today." "Well," said the man, "I am that beggar, but I thought I would put on a new suit of clothes before I came to see you." "I don't want you," was the artist's reply, "I want a beggar." And so a great many people come to God with their self-righteousness, instead of coming in their raggedness. Why, someone has said, "It is only the ragged sinners that open God's wardrobe. If you want to start out to get a pair of shoes from a passerby, you would start out barefooted, wouldn't you?

I remember a boy to whom I gave a pair of boots, and I found him shortly after in his bare feet again. I asked him what he had done with them, and he replied that when he was dressed up it spoiled his business; when he was dressed up no one would give him anything. By keeping his feet naked he got as many as five pairs of boots a day. So if you want to come to God, don't dress yourself up. It is the sinners God wants to save. Come to Him after you have cast off your self-righteousness and the Son of God will receive you.

I remember some years ago of a man who had gone to sea. He led a wild, reckless life. When his mother was alive, she was a praying mother. Ah, how many men have been saved by their mothers after they have gone up to heaven; perhaps her influence made him think sometimes. When at sea a desire of leading a better life came over him, and when he got on shore, he thought he would join the Free Masons. He made application, but upon investigation, his character proved he was only a drunken sailor, and he was blackballed. He next thought of joining the Odd Fellows and applied, but his application met with a like result. While he was walking up Fulton Street one day a little tract was given him – an invitation to the prayer meeting. He came, and Christ received him. I remember him getting up in the meeting and telling how the Free Masons had blackballed him, how the Odd Fellows had blackballed him, and how Christ had received him as he was. A great many orders and societies will not receive you, but I tell you He will receive you, vile as you are – He, the Savior of sinners – He, the Redeemer of the lost world – He bids you come just as you are.

Ah, but there is another voice coming down from the gallery yonder, "I have intellectual difficulties; I cannot believe." A man came to me some time ago and said, "I cannot." "Cannot what?" "Well," said he, "I cannot believe." "Who?" "Well," he repeated, "I cannot believe." "Who?" I asked. "Well, I can't believe myself." "Well, you don't want to." Make yourself out false every time but believe in the truth of Christ. If a man says to me, "Mr. Moody, you have lied to me; you have dealt falsely with me," it may be so, but no man on the face of the earth can ever say that God ever dealt unfairly, or that He lied to him. If God says a thing, it is true. We don't ask you to believe in any man on the face of the earth, but we ask you to believe in Jesus Christ, who never lied – who never deceived anyone. If a man says he cannot believe Him, he says what is untrue.

"Ah, well, all those excuses don't apply to me," says another; "I can't feel." That is the very last excuse. When a man comes with that excuse, he is getting pretty near to the Lord. We are having a body of men in England giving a new translation of the Scriptures. I think we should get them to put in a passage relating to feeling. With some people it is feel, feel, feel all the time.

What kind of feeling have you got? Have you got a desire to be saved – have you got a desire to be present at the marriage supper? Suppose a gentleman asked me to dinner. I say, "I will see how I feel." "Sick?" he might ask. "No, it depends on how I feel." That is not the question – it is whether I will accept the invitation or not. The question with us is, Will we accept salvation – will you believe? There is not a word about feelings in the Scriptures.

When you come to your end, and you know that in a few days you will be in the presence of the Judge of all the earth, you will remember this excuse about feelings. You will be saying, "I went up to the Tabernacle, I remember, and I felt very good. Before the meeting was over, I felt very bad, and I didn't feel I had the right kind of feeling to accept the invitation." Satan will then say, "I made you feel so." Suppose you build your hopes and fix yourself upon the Rock of Ages, the devil cannot come to you. Stand upon the Word of God, and the waves of unbelief cannot touch you; the waves of persecution cannot assail you. The devil and all the fiends of hell cannot approach you if you only build your hopes upon God's word. Say, "I will trust Him, though He slay me – I will take God at His word."

I haven't exhausted all the excuses. If I had, you would make more before tomorrow morning. What has to be done with all the excuses is to bundle them all up and label them "Satan's lies." There is not an excuse, but it is a lie. When you stand at the throne of God, no man can give an excuse. If you have got a good excuse, don't give it up for anything I have said; don't give it up for anything your friend may have said. Take it up to the bar of God and state it to Him. But if you have not got a good excuse – an excuse that will stand eternity – let it go tonight and flee to the arms of a loving Savior. It is easy enough to excuse yourself to hell, but you cannot excuse yourself to heaven. If you want an excuse, Satan will always find one ready for you. Accept the invitation now, my friends. Let your stores be closed till you accept this invitation; let your households go till you accept this invitation. Do not let the light come, do not eat, do not drink till you accept the most important thing to you in this wide world. Will you stay tonight and accept this invitation? Don't make light of it. I can imagine some of you saying, "I never get so low as to make light of religion."

Suppose I got an invitation to dinner from a citizen of Chicago for tomorrow, and I don't answer it – I tear the invitation up. Would not that be making light of it? Suppose you pay no attention to the invitation tonight – is not that making light of it? Would anyone here be willing to write out an excuse something like this: "The Tabernacle, Oct. 29. To the King of Heaven: While sitting in the Tabernacle today, I received a very pressing invitation from one of your servants to sit at the marriage ceremony of the Son of God. I pray you have me excused." Is there a man or woman in this assembly who would take their pen and write their name at the bottom of it? Is there a man or woman whose right hand would not forget its cunning and whose tongue would not cleave to their mouth if they were trying to do it? Well, you are doing this if you get up and go right out after you have heard the invitation. Who will write this: "To the Lord of lords and King of Glory: While sitting in the Tabernacle this beautiful Sabbath evening, Oct. 29, 1876, I received a pressing invitation from one of your servants to be present at the marriage supper. I hasten to accept." Will anyone sign this? Who will put their name to it? Is there not a man or woman saying, down deep in their soul, "By the grace of God I will sign it." "I will sign it by the grace of God and will meet that sainted mother who has gone there." "I will sign and accept that invitation and meet that loving wife or dear child." Are there not some here tonight who will accept that invitation?

I remember, while preaching in Glasgow, an incident occurred which I will relate. I had been preaching there several weeks, and the night was my last one, and I pleaded with them as I had never pleaded there before. I urged those people to meet me in that land. It is a very solemn thing to stand before a vast audience for the last time and think you may never have another chance of asking them to come to Christ. I told them I would not have another opportunity, and urged them to accept, and just asked them to meet me at that marriage supper. At the conclusion, I soon saw a tall, young lady coming into the inquiry room. She had scarcely come in when another tall, young lady came in, and she went up to the first and put her arms round her and wept.

Pretty soon another young lady came and went up to the first two and just put her arms round them both. I went over to see what it was, and found that, although they had been sitting in different parts of the building, the sure arrow of conviction went down to their souls and brought them to the inquiry room. Another young lady came down from the gallery and said, "Mr. Moody, I want to become a Christian." I asked a young Christian to talk to her, and when she went home that night about ten o'clock – her mother was sitting up for her – she said, "Mother, I have accepted the invitation to be present at the marriage supper of the Lamb." Her mother and father laid awake that night talking about the salvation of the child. That was Friday night, and next day, Saturday, she was unwell, and before long her sickness developed into scarlet fever. A few days after I got this letter: – "Mr. Moody – Dear Sir: It is now my painful duty to inform you that the dear girl concerning whom I wrote to you on Monday, has been taken away from us by death. Her departure, however, has been signally softened to us, for she told us yesterday she was 'going home to be with Jesus;' and after giving messages to many, told us to let Mr. Moody and Mr. Sankey know that she died a happy Christian.

"My dear sir, let us have your prayer that consolation and needed resignation and strength may be continued to us, and that our two dear remaining little ones may be kept in health if the Lord wills. I repeated a line of the hymn, 'In the Christian's home in glory, There remains a land of rest,' when she took it up at once, and tried to sing, 'When the Savior's gone before to fulfil my soul's request.' This was the last conscious thing she said. I should say that my dear girl also expressed a wish that the lady she conversed with on Friday evening should also know that she died a happy Christian."

When I heard this, I said to Mr. Sankey, "If we do nothing else, we have been paid for coming across the Atlantic. There is one soul we have saved whom we will meet on the resurrection morn."

Oh, my dear friends, are there not some here tonight who will decide this question? Do accept this invitation. Let the sickness come, let sorrow come; you will be sure of meeting at the marriage supper of the Lamb. Blessed is he who shall be found at that marriage feast.

The Prophet Daniel

First Address

I want to talk about the life of the prophet Daniel. The name means "God with him"; not the public with him, not his fellow men, but God. Therefore, he had to report himself to God, and hold himself responsible to Him. I do not know just what time Daniel went down to Babylon. I know that in the third year of King Jehoakim, Nebuchadnezzar took 10,000 of the chief men of Jerusalem and carried them captive down to Babylon. I am glad these chief men who stirred on the war were given into the great king's hands. Unlike too many of the ringleaders in our great war, they got the punishment on their own heads. Among the captives were four young men. They had been converted, doubtless under Jeremiah, the "weeping prophet," that God had sent to the children of Israel. Many had mocked him when he lifted up his voice against their sins. They had laughed at his tears and told him to his face, as many say of us, that he was getting up a false excitement. But these four young men listened and had the backbone to come out for God.

And now, after they were come to Babylon, the king said a number of the young men should be educated and ordered the same kinds of meat and wine set before them that were used in his own palace, and that at the end of a year they should be brought before him. Daniel and his three friends were among these. Now, no young man ever comes to the city but has great temptation cross his path as he enters it. And just at this turning point in his life, as in Daniel's, must lie the secret of his success.

If you see success in statesmen, in lawyers, or men in any walk in life, you ask the secret of it, and you find it in this same time of youth. Jacob turned away from God, and David turned away from God, but only just in proportion as they had not fully and entirely given themselves up to Him when they were young men. Yes, that was the secret of this young man Daniel's success; he took his stand with God right on his entering the gate of Babylon and cried to God to keep him steadfast. And he needed to cry hard. A law of his and his nation's God was that no man should eat meat offered to idols; but now comes the king's first edict, that this young man should eat the meat he himself did. I do not think it took young Daniel long to make up his mind. The law of God forbade it, and he would not do it. "He purposed in his heart" – in his heart, mark that – that he would not defile himself. He did not do it in his head but love in his heart prompted him.

If some Chicago Christians could have advised Daniel, they'd have said, "Don't you do it; don't set aside the meat. That would be a species of Phariseeism. The moment you take your stand and say you won't eat it, you say in effect you are better than other people." That is the kind of talk too often heard now. Oh, yes, "When you are in Rome do as the Romans do." They would have insisted to the poor, young captive that he might, and ought to, carry out the commandments of his God when he was in his own country, but not there where he was a poor slave; he could not possibly carry along his religion down there to Babylon. Thank God, this young man said he would not eat, and ordering the meat taken away, got the eunuch to bring him vegetables. And behold, when Daniel came before the king, the eunuch's fears were gone, for the faces of Daniel and the rest of the dear boys were fairer and fatter than any that the king looked down upon. They hadn't noses, like too many in our streets, as red as if they were just going to blossom. It is God's truth, and Daniel tested it, that cold water, with a clear conscience, is better than wine.

The king one day had a dream, and all the wise men were called. But they all said, "We cannot interpret it, it is too hard." The king in wrath, threatened them, and still getting no answer, made an edict that all the wise men should be put to death. And the officers came to Daniel with the rest of the wise men, but Daniel was not afraid. I can imagine he prayed to God, falling low on his knees with his face to the earth, and asked Him what to do; and then he crawled into bed and slept like a child. We would hardly sleep well under such circumstances. And in his sleep God told him the meaning of the dream. There must have been joy among the wise men that one of their number had found it, and that the king would save their lives. And he is brought before the king, and cries out, "O king, while you were lying with your head on your pillow, you dreamed, and in your dream you saw a great image." I can imagine at these opening words how the king's eyes flashed, and how he cried out with joy, "Yes! That is it, the whole thing comes back to me now!"

And then Daniel, in a deathlike stillness, unfolded all the interpretation, and told the king that the golden head of the great image represented his own government. I suppose Babylon was the biggest city ever in the world. It was sixty miles around. Some writers put the walls from sixty-five to eighty-five feet high and twenty-five feet wide; four chariots could ride abreast on top of them. A street fifteen miles long divided the grand city and hanging gardens in acres made the public parks. It was like Chicago – so flat that they had to resort to artificial mounds; and, again like Chicago, the products of vast regions flowed right into and through it.

This great kingdom Daniel told the king was his own; but he said a destroying kingdom should come, and afterward a third and fourth kingdom, when at the last, the God of heaven should set up His kingdom. And Daniel himself lived to see the first overthrown, when the Medes and Persians came in. Centuries after came Alexander and then the Romans. I believe in the literal fulfilment, so far, of Daniel's God-given words, and in the sure fulfilment of the final prophecy of the "stone cut out of the mountains without hands," that by and by shall grind the kingdoms of this world into dust and bring in the kingdom of peace. Then will be the millennium, and Christ will sway His scepter over all the earth. Well, the king was very much pleased. He gave him a place near the throne, and he became one of the chief men of the world, and all his three friends were put in high office. God had blessed them signally, and he blessed them still more, and that was perhaps a harder thing – in keeping them true to Him in their prosperity. Yet their faith and fortunes waxed strong together.

Time went on, and now we reach a crisis indeed. "Nebuchadnezzar, the king," we read, "made an image of gold, one hundred and ten feet high and nine feet wide." It was not gilded, but solid gold. When Babylon was pillaged the second time, a single idol was found in the temple that was worth between two and three million pounds sterling. The king's monstrous image was set up in the plains of Dura, near to the city. I suppose he wanted to please his kingly vanity by inaugurating a universal religion.

When the time came for the dedication, I do not suppose Daniel was there. He was perhaps in Egypt or some other province, on affairs of the empire. Counsellors, satraps, high secretaries, and the princes of the people were ordered to hasten to the dedication, and when they should hear the sound of the cornet, flute, and psaltery announce that the great idol was consecrated, they were to bow down and worship it. Perhaps they called the ceremony the unveiling of the monument, as we should say, but one command is certain, that at the given signal all the people were to fall to the earth in worship. But in the law of God there is something against that: "Thou shall have no other gods but Me." God's law went right against the king's. Oh, would all of us have Daniel's three friends to do the right thing at any hazard! Would none of us, without backbone, have advised him to just bow down a little so that no one would notice it, or to merely bow down but not worship it!

The hour came, and Daniel's friends refused to bow down. They refused utterly to bend the knee to a god of gold. How many cry out in this city, "Give me gold, give me money, and I will do anything." Such may think that men in Nebuchadnezzar's time should not bow down to a golden idol, but they themselves are every day doing just that very thing. Money is their golden image, or position, or golden ambition. Well, the informers came to the king, and told him that Shadrach, Meshach, and Abednego had stood with unbended knee, and straightway they were hurried before him, the old king speechless with rage and gesturing his commands. I can imagine that one last chance was given them, after the king finally regained his voice, and that one of them, probably Meshach, spoke up in respectful but firm voice, that they must obey God rather than man. At once the raging king cried out, "What is your God that He can deliver you out of our hands?" And in the same breath screamed a command to bind them hand and foot and cast them into the fiery furnace and make it seven times hotter than ever.

The command was instantly executed, and the flames leaped out from the door and consumed the officers who cast them in. But Jesus was with His servants as the flames wreathed about them, and soon word was brought to the king that four men walked about in the flames. Yes, they walked there with Jesus – they didn't run – as in a green pasture and beside still waters. And directly the king rushed up and cried, "You sons of the living God, come forth!" And behold, even the hair of their heads was not singed. Then made the king a royal edict, that all in his realm should reverence the God of Meshach, Shadrach, and Abednego.

These glorious heroes braved even death because God was with them. Oh, friends, we want to be Christians with the same backbone, men and women who stand up for the right and never mind what the world may say. I believe, before God, there would be ten thousand conversions in Chicago in the next twenty-four hours had we only a perfect consecration. God grant it us out of the abundance of His grace. I cannot go on now but will finish about Daniel next Sunday morning. Let us pray.

The Prophet Daniel

Second Address

Last Sunday morning we got to the second dream of King Nebuchadnezzar. This morning we will just take up where we broke off. The king had a dream, and he was greatly troubled. This time the particulars of the dream had not gone from him. They stood out vivid and clear in his mind as he sent out to fetch the wise men and called to them to give him the interpretation. But they cannot give it. When he had his first dream, he had summoned these same soothsayers, but they had stood silent. And now they stand silent again as the second dream is told them; they cannot interpret it.

Then once again he sends for the prophet Daniel, that he had named after one of his gods, Belteshazzar. And the young prophet comes before the king, and as quick as the king sees him, he feels sure that he will now get the meaning. Calling out from his throne, he tells how he had dreamed a dream, wherein he saw a tree in the midst of the earth, with branches that reached to heaven, and the sight thereof to the ends of the earth. The beasts of the field had shelter under it, and the fowls of the air dwelt in the boughs thereof; and the tree was very fair and had much fruit, and all flesh was fed on it. Then, lowering his voice, he tells how as he gazed, he saw a watcher and a holy one come down from heaven, who cried aloud, "Hew down the tree." "And now," cries the king, "can you tell me the interpretation?" And for a time, Daniel stands still and motionless. Does his heart fail him? The record simply says that, "For one hour he was astonished." The ready words doubtless rush to his lips, but he hates to let them out; he doesn't want to tell how the king's kingdom and mind are going to depart from him, and he is to wander forth to eat grass like a beast.

The king, too, hesitates. A dark foreboding for a time gets the better of curiosity. But, directly, he nerves himself to hear the worst, and speaks very kindly, "Do not be afraid to tell me, oh Daniel; let not the dream or its interpretation trouble you." And at last Daniel speaks, "Oh, king, you are the man; God has exalted you over every king, and over all the world, but you shall be brought low; you shall be driven out from men and eat grass among the beasts of the field; but your kingdom – as the great watcher spared the stump of the tree – shall afterwards return to you. Wherefore, O king, break off your sins by righteousness and your iniquities by showing mercy to the poor, if it may be a lengthening of your tranquility."

And straightway the king repented in sackcloth and ashes, and so God stayed the doom. But twelve months from that time we see Nebuchadnezzar walking in his palace and boasting, "Is not this my great Babylon that I have built by the might of my power and for the honor of my majesty!" And behold, while he yet spoke a voice came from heaven, saying, "Your kingdom has departed," and undoubtedly God then touched his reason, and straightway he ran madly through the gates to eat grass.

But his kingdom had not passed from him forever, and according to the prophet's word, at the end of seven years, or possibly seven months, his reason came back, and he returned to his palace, and all his princes and officers gathered about him. Then immediately he sent out a new proclamation, and its closing words show his repentance and how Daniel had brought this mighty king to God.

"And at the end of the days, I, Nebuchadnezzar, lifted up my eyes unto heaven, and my understanding returned unto me, and I blessed the Most High, and I praised and honored Him that lives forever, whose dominion is an everlasting dominion, and his kingdom is from generation to generation.

At the same time my reason returned unto me; and for the glory of my kingdom, my honor and brightness returned unto me; and my counsellors and my lords sought unto me. I was established in my kingdom, and excellent majesty was added unto me.

Now I, Nebuchadnezzar, praise and extol the King of heaven, all whose works are truth, and His ways judgment; and those that walk in pride He is able to abase."

And then he passes from the stage; this is the last record of him, and undoubtedly, he and Daniel now walk the crystal pavement together. Oh, that mighty monarch was led to the God of the Hebrews by the faith of this Hebrew slave, and just because he had a religion and dared to make it known.

But now we lose sight of the prophet for a few years, perhaps fifteen or twenty. The next we hear is that Belteshazzar is on the throne, possibly as regent. He is believed to have been a grandson of Nebuchadnezzar. One day he said he would make Daniel the third ruler of the people if he would tell him the handwriting on the wall. He was probably second himself, and Daniel would be next to him. Of this prince we have only one glimpse. The feast scene is the first and last we have of him, and it is enough. It was a great feast, and fully a thousand of his lords sat down together. Feasts in those days sometimes lasted six months. How long this one lasted we don't know.

The king caroused with his princes and satraps and all the mighty men of Babylon, drinking and rioting and praying to gods of silver and gold and brass and stubble, just what we're doing today if we bow the knee to the gods of this world. And the revelers, growing more evil, even go into the temple and lay sacrilegious hands on the sacred vessels brought away from Jerusalem, and drank out of them, drank toasts to idols and harlots. And undoubtedly as they are drinking, they scoff at the God of Israel. I see them swearing and rioting when – the king turns pale and trembles from head to foot. Above the golden candlesticks, on a bare space on the wall, he sees the writing of the God of Zion. He distinctly sees the terrible finger. His voice shakes with terror, but manages to falter out, "Bring in the wise men. Any man that can read the handwriting I will make third ruler of the kingdom. And they come trooping in, but there is no answer, none of them can read it. They are skilled in Chaldean lore, but this stumbles them. At last, the queen comes in and whispers, "Oh king, there is one man in the kingdom that can read that writing. When your grandfather could not interpret his dreams he sent for Daniel, the Hebrew, and he knew all about them. Can we not find him?"

And they did find him, and now we see the man of God again standing before a king's throne. To the king's hurried promises of gifts and honors he replies, "You can keep your rewards," and quietly turns his eyes on the writing. And he reads it at the first glance, for it is his Father's hand-writing. "Mene," he says, "your kingdom has departed from you." "Tekel, you are weighed in the balance and found wanting." Oh sinner, what if God should put you in the balance, and you have not got Christ in your soul! How that word of doom must have rung through the palace that night! "Upharsin, your kingdom is divided. It is given over to the hands of the enemy."

And the destruction did not tarry. The king recovered himself, banished his fears, the dream and its interpretation is idle, and went on drinking in his hall. He thought he was perfectly secure. He thought the great walls of Babylon perfectly safe. But there was Darius besieging the city; the enemy was right upon him. Was that safe? Oh, sinners of Chicago, death and hell are right on you! Death and hell, I say. And they are just as close, may be, as the slayer's sword to those midnight revelers. While they reveled, the river Euphrates, that flowed under the walls was turned into another channel. The hosts of Medes and Persians rushed through, unobstructed, and in a few minutes more battered down the king's gate and broke through the palace guard into the inmost palace chamber. The king was slain, and his blood flowed in that banquet hall.

We are next told Darius took the throne and set over the people 120 rulers, and over these, three presidents, of whom Daniel was first. And so we find him in office again. I do not know how long he was in that position. But by and by a conspiracy took head among his fellow officers to get rid of him. They got jealous and said, "Let's see if we can't get this man removed; he's bossed us long enough, the sanctimonious old Hebrew." And then he was so impracticable, they couldn't do anything with him.

There were plenty of collectors and treasurers, but he kept such a close eye on them that they only made their salaries. There was no plundering of the government with Daniel at the head. He was president of the princes and all revenue accounts passed before him. I can overhear the plotters whispering, "If we can only put him out of the way, we can make enough in two or three years to retire from office, have a city house in Babylon, and two or three villas in the country, have enough for all our days. We can go down to Egypt and see something of the world. As things are now, we can only get our exact dues, and it will take years to get anything respectable – yes, let's down with this pious Jew." Well, they worked things so as to get an investigating committee hoping to catch him in his accounts. But they found no occasion nor fault against him. If he had put any relatives in office, it would have been found out; if he had been guilty of embezzlement, or in any way broken the unalterable statutes of the kingdom, it would have come to light. Oh, what a bright light was that, standing alone in that great city for God and the majesty of law!

But at last they struck on one weak point, they called it – he would worship no one but the God of Israel. The law of his God was his only assailable side. "If we can only get Darius," the conspirators plotted, "to forbid anyone making a request for thirty days except from the king himself, we shall trap him, and then can cast him among the lions; we will take good care to have the lions hungry." And the hundred and twenty princes took long council together. "Take care," they said. "You must draw up the paper which is to be signed by the king with a deal of care and discretion. The king loves him, and he has influence. Don't speak of the movement outside of this meeting; it might come to the ears of the king, and we must talk to the king ourselves."

When the mine is all ready, the hundred and twenty princes come to the king and open their business with flattering speech. If people come to praise me, I know they've something else coming – they've got a purpose for telling me I am a good man. And so we naturally hear these men saying, "King Darius, live forever." They tell him how prosperous the realm is and how much the people think of him. And then they tell him, in the most plausible manner that ever was, that if he would be remembered by children's children to all ages, just to sign this decree; it would be a memorial of his greatness and goodness for ever.

And the king replies graciously: "What is the decree you wish me to sign?" and casting his eye over the paper, goes on, "I don't see any objection to that." In the pleasure of granting a request he thinks nothing of Daniel, and the princes carefully refrain from jogging his memory. And he asks for his signet ring and gives the royal stamp. The edict has become one of the laws of the Medes and Persians, that alter not. It reads: "Any man that worships any God but me for thirty days shall be cast into the lion's den."

The news spreads all through the city; it comes out perhaps in the Babylon *Inter-ocean*, and quickly gets to the ears of Daniel. I can imagine some of them going to the prophet and advising him about the edict. "If you can only get out of the way for a little time, if you can just quit Babylon for thirty days, it will advance your own and the public interest together. You are the chief secretary and treasurer, in fact, you are the chief ruler in the government. You are an important man and can do as you please. Well, now, just you get out of Babylon. Or, if you will stay in Babylon, don't let them catch you on your knees; at all events, don't pray at the window towards Jerusalem. If you will pray, close that window, pull down the curtain, and put something in the keyhole."

How many young men there are who don't dare to pray before their roommates; they've no moral courage. How many young men say to me, "Mr. Moody, don't ask me to get down on my knees at this prayer meeting." They lack moral courage. Oh, thousands of men have been lost for want of moral courage, to dare to get down on their knees and pray to God. The idea of policy coming in here is all wrong. I can imagine how that old prince, Daniel, now in his gray hairs, would view such a thought, that he is going to desert his God in his old age. All the remonstrances that must have been made fell dead; he just went on praying as usual, three times a day, with his face towards Jerusalem.

Our businessmen, too many of them, "don't have any time to pray," business is so pressing. But this old prophet found plenty of time, though secretary and treasurer of the most important empire in the world. And, besides his own business, he had to attend, doubtless, to much belonging of right to those hundred and twenty. But he would never have been too busy or ashamed at a prayer meeting to stand up for God. He had a purpose, and he dared to make it known. He knew Whom he worshipped. The idea of looking back to church records of years ago to see whether a man has professed religion is all wrong. In Babylon they knew whom Daniel believed on; these hundred and twenty knew the very day after the passage of the edict. He knows they are watching near his window when the hour comes for prayer. He can see two men close at his side and knows they are spies; perhaps they may be taking down every word he says for the papers.

The moment comes, and he falls on his knees, and in tones louder than ever makes his prayer to the God of Israel, Abraham, Isaac, and Jacob. He doesn't omit to pray for the king. It is right to pray for our rulers. If we quit praying for our rulers, our country will go to pieces. The reason they are not better oftentimes is just because we do not pray for them. And now the spies rush to the king and say: "O, Darius, live forever. Do you know there is a man in your kingdom that won't obey you?" "Won't obey me! Who is he?" "Why, that man Daniel." And the king says, "I know he won't bow down and worship me; I know that he worships the God of heaven.

Then the king sets his heart to deliver Daniel from the hands of those one hundred and twenty men. But they come to him and say, "If you want to break your law, your kingdom will depart and your subjects will no longer obey you. You must deliver him to the lions' den." And Darius is compelled, and at last, gives the word to have him sent away and cast into the lions' den, and these men take good care to have the den filled with the hungriest beasts in Babylon.

He is thrown headlong into the den, but the angel of God flies down, and Daniel lights unharmed on the bottom. The lions' mouths are stopped. They are as harmless as lambs. The old prophet at the usual hour drops on his knees and prays with his face towards Jerusalem, as calmly as in his chamber. And when it gets later, he just lays his head on one of the lions and goes to sleep, and undoubtedly, no one in all Babylon slept sweeter than Daniel in the lions' den.

In the palace, the king cannot sleep. He orders his chariot, and early in the morning rattles over the pavement and jumps down at the lions' den. I see him alight from his chariot in eager haste and hear him cry down through the mouth of the den, "Oh, Daniel, servant of the living God, is your God, whom you revere continually, able to deliver you from the lions?" Hark! Why, it is a resurrection voice! It is Daniel saying, "My God is able; He has sent one of His angels and has shut the lions' mouths." I can see them now just embrace each other, and together they jump into the chariot and away they go back to the palace to breakfast. But I am overstepping my time. Let us pray.

The Prophet Daniel

Third Address

I want to say some further things about Daniel. I want to refer to how an angel came to him, and, as we read in the 12th chapter of Daniel, told him he was a man greatly beloved. Another angel had come to him with the same message. It is generally thought this last angel was the same one spoken of in the 1st chapter and 13th verse of Revelation, as coming to John when banished at the Isle of Patmos. People thought he was sent off there alone; but no, the angel of God was with him. And so with Daniel. Here in the 10th chapter and 5th verse he says, "Then I lifted up my eyes, and looked, and behold, a certain man clothed in linen," and otherwise arrayed as God's messenger, who cried, 'Oh, Daniel, a man greatly beloved, understand the words which I speak unto you, and stand upright, for unto you am I now sent.'" It was Daniel's need that brought Him from the glory land. It was the Son of God right by his side in that strange land. And that was the second time that the word came to him that he was greatly beloved. Yes, three times a messenger came from the throne of God to tell him this.

I love to speak of that precious verse in the 11th chapter – the 32nd verse: "The people that do know their God shall be strong and do exploits," and also of the 12th chapter and 2nd and 3rd verses: "And many of them that sleep in the dust of the earth shall awake, some to everlasting life, and some to shame and everlasting contempt; and they that be wise shall shine as the stars of the firmament; and they that turn many to righteousness as the stars for ever and ever."

This was the angel's comfort to Daniel, and a great comfort it was. The fact with all of us is that we like to shine. There is no doubt about that. Every mother likes her child to shine. If her boy shines at school by getting to the head of his class, the proud mother tells all the neighbors, and I suppose she has a right to. But it is not the great of this world that will shine the brightest. For a few years they may shed bright light, but they go out in darkness, without an inner lightness. Supplying the brightness, they go out into black darkness and make it light. Where are the great men who did not know Daniel's God? Did they shine long? Why, we know of Nebuchadnezzar and the rest of them scarcely a thing, except as they fill in the story about these humble men of God. We are not told that statesmen shall shine; they may for a few years or days, but they are soon forgotten.

Look at those great ones who passed away in the days of Daniel. How wise in counsel they were, how mighty and victorious over hundreds of nations; what gods upon earth they were! Yet their names are forgotten and written in the grave. Philosophers, falsely so-called, do they live? Behold men of science – scientific men they call themselves – going down into the bowels of the earth, digging away at some carcass and trying to make it talk against the voice of God. They shall go down to death by and by, and their names shall rot. But the man of God shines. Yes, he it is who shall shine as the stars forever and ever. This Daniel has been gone for 2,500 years, but still increasing millions read of his life and actions. And so it shall be to the end; he will only get better known and better loved; he shall only shine the brighter as the world grows older. Of a truth they that be wise and turn many to righteousness shall shine on, like stars, to eternity.

And this blessed, thrice blessed, happiness, like all the blessings of God's kingdom is for everyone. Even without the first claim to education or refinement you can shine if you will. One of you sailors there can shine forever if you only go to work for the kingdom. The Bible doesn't say the great shall shine, but they that turn many to righteousness. A false impression has got hold of many of God's people. They have got the idea that only a few can talk about God's affairs. Nine-tenths of the people say, if anything is to be done for the souls of men, "Oh, the ministers must do it." It doesn't enter into the heart of the people that they have any part in the matter. It is the devil's work to keep Christians from the blessed luxury of winning souls to God. Anyone can do this work.

A little girl only eleven years old came to me in a Sunday school and said: "Won't you please pray that God will make me a winner of souls?" I felt so proud of her, and my pride was justified, for she has become one of the best winners of souls in this country. Oh, suppose she lives threescore years and goes on winning four or five souls every year; at the end of her journey there will be three hundred souls on the way to glory. And how long will it be before that little company swells to a great army. Don't you see how that little mountain rill keeps swelling till it carries everything before it. Little trickling streams have run into it, till now, a mighty river, it has great cities on its banks, and the commerce of all nations floating on its waters. So when a single soul is won to Christ you cannot see the result. One multiplies to a thousand, and that into ten thousand. Perhaps a million shall be the fruit; we cannot tell. We only know that the Christian who has turned so many to righteousness shall indeed shine for ever and ever. Look at those poor fishermen, Jesus's disciples, how unlettered. They were not learned men but great in winning souls. So not a child here but can work for God.

The one thing that keeps people from work is that they don't have the desire. If a man has this desire, God soon qualifies him; and what we want is God's qualification. It must come from Him. I have been thinking what shall be done for the next thirty days that I continue to preach here. If I should just put it to vote, and asked all Christians who wanted prayers to rise, all of you, I know, would rise. There are at least 3,000 Christians here. Now, is it too much to ask that 3,000 Christians will each lead one soul to Christ this coming week? The Son of God died on the cross for you. Right here in this Tabernacle you can tell those weeping over their sins about God and heaven. How many times I have watched just to see if Christians would speak to these sorrowing ones! If we only had open-eyed watchers for souls, there wouldn't be a night but five hundred or a thousand inquirers would crowd into the inquiry rooms. These anxious inquirers are at every meeting, just waiting to have warm-hearted Christians bring them to Christ. They are timid but will always listen to one speaking to them about Christ. Suppose each one of you now prayed, "Give me some soul this week for my hire." What would be the result? This room would not hold the multitude sending up shouts of praise to God and making heaven glad. Where there is an anxious sinner there is the place for the Christian.

A little bed-ridden boy I knew kept mourning that he couldn't work for Jesus. The minister told him to pray and pray he did; and the persons he prayed for one by one felt the load of their sins and professed Christ. When he heard that such a one had not given in, he just turned his face to the wall and prayed harder. Well, he died, when by his little memorandum it was found that he had prayed for fifty-six persons daily by name, and before he was buried all of them had given their hearts to Jesus. Tell me that little boy won't shine in the kingdom of God! These little ones can be used by God.

I remember a good many years ago I resolved I wouldn't let a day pass without talking to someone about their soul's salvation. And it was in that school God qualified me to speak the gospel. If we were faithful over small things, God will promote us. If God says, "Speak to that young man," obey the word, and you will be given by and by plenty of souls. I went down past the corner of Clark and Lake streets one day, and fulfilling my vow, on seeing a man leaning up against a lamp post, I went up to him and said, "Are you a Christian?" He damned me and cursed me and said to mind my own business. He knew me, but I didn't know him. He said to a friend of his that afternoon that he had never been so insulted in his life and told him to say to me that I was damning the cause I pretended to represent.

Well, the friend came and delivered his message. "Maybe I am doing more hurt than good," I said. "Maybe I am mistaken, and God hasn't shown me the right way." That was the time I was sleeping and living in the Young Men's Christian Association rooms, where I was then president, secretary, janitor, and everything else. Well, one night after midnight I heard a knock at the door. And there on the step leading into the street stood this stranger I had made so mad at the lamp post, and he said he wanted to talk to me about his soul's salvation.

He said, "Do you remember the man you met about three months ago at a lamp post and how he cursed you? I have had no peace since that night; I couldn't sleep. Oh, tell me what to do to be saved." And we just fell down on our knees, and I prayed, and that day he went to the noon prayer meeting and openly confessed the Savior, and soon after went to the war a Christian man. I do not know but he died on some Southern battlefield or in a hospital, but I expect to see him in the kingdom of God. Oh, how often have I thanked God for that word to that dying sinner that He put into my mouth!

God's business is not to be done wholesale. Think of the Master Himself talking just to Nicodemus, and then how He talked to that poor woman at the well of Samaria. Some of Christ's greatest utterances were delivered to congregations of one or two. How many are willing to speak to tens of thousands but not to speak to a few! I knew a man who was going to get rich and do large things for God, but he never did anything. He wouldn't do little things, that was the error. Oh, be willing, Christians, to be built into the temple, as a polished capstone, or just a single brick – no matter just how, but somehow. Say to yourself in your home, in your Sunday school classes, in your daily rounds, "I'll not let this sun go down till I lead one soul to Christ." And then, having done all, shall you shine as gems in the great white throne forever and ever.

I want to tell you how I got the first impulse to work solely for the conversion of men. For a long time after my conversion, I didn't accomplish anything. I hadn't got into my right place, that was it. I hadn't thought enough of this personal work. I'd get up in prayer meeting, and I'd pray with the others, but just to go up to a man and take hold of his coat and get him down on his knees, I hadn't yet got round to that. It was in 1860 that the change came.

In the Sunday school I had a pale, delicate, young man as one of the teachers. I knew his burning piety and assigned him to the worst class in the school. They were all girls, and it was an awful class. They kept gadding around in the schoolroom and were laughing and carrying on all the while. And this young man had better success than anyone else. One Sunday he was absent, and I tried myself to teach the class, but couldn't do anything with them; they seemed farther off than ever from any concern about their souls. Well, the day after his absence, early

Monday morning, the young man came into the store where I worked, and tottering and bloodless, threw himself down on some boxes.

"What's the matter?" I said. "I have been bleeding at the lungs, and they have given me up to die," he said. "But you are not afraid to die?" I questioned. "No," said he. "I am not afraid to die, but I have got to stand before God and give an account of my stewardship, and not one of my Sunday school scholars has been brought to Jesus. I have failed to bring one and haven't any strength to do it now." He was so weighed down that I got a carriage and took that dying man in it, and we called at the homes of every one of his scholars. To each one he said, as best his faint voice would let him, "I have come to just ask you to come to the Savior," and then he prayed as I never heard before. And for ten days he labored in that way sometimes walking to the nearest houses. And at the end of that ten days every one of that large class had yielded to the Savior.

Full well I remember the night before he went away (for the doctors said he must hurry to the South), how we held a true love feast. It was the very gate of heaven, that meeting. He prayed and they prayed; he didn't ask them. He didn't think they could pray. And then we sang "Blest Be the Tie that Binds." It was a beautiful night in June that he left on the Michigan Southern, and I was down to the train to help him off. And those girls, every one, gathered there again, all unknown to each other; and the depot seemed a second gate to heaven, in the joyful, yet tearful, communion and farewells between those newly-redeemed souls and him whose crown of rejoicing it will be that he led them to Jesus. At last the gong sounded, and supported on the platform, the dying man shook hands with each one and whispered, "I will meet you yonder."

Some of the very best, most constant teachers I had before going to Europe were converted at that time, and they, in their turn, have gathered many sheaves. I myself was led by this incident, this wonderful blessing of God on individual effort, to throw up my business and give my whole strength to God's work. Shall not that young man have a high place, a place very near the Savior of men, in the day when He makes up His jewels? Oh, friends, if you want to shine in the kingdom of God, work for Him today. Shall we not, every one, go out of this building saying, "I will try to bring one soul to Christ today?"

To the Afflicted

If I were to ask this audience what Christ came into this world for, every one of you would say to save sinners, and then you would stop. A great many think that is all Christ came to do – to save sinners. Now, we are told that he came, to be sure, to "seek and save that which was lost," but he came to do more. He came to heal the brokenhearted. In that 18th verse of the 4th chapter of Luke, which I read to you last night, He said that the Spirit of the Lord was upon Him, and that He was anointed to preach the gospel to the poor, and in the next sentence He tells us, He is sent to heal the brokenhearted. In another place we are told He came into the world to declare who the Father was and reveal Him to the sons of men.

Tonight, I want to take up this one thought – that Christ was sent into the world to heal the brokenhearted. When the Prince of Wales came to this country a few years ago, the whole country was excited as to his purpose. What was his object in coming here? Had he come to look into our republican form of government, or our institutions, or was it simply to see and be seen? He came and he went without telling us what he came for. When the Prince of Peace came into this dark world, He did not come in any private way. He tells us that He came, not to see and be seen, but to "seek and save that which was lost," and also "to heal the brokenhearted." And in the face of this announcement, it is a mystery to me why those who have broken hearts will carry them year in and year out, rather than just bring them to this Great Physician. How many men in Chicago are just going down to their graves with a broken heart? They have carried their hearts weighted with trouble for years and years, and yet, when they open the Scriptures, they can see the passage telling us that He came here for the purpose of healing the brokenhearted. He left heaven and all its glory to come to the world – sent by the Father, He tells us, for the purpose of healing the brokenhearted.

You will find, my friends, that there is no class of people exempt from broken hearts. The rich and the poor suffer alike. There was a time, when I used to visit the poor, that I thought all the broken hearts were to be found among them, but within the last few years I have found there are as many broken hearts among the learned as the unlearned, the cultured as the uncultured, the rich as well as the poor. If you could but go up one of our avenues and down another and reach the hearts of the people and get them to turn out their whole story, you would be astonished at the wonderful history of every family.

I remember a few years ago I had been out of the city for some weeks. When I returned, I started out to make some calls. The first place I went to I found a mother, her eyes red with weeping. I tried to find out what was troubling her, and she reluctantly opened her heart and told me all. She said, "Last night my only boy came home about midnight, drunk. I didn't know that he was addicted to drunkenness, but this morning I found out that he has been drinking for weeks, and" she continued, "I would rather have seen him laid in the grave than have him brought home in the condition I saw him in last night." I tried to comfort her as best I could when she told me her sad story.

When I went away from that house I didn't want to go into any other house where there was family trouble. The very next house I went to, however, where some of the children who attended my Sunday school resided, I found that death had been there and laid his hand on one of them. The mother spoke to me of her afflictions and brought to me the playthings and the little shoes of the child, and the tears trickled down that mother's cheeks as she related to me her sorrow. I got out as soon as possible and hoped I should see no more family trouble that day.

The next visit I made was to a home where I found a wife with a bitter story. Her husband had been neglecting her for a long time, "and now," she said, "he has left me, and I don't know where he has gone. Winter is coming on, and I don't know what is going to become of my family." I tried to comfort her and prayed with her and endeavored to get her to lay all her sorrows on Christ.

The next home I entered I found a woman crushed and brokenhearted. She told me her boy had forsaken her, and she had no idea where he had gone. That afternoon I made five calls, and in every home, I found a broken heart. Every one had a sad tale to tell, and if you visited any home in Chicago you would find the truth of the saying, that "there is a skeleton in every house." I suppose while I am talking, you are thinking of the great sorrow in your own bosom. I do not know anything about you, but if I came round to every one of you, and you were to tell me the truth, I would hear a tale of sorrow.

The very last man I spoke to last night was a young mercantile man, who told me his load of sorrow had been so great, that many times during the last few weeks he had gone down to the lake and had been tempted to plunge in and end his existence. His burden seemed too much for him. Think of the broken hearts in Chicago tonight! They could be numbered by hundreds – yea, by thousands. All over this city are broken hearts. If all the sorrow represented in this great city was written in a book, this building couldn't hold that book, and you couldn't read it in a long lifetime.

This earth is not a stranger to tears, neither is the present the only time when they could be found in abundance. From Adam's days to ours, tears have been shed, and a wail has been going up to heaven from the brokenhearted. And I say it again, it is a mystery to me how all those broken hearts can keep away from Him Who has come to heal them. For six thousand years that cry of sorrow has been going up to God. We find the tears of Jacob put on record, when he was told that his own son was no more. His sons and daughters tried to give him comfort, but he refused to be comforted. We are also told of the tears of King David. I can see him, as the messenger brings the news of the death of his son, exclaiming in anguish, "O, Absalom, my son, would that I had died for you!" And when Christ came into the world, the first sound He heard was woe – the wail of those mothers in Bethlehem. From the manger to the cross, He was surrounded with sorrow. We are told that He often looked up to heaven and sighed. I believe it was because there was so much suffering around Him. It was on His right hand and on His left – everywhere on earth, and the thought that He had come to relieve the people of the earth of their burdens, and so few would accept Him, made Him sorrowful. He came for that purpose. Let the hundreds of thousands just cast their burdens on Him. He has come to bear them as well as our sins. He will bear our griefs and carry our sorrows. There is not a burdened son of Adam in Chicago who cannot but be freed if he will only come to Him.

Let me call your attention to this little word "sent." "He has sent me." Take your Bibles and read about those who have been sent by God, and one thought will come to you – that no man who has ever been sent by God to do His work has ever failed. No matter how great the work, how mighty the undertaking; no matter how many difficulties had to be encountered, when they were sent from God, they were sure to succeed.

God sent Moses down to Egypt to bring 3 million people out of bondage. The idea would have seemed absurd to most people. Fancy a man with an impediment in his speech, without an army, without Generals, and with no record bringing 3 million people from the power of a great nation like that of the Egyptians. But God sent him, and what was the result? Pharaoh said they should not go, and the great king and all his army were going to prevent them. But did he succeed? God sent Moses and he didn't fail.

We find that God sent Joshua to the walls of Jericho, and he marched around the walls, and at the proper time those walls came tumbling down and the city fell into his hands. God sent Elijah to stand before Ahab, and we read the result. Samson and Gideon were sent by God, and we are told in the Scriptures what they accomplished, and so all through the word we find that when God sent men they have never failed. Now, do you think for a moment that God's own Son, sent to us, is going to fail? If Moses, Elijah, Joshua, Gideon, Samson, and all these mighty men sent by God succeeded in doing their work, do you think the Son of Man is going to fail? Do you think, if He has come to heal broken hearts, He is going to fail? Do you think there is a heart so bruised and broken that can't be healed by Him? He can heal them all, but the great trouble is that men won't come.

If there is a broken heart here tonight, just bring it to the Great Physician. If you break an arm or a leg, you run off and get the best physician. If you have a broken heart, you needn't go to a doctor or minister with it; the best physician is the Great Physician. In the days of Christ, they didn't have hospitals or physicians as we have now. When a man was sick, he was taken to the door, and the passers-by prescribed for him. If a man came along who had had the same disease as the sufferer, he just told him what he had done to get cured. I remember I had a disease for a few months, and when I recovered if I met a man with the same disease, I had to tell him what cured me. I could not keep the prescription all to myself. When He came there and found the sick at their cottage door, the sufferers found more medicine in His words than there was in all the prescriptions of that country. He is a mighty physician, who has come to heal every wounded heart in this building and in Chicago tonight. You needn't run to any other physician. The great difficulty is that people try to get some other physician – they go to this creed and that creed, to this doctor of divinity and that one, instead of coming directly to the Master. He has told us that His mission is to heal the broken hearts, and if He has said this, let us take Him at His word and just ask Him to heal.

I was thinking today of the difference, when trouble comes upon them, between those who know Christ and those who know Him not. I know several members of families in this city who are just stumbling into their graves over trouble. I know two widows in Chicago who are weeping and moaning over the death of their husbands, and their grief is just taking them to their graves. Instead of bringing their burdens to Christ, they mourn day and night, and the result will be that in a few weeks or years at most, their sorrow will take them to their graves, when they ought to take it all to the Great Physician. Three years ago, a father took his wife and family on board that ill-fated French steamer. They were going to Europe and when out on the ocean, another vessel ran into her and she went down.

When I was preaching in Chicago, that mother used to bring her two children to the meetings every night. It was one of the most beautiful sights I ever looked on, to see how those little children used to sit and listen and to see the tears trickling down their cheeks when the Savior was preached. It seemed as if nobody else in that meeting drank in the truth as eagerly as those little ones. One night when an invitation had been extended to all to go into the inquiry room, one of these little children said, "Mamma, why can't I go in too?" The mother allowed them to come into the room, and some friend spoke to them, and to all appearances they seemed to understand the plan of salvation as well as their elders.

When that memorable night came, that mother went down and came up without her two children. Upon reading the news I said, "It will kill her," and I quitted my post in Edinburgh – the only time I left my post on the other side – and went down to Liverpool to try and comfort her. But when I got there, I found that the Son of God had been there before me, and instead of me comforting her, she comforted me. She told me she could not think of those children as being in the sea; it seemed as if Christ had permitted her to take those children on that vessel only that they might be wafted to Him and had saved her life only that she might come back and work a little longer for Him. When she got up the other day at a mothers' meeting in Farwell Hall and told her story, I thought I would tell the mothers of it the first chance I got. So if any of you have some great affliction, if any of you have lost a loved and loving father, mother, brother, husband, or wife, come to Christ, because God has sent Him to heal the brokenhearted.

Some of you, I can imagine, will say, "Ah, I could stand that affliction; I have something harder than that." I remember a mother coming to me and saying, "It is easy enough for you to speak in that way; if you had the burden that I've got, you couldn't cast it on the Lord." "Why, is your burden so great that Christ can't carry it?" I asked. "No, it isn't too great for Him to carry, but I can't put it on Him." "That is your fault," I replied. I find a great many people with burdens who, rather than just come to Him with them, strap them tighter on their backs and go away staggering under their load. I asked her the nature of her trouble, and she told me, "I have an only boy who is a wanderer on the face of the earth. I don't know where he is. If I only knew where he was, I would go round the world to find him. You don't know how I love that boy.

This sorrow is killing me." "Why can't you take him to Christ? You can reach Him at the throne, even though he be at the uttermost part of the world. Go tell God all about your trouble, and He will take away his, and not only that, but if you never see him on earth, God can give you faith that you will see your boy in heaven."

And then I told her of a mother who lived down in the southern part of Indiana. Some years ago, her boy came up to this city. He was a moralist. My friends, a man has to have more than morality to lean upon in this great city. He hadn't been here long before he was led astray. A neighbor happened to come up here and found him one night in the streets, drunk. When that neighbor went home, at first, he thought he wouldn't say anything about it to the boy's father, but afterwards he thought it was his duty to tell.

So in a crowd in the street of their little town, he just took that father aside and told him what he had seen in Chicago. It was a terrible blow. When the children had been put to bed that night, he said to his wife, "Wife, I have bad news. I have heard from Chicago today." The mother dropped her work in an instant and said, "Tell me what it is." "Well, our son has been seen drunk on the streets of Chicago." Neither of them slept that night, but they took their burden to Christ. About daylight the mother said, "I don't know how, I don't know when or where, but God has given me faith to believe that our son will be saved and will never come to a drunkard's grave." One week after, that boy left Chicago. He couldn't tell why – an unseen power seemed to lead him to his mother's home, and the first thing he said on coming over the threshold was, "Mother, I have come home to ask you to pray for me," and soon after he came back to Chicago a bright and shining light. If you have got a burden like this, fathers, mothers, bring it to Him and cast it on Him, and He, the Great Physician, will heal your broken hearts.

I can imagine again some of you saying, "How am I to do it?" My friends, go to Him as a personal friend. He is not a myth. What we want to do is to treat Christ as we treat an earthly friend. If you have sins, just go and tell Him all about them; if you have some great burden, "Go bury thy sorrow," bury it in His bosom. If you go to people and tell them of your cares, your sorrows, they will tell you they haven't time to listen. But He will not only hear your story, however long it be, but will bind your broken heart up. Oh, if there is a broken heart here tonight, bring it to Jesus, and I tell you upon authority, He will heal you. He has said He will bind your wounds up – not only that, but He will also heal them.

During the war I remember of a young man, not 20, who was court-martialed down in the front and sentenced to be shot. The story was this. The young fellow had enlisted; he was not obliged to, but he went off with another young man. They were what we would call "chums." One night this companion was ordered out on picket duty, and he asked the young man to go for him. The next night he was ordered out himself, and having been awake two nights, and not being used to it, fell asleep at his post, and for the offence he was tried and sentenced to death. It was right after the order issued by the President that no interference should be allowed in cases of this kind. This sort of thing had become too frequent, and it must be stopped.

When the news reached the father and mother in Vermont, it nearly broke their hearts. The thought that their son should be shot was too great for them. They had no hope that he would be saved by anything they could do. But they had a little daughter who had read the life of Abraham Lincoln and knew how he loved his own children, and she said, "If Abraham Lincoln knew how my father and mother loved my brother, he wouldn't let him be shot." That little girl thought this over and made up her mind to go and see the President.

She went to the White House, and the sentinel, when he saw her imploring looks, passed her in, and when she came to the door and told the private secretary that she wanted to see the President, he could not refuse her. She came into the chamber and found Abraham Lincoln surrounded by his generals and counsellors, and when he saw the little country girl, he asked her what she wanted. The little maid told her plain, simple story – how her brother, whom her mother and father loved very dearly, had been sentenced to be shot. How they were mourning for him, and if he were to die in that way it would break their hearts.

The President's heart was touched with compassion, and he immediately sent a dispatch canceling the sentence and giving the boy a parole so that he could come home and see that father and mother. I just tell you this to show you how Abraham Lincoln's heart was moved by compassion for the sorrow of that father and mother, and if he showed so much, do you think the Son of God will not have compassion upon you, sinner, if you only take that crushed, bruised heart to Him? He will read it. Have you got a drunken husband? Go tell him. He can make him a blessing to the church and to the world. Have you a profligate son? Go take your story to Him, and He will comfort you and bind up and heal your sorrow. What a blessing it is to have such a Savior. He has been sent to heal the brokenhearted. May the text, if the sermon doesn't, reach everyone here tonight, and may every crushed, broken, and bruised heart be brought to that Savior, and they will hear His comforting words. He will comfort you as a mother comforts her child if you will only come in prayer and lay all your burdens before Him.

Spiritual Blindness

You who have been here during the week have heard me speaking on the 4th chapter of Luke and 18th verse. I spoke on the first three clauses of that verse, and we have now come to the next clause in which he tells us that he came to give sight to the blind – for the recovery of sight to the blind. Paul tells us in his epistle to the Corinthians 4th chapter and 3rd verse: *"But if our gospel be hid, it is hid to them that are lost; in whom the god of this world has blinded the minds of them which believe not lest the light of the glorious gospel of Christ, who is the image of God, should shine unto them."* "If the gospel be hid…in whom the god of this world has blinded." Now you may see this world is just one, large blind asylum – it is full of blind people.

Last Wednesday night I tried to tell you that the world was full of broken hearts; last night I tried to tell you that the world was full of captives, bound hand and foot in sin, and tonight I tell you that it is full of blind people. Not only blind, but bound and brokenhearted. You might say that nearly all those in the world come under the three heads. Now just look at the contrast between Satan and Christ. Satan breaks men's hearts, but Christ binds them up. Satan binds the people of this earth hand and foot, but Christ breaks the fetters and sets them free. Satan makes us blind, but Christ opens our eyes. He came to do this, and just see how He was received. He went into that synagogue at Nazareth and preached this glorious gospel. He commenced by telling them that the spirit of the Lord was upon Him and went on to tell them that He had come to save them; what did they do? They thrust Him out of the city and took Him to the brow of the hill and would have hurled Him into hell if they could.

And men have been as bitter toward the gospel all along these 1,800 years. Why, some men would tear the preacher from limb from limb if it weren't for the law. Then we find when He goes to Bethany and raising up the brother of Martha and Mary and binding up broken hearts as he went along and preaching mercy, they want to kill Him. We find Him in the 3rd chapter of Mark setting the captive free. Here we find a man possessed of demons, whom no one could cure, set at liberty by the Son of Man, and in the healing, because they lost a few swine, they told Him to depart from their coasts. Then we find Him just a few days before His death, almost on His way to Calvary, giving sight to that blind man. And for all this they take Him to that mount and nail Him to a cross. Oh, what blindness!

We are told that there are 3 million people in the world who are called blind. Everyone calls them blind because they haven't their natural sight. But do you ever think how many are spiritually blind in this world? Why, if there are 3 million people in the world who have not their natural sight, how many do you suppose are spiritually blind? We sympathize with those who have lost their sight. Nothing appeals to our sympathy so readily. I believe I could raise thousands of dollars among you by telling you about some blind person who is suffering for the necessaries of life through their affliction. How many of you wouldn't put your hand in your pockets and give liberally? How it moves our compassion – how it moves our hearts as we see the blind men, women, or children in the streets. How your heart goes out to those poor unfortunates.

I was at a meeting in London, and I heard a man speaking with wonder, but power and earnestness. "Who is that man?" I asked, my curiosity being excited. "Why, that is Dr.--. He is blind." I felt some interest in this man, and at the close of the meeting I sought an interview, and he told me that he had been stricken blind when very young. His mother took him to a doctor and asked him about his sight. "You must give up all hope," the doctor said. "Your boy is blind and will be forever." "What, do you think my boy will never see?" asked his mother. "Never again." The mother took her boy to her bosom and cried, "Oh, my boy, who will take care of you when I am gone – who will look to you!" forgetting the faithfulness of that God she had taught him to love. He became a servant of the Lord and was permitted to print the Bible in twelve different languages, printed in the raised letters, so that all the blind people could read the Scriptures themselves.

He had a congregation, my friends, of 3 million people, and I think that blind man was one of the happiest beings in all London. He was naturally blind, but he had eyes to his soul and could see a bright eternity in the future. He had built his foundation upon the living God. We pity those who have not their natural sight, but how you should pity yourself if you are spiritually blind. If we could get all the blind, spiritually, in this city! You talk about those great political meetings; they would be nothing to the crowd you would collect. Why, just look at all the men in this city who are blind, and many of them are in the churches. This has been the trouble with men always. Christ couldn't get men to understand they were blind; He couldn't even get His disciples to open their eyes until after He went up to heaven. And then they received the spiritual truth. How many are the professed children of God we read of in the Book of Revelation?

I think tonight I might pick up some of the different classes who are blind. I am somewhat acquainted with the rich men of this city, and I don't think it would take long to prove that the leading men of this city are blind – blind to their own interests. Take a man just spending all his strength and energies to get money. He is money blind. He is so blind in his pursuit that he cannot see the God of heaven. Money is his god. His cry is continually, "Money! Money!" and it is the cry of many here in Chicago. They don't care about God, don't care about salvation, don't heed their eternal condition so long as they get money, money, money. And a great many of them have got it. But how lean their souls are. God has given them the desire of their heart, but He has given them leanness of soul.

I heard of a man who had accumulated great wealth, and death came upon him suddenly and he realized, as the saying is, that "there was no bank in the shroud," that he couldn't take anything away with him.

We may have all the money on earth, but we must leave it behind us. He called a lawyer in and commenced to will away his property before he went away. His little girl couldn't understand exactly where he was going, and she said, "Father, have you got a home in that land you are going to?" The arrow went down to his soul. "Got a home there?" The rich man had hurled away God and neglected to secure a home there for the sake of his money, and he found it was now too late. He was money mad, and he was money blind. It wouldn't be right for me to give names, but I could tell you a good many here in Chicago who are going on in this way – just spending all their lives in the accumulation of what they cannot take with them. This is going on while how many poor people are suffering for the necessaries of life. These men don't know they are blind – money is their god.

There is another class who don't care so much for money. We might call them business blind. It is business, business, business with them all the time. In the morning they haven't time to worship. They must attend to business; must get down to the store. Down they run and haven't time to get home to dinner. They mustn't let anyone get ahead of them. They get home late at night, and their families have gone to bed. They scarcely ever see their children. It is all business with them.

A man told me not long ago, "I must attend to my business. That is my first consideration and see that none gets ahead of me." That is his god. I don't care if he is an elder or a deacon in the church. That is his god. The god of business has blinded him. Look at the merchant prince who died the other day. Men called him a clever, shrewd man. Call that shrewdness – to pile up wealth for a lifetime and leave no record behind so that we know he has gone to heaven? He rose above men in his business; he devoted his whole soul to it, and the world called him a power among men. The world called him great. But let the Son of God write his obituary; let him put an epitaph on his tombstone, and it would be, "You fool." Man says, "I must attend to business first"; God says, "Seek first the kingdom of God." I don't care what your business may be; it may be honorable, legitimate, and all that, and you think you must attend to it first. Bear in mind that God tells every man to seek His kingdom first.

There is another class of people who are blind. They don't care so much about riches They are not very ambitious to become rich, they don't spend their lives in business matters. They are politically blind. They are mad over politics, they are bound up in the subject. There will be a great many broken hearts in a week hence. They have got their favorite candidate to attend to and they cannot find time to worship God. How little prayer there has been about the election. There has been a good deal of work, but how much praying has been done? We want prayer to go up all over our land that high and honest men may rule over us. But they are so excited over this election that they have no time to pray to the God of heaven. They are politically blind. How many men within our recollection who have set their hearts upon the Presidential chair have gone down to the grave with disappointment? They were poor, blind men, and the world called them great. Oh, how foolish, how blind. They didn't seek God; they only sought one thing – greatness – position and office. They were great, brilliant, clever men, but when they were summoned into the presence of their God, what a wreck. Men so brilliant might have wielded an influence for the Son of God that would have lived in the hearts of the people for generations to come, and the streams of their goodness might have flowed long after they went to heaven. But they lived for the world and their works went to dust.

But a great number of people don't care for business or politics. They only want a little money so as to get pleasure. How many men have been blinded by pleasure. A lady told me in the inquiry room she would like to become a Christian, but there was a ball coming on, and she didn't want to become a Christian until after the ball. The ball was worth more to her than the kingdom of God. For this ball she would put off the kingdom of God until it was over, forgetting that death might come to her in the meantime and usher her into the presence of God. How blind she was, and many are just like her. The kingdom of God is offered to them without money and without price, and yet for a few days of pleasure they forfeit heaven and everything dear to their eternity.

I was talking to a lady who, with the tears running down her cheeks upon my speaking to her, said, "The fact is, if I become a Christian, I have to give up all pleasure. I cannot go to a theatre, I cannot read any novels, I cannot play cards. I have nothing else to do." Oh, what blindness! Look at the pleasure of being taken into the Lord's vineyard and the joy and luxury of working for Him and leading souls to Christ. And people with their eyes wide open would rather bend down to the god of pleasure than become Christians.

Then there is the god of fashion. How many women just devote their lives to it. They want to see the latest bonnet, the latest cloak, the latest dress. They can't think of anything else. Said a lady to me, "I am always thinking of fashion; it doesn't matter if I get down on my knees to pray, I am always thinking of a new dress." You may laugh at this, but it's true. Pleasure in the ballroom and fashion is the god of a great many people. Oh, that we may lift our eyes to something nobler. Suppose you don't have so many dresses and give something to the poor, you will have something then which will give you joy and comfort that will last you always. I pity the man or woman who lives for the day like the butterfly – those whose minds are fixed upon fashion and pleasure and have no time to look to their perishing soul.

A good many people don't know they are hid. Look at that young man. You call him a fast young man. He has got a salary of $1,000, and it costs him $3,000 to live. Where does he get the money? Where does it come from? His father cannot give it him because he is poor. His employer begins to get suspicious. "I only give him $1,000 a year, and he is living at the rate of $3,000." By and by he looks into his account book and finds it overdrawn. Thus he is ruined – character blasted. Oh, how many are of this stamp in Chicago! It is only a question of time. How many young men have we got just living beyond their income – taking money out of their employer's drawer. They say, "Well, I am going to the theater tonight, and I will just take a dollar; will put it back next week." But when next week comes, he hasn't put it back, and takes another dollar. He has taken $2 now. He keeps on draw, draw, drawing, when by and by it all comes out. He loses his place, doesn't get any letters of recommendation, and the poor man is ruined.

My friends, this is not the description of an isolated case. This class is all over the country. I wish I could send you the letters I get about just such cases. I got one the other day from a young mother with a family of beautiful children. She told me how happy they had lived – husband, wife, and children, and how one night her husband came home excited, his face white with terror, and said, "I've got to fly from justice. Goodbye." He has gone from her, and she said it seemed as if she could die; her husband, disgraced and starving, couldn't get anything to do. Her cry seemed to be "Help, help me." Is not the country full of such cases? Is it not blindness and madness for men to go on in this way? If anyone is here tonight following in the way of these men, I pray God your eyes may be opened before you are led to death and ruin.

You know we had a full meeting today, and the subject was intemperance. How many young men are there who spend their time in the saloons of the city. I am afraid many will be led astray next Tuesday. I always dread an election day – I generally see so many young men beastly drunk. They are led away, and that is another quick road down to hell. May the young men see the folly of this, and on that day stand firm. May God open your eyes. How many young men are there whose characters have been blasted by strong drink. How many brilliant men in the Chicago bar have gone down to death by it. Some of the noblest statesmen, some of the most brilliant orators and men of all professions have been borne down to the drunkard's grave. May God open your eyes to show the folly of tampering with strong drink.

Now, many men say, "I am not going down to the grave of a drunkard." They think they have strength to stop when they like. When it gets hold, there is nothing within us by which we can save ourselves. He alone can give you power to resist the cup of temptation: He alone can give you power to overcome its influence if you only will believe Him. The god of this world has been trying to make you believe that man can do it himself, and Christ will have nothing to do with him. The god of this world is a liar. I come with authority to tell you – I don't care how far gone you are; don't care how blessed you may be – that the Son of God can and will save you if you only believe Him. If there is one here tonight under the power of strong drink, come tonight. We lift up our voice to warn you.

Look at that man in a boat on Niagara River. He is only about a mile from the rapids. A man on the bank shouts to him, "Young man, young man, the rapids are not far away, you'd better pull for the shore." "You attend to your own business; I will take care of myself," he replies. Like a great many people here, and ministers, too, they don't want any evangelist here – don't want any help, however great the danger ahead. On he goes, sitting coolly in his boat. Now he has got a little nearer, and a man from the bank of the river sees his danger, and shouts, "Stranger, you'd better pull for the shore; if you go further, you'll be lost. You can be saved now if you pull in." "Mind your business, and you'll have enough to do; I'll take care of myself."

Like a good many men, they are asleep to the danger that's hanging over them while they are in the current. And I say, drinking young man, don't you think you are standing still. You are in the current, and if you don't pull for a rock of safety you will go over the precipice. On he goes. I can see him in the boat laughing at the danger. A man on the bank is looking at him, and he lifts up his voice and cries, "Stranger, stranger, pull for the shore! If you don't you will lose your life!" and the young man laughs at him – mocks him. That is the way with hundreds in Chicago. If you go to them and point out their danger, they will jest and joke at you. By and by he says, "I think I hear the rapids – yes, I hear them roar," and he seizes his oars and pulls with all his strength, but the current is too great. Nearer and nearer he is drawn on to that abyss, until he gives one unearthly scream and over he goes. Ah, my friends, this is the case with hundreds in this city. They are in the current of riches, of pleasure, of drink, that will take them to the whirlpool. Satan has got them blindfolded, and they are on their road to the bottomless pit.

We hear some men say in a jesting way, "Oh, we are sowing our wild oats; we will get over this by and by." I have seen men reap their wild oats. It's all well enough sowing, but when it comes to the reaping it's a different thing. I remember I went home one night and found all the people in alarm. They had seen a man come running down the street, and as he approached the house, he gave an unearthly roar, and in terror they bolted the door. He came right up to my door, and instead of ringing the bell, just tried to push the door in. They asked him what he wanted, and he told them he wanted to see me. They said I was at the meeting, and away he ran, and they could hear him groan as he disappeared.

I was coming along North Clark Street, and he shot past me like an arrow. But he had seen me and turned and seized me by the arm, saying eagerly, "Can I be saved tonight? The devil is coming to take me to hell at one o'clock tonight." "My friend, you are mistaken." I thought the man was sick. But he persisted that the devil had come and laid his hand upon him and told him that he might have till one o'clock, "and," said he, "Won't you go up to my room and sit with me?" I got some men up to his room to see to him. At one o'clock the devils came into that room, and all the men in that room could not hold him. He was reaping what he had sown. When the Angel of Death came and laid his cold hand on him, oh, how he cried for mercy – how he beseeched for pardon. Ah, yes, young men, you may say in a laughing and jesting way you are sowing your wild oats, but the reaping time is coming. May God show you tonight what folly it is – what a miserable life you are leading. May we lift our heart here to the God of all grace, so that we may see our lost and ruined condition if we do not come to Him. Christ stands ready and willing to save – to save tonight all those who are willing to be saved. Let us pray.

Repentance

You will find my text tonight in the 17th chapter of Acts, part of the 30th verse: *"And now commands all men everywhere to repent."* I have heard a number of complaints about the preaching here in the Tabernacle, that repentance has not been touched upon. The fact is that I have never had very great success in preaching upon repentance. When I have preached it, people haven't repented. I've had far more success when I've preached Christ's goodness. But tonight, I will preach about repentance, so you will have no more cause of complaint. I believe in repentance just as much as I believe in the Word of God.

When John the Baptist came to preach to that Jewish nation, his one cry was, "Repent! Repent!" But when Christ came, he changed it to, "The blood of the Lamb takes away the sin of the world." I would rather cry, "The blood of the Lamb takes away the sin of the world," than talk about repentance. And when Christ came, we find Him saying, "Repent," but He soon pointed them to something higher – He told them about the goodness of God. It is the goodness of God that produces repentance.

When, upon the Day of Pentecost they asked what to do to be saved, we find Him telling men, "Repent, every one of you." When Christ sent His disciples out to preach, two by two, we find the message He gave them to deliver was, "Repent, for the kingdom of heaven is at hand." It is clearly preached throughout the Scriptures. There is a good deal of trouble among people about what repentance really is. If you ask people what it is, they will tell you, "It is feeling sorry." If you ask a man if he repents, he will tell you, "Oh, yes; I generally feel sorry for my sins." That is not repentance. It is something more than feeling sorry. Repentance is turning right about and forsaking sin. I wanted to speak on Sunday about that verse in Isaiah, which says, "Let the guilty forsake his way, and the unrighteous man his thoughts." That is what it is. If a man doesn't turn from his sin, he won't be accepted of God, and if righteousness doesn't produce a turning about – a turning from bad to good – it isn't true righteousness.

Unconverted people have got an idea that God is their enemy. Now, let me impress this, and I told you the same the other night. God hates sin with a perfect hatred. He will punish sin wherever He finds it, yet He at the same time loves the sinner and wants him to repent and turn to Him. If men will only turn, they will find mercy and find it just the moment they turn to Him. You will find men sorry for their misdeeds. Cain, no doubt, was sorry, but that was not true repentance. There is no cry recorded in the Scriptures as coming from him, "O my God, O my God, forgive me." There was no repentance in his only feeling sorry.

Look at Judas. There is no sign that he turned to God, no sign that he came to Christ asking forgiveness. Yet, probably, he felt sorry. He was, very likely, filled with remorse and despair; but he didn't repent. Repentance is turning to Him who loved us and gave Himself for us. Look at King Saul and see the difference between him and King David. David fell as low as Saul and a good deal lower – he fell from a higher pinnacle, but what was the difference between the two? David turned back to God and confessed his sin and got forgiven. But look at King Saul. There was no repentance there, and God couldn't save him till he repented. You will find all through the Scriptures, where men have repented, God has forgiven them.

Look at that publican when he went up to pray. He felt his sin so great that he couldn't look up to heaven – all he could do was to smite his heart and cry, "God, forgive me a sinner!" There was turning to God – repentance, and that man went down to his home forgiven. Look at that prodigal. His father couldn't forgive him while he was still in a foreign land and squandering his money in riotous living, but the moment he came home repentant, how soon that father forgave him – how quick he came to meet him with the word of forgiveness. It wouldn't have done any good to forgive the boy while he was in that foreign country unrepentant. He would have despised all favors and blessings from his father. That is the position the sinner stands toward God. He cannot be forgiven and get His blessing, until he comes to God repenting of all his sins and asking the blessing.

Now, we read in Scripture that God deals with us as a father deals with a son. Fathers and mothers, you who have children, let me ask by way of illustration, suppose you go home, and you find that while you have been here, your boy has gone to your private drawer and stolen $5 of your money. You go to him and say, "John, did you take that money?" "Yes, father, I took that money," he replies. When you hear him saying this without any apparent regret, you won't forgive him. You want to get at his conscience; you know it would do him an injury to forgive him unless he confesses his wrong. Suppose he won't do it. "Yes," he says, "I stole your money, but I don't think I've done wrong." The mother cannot, the father cannot forgive him, unless he sees he has done wrong and wants forgiveness.

That's the trouble with the sinners in Chicago. They've turned against God, broken His commandments, trampled His law under their feet, and their sins hang upon them; until they show signs of repentance their sin will remain. But the moment they see their iniquity and come to God, forgiveness will be given them, and their iniquity will be taken out of their way. Said a person to me the other day, "It is my sin that stands between me and Christ." "It isn't," I replied, "it's your own will." That's what stands between the sinner and forgiveness. Christ will take all your iniquities away if you will. Men are so proud that they won't acknowledge and confess before God. Don't you see on the face of it, if your boy won't repent, you cannot forgive him, and how is God going to forgive a sinner if he doesn't repent? If He were allowing an unrepentant sinner into His kingdom, there would be war in heaven in twenty-four hours. You cannot live in a house with a boy who steals everything he can lay his hands on. You would have to banish him from your house.

Look at King David with his son Absalom. After he had been sent away, he gets his friends to intercede for him to get him back to Jerusalem. They succeeded in getting him back to the city, but someone told the king that he hadn't repented, and his father would not see him. After he had been in Jerusalem some time, trying his best to get into favor and position again without repentance, he sent a friend, Joab, to the king, and told him to say to his father, "Examine me, and if you find no iniquity in me, take me in." He was forgiven, but the most foolish thing King David ever did was to forgive that young prince. What was the result? He drove him from the throne. That's what the sinner would do if he got into heaven unrepentant. He would just drive God from the throne – tear the crown from Him. No unrepentant sinner can get into the kingdom of heaven.

Ah, some people say, "I believe in the mercy of God; I don't believe God will allow one to perish. I believe everyone will get to heaven. Look at those who lived before the flood. Do you think He swept all those sinners, all those men and women who were too wicked to live on earth – do you believe He swept them all into heaven, and left the only righteous man to wade through the flood? Do you think He would do this? Yet many men believe all will go into heaven. The day will come when you will wake up and know that you have been deceived by the devil. No unrepentant sinner will ever get into heaven; unless they forsake their sin, they cannot enter there.

The law of God is very plain on this point: "Except a man repent." That's the language of Scripture. And when this is so plainly set down, why is it that men fold their arms and say, "God will take me into heaven anyway." Suppose a governor elected today comes into office in a few months and he finds a great number of criminals in prison, and he goes and says, "I feel for those prisoners. They cannot stay in jail any longer." Suppose some murders have been committed, and he says, "I am tender hearted, I can't punish those men," and he opens the prison door and lets them all out. How long would that governor be in his position? These very men who are depending on the mercy of God would be the first to raise their voice against that governor. These men would say, "These murders must be punished, or society will be imperiled; life will not be safe," and yet they believe in the mercy of God whether they repent or not. My dear friends, don't go on under that delusion; it is a snare of the devil. I tell you the Word of God is true, and it tells us, "Except a man repent," there is not one ray of hope held out. May the Spirit of God open your eyes tonight and show you the truth – let it go into your hearts." Let the wicked forsake his way and the unrighteous his thoughts.

Now, my friends, repentance is not fear. A great many people say I don't preach up the terrors of religion. I don't want to – don't want to scare men into the kingdom of God. I don't believe in preaching that way. If I did get some in that way, they would soon get out. If I wanted to scare men into heaven, I would just hold the terror of hell over their heads and say, "Go right in." But that's not the way to win men. They don't have any slaves in heaven. They are all sons, and they must accept salvation voluntarily. Terror never brought a man in yet. Look at a vessel tossed upon the billows, and sailors think it is going to the bottom and death is upon them. They fall down on their knees, and you would think they were all converted. They ain't converted; they're only scared. There's no repentance there, and as soon as the storm is over and they get on shore, they are the same as ever. All their terror has left them – they've forgotten it, and they fall into their old habits. How many men have, while lying on a sick bed, thought they saw the terrors of death gathering around them, and made resolutions to live a new life if they only get well again; but the moment they get better they forget all about their resolutions. It was only scare with them; that's not what we want to feel. Fear is one thing, and repentance is another. True repentance is the Holy Spirit showing sinners their sin. That's what we want. May the Holy Spirit reveal to each one here tonight out of Christ their lost condition unless they repent.

If God threw Adam out of Eden on account of one sin, how can you expect to get into the heavenly paradise with ten thousand? I can imagine someone saying, "I haven't got anything to repent of." If you are one of those Pharisees, I can tell you that this sermon will not reach your heart. I would like to find one man who could come up here and say, "I have no sin." If I were one of those who thought I had no sin to repent of, I'd never go to church; I would certainly not come up to the Tabernacle. But could you find a man walking the streets of Chicago who could say this honestly? I don't believe there's a day passed over my head during the last twenty years but when night came, I found I had some sin to repent of.

It is impossible for a man to live without sinning. There are so many things to draw away the heart and affections of men from God. I feel as if I ought to be repenting all the time. Is there a man here who can say honestly, "I have not got a sin that I need ask forgiveness for? I haven't one thing to repent of?" Some men seem to think that God has got ten different laws for each of those ten commandments, but if you have been guilty of breaking one, you are guilty of breaking all. If a man steals $5 and another steals $500, the one is as guilty of theft as the other. A man who has broken one commandment of God is as guilty as he who has broken ten.

If a man doesn't feel this and come to Him repentant and turn his face from sin toward God, there is not a ray of hope. Nowhere can you find one ray from Genesis to Revelation. Don't go out of this Tabernacle saying, "I have nothing to repent of." I heard of a man who said he had been converted. A friend asked him if he had repented. "No," said he, "I never trouble my head about it." My friends, when a man becomes converted, the work has to be a little deeper than that. He has to become repentant and try to atone for what he has done. If he is at war with anyone, he has to go and be reconciled to his enemy. If he doesn't, his conversion is the work of Satan. When a man turns to God, he is made a new creature – a new man. His impulses all the time are guided by love. He loves his enemies and tries to repair all wrong he has done. This is a true sign of conversion. If this sign is not apparent, his conversion has never got from his head to his heart. We must be born of the Spirit, hearts must be regenerated – born again. When a man repents and turns to the God of heaven, then the work is deep and thorough. I hope that everyone here tonight will see the necessity of true repentance when they come to God for a blessing, and may the Spirit move you to ask it tonight.

I can imagine some of you saying, "How am I to repent tonight?" My friends, there are only two parties in the world. There has been a great political contest here today, and there have been two sides. We will not know before forty-eight hours which side has triumphed. There is great interest now to know which side has been the stronger. Now, there are two parties in this world – those for Christ and those against Him, and to change to Christ's party is only moving from the old party to the new. You know that the old party is bad, and the new one is good, and yet you don't change.

Suppose I was called to New York tonight and went down to the Illinois Central Depot to catch the ten o'clock train. I go on the train, and a friend should see me and say, "You are on the wrong train for New York. You are on the Burlington train." "Oh, no," I say, "you are wrong; I asked someone, and he told me this was the right train." "Why," this friend replies, "I've been in Chicago for twenty years and know that you are on the wrong train." The man talks and at last convinces me, but I sit still, although I believe I am in the wrong train for New York, and I go on to Burlington. If you don't get off the wrong train and get on the right one, you will not reach heaven. If you have not repented, seize your baggage tonight and go to the other train.

If a man is not repentant, his face is turned away from God. The moment his face is turned toward God peace and joy follow. There are a great many people hunting after joy, after peace. Dear friends, if you want to find it tonight, just turn to God, and you will get it. You need not hunt for it any longer; only come and get it. When I was a little boy, I remember I tried to catch my shadow. I don't know if you were ever so foolish, but I remember running after it and trying to get ahead of it. I could not see why the shadow always kept ahead of me.

Once I happened to be racing with my face to the sun, and I looked over my head and saw my shadow coming back of me, and it kept behind me all the way. It is the same with the Sun of Righteousness. Peace and joy will go with you while you go with your face toward Him, and these people who are getting at the back of the Sun are in darkness all the time. Turn to the light of God and the reflection will flash in your heart. Don't say that God will not forgive you. It is only your will which keeps His forgiveness from you.

My sister, I remember, told me her little boy said something naughty one morning. His father said to him, "Sammy, go and ask your mother's forgiveness." "I won't," replied the child. "If you don't ask your mother's forgiveness, I'll put you to bed." It was early in the morning – before he went to business, and the boy didn't think he would do it. He said, "I won't," again. They undressed him and put him to bed. The father came home at noon expecting to find his boy playing about the house.

He didn't see him about and asked his wife where he was. "In bed still." So he went up to the room, sat down by the bed, and said: "Sammy, I want you to ask your mother's forgiveness." But the answer was, "No." The father coaxed and begged but could not induce the child to ask forgiveness. The father went away expecting certainly that when he came home at night the child would have got all over it.

At night, however, when he got home, he found the little fellow still in bed. He had lain there all day. He went to him and tried to get him to go to his mother, but it was no use. His mother went and was equally unsuccessful. That father and mother could not sleep that night. They expected every moment to hear the knock at their door by their little son. Now they wanted to forgive the boy. My sister told me it was just as if death had come into their home. She never passed through such a night. In the morning she went to him and said, "Now, Sammy, you are going to ask my forgiveness," but the boy turned his face to the wall and wouldn't speak. The father came home at noon and the boy was as stubborn as ever. It looked as though the child was going to conquer. It was for the good of the boy that they didn't want to give him his own way. It is a great deal better for us to submit to God than have our own way. Our own way will lead us to ruin; God's way leads to life everlasting.

The father went off to his office, and that afternoon my sister went in to her son about four o'clock and began to reason with him, and, after talking for some time, she said, "Now, Sammy, say 'mother.'" "Mother," said the boy. "Now say 'for.'" "For." "Now just say 'give.'" And the boy repeated, "give." "Me," said the mother. "Me," and the little fellow fairly leaped out of bed. "I have said it," he cried; "take me down to papa, so that I can say it to him." Oh, sinner, go to Him and ask His forgiveness. This is repentance. It is coming in with a broken heart and asking the King of heaven to forgive you. Don't say you can't. It is a lie. It is your stubborn will – it is your stubborn heart.

Now let me say here tonight, you are in a position to be reconciled to God now. You are not in a position to deny this reconciliation a week, a day, an hour. God tells you now. Look at that beautiful steamer *Atlantic*. There she is in the bay groping her way along a rocky coast. The captain doesn't know, as his vessel plows through that ocean, that in a few moments it will strike a rock and hundreds of those on board will perish in a watery grave. If he knew, in a minute he could strike a bell and the steamer would be turned from that rock and the people would be saved. The vessel has struck, but he knows now too late. You have time now. In five minutes, for all you and I know, you may be in eternity. God hangs a mist over our eyes as to our summons. So now God calls – now everyone repent, and all your sins will be taken from you. I have come in the name of the Master to ask you to turn to God now. May God help you to turn and live. Let us pray.

What Christ Is to Us

Now I am not going to take a text tonight. I am going to take a subject, and that subject will be "What Christ is to Us." If you say when I get through that Christ is not what I try to make Him out to be, it will be your own fault and no one else's, because He is a thousand times more to every soul here than I can make Him out to be tonight. A man cannot tell what Christ is in a few moments – cannot begin to express what Christ is to us. I remember talking on the same subject at a meeting in the north of England. I felt that I had not said enough about Him when I got through.

When I went home, I went with a Scotchman. I was complaining and groaning over the meeting and told him I had only got half through with my subject, when the Scotchman turned to me and said, "Ye dinna expect to tell a'aboot Christ in one hour, d'ye? Why, 'twould tak a'eternity to do it, man." I thought I could get through in an hour, but, my friends, it cannot be done. I'm not going to talk to you an hour tonight, however, and now I would like to call your attention to the 2nd chapter of Luke and 11th verse: "For unto you is born this day in the city of David a Savior which is Christ the Lord." That's what Christ offers to be to every soul that comes into this world. God gives Him to the world, "Unto you is born this day a Savior." God gave Him to free us from our sins; that is what Christ came into the world to do. To get Him, we must first meet Him at Calvary as our Jesus, our purifier, our sanctification, our redemption. We must first pass Calvary before we can see Him as our Savior. And He wants you to come there – He wants to be a Savior to every soul in Chicago. He is not only a Savior who takes us from the pit of hell, but He delivers us from sin.

A great many people have a wrong idea of Christ. They think He only saves us from hell, but He keeps us from sin day by day. God knew a great deal better what the world needed than us. Therefore, He gave us Christ, not only to save us from death, but also to free us from sin. He is not only a Savior; he is a Redeemer. Redemption is more real than salvation.

I asked a man some time ago why he thought so much about a certain man. I noticed that he could not speak of him but tears came into his eyes, and so I asked him, "Why is it that you love that man as you do?" "Why, Mr. Moody," he said, "that man saved me." He told me in confidence how he got involved, how he took what did not belong to him, thinking he could replace it in a few weeks, but when the time came found he could not. In a week or two exposure would come, and it would be sure ruin to him, wife, and family. He told how he went to a friend and poured out his heart, and how that friend advanced him the money and paid the debt, "and," he added, "I would be willing to lay down my life for that friend. He saved me." It was out of gratitude to that man that he was willing to give his life for him. When we appreciate what redemption is and what Christ has done for us, we are willing to lay down our life for Him – sacrifice everything for His sake.

Redemption is more. It is buying back, for we are told in Galatians, "He has redeemed us from the curse." The curse of the law rests upon every son of Adam – "He has redeemed us from the curse of the law." Redemption is buying back. He has bought us back from sentence of justice. We belong to Him – "He has redeemed us by His blood." I remember I was going from my home to preach in a neighboring village. My brother was with me, and I saw a young man driving before us. I said to my brother, "Who is that young man? I've never seen him before." "Do you see that farm, those beautiful buildings, do you see all these fields, and the pasture? That is his farm. His father was a drunkard and squandered his money, buried his home in debt, and died. His mother had to go to the poorhouse. That young man went away, earned money, came back, redeemed the farm, took his mother from the poorhouse, and he is looked upon as one of the noblest young men in the country." That's what Christ is doing for us. Adam sold us very cheap, and Christ comes and redeems us – does it without any cost. He is more than a savior and a redeemer – He is a deliverer.

A great many people go to Calvary and believe He is their Redeemer, but they forget that He came to deliver us from all temptation, from all appetite, from all lust. Now, when God put the children of Israel behind the blood at Goshen, they were safe. When they came to the Red Sea, and they heard the King of Egypt with his mighty army, his horsemen, and his chariots come rolling on to their destruction, it was then that the God of heaven showed His power as a deliverer. He said to Moses, "Stretch out your rod," and the sea opened and His chosen people passed over in safety. God is a deliverer to all His children, whatever you may be. He is a great physician to us all, and He will deliver you from all your difficulties.

In the 5th chapter of Mark, we see him as a deliverer. I do not think that God ever found harder cases in Chicago, than those were there. We have got hospitals for the incurables, and if they had had them in those days, these cases would have been put there. First look at that man who had his dwelling in the tombs. They tried to tame him, but he snapped the chains as Samson did the pillars. They tried to bind him, they tried to keep him clothed, but he tore his garments into shreds. There he was, a wild man and a terror to everybody. The children were afraid of him, and the women and men, hearing his cries at night, dreaded to go near that spot. There he was, a slave of the devils. But Christ came to that part of the country. See how they tried to chain him, to bind him, to tame him; but they all failed. But Christ came, and with one word, delivered him. One word, and those devils forsook him. And his countrymen hearing of the incident, came out. They did not go out to see what Christ had been doing, but they came out to look for their swine.

A good many men here in Chicago value swine more than they do the salvation of souls. Let pork go up or down and see what a commotion there would be. But if there are souls to save here tonight, they would never trouble themselves. They came out to see the swine, and there they found the wild man sitting at the feet of Jesus, clothed, and in his right mind. When the man found himself delivered, he wanted to go with the Savior. That was gratitude. Christ had saved him, had redeemed him. He had delivered him from the hand of the enemy. And this man cried, "Let me follow You round the world; where You go I will go." But the Lord said, "You go home and tell your friends what good things the Lord has done for you." And he started home. I would like to have been in that house when he came there. I can imagine how the children would look when they saw him and say, "Father is coming." "Shut the door!" the mother would cry. "Look out! Fasten the windows! Bolt every door in the house!"

Many times he very likely had come home and abused his family, broken the chairs and tables, turned the mother into the street, and alarmed all the neighbors. They see him now coming down the street. Down he comes till he gets to the door, and then gently knocks. You don't hear a sound as he stands there. At last he sees his wife at the window, and he says, "Mary!" "Why," she says, "why he speaks as he did when I first married him; I wonder if he has got well?" So she looks out, and says, "John, is that you?" "Yes, Mary," he replies, "it's me. Don't be afraid anymore, I'm well now." I see that mother, how she pulls back the bolts of that door, and looks at him. The first look is sufficient, and she springs into his arms, and clings about his neck. She takes him in and asks him a hundred questions – how it all happened – all about it. "Well, just take a chair, and I'll tell you how I got cured." The children hang back and look amazed. He says, "I was there in the tombs, you know, cutting myself with stones and running about in my nakedness, when Jesus of Nazareth came that way. Mary, did you ever hear of Him? He is the most wonderful man. I've never seen a man like him. He just ran in and told those devils to leave me, and they left me. When He had cured me, I wanted to follow Him, but He told me to come home and tell you all about it." The children by and by gather about his knee, and the elder ones run to tell their playmates what wonderful things Jesus has done for their father. Ah, my friends, we have got a mighty deliverer – don't care what affliction you have. He will deliver you from it. The Son of God, who cast out those devils, can deliver you from your besetting sin.

A man told me last night, in speaking about drunkards, the trouble is that the passion for drink becomes a disease, and when it does, there is no hope. That man didn't know the gospel, my friend. Christ is a physician who has never lost a case yet. We've got a great many fine physicians– how many of them can say, "I have never lost a case." Christ has never failed, and He has had some pretty hard cases. Just look at that woman suffering for years from an issue of blood. Probably she had visited all the physicians around – had gone clear up to Damascus and down to Egypt. Perhaps she had spent all her money in trying to get better, but instead had only grown worse. That's just the case with Christians today. Instead of her coming to Christ, she went to the physicians around. I can imagine one of her friends coming in and saying, "Have you ever heard of Jesus of Nazareth?" "No." "Well, He is a great prophet. I have never seen Him myself, but they tell me He is in Jerusalem doing wonderful things. I heard of a man who was troubled with leprosy and another with palsy, and they went to Him, and in a moment were cured. They say, too, He gives sight to blind men." As her friend tells her these things, a ray of hope breaks upon the poor woman's soul, and she questions the friend further. "Yes, and I heard of another cure of a poor cripple who had been lame for years, so lame that he had to be carried to the prophet. When they got there, they found such a crowd that they had to cut a hole in the roof and let him down, and whenever He saw him, He just touched him, and he was healed." "He must be a great physician. How much does He charge?" "Doesn't charge you anything." And this is the trouble with a great many people today. They think they have something to do for the Lord – something to give him in return for the salvation He offers. "Do you mean to tell me He don't charge anything?" "Yes, I tell you. He cures all the people who come to Him for nothing!" "I never heard of such a thing in my life. Whenever He comes here, I am going to see Him." By and by she hears that He is passing through her town, and she prepares to go. Her children probably come to her and urge her not to go. "Don't go to any more physicians. You've been running after too many, and they've only made you worse." But she gives them a deaf ear. She wants to be blessed. I don't know what they called the women's garments in those days, but we will come down to the present. She gets down her old shawl. The doctor took all her money, and she can't afford to buy a new one.

When she gets to where He is, she finds a crowd around Him – perhaps four or five times as many people as we have here. I can see that woman elbowing her way through the crowd as she says to herself, "If I can only get near that man, I know by His look He can bless me." There she goes, pushing her way through the crowd of able-bodied men standing between her and the Savior. "Why don't you go away or stand still?" they say to her. "There are plenty more beside you who want to get near Him." But she keeps on, and by and by she is just about to touch Him, when someone is thrust in between her and the Savior, and she is driven back.

But she works her way on, and comes near enough again, and I can see that thin, pale hand as it comes from under that shawl, and it creeps to His garment – lo, in a moment, she is well. Someone has said that He has got more medicine in this garment than there is in all the apothecaries' stores of the world. A mighty physician! If you have a sick soul, come up to Him. There is no case too bad for Him. I don't care if you have some sin to which you are a slave – He can heal you of it. Yes, my friends, He is a mighty physician, and can save all who come and seek His aid. I can imagine some of you say, "I am a good deal worse than any you have spoken of. I am dead to everything that is pure and holy. I come here night after night, and those remarks never touch me. Those sweet songs never thrill me. I am dead."

Well, right here we find the story of one who was dead, Jairus' daughter. When He came to the house, they said He was too late. You and I have been too late, but Christ never. They forgot He was the Resurrection and the Life. When He went into that room with Peter and John, among the weeping mourners, He just said to that dead girl, "Damsel, I say unto you, arise," and she was awakened from the sleep of death. If there is a dead soul here tonight, He can save you. He said at the creation, "Let there be light," and lo! the light appeared. If He commands your dead souls to live, they will surely live. Let your prayers be going up to God that your dead souls may be filled with the light of His presence. He said to that woman's son, "Young man, arise." Why, He could raise men out of the stones in the street. There is no limit to the power of the Lord God of Israel. If there is a dead soul here, He can fill it with purity. Our Savior, our Redeemer, our Deliverer, our Physician is able to do this. He can quicken dead souls. He can make them alive.

You know when He took the children of Israel through the Red Sea and into the wilderness, He became their way. You hear people sometimes saying, "If I become a Christian, I don't know what church I will join. I find the Roman Catholic Church saying that they are the only true church – the only Apostolic Church – and unless I join it, they say I cannot enter heaven. Then the Baptists tell me I cannot get into heaven unless I become immersed; the Episcopalian Church claims to be the only true church. So with the Presbyterians, Methodists, and I don't know really what way to take." Thank God, we need not be in darkness about that. He tells us, "I am the way." The greatest mistake of the present day is the following of this creed and that one, this and that church, and a great many listen to the voice of the Church instead of the voice of God. The Catholic Church, or any other, never saved a soul. The Son of God is the Savior of the world.

The very name of Jesus can save His people from their sins. He is a real, personal Savior, and if a man wants to become a Christian, let him put his eyes on that Savior and he will be saved. You know that the children of Israel had a cloud going ahead of them. When the cloud moved, they moved. When it stopped, they stopped. And when it started, they followed it. So, my friends, it is Jesus that is our way, and if we follow His footsteps we will be in the right Church. Who could have led those chosen people through that wilderness better than God Almighty? He knew of all dangers and difficulties.

When they wanted bread, He opened His hand and gave it them; when they wanted water, He commanded Moses to strike a rock, and, lo, the crystal stream gushed forth. Who could better lead them through the wilderness, and Who could better lead us to heaven than Jesus? A great many people don't like the old way our fathers taught. Well, the people in the days of Jeremiah didn't like the old way; they hated it, and so He put them in slavery for seventy years. The good, old way our fathers taught is better than our own way. People say this Bible was good enough for ancient days, but we have men of culture, of science, of literature now, and its value has decreased to the people of our day. Now, give me a better book and I will throw it away.

Has the world ever offered us a better book? These men want us to give up the Bible. What are you going to give us in its place? Oh, how cruel infidelity is to tell us to give up all the hope we have – to throw away the only book which tells us the story of the resurrection. They try to tell us it is all a fiction, so that when we lay our loved ones in the grave, we bid them farewell for time and eternity. Away with this terrible doctrine. The Bible of our fathers and mothers is true, and the good, old way is true. When man comes and tries to draw us from the old to the new way, it is the work of the devil. But men say we have outgrown this way. Why don't men outgrow the light of the sun? They shouldn't let the light of the sun come into their buildings – should have gas; the sun is old, and gas is a new light. There is just as much sense in this as to take away the Bible. How much we owe the blessed Bible! Why, I don't think human life would be safe in this city if it wasn't for it. Look at the history of the nations where the Bible has been trampled underfoot.

Only a few years ago France and England were pretty nearly equal. England threw the Bible open to the world, and France tried to trample it. Now the English language is spoken around the world, and its prosperity has increased, while it stands foremost among nations. But look at France. It has gone down and down with anarchy and revolution. Let us not forsake the old way. The Chief Shepherd has gone in through the gates and tells us to come in through Him.

When I was in Dublin, I heard of a little boy who, while being taught in one of the mission schools, had found Christ. When he got home, he tried to talk to his father and mother about his Redeemer. The little fellow sickened and died, and when I was there, four years after the death of that boy, the father might have been seen night after night reading his Bible. If you had asked him what he was looking for, he would have told you he was looking for the way his little son had taken to get into heaven. He was trying to find the way. My friends, our elder Brother has gone before us, and has taken His seat at the right hand of His God, and He won't leave us in darkness.

I remember, a number of years ago, I went out of Chicago to try to preach. I went down to a little town where was being held a Sunday school convention. I was a perfect stranger in the place, and on my arrival, a man stepped up to me and asked me if my name was Moody.

I told him it was, and he invited me to his house. When I arrived, he said he had to go to the convention and asked me to excuse his wife, as she, not having a servant, had to attend to her household duties. He put me into the parlor and told me to amuse myself as best I could till he came back. I sat there, but the room was dark, and I could not read, and I got tired. So I thought I would try and get the children and play with them. I listened for some sound of childhood in the house but could not hear a single evidence of the presence of little ones.

When my friend came back, I said, "Haven't you any children?" "Yes," he replied, "I have one, but she's in heaven, and I am glad she is there, Moody." "Are you glad that your child is dead?" I inquired. He went on to tell me how he had worshipped that child; how his whole life had been bound up in her, to the neglect of his Savior. One day he had come home and found her dying. Upon her death, he accused God of being unjust. He saw some of his neighbors with their children around them. Why hadn't he taken some of them away? He was rebellious.

After he came home from her funeral he said, "All at once I thought I heard her little voice calling me, but the truth came to my heart that she was gone. Then I thought I heard her feet upon the stairs, but I knew she was lying in the grave. The thought of her loss made me almost mad. I threw myself on my bed and wept bitterly. I fell asleep, and while I slept, I had a dream, but it almost seems to me like a vision. I thought I was going over a barren field, and I came to a river so dark and chill-looking that I was going to turn away, when all at once I saw, on the opposite bank, the most beautiful sight I ever looked at. I thought death and sorrow could never enter into that lovely region. Then I began to see beings all so happy looking, and among them I saw my little child. She waved her little angel hand at me and cried, 'Father! Father! Come this way!' I thought her voice sounded much sweeter than it did on earth. In my dream I thought I went to the water and tried to cross it but found it deep and the current so rapid that I thought if I entered, it would carry me away from her forever. I tried to find a boatman to take me over, but couldn't, and I walked up and down the river trying to find a crossing, and still she cried, 'Come this way!' All at once I heard a voice come rolling down, 'I am the way, the truth, and the life; no man comes unto the Father but by me.' The voice awoke me from my sleep, and I knew it was my Savior calling me and pointing the way for me to reach my darling child. I am now superintendent of a Sunday school; I have made many converts. My wife has been converted, and we will, through Jesus as the way, see one day our child."

Am I not speaking to some father tonight who has some loved one in yonder land? Am I not speaking to some mother who has a little one in that happy land? And if you could but hear their voice would they not be, "Come right this way?" Am I not speaking to some here who have representatives there? There's not a son here, if he could hear his mother's voice, but who would be told to come right that way. Thank God, we have all our elder Brother there. Nearly 1,900 years have passed since He went there, but He is as constant to us now as He was when first He went there. Dear friends, as He calls us up to Him, let us turn our backs to this world. Let us take Christ as our Redeemer, as our Deliverer, as our Physician, as our Way, as our Truth, and as our Light. May the blessing of heaven fall upon us all tonight and may every man and woman here who is out of the kingdom, accept Him and press into His dominions. Let us pray.

Christ the Good Shepherd

You that were here last night may remember that I was talking about what Christ was to us. I did not finish that subject and want to take it up again. I want to speak of Christ now as our keeper. Many people in the inquiry rooms complained that they could not hold out; they commenced all right but could not hold out. Of course, they could not if they tried to do so of themselves. But thank God, they have a keeper. A man, when asked what persuasion he was, replied that he was of the same as St. Paul was, and he said, "I believe that He is able to keep that which is committed to Him." That is a good denomination, and I recommend it to your attention. What is this keeping? What does it consist of? If one of you had $100,000 in your pocket and knew that fifteen or twenty thieves had their eyes on you and wanted to rob you, what would you do? You would find a safe bank and put it in there and feel safe. Now, every one of you has a precious soul which the devil is striving to rob you of, and you cannot be safe until you have given it into Christ's keeping.

The Lion of the tribe of Judah is the only one that can safely keep us. What does the Word say? "I am the light of the world; if any man follow me he shall have the light of life." Why are so many of us in darkness? Because we will not follow the light – will not follow Christ. It does not matter who it is; a man of talent and intellect is no better than anyone else if he does not walk in the light.

I remember during the second year of the war, when things looked very bad for the country, they had a meeting, and everyone spoke gloomily and hung their heads like so many bulrushes. One old man, though gray-bearded and with a face that literally shone – a man who looked like Moses – and he commenced to upbraid them that they did not look toward the light; that they should remember that if it was dark around them it was light higher up where their elder Brother was, and it only rested with them to climb higher. There is no darkness where Jesus is. Let us ask ourselves, let each one ask, "Am I a light in my family, among my companions?" The Word said, "You are the light of the world." Are you, brethren? Just consider over it. Let us keep our loins girded and our lamps burning, or people will stumble over us. Oh, my friends, if the light in us be darkness, how great is that darkness. If we would light the world up we must borrow the light; we must take no glory to ourselves but merely reflect the light of Jesus Christ. The Bible does not say, "Make your light shine before men," but "Let your light shine." Let it shine. What a concession to them, such sinners as they were. God supplies us with it for the asking. Oh, my friends, will you not ask for it? And when you once have it, hundreds of thousands of others will see it and want it as well. Keep your lower lights burning, as Mr. Sankey has sung to you.

Now I also like to think of Christ as a shepherd. The duty of a shepherd is to take care of his sheep. When a bear attacked David's flock, he seized his spear and slew the intruder, and your Shepherd will take as much care of you. Oh, what joy in the news to those who can say, "the Lord is my shepherd." Think of the shepherd carefully counting his sheep at the close of the day; one is missing. What does he do? Is he content with his ninety and nine, leave the missing? No, he safely houses the others, and then goes in search of the one which is missing. Can you not see him hunting for the lost one, going over mountains and rocks and crossing brooks, and what joy there is when the wanderer is found. Oh, what a shepherd is that. He wants to be a shepherd to all you here tonight. Will you not accept Him?

The man who saw a shepherd calling his sheep by name, wondered if he could tell one from another, they all looked so much alike. When he enquired on the matter he was pointed to several little defects on the sheep; one had a black spot, another a torn ear, another a bad toe. One was cross-eyed, and so on. You see, the shepherd knew his sheep by their defects, and I think it is so with our heavenly Father. He knows us all by our defects; and yet with all our faults He loves us. You may ask, if He loves me, why does He afflict me? Well, now, I once saw a drove of sheep looking very tired and weary, being hurried on by a shepherd and his dogs, and when they wanted to stop and drink at a brook by the wayside, they were not allowed to but driven on. I felt that it was very unkind of that shepherd. But by and by they stopped before a pair of handsome gates, and the flocks were turned into beautiful green pastures with a clear stream running through them. Then I knew that I had been hasty; that the shepherd had not been unkind, but kind, in not allowing his sheep to drink from that muddy stream in the road, for he had been saving them and taking them on to something better. So with our heavenly Father, our Shepherd. He is compelled to afflict us sometimes while leading us into green pastures. Oh, brethren, let us give thanks that we have such a good shepherd to guide and protect us, and though these afflictions may come upon us and seem hard at the time, let us remember His great mercy and lovingkindness, and bow and kiss the rod. Let us look to God for His blessing.

What Shall I Do to Be Saved?

My sermon tonight grows out of the question of the jailer to Paul and Silas, *"What shall I do to be saved?"* A man out of a job always wants to know what to do to get his bread. How to get one's heavenly bread is more important. What shall a man do to be saved? Why, just believe on the Lord Jesus Christ. A man is not saved by doing. The sinner is not under the law, but under grace – the full, forgiving grace of Jesus. Salvation is a gift. It can't be earned. A man will not be saved at all except by taking this priceless boon as a gift. The Christian should then work for God because God has saved him. Faith without works is dead, but works are the fruit and not the seed of God's gift of salvation. A guilty sinner should have the glad news dinned into his ears over and over again. Just let him accept Christ, and He saves him.

If any poor sinner would just believe this, he could be saved before the benediction is pronounced. The Philippian jailer was saved, with all his house, that first night on meeting the apostle. Oh, will not some dying soul catch hold of the offered salvation! A man just going over the rapids of Niagara would see death just an instant off, and would cry out, "Help! Help!" with all his force. Will, then, the apathetic soul within him be silent? God forbid! May God show the poor, blind eyes the yawning gulf just ahead! Seize the hand of Christ! Lay hold, that is all. He will do the rest. He comes right down to you in your chair there and entreats.

Let Him save you! His pleading voice sounds in your ears! O turn not away! Christ's ability to do all things is unquestioned. He can save as easily as He said, "Let there be light." And He is as willing as able. Every obstacle, then, is out of the way, and all that is needed is just self-surrender. Eternal life is the prize. Oh, look and live; lay hold and be saved. An aged woman, fallen into a pit, had exhausted every means to get out, but slipped back farther and farther after every effort. A star caught her gaze as she lay resigned to death at the bottom. Fainting away, she still saw the star in her sleep. She awoke, and the star meant to her the salvation of Christ, and right then and there she caught hold of Jesus' love. And lo! Her limbs carried her right out of the pit. She had taken the Lord's hand, and as He always will, He lifted her up, even from the death of this world. Can not the saving hand be taken by everyone present? You should not be content with mere trying to be Christians. Trying won't do. A decisive act of the will is needed, and then prompt obedience to the new resolution. Only resolve to take the water of life, and then put the cup at once to your lips. The drowning man seized the slab of wood as soon as he saw it. He didn't say, "I'll try," but he just seized hold. God's free gift is to drowning sinners.

Tonight, will you not take God at His word, and become Christians? Some might answer they are too sinful, but it is just the sins that need forgiveness. The drunkard, the open blasphemer, the worst sinners are precisely the ones that need Jesus most. The well don't need Him. A certain man who had cursed more of his neighbors than any hundred men together in the country was saved by a single lecture from the speaker. It didn't matter, the poor blasphemer was told, if he had even cursed his wife and children at every meal and cursed the mother who bore him, if he would just get down on his knees and cry for pardon; that, just like the thief on the cross, the worst sinner can be forgiven by God's beloved Son and he could be saved if only he wanted to be. And that man took Christ at His word, and he is now a pillar of the church. Like a little child, cry out in bitter repentance, and just like a child believe the absorbing words, "Your sins are forgiven." Jesus is the way of life. Oh, will not thousands press into the way of heaven this very night? The gate is yet open. Hasten ere it close.

Christ's Command

You'll find my text tonight in the 16th chapter of Mark, 15th and 16th verses: *"And He said unto them, Go into all the world and preach the gospel to every creature. He that believes and is baptized, shall be saved; but he that believes not shall be damned."* I like these kinds of texts – they've got such a sweep in them; they take in everybody. You know the great difficulty is to make all people believe that you are preaching to them individually. A text like this tonight takes in everyone. It says, "Go into all the world and preach the gospel to every creature; don't leave out one." When He delivered this command to His followers, He was on His way home – to the land where all knew Him, and all loved Him.

Gethsemane, with its hours of agony and blood, was over. He could now look beyond it. He had been brought before Pilate and before the Sanhedrim, and had been tried and condemned. All that was past. Calvary, with all its horrors, was over, and the empty sepulcher lay behind Him. He stood with a little body of believers around Him, with a little handful of men, who had stood by Him in His conflict with the Pharisees and priests, and now He was giving them His parting words – a mission as it were. It was the Captain of our salvation, telling His warriors what to do after He was gone. In a few minutes He was to be caught up into heaven. They were the words of a resurrected man – a man who had gone down and sounded the depths of the grave; a man who had gone down and conquered the lion of hell, and now stood on resurrection ground as He said, "Go into all the world and preach the gospel to every creature. He that believes and is baptized shall be saved, but he that believes not shall be damned."

Now I want to ask you the question. Do you believe that He would send those men out to preach the gospel to every creature unless He wanted every creature to be saved? Do you believe He would tell them to preach it to people without giving people the power to accept it? Do you believe that the God of heaven is mocking men by offering them this gospel and not giving them the power to take hold of it? Do you believe He will not give men power to accept this salvation as a gift? Man might do that, but God never mocks men. And when He says, "Preach the gospel to every creature," every creature can be saved if he will. For 1,800 years the heralds of the cross have been crossing seas and fording rivers, have been enduring hardships and persecution, in testifying to the people these glorious truths of the gospel. Their spirits have gone up amid flames and tortures, and they have died in prison because of their preaching of the gospel.

Today we live in an open land, where the gospel is as free as the air. Remember that it cost all God had to give it, and every poor, miserable sinner on the earth can be saved for nothing. It is free to all, but don't forget that it cost God the Son of His love, the Son of His bosom, to redeem a rebellious world. If you are saved bear this in mind, that it is a free gift, but it cost God everything. Its reading is that whosoever believes it within the sound of my voice can have it. Some people come to me and say, "Mr. Moody, don't you feel a great responsibility when you come before an audience like this – don't you feel a great weight upon your shoulders?" "Well," I say, "no; I cannot convert men. I can only proclaim the gospel." Not only that, but I tell you that God gives me a mission to preach it to every creature – I don't care to what nationality you belong, what has been your early training, how far you are sunk in iniquity – I don't care who or what you may be, I tell you tonight you have either to receive the gospel and be saved or reject it and be damned. That's the Scripture.

I was talking to a man this morning, and I asked him, "Would you like to become a Christian?" "No, sir." "You would rather be damned, eh?" "Well, I wouldn't exactly like to put it that way," he replied. "Well," I said, "that's the way you're putting it." My friends, let's put it in plain

English, so that we can get hold of it. Are there any here tonight who are willing to say coolly and calmly and deliberately, "I don't want salvation as a gift; I don't want to be saved?" Would you rather go down fighting God and the Son of His love than accept Him and be saved?

Now, the invitation is to everyone. "Go into all the world and preach the gospel to every creature." It is so hard to make people believe it is for them – to make them take it right home.

Mr. Spurgeon told me that he once went to his orphanage on a visit. He said that a great many of those orphans had uncles and aunts and cousins and sisters who brought them Christmas presents. While he was on this visit, a little boy came to him and said, "Mr. Spurgeon, will you let me talk to you a minute?" "Yes, my boy, what is it you want?" "Well," said he, "Mr. Spurgeon, suppose you were a poor little boy and had no aunts or cousins or sisters or brothers, and had nobody to bring you any presents, and you saw others who had uncles and aunts and cousins and sisters who brought presents to them, wouldn't you feel bad?" "Why, yes," replied Mr. Spurgeon. "That's me; that's me," said the boy. He got Mr. Spurgeon right down to the point, and so if men would just say, "This gospel is for us; I believe it is for myself," there would be hope for them being saved. Now, I don't see how you can get away from this text tonight, it is put so plain.

Don't reject it any longer, my friends. Every time you hear it, your heart is getting harder and harder, and you will, the longer you keep away, have more difficulty in bending your will to its acceptance. I tell you, you will have to do either of two things tonight – reject it or receive it. I remember a man, upon hearing this, getting up in a furious passion and stamping up and down. "The idea of anyone saying we've got to receive it or reject it." He didn't like the plain statement. Well, my friends, can we tell you anything else? The audience must be divided into two classes, those who will receive it and those who will reject it. It is for you to decide on which side you will be. As many as receive it He will give power to become the sons and daughters of men.

The question is, what are you going to do with God's gift tonight? The question comes home to everyone within this building. What are you going to do with the gift of God's love? You must either trample Him under your feet and make light of what He has offered us, or you must receive Him as our Way, our Truth, our Light. I was down at the Ohio Penitentiary a few years ago, and the chaplain said to me, "I want to tell you a scene that occurred some time ago. Our commissioner went to the governor of the state and asked him if he wouldn't pardon out five men at the end of six months who stood highest on the list for good behavior. The governor consented, and the record was to be kept secret; the men were not to know anything about it.

"The six months rolled away and the prisoners were all brought up – 1,100 of them – and the president of the commission came up and said, 'I hold in my hand pardons for five men.' I never witnessed anything like it. Every man held his breath, and you could almost hear the throbbing of every man's heart. 'Pardons for five men,' and the commissioner went on to tell the men how they had got these pardons – how the governor had given them, but the chaplain said the surprise was so great that he told the commissioner to read the names first and tell the reason afterward. The first name was called – 'Reuben Johnson' – and he held out the pardon, but not a man moved.

He looked all around, expecting to see a man spring to his feet at once; but no one moved. The commissioner turned to the officer of the prison and inquired, 'Are all the convicts here?' 'Yes,' was the reply, 'Reuben Johnson, come forward and get your pardon; you are no longer a criminal.' Still no one moved. The real Reuben Johnson was looking all the time behind him and around him to see where Reuben was. The chaplain saw him standing right in front of the commissioner and beckoned to him, but he only turned and looked around him, thinking that the chaplain must mean some other Reuben.

"A second time he beckoned to Reuben and called to him, and a second time the man looked around. At last, the chaplain said to him, 'You are the Reuben.' He had been there for nineteen years, having been placed there for life, and he could not conceive it would be for him. At last, it began to dawn upon him, and he took the pardon from the commissioner's hand, saw his name attached to it, and wept like a child." This is the way that men make out pardons for men; but thank God, we have not to come tonight and say we have pardons for only five men – for those who behaved themselves. We have assurance of pardon for every man. "Whosoever will let him drink of the water of life" – it is offered to every thief and harlot, to every gambler and drunkard; salvation for everyone. Salvation is offered to every man, woman, and child.

I can just imagine the scene as those warriors of the cross stood around Christ, the tears trickling down the cheeks of Peter as he says upon hearing the command, "You don't mean, when you command us to preach to every creature, that we are to tell the gospel to those unbelievers – those murderers in Jerusalem?" "Yes, go first to those Jerusalem sinners." And at that scene of Pentecost, I can imagine a man coming up and saying, "Peter, I am the man that spat in His face. You don't mean to say I can be saved?" "Yes, every one of you, for He told me before He left, "Preach the gospel to every creature."

Another man comes up and says, "Peter, I am he who made the crown of thorns; do you think I can be saved?" "Yes, He will give you in return the crown of life." "I am the man," says another, "who drove the spear into His side." "Yes, I know it," replies Peter, "for I saw you doing it, but even you can be saved." My friends, if those Jerusalem sinners can be saved there is hope for the sinners of Chicago. One man, in drawing that scene, said he could fancy Peter saying, "Surely You don't mean that we are to go back to Jerusalem and preach to those men who sacrificed You – who spat in Your face?" "Yes, hunt them up. Hunt up the man who drove the spear into My side, and tell him in its place I will put a scepter in his hand if he will accept salvation from Me; unto that man who made a crown of thorns for My head, say I will give a crown of glory; tell them there is forgiveness for all." Oh, my friend, the gospel is for every creature. Take salvation as a gift. It is for you. God says plainly He does not will anyone to death – He wants all to be saved.

When I was East a few years ago, Mr. George H. Stewart told me of a scene that occurred in a Pennsylvania prison when Governor Pollock, a Christian man, was governor of that state. A man was tried for murder, and the judge had pronounced sentence upon him. His friends had tried every means in their power to procure his pardon. They had sent deputation after deputation to the governor, but he had told them all that the law must take its course.

When they began to give up all hope, the governor went down to the prison and asked the sheriff to take him to the cell of the condemned man. The governor was conducted into the presence of the criminal, and he sat down by the side of his bed and began to talk to him kindly – spoke to him of Christ and heaven, and showed him that although he was condemned to die on the morrow by earthly judges, he would receive eternal life from the Divine Judge if he would accept salvation. He explained the plan of salvation, and when he left him, he committed him to God.

When he was gone, the sheriff was called to the cell by the condemned man. "Who was that man," asked the criminal, "who was in there and talked so kindly to me?" "Why," said the sheriff, "that was Governor Pollock." "Was that Governor Pollock? O, Sheriff, why didn't you tell me who it was? If I had known that was him, I wouldn't have let him go out till he had given me pardon. The governor has been here – in my cell – and I didn't know it," and the man wrung his hands and wept bitterly. My friends, there is one greater than a governor here tonight to tell you He is here. You haven't got to go to heaven to bring Him down. He is here now waiting for your acceptance. You can be saved for time and eternity if you will. My friends, what will you do? Accept Him and receive the crown of glory, or reject Him and be lost? It rests with you to decide.

The Conversion of Saul

You who were here last night know that I was speaking on the prodigal son. Tonight, I want to take up another man for my text – the one we have been speaking about; a much harder case than the prodigal, because he didn't think he needed a Savior. You needn't have talked a great while to that prodigal before you could have convinced him that he needed a Savior. It is easy to reach a prodigal's heart when he reaches the end of his rope. This man stood high in the estimation of the people – he stood, as it were, at the top rung of the ladder, while the prodigal was at the bottom. This man was full of self-righteousness, and if you had tried to pick out a man in Jerusalem as a hopeless case, so far as accepting Jesus of Nazareth as a Savior, you would have picked out Saul. He was the most utterly hopeless case you could have found. I would sooner have thought of the conversion of Pilate than of this man.

When they were putting to death the martyrs to the cross, he had cheered on the murderers. But in spite of all this we find the Son of God coming and knocking at his heart, and it was not long before he received Him as his Savior. You can see him as he goes to the chief priests of Jerusalem, getting the necessary documents that he might go to Damascus, that he might go to the synagogue there and get all who were calling upon the Lord Jesus Christ cast into prison. He was going to stamp out the teachers of the new gospel. One thing that possibly made him so mad was that when the disciples were turned out of Jerusalem, instead of stopping, they went all around and preached.

Philip went down to Samaria, and probably there was a great revival there. News had come from Damascus that the preachers had actually reached that place. This man was full of zeal and full of religion. He was a religious man, and no doubt he could say a prayer as long as anyone in Jerusalem. He had kept the laws faithfully and been an honest and upright man. The people then would never have dreamed of him requiring a Savior. A good many people right here in Chicago would say, "He is good enough. To be sure he doesn't believe in Jesus Christ, but he is a good man." And there's a good many in Chicago who don't believe in Him. They think if they pay their debts and live a moral life, they don't need to be converted. They don't want to call upon Him; they want to get Christ and all his teaching out of the way as this man did. That's what they have been trying to do for eighteen centuries. He just wanted to stamp it out with one swoop. So he got the necessary papers, and away he went down to Damascus.

Suppose as he rode out of the gate of Jerusalem on his mission anyone had said to him, "You are going down to prosecute the preachers of Christ, but you'll come back a preacher yourself." If a man said this, he would not have had his head on his shoulders five minutes. He would have said, "I hate Him; I abhor Him; that's me." He wanted to get Christ and his disciples out of the way. He was no stranger to Christ; he knew His working. For as Paul said to Agrippa, "This thing was not done in a corner." He knew all about Christ's death. Probably he was acquainted with Nicodemus and the members of the Sanhedrim who were against Christ. Perhaps he was acquainted with Christ's disciples and with all their good deeds. Yet he had a perfect hatred for the gospel and its teachers, and he was going down to Damascus just to have all those Christians put in prison.

You see him as he rides out of Jerusalem with his brilliant escort, and away he goes through Samaria, where Philip was. He wouldn't speak to a Samaritan, however. The Jews detested the Samaritans. The idea of him speaking to an adulterous Samaritan would have been ridiculous to him. So he rode proudly through the nation, with his head raised, breathing slaughter to the children of God. Damascus was about 138 miles from Jerusalem, but we are not told how long he took for that journey.

Little did he think that 1,900 years after, that in this country, then wild, there would be thousands of people gathered just to hear the story of his journey down to Damascus. He has arrived at the gates of the city and he has not got cooled off, as we say. He is still breathing revenge. See him as he stands before that beautiful city. Someone has said that this is the most beautiful city in the world, and we are told that when Mohammed came to it, he turned his head away from it lest the beauty of it would take him from his god. So this young man comes to the city, and he tells us the hour when he reached it. He never forgets the hour, for it was then that Christ met him. He says he "saw in the way a light from heaven above the brightness of the sun;" he saw the light of heaven and a glimpse of that light struck him to the ground. And when God speaks to the sinner, that's where he ought to be. Every man ought to fall on his face. From that light a voice called, "Saul, Saul." Yes, the Son of God knows his name.

Sinner, God knows your name. He knows all about you. He knows the street you live in, the number of your house, because He told where Ananias lived when Paul went there. "Saul, Saul, why do you persecute Me?" How the words must have gone down to his soul. He stopped. The words were to him. And I find preaching is not attended with much good till men just stop and take the gospel to themselves. May every sinner here tonight hear Christ calling you by name. We want a personal Christ. Well, when the question was put to him, "Why do you persecute Me?" could he give a reason? Is there any sinner can give a reason for persecuting Christ? Oh, why do you persecute Christ? I can imagine some of you saying, "I never persecuted Christ. I have a great many sins; I swear sometimes, sometimes drink, but I always speak respectfully of Christ."

Do you? Do you never speak disrespectfully of His disciples and God's children? Remember if you speak disrespectfully of them, you treat Him with disrespect. When Christ asked him this question, "Why do you persecute Me?" He might have added, "I lived on the earth thirty years, and I never did you any hurt. I never did you any injury, I never even injured your friends. I came into the world to bless you. Why do you persecute Me?" Why, my friends, all the blessings you ever got came from Him, why can't you live for Him. Why do you go on hating Christ? Is there a man in this assembly who can give a reason why he doesn't love Him? Is there any reason to be found in the wide, wide world why men and women should not love Christ?

I remember hearing of a Sunday school teacher who had led every one of her children to Christ. She was a faithful teacher. Then she tried to get her children to go out and bring other children into the school. One day one of them came and said she had been trying to get the children of a family to come to the school, but the father was an infidel, and he wouldn't allow it. "What is an infidel?" asked the child. She had never heard of an infidel before. The teacher went on to tell her what an infidel was, and she was perfectly shocked.

A few mornings after, the girl happened to be going past a post office on her way to school, and she saw the infidel father coming out. She went up to him and said, "Why don't you love Jesus?" If it had been a man who had said that to him, probably he would have knocked him down. He looked at her and walked on. A second time she put the question, "Why don't you love Jesus?" He put out his hand to put her gently away from him, when on looking down, he saw her tears. "Please, sir, tell me why you don't love Jesus?" He pushed her aside and away he went. When he got to his office, he couldn't get this question out of his mind. All the letters seemed to read, "Why don't you love Jesus?" All the men in his place of business seemed to say, "Why don't you love Jesus?"

When he tried to write, his pen seemed to shape the words, "Why don't you love Jesus?" He couldn't rest, but on the street, when he went to mingle with the businessmen, he seemed to hear a voice continually asking him, "Why don't you love Jesus?" He thought when night came, and he got home with his family he would forget it, but he couldn't. He complained that he wasn't well and went to bed. But when he laid his head on the pillow that voice kept whispering, "Why don't you love Jesus?" He couldn't sleep. By and by, about midnight, he got up and said, "I will get a Bible and find where Christ contradicts Himself and then I'll have a reason," and he turned to the book of John.

My friends, if you want a reason for not loving Christ, don't turn to John. John knew Him too long. I don't believe a man can read the gospel of John without being turned to Christ. Well, he read through and found no reason why he shouldn't love Him, but he found many reasons why he should. He read this book and before morning he was on his knees, and that question put by that little child led to his conversion. My friends, if you make up your minds not to go to sleep tonight without a good reason why you shouldn't love Him, you will love Him. There is no reason, as I said before, in the wide, wide world, why you shouldn't love Christ. Go down to the dark corners of the earth – even to hell and ask them there if they can give you any reason for not loving Christ. My friends, the lost spirits can give you no reason. Neither in earth nor in hell can any reason be found for not loving Him. Tonight, put this question to yourselves, "What keeps me from coming to Christ?" "Saul, Saul, why do you persecute Me?" Oh, may the question go down to our hearts tonight, and may you not sleep till you can look up and say, "Christ is my Savior, He is my Redeemer," and until you can see your title clear for one of those mansions He has gone to prepare.

When this question was put to Saul, "Why do you persecute me?" he supplemented it by saying, "It is hard for you to kick against the pricks." The thought I want to call attention to is this: "It is hard for thee to kick against the pricks." You and I would not have had any compassion upon Saul if we had been in Christ's place. We would have said the hardship is upon the poor Christians in Damascus. But the Lord saw differently. He said, "It is hard for you to kick against the pricks." In those days when they didn't drive their camels with whips, they had a piece of stick with a sharp piece of steel at the end called a prick, and it was applied to the animal.

A lady said to me some time ago, "It is easy to sin, but it is hard to do right," or, in other words, it is hard to serve God and easy to serve the devil. I think you will find hundreds of people in Chicago who think this way. There is not a lie which ever came from hell so deceptive as this. It is as false as any lie the devil ever uttered. We want to drive that lie back where it came from. My friends, it is not true. God is not a hard master. He is a lenient one. What did Christ say to Saul? "It is hard for you to kick against the pricks." There is a period at which the sinner arrives when he sees the truth of this. How many men have said to me, "Mr. Moody, the way of the transgressor is pretty hard." It is a common expression. I have been with men in court and in prison who have said this. It is not a hard thing to serve God if you are born of God, but, my friends, it is a hard thing to serve Satan. The way of sin grows darker and harder to a man the longer he is in it. Before I came down, I took up a paper, and the first thing I saw was an account of a Boston man who had forged funds, and it closed by saying his path was a hard, flinty one.

Now, take up any class of sinners in Chicago. We've representatives here tonight. Take the harlot. Do you think her life is an easy one? It is very short. The average one is seven years. Just look at her as she comes up to the city from the home where she has left sisters and a mother as pure as the morning air. She came down to the city and is now in a low brothel. Sometimes her mind goes back to the pure home where her mother prayed for her; where she used to lay down her head on that mother's bosom, and she used to press the sweet face of her child to her own. She remembers when she went to Sunday school; remembers when her mother tried to teach her to serve God, and now she is an exile. She doesn't want to go home. She is full of shame. She looks into the future and sees darkness before her. In a few short years she dies the death of a harlot, and she is laid away in an unknown grave. All the flattery of her lovers is hollow and false. Is her life a happy one?

Ask a harlot tonight, and she will tell you the way of the transgressor is hard, and then ask the pure and virtuous if Christ is a hard master. Go ask that drunkard if his way is an easy one. Why, there was a man whom I knew who was an inveterate drinker. He had a wife and children. He thought he could stop whenever he felt inclined, but he went the ways of most moderate drinkers. I had not been gone more than three years, and when I returned, I found that that mother had gone down to her grave with a broken heart, and that man was the murderer of the wife of his bosom. Those children have all been taken away from him, and he is now walking up and down those streets homeless. But four years ago, he had a beautiful and a happy home with his wife and children around him. They are gone, probably he will never see them again. Perhaps he has come in here tonight. If he has, I ask him, "Is not the way of the transgressor hard?" Is it not hard to fight against Him? Do not go against your Maker. Don't believe the devil's lies; don't think

God is a hard master. If you persist in wrongdoing, you will find out the truth of what was said to Saul, "It is hard for you to kick against the pricks."

Look again at that rum seller. When we talk to him, he laughs at us. He tells us there is no hell, no future – there is no retribution. I've got one man in my mind now who ruined nearly all the sons in his neighborhood. Mothers and fathers went to him and begged him not to sell their children liquor. He told them it was his business to sell liquor, and he was going to sell liquor to everyone who came. The place was a blot upon the neighborhood as dark as hell. But that man had a father's heart. He had a son. He didn't worship God, but he worshipped that boy. He didn't remember that whatsoever a man sows so shall he reap. My friends, they generally reap what they sow. It may not come soon, but the retribution will come. If you ruin other men's sons, some other man will ruin yours. Bear in mind God is a God of equity; God is a God of justice. He is not going to allow you to ruin men and then escape yourself. If we go against His laws, we suffer.

Time rolled on and that young man became a slave to drink, and his life became such a burden to him that he put a revolver to his head and blew his brains out. The father lived a few years, but his life was as bitter as gall, and he then went down to his grave in sorrow. Ah, my friends, it is hard to kick against the pricks. You may go out of the Tabernacle laughing at everything I say, but it is true as the God in heaven that the day of retribution will come. It is only a question of time. See that false-hearted libertine! The day is coming when he will reap what he is sowing. He may not be called to reap it in this world, but he will be brought up before that bar of heaven, and there the harvest will be seen. These men who have got smooth, oily tongues go into society and play their part and still walk around. If a poor woman falls, she's ruled out, but these false-hearted libertines still go up and down the world. The eyes of justice may not find them out. They think themselves secure, but they are deceiving themselves. By and by the God of heaven will summon them to give an account. They say then that God will not punish them, but the decree of heaven, has gone forth, "Whatsoever a man sows so shall he reap."

One week ago, I preached on the text, "Christ came to heal the brokenhearted." I told you just before I came down that I had received a letter from a brokenhearted wife. Her husband one night came in, to her surprise, and said he was a defaulter and must fly, and he went she knew not where. He forsook her and two children. It was a pitiful letter, and the wail of that poor woman seems to ring in my ears yet. That night, up in that gallery, was a man whose heart began to beat when I told the story, thinking it was him I meant, till I came to the two children. When I got through, I found that he had taken money which did not belong to him, intending to replace it, but he failed to do so and fled. He said, "I have a beautiful wife and three children, but I had to leave her and come to Chicago where I have been hiding. The governor of the state has offered a reward for me."

My friends, a week ago this poor fellow found out the truth of this text. He was in great agony. He felt as if he could not carry the burden, and he said, "Mr. Moody, I want you to pray with me. Ask God for mercy for me." And down we went on our knees. I don't know if ever I felt so deeply for a man in my life. He asked me if I thought he should go back. I told him to ask the Lord, and we prayed over it. That was Sunday evening, and I asked him to meet me on the Monday evening. He told me how hard it was to go back to that town and give himself up and disgrace his wife and children. They would give him ten years. Monday came and he met me and said, "Mr. Moody, I have prayed over this matter, and I think that Christ has forgiven me, but I don't belong to myself. I must go back and give myself up. I expect to be sent to the penitentiary, but I must go." He asked me to pray for his wife and children and he went off. He will be there now in the hands of justice. My friends, don't say the way of the transgressor is not hard. It is hard to fight against sin, but it is a thousand times harder to die without hope. Will you not just accept Christ? Take Christ as your hope, your life, your truth. Let us pray.

Naaman

We have for our subject this evening "Naaman." We are told in this chapter that we have just read that he was a great man, but he was a leper and that spoiled him. He was a successful man, yet he was a leper. He was a very valiant man, but he was a leper. He was a very noble man, yet he was a leper. What a blight that must have cast on his path. It must have haunted him day and night. He was a leper, and there was no physician in Syria that could help him. It was an incurable disease, and I suppose he thought he would have to go down to the grave with that loathsome disease.

We read that several companies had gone down to the land of Israel and brought down to Syria some poor captives, and among them was a little girl, who was sent to wait on Naaman's wife. I can imagine that little maid had a praying mother who had taught her to love the Lord, and when she got down there, she was not ashamed to own her religion – she was not ashamed to acknowledge her Lord.

One day, while waiting on her mistress, I can think of her saying, "Would to God your husband was in Samaria. There is a prophet there who would cure him." I can imagine her looking at the girl when she said this, "What! A man in Israel can cure my husband? You must be dreaming. Did you ever hear of a man being cured of the leprosy?" "No," the girl might have said, "but that is nothing. Why, the prophet in Samaria has cured many persons worse than your husband." And perhaps she told her about the poor woman who had such an increase of oil, and how her two boys were saved from slavery by the prophet, and how he had raised the child of that poor woman from the dead, and "if the prophet can raise anybody from the dead, he can cure your husband." This girl must have had something about her to make those people listen to her; she must have shown her religion in her life. Her life must have been consistent with her religion to make them believe her.

We read that Naaman has faith in her word, and he goes to the king and tells him what he intends to do. And the king says, "I will tell you what I will do. I will give you letters to the king of Israel, and of course, if any cure is to be effected, the king will know how to obtain it." Like a great many men nowadays, they think if there is anything to be got it is to be got from the king and not from his subjects. And so you see this man starting out to the king of Israel with all his letters and a very long purse. I cannot find just now how much it was, but it must have been something like $500,000. The sum was a very large one, likely. He was going to be liberal. He was not going to be small. Well, he got all his money and letters together and started.

There was no small stir as Naaman swept through the gates of Syria that day with his escort. He reaches Samaria and sends a messenger to the king announcing his arrival. The messenger delivers the letter to the king, and the first thing he does is to open the letter and begin to read it. I can see his brow knit as he goes on. "What is this?" he exclaims. "What does this mean? This man means war. This Assyrian king means to have a war with me. Who ever heard of such a thing as a man cured of leprosy?" and he rent his mantle.

Everyone knew something was wrong when the king rent his mantle, and the news spread through the streets that they were on the eve of a war. The air was filled with war; everybody was talking about it. No doubt the news had gone abroad that the great general of Assyria was in the city, and he was the cause of the rumors, and by and by it reached the prophet Elisha that the king had torn his mantle, and he wanted to know the cause.

When he had heard what it was, he just told the king to send Naaman to him. Now you see the major general riding up in grand style to the prophet's house. He probably lived in a small and obscure dwelling.

Perhaps Naaman thought he was doing Elisha a great favor by calling on him. He had an idea that he was honoring this man who had no influence or position. So he rides up. A messenger is sent in to announce Major General Naaman of Damascus. But the prophet doesn't even see him. He simply tells the servant to say to him, "Go and wash in the Jordan seven times."

When the messenger comes to Naaman and tells him this, he is as mad as anything. He considers it a reflection upon him – as if he hadn't kept his person clean. "Does the man mean to insinuate that I haven't kept my body clean – can't I wash myself in the waters of Damascus? We've much better water than they have here. Why, if we had the Jordan in Syria we'd look upon it as a ditch. The idea – wash in that contemptible river." He's full of rage as he can be, and he said, "Behold, I thought." That's the way with sinners; they always say they thought. In this expression we can see he had thought of some plan, had marked out a way for the Lord to heal him.

That is the way with nearly every man and woman in Chicago. They've got a plan drawn out, and because God does not come and save them according to their plan, they don't take Him. Keep this in mind, "My ways are not your ways, nor My thoughts your thoughts." If you look for Him to come in that direction, He will come the other way. "My ways are not your ways." He thought. My friends, no man gets into the kingdom of God till he gives up his thoughts. God never saved a man till he gave up his own thoughts and takes up God's. Yes, Naaman thought that the moment the prophet knew he was outside he would come out and bow and scrape and say he was glad to see such a great and honorable man from Syria. Instead of that he merely sent out a messenger to tell him to go and wash in the Jordan seven times.

When we were in Glasgow, we had an employer converted, and he wanted to get a man in his employ to come to our meetings, but he wouldn't come. If he was going to be converted he wouldn't be converted by those meetings. You know when a Scotchman gets an idea into his head, he is the most stubborn man you can find. He was determined not to be converted by Moody and Sankey. Like a good many here, they say, "If I'm going to be converted, I ain't going to be converted down in that old tabernacle." The employer talked and talked to this man but couldn't get him to come. Well, we left Glasgow, and got away up to the north of Scotland – in Inverness – and he sent this man up there on business, thinking he might be induced to go into the meetings.

One night we were singing "On the Banks of that Beautiful River," and he happened to be passing and wondered where the sweet sounds were coming from. He came up finally, and I happened to be preaching that night on the very text, "I thought." He listened and soon did not know exactly where he was. He was convicted; he was converted and became a Christian. "I thought," how many people have said, "I'd never be converted by these meetings," "I'll never be converted in the Baptist Church," "I will never be converted in the Presbyterian Church." A man makes up his mind not to go there, and he goes. A man must yield his own way to that of God. Now, you can see all along that Naaman's thoughts were altogether different from those of God. He was going to get the grace of God by showing favors, and a good many men now think they can buy their way into the kingdom of God. My friends, we cannot buy the favor of heaven with money. If you get a seat in the kingdom of heaven, you have to accept salvation as a gift.

Then another thing he thought. He thought he could get what he wanted by taking letters to the king, not the prophet. The little maid told him of the prophet, yet he was going to pass the prophet by. How many people would go into the kingdom of God if it wasn't for pride! He was too proud to go to the prophet. But pride, if you will allow me the expression, got a knock on the head on this occasion. It was a terrible thing for him to think of obeying, going down to the Jordan and dipping seven times. He had got better rivers in Damascus, in his own wisdom, and says, "Can I not wash there and be clean?" He was angry, but when he got over it, he listened to his servants. I would rather see people angry than see them go to sleep. I would rather see a man get as angry as possible at anything that I may say than send him to sleep. When a man's asleep there's no chance of reaching him, but if he is angry, we may get at him. It is a good thing for a man to get angry sometimes, for when he cools off, he generally listens to reason.

So his servant came to him and said, "Suppose he had bid you do some great thing, would you not have done it?" Probably had he told him to take cod liver oil for ten years, he would have done it. If he had told him that he wanted as much money as Naaman had brought up, that would have been all right. But the idea of literally doing nothing – just to go down to the Jordan and wash himself – it was so far below his calculations that he thought he was being imposed upon.

It is so in our days. How many people expect to get salvation by some sudden shock, some great event happening to them, or some sudden flash of light to break upon them. Some think that God's plan of salvation requires months to find out. They go on stumbling over its simplicity. And so his servant said, "If the prophet had bid you do some great thing, would you not have done it? Hadn't you just better go down and wash in Jordan?" Perhaps he said, "If I go down to the Jordan and am not cured, what will my enemies say when I go back to Damascus?" But he was influenced by the servant, and he went. That was one good thing in Naaman's character – he was influenced by a humble messenger. A good many people won't accept a messenger, because he is not refined and cultured and educated.

My friends, never mind who brings the message. It is the message you want, not the messenger. If a boy were to bring me a telegraphic message with good news, I wouldn't notice the boy, wouldn't look to see whether he was white or black. It would be the message I would want. And so it was with Naaman. It was a little Hebrew girl who first told him to come to Samaria, and now he was told to wash by his servant. So he goes down and dips into the waters. The first time he rose he said, "I'd just like to see how much my leprosy has gone." And he looks, but not a bit has left him. "Well, I'm not going to get rid of my leprosy in this way; this is absurd." "Well," said the servant, "do just as the man of God tells you; obey him." And this is just what we are told to do in the Scriptures, to obey Him. The first thing we have to learn is obedience. Disobedience was the pit Adam fell into, and we have to get out of it by obedience.

Well, he goes into the water a second time. If some Chicago Christians had been there, they would have asked, sneeringly, "Well, how do you feel now?" He didn't see that he was any better, and down he went a third time, but when he looked at himself, he had just as much leprosy as ever. Down he goes a fourth, fifth, and sixth time. He looks at himself, but not a speck of it is removed. "I told you this," he says to his servant.

"Look here. I'm just the same as ever." "But," says the servant, "you must just do what the man of God tells you to do – go down seven times."

He takes the seventh plunge and comes out. He looks at himself, and behold, his flesh is as that of a little child. He says to his servant, "Why, I never felt as good as I do today. I feel better than if I had won a great battle. Look! I'm cleansed. Oh, what a great day this is for me! The leprosy has gone." The waters to him had been as death and judgment, and he had come out resurrected – his flesh as that of a little child. I suppose he got into his chariot, and away he went to the man of God. He had lost his temper, he had lost his pride, and he had lost his leprosy. That is the way now. If a man will only lose his pride, he will soon see his leprosy disappear – the leprosy will go away with his pride. I believe the greatest enemies of men in this world are unbelief and pride. I believe hundreds and thousands in Chicago would press into the kingdom of God if it were not for their pride.

He goes back to the man of God and takes his silver and gold. He offers him money. "I don't want your money," replies the prophet. If he had taken money, it would have spoiled the beautiful story. Naaman had to take back everything he brought from Damascus but his leprosy. The only thing that the sinner has that God wants is his sins, and if you let Him take them tonight, He will. Get rid of your leprosy; He will take it. Never mind your feelings. No soul in this audience will go down to the dark caverns if he is willing to obey God. And now the question comes to you all tonight. Will you obey Him? You don't have to go a thousand miles away and dip into a Jordan, but just believe where you sit – believe on the Lord Jesus Christ. "Come unto me all ye that labor and are heavy laden, and I will give you rest." Is there anything to hinder you from obeying God now? He will give you power to accept Him. Do you believe He would offer you salvation without giving you the power to obey Him? Don't go from this hall with any such delusion, my friends.

Don't go home from this Tabernacle with this leprosy thinking that you cannot get rid of it. If sin is better to you, then of course, hold on to it – if leprosy is worth more to you than to be purified, then keep it. Naaman could have gone back with his leprosy if he hadn't met that prophet and gone down to the Jordan. If you go out of the Tabernacle tonight without accepting Him, you go out as a sinner, and if death comes, as it may, suddenly upon you, there is no assurance in the Bible that you can pass through the pearly gates. There is no leprosy there; you must leave it here. If a leper was to get into the kingdom of heaven, all heaven would be affected by him. There is a fountain opened in the house of David for the lepers. This night you can be saved if you will. The door is open – on the hinge; the battle is fought on this fact, if you will – not because you can't.

Oh, but you say, "I've tried." Naaman might have said, "I have tried" too. Probably he had tried all the physicians in his country, but Naaman couldn't be cured. He couldn't cure himself. When Christ said to that man who had a withered hand hanging at his side, "Stretch out your hand," he might have said, "I've tried to stretch it out for twenty years, and I can't do it." But when the command was given him, the power came also. All that was wanted was the will of the man. My friends, if you don't accept the gospel and obey it, and you go down to death, there is not a ray of hope that you will escape the punishment held out in the Bible. There is not a word in the Bible to lead you to believe that you will escape condemnation if you go down to the grave with that leprosy.

Do you think, I ask again, that He will ask you to repent and accept eternal life without giving you the power? The moment you obey, that moment the blessing comes. Who will accept Him tonight? I wish I could believe for you all, but I cannot. I would have you all come into the kingdom of God tonight. One of two things you have got to do – either accept the remedy He offers you, and be saved, or spurn the remedy, as Naaman was going to do, and go home with your sins. May God open your eyes to see the necessity of being saved by this great remedy. Let us pray.

How to Study the Bible

First Address

One thing I have noticed in studying the Word of God, and that is, when a man is filled with the Spirit, he deals largely with the Word of God; whereas, the man who is filled with his own ideas, refers rarely to the Word of God. He gets along without it, and you seldom see it mentioned in his discourses. A great many use it only as a textbook. They get their text from the Bible and go on without any further allusion to it. They ignore it. But when a man is filled with the Word, as Stephen was, he cannot help speaking Scripture.

You will find that Moses was constantly repeating the commandments. You will find, too, that Joshua, when he came across the Jordan with his people, there they stood and the law of the Lord God was read to them. And you will find all through Scripture the man of God dealing much with His Word. Why, you will find Christ constantly referring to them saying, "Thus says the Scriptures." Now, as old Dr. Bonar of Glasgow said, "The Lord didn't tell Joshua how to use a sword, but He told him how he should meditate on the Lord day and night, and then he would have good success." When we find a man meditating on the words of God, my friends, that man is full of boldness and is successful. And the reason why we have so little success in our teaching is because we know so little of the Word of God. You must know it and have it in your heart. A great many have it in their head and not in their heart. If we have the Spirit of God in our heart, then we have something to work upon. He does not use us because He is not in us. Know, as we come to this word today, as Mr. Sankey has been singing, "No word He hath spoken, Was ever yet broken."

Let us take this thought in John 10:35, "And the Scripture cannot be broken." There is a great deal of infidelity around, and it has crept into many of the churches, too. These doubters take up the Bible and wonder if they can believe it all – if it is true from back to back, and a good many things in it they believe are not true. I have a good deal of admiration for that black man who was approached by some infidel – some skeptical man who told him, "Why, the Bible is not true; all scientific men tell us that now. It's only a bundle of fables." "Bible ain't true?" replied the man. "Why, I was a blasphemer and a drinker, and that book just made me stop swearing, drinking, lying, and blaspheming and you say it ain't true." My friends, the black man had the best of the argument. Do you think if the Bible were a bad book it would make men good? Do you think if it were a false book it would make men good? And so let us take our stand on the black man's platform and be convinced that it is true. When we take it into our hands, let us know that it is the Word of God and try to understand it. Many of the passages appear to us difficult to understand, but if we could understand it clearly from back to back at first, it would be as a human book, but the very fact that we cannot understand it all at once is the highest proof that it is the Word of God.

Now, another thought is that a great many people read it, but they read it as a task. They say, "Well, I've read it through, I know all that's in it," and lay it aside. How many people prefer the morning paper in order to get news. They prefer it, but it is a false idea. This Bible is the only newspaper. It tells you all that has taken place for the last 6,000 years, and it tells you all the news of the future. Why, 1,700 years before Christ, the people were told in it of the coming of Christ. They knew He was coming. The daily papers could not tell us of this. They may be written by learned men, brilliant editorial writers, but they couldn't have told this. If you want news, study the Bible – the blessed, old Bible, and you will find it has all the news of the world.

Now we come to the question, how to study it? A great many read it as I used to read it, just to ease my conscience. I had a rule before I was converted to read two chapters a day. If I didn't do it before I retired for the night, I used to jump out of bed and read them, but if you had asked me fifteen minutes after what I had read, I could not have told you. Now this is the trouble with many – they read with the head and not with the heart. A man may read his Bible, but when he has closed it you may ask him what chapter he read last, and he cannot tell you. He sometimes puts a mark in it to tell him; without the mark he doesn't know, his reading has been so careless. It is to keep him from reading it again. Just as I used to do when hoeing corn. I used to put a stick in the furrow to mark the place where I had hoed last.

A good many people are just like this. They pick up a chapter here, and there is no connection in their reading, and consequently don't know anything about the Word of God. If we want to understand it, we've got to study it – read it on our knees, asking the Holy Spirit to give us the understanding to see what the Word of God is, and if we go about it that way, and turn our face as Joshua did, in prayer, and set ourselves to study these blessed and heavenly truths, the Lord will not disappoint us, and we will soon know our Bible, and when we know our Bible ,then it is that God can use us.

Let me say there are three books which every Christian ought to have, and if you haven't them, go and buy them before you get your tea. The first is a good Bible – a good large-printed Bible. I don't like those little-printed ones which you can scarcely see   get one in large print. A good many object to a large Bible because they can't carry it in their pocket. Well, if you can't carry it in your pocket, it is a good way to carry it under your arm. It is showing what you are – it is showing your flag. Now a great many of you are coming in from the country to these meetings, and when you get on the cars, you see people who are not ashamed to sit down and play cards. I don't see why the children of God should be ashamed of carrying their Bible under their arms in the cars. "Ah!" some say, "that is the spirit of a Pharisee." It would be the pharisaical spirit if you hadn't dipped down into heavenly truths, if you haven't the Spirit of God with you. Some say, "I haven't it." Suppose you don't read so many of these daily papers and read a little oftener the Bible. Some say, "I haven't time." Take time.

I don't believe there is a businessman in Chicago who couldn't find an hour a day to read his Bible if he wanted to. Get a good Bible, then a good concordance, and then a scriptural textbook. Whenever you come to something in the Word of God that you don't know, hunt for its meaning in those books. Suppose after the meeting I am looking all over the platform and Dr. Kittredge says, "What are you looking for?" and I answer, "Oh, nothing, nothing." He would go off. If he thought I hadn't dropped something, he wouldn't stay. But suppose I had lost a very valuable ring which some esteemed friend had given me, and I told him this. He would stay with me, and we would move this organ and those chairs, and look all over, and by looking carefully, we would find it. If a man hunts for truths in the Word of God and reads it as if he were looking for nothing particular, he will get nothing. When the men went to California in the gold excitement, they went to dig for gold, and they worked day and night with a terrible energy just to get gold. Now, my friends, if they wanted to get the pure gold, they had to dig for it, and when I was there, I was told that the best gold was gotten by digging deep for it. So the best truths are got by digging deep for them.

When I was in Boston, I went into Mr. Prang's chromo establishment. I wanted to know how the work was done. He took me to a stone several feet square, where he took the first impression, but when he took the paper off the stone, I could see no sign of a man's face; the paper was just tinged. I said I couldn't see any sign of a man's face there. "Wait a little," he said. He took me to another stone, but when the paper was lifted, I couldn't see any impression yet. He took me up, up to eight, nine, ten stones, and then I could see just the faintest outlines of a man's face. He went on till he got up to about the twentieth stone, and I could see the impression of a face, but he said it was not very correct yet. Well, he went on until he got up, I think, to the twenty-eighth stone, and a perfect face appeared, and it looked as if all it had to do was to speak and it would be human. If you read a chapter of the Bible and don't see anything in it, read it a second time, and if you cannot see anything in it read it a third time. Dig deep. Read it again and again, and even if you have to read it twenty-eight times, do so, and you will see the man Christ Jesus, for He is in every page of the Word, and if you take Christ out of the Old Testament you will take the key out of the Word.

Many men in the churches nowadays are saying that they believe the teachings in the New Testament are to be believed, but those in the Old are not. Those who say this don't know anything about the New. There is nothing in the Old Testament that God has not put His seal upon. "Why," some people say to me, "Moody, you don't believe in the flood. All the scientific men tell us it is absurd." Let them tell us. Jesus tells us of it, and I would rather take the word of Jesus than that of any other one. I haven't got much respect for those men who dig down for stones with shovels in order to take away the Word of God. Men don't believe in the story of Sodom and Gomorrah, but we have it sealed in the New Testament. "As it was in the days of Sodom and Gomorrah." They don't believe in Lot's wife, but He says, "Remember Lot's wife." So there is not a thing that men today criticize but the Son of God endorses. They don't believe in the swallowing of Jonah. They say it is impossible that a whale could swallow Jonah – its throat is too small. They forgot that the whale was prepared for Jonah; as a woman once said, "Why, God could prepare a man to swallow a whale, let alone prepare a whale to swallow a man." We find that He endorses all the points in the Old Testament, from Genesis to Revelation. We have only one book – we haven't two.

The moment a man begins to cut and slash away, it all goes. Some don't believe in the first five books. They would do well to look into the 3rd chapter of John where they will see the Samaritan woman at the well looking for the coming of Christ from the first five books of Moses. I tell you, my friends, if you look for Him you will find Him all through the Old Testament. You will find Him in Genesis – in every book in the Bible. Just turn to Luke 24:27, you will find Him, after He had risen again, speaking about the Old Testament prophets, "And beginning at Moses, and all the prophets, he explained unto them in all the Scripture the things concerning Himself." Concerning Himself. Doesn't that settle the question? I tell you I am convinced in my mind that the Old Testament is as true as the New.

"And He began at Moses and all the prophets." Mark that, "all the prophets." Then in the 44th verse, "And He said unto them, these are the words which I spoke unto you, while I was yet with you, that all things must be fulfilled which were written in the law of Moses and in the prophets and in the psalms concerning Me. Then opened He their understanding that they might understand the Scripture." If we take Christ out of the Old Testament what are you going to do with the psalms and prophets? The book is a sealed book if we take away the New from it. Christ unlocks the Old and Jesus the New. Philip, in teaching the people, found Christ in the 53rd chapter of Isaiah, "All we, like sheep, have gone astray; we have turned every one to his own way, and the Lord has laid on him the iniquity of us all." Why, the early Christians had nothing but the Old Testament to preach the gospel from – at Pentecost they had nothing else. So if there is any man or woman in this assembly who believes in the New Testament, and not in the Old, dear friends, you are deluded by Satan, because if you read the Word of God you will find him spoken of throughout both books. I notice if a man goes to cut up the Bible and comes to you with one truth and says, "I don't believe this, and I don't believe that," I notice when he begins to doubt portions of the Word of God that he soon doubts it all.

Now the question is how to study the Bible. Of course, I cannot tell you how you are to study it, but I can tell you how I have studied it and that may help you. I have found it a good plan to take up one book at a time. It is a good deal better to study one book at a time than to run through the Bible. If we study one book and get its key, it will, perhaps, open up others. Take up the book of Genesis, and you will find eight beginnings; in other words, you pick up the key of several books. The gospel was written that man might believe on Jesus Christ, and every chapter speaks of it. Now, take the book of Genesis; it says it is the book of beginnings. That is the key. The book of Exodus – it is the book of redemption; that is the keyword of the whole. Take up the book of Leviticus, and we find that it is the book of sacrifices. And so on through all the different books; you will find each one with a key.

Another thing: we must study it unbiased. A great many people believe certain things. They believe in certain creeds and doctrines, and they run through the book to get Scripture in accordance with them. If a man is a Calvinistic man, he wants to find something in accordance with his doctrine. But if we go to seek truth, the Spirit of

God will come. Don't seek it in the blue light of Presbyterianism, in the red light of Methodism, or in the light of Episcopalianism, but study it in the light of Calvary.

Another way to study it is not only to take one book at a time, but I have been also wonderfully blessed by taking up one word at a time. Take up the word and go to your concordance and find out all about it. I remember I took up the word "love," and turned to the Scriptures and studied it, and got so that I felt I loved everybody. I got full of it. When I went on the street, I felt as if I loved everybody I saw. It ran out of my fingers. Suppose you take up the subject of love and study it up. You will get so full of it that all you have got to do is to open your lips and a flood of the love of God flows upon the meeting. If you go into a court, you will find a lawyer pleading a case. He gets everything bearing upon one point, heaped up so as to carry his argument with all the force he can, in order to convince the jury. Now it seems to me a man should do the same in talking to an audience; just think that he has a jury before him, and he wants to convict a sinner. If it is love, get all you can upon the subject and talk love, love.

Take up the word grace. I didn't know what Calvary was till I studied grace. I got so full of the wonderful grace that I had to speak. I had to run out and tell people about it. If you want to find out those heavenly truths, take up the concordance and heap up the evidence, and you cannot help but preach. Take heaven; there are people all the time wondering what it is and where it is. Take your concordance and see what the Word of God says it is. Let these men who are talking against blood look into the Word of God, and they will find if it doesn't teach that, it teaches nothing else. When we preach about that some people think we are taking our own views. But the Word says, "The life of all flesh is in the blood, and without blood there is no remission." The moment a man talks against blood, he throws out the Bible.

Take up Saul, study him. You will find hundreds of men in Chicago just like him. Take up Lot, study that character. Let me say right here that if we are going to have, and I firmly believe in my soul that we are going to have, a revival in the Northwest – if we are going to have it, you must bring the people to the study of the Word of God. I have been out here for a good number of years, and I am tired and sick of these spasmodic meetings; tired of the bonfires which, after a little, are reduced to a bundle of shavings. When I see men speaking to inquirers in the inquiry room without holding the Word of God up to them, I think their work will not be lasting. What we want to do is to get people to study the Word of God in order that the work may be thorough and lasting. I notice when a man is brought coolly and calmly and intelligently, that man will have a reason for being a Christian. We must do that; we must bring a man to the Word of God if we don't want this western country filled with backsliders.

Let us pray that we will have a Scriptural revival, and if we preach only the Word in our churches and in our Sunday schools, we will have a revival that will last to eternity. Let us turn back to one of the Old Testament revivals, when the people had been brought up from Babylon. Look at the 8th chapter of Nehemiah: "And Ezra, the priest, brought the law before the congregation, both of men and women, and all that could hear with understanding, upon the first day of the seventh month, and he read therein, before the street that was before the water gate, from morning until midday, before the men and women and those that could understand, and the ears of the people were attentive unto the book of the law." No preaching there; he merely read the Word of God – that is, God's Word – not man's.

A great many of us prefer man's word to that of God. We are running after eloquent preachers – after men who can get up eloquent moral essays. They leave out the Word of God. We want to get back to the Word of God. They had an all-day meeting there, something like this, "And Ezra opened the book in the sight of all the people, for he was above all the people; and when he opened it all the people stood up." I can see the great crowd standing up to listen to the prophet, just like young robins taking in what the old robins bring them. "And Ezra blessed the Lord, the great God, and all the people answered, Amen, Amen. With lifting up their hands they bowed their heads and worshipped the Lord with their faces to the ground…So they read in the book of law of God distinctly, and gave the sense, and caused them to understand the reading."

Now, it strikes me it is about the height of preaching to get people that understand the reading of the Word. It would be a great deal better if a preacher would sometimes stop when he had a remark, and say, "Mr. Jones, do you understand that?" "No, I don't," and then the preacher might make it a little plainer, so that he could understand it. There would be a great difference in the preaching in some of the churches. He would talk a little less about metaphysics and science and speak about something else. "Then he said unto them, Go your way, eat the fat and drink the sweet, and send portions unto them for whom nothing is prepared, for this day is holy unto our Lord, neither be sorry, for the joy of the Lord is your strength." "For the joy of the Lord is your strength." If you will show me a Bible-Christian living on the Word of God, I will show you a joyful man. He is mounting up all the time. He has got new truths that lift him up over every obstacle, and he mounts over difficulties higher and higher, like a man I once heard of who had a bag of gas fastened on either side, and if he just touched the ground with his foot over a wall or a hedge, he would go over it; and so these truths make us so light that we bound over every obstacle.

And when we have those truths our work will be successful. Just turn over to Jeremiah 20:9, to this blessed old prophet. There was a time when he was not going to speak about the Word of God anymore. Now, I just want to show you this, when a man is filled with the Word of God you cannot keep him still. If a man has got the Word, he must speak or die. "Then I said, I will not make mention of Him, nor speak any more in His name, but His word was in my heart as a burning fire shut up in my bones, and I was weary with forbearing, and I could not stay." It set him on fire, and so a man filled with the Word of God is filled as with a burning fire, and it is so easy for a man to work when he is filled with the Word of God.

I heard of a man the other week who was going to preach against the blood. I was very anxious to see what he would say about it, and I got the paper the next morning and I found there was nothing else there than Scriptural quotations. I said that was the very best thing he could do. As we see in the 23rd chapter of Jeremiah, "Is not my word like as a fire, says the Lord, that breaks the rock in pieces?" Those hard, flinty rocks will be broken if we give them the Word of God. Those men in the Northwest that we cannot reach by our own words, give them this and see if they cannot be reached. Not only that, if we are full of Scripture ourselves, give them what God says, you will find it easy to preach. You will say we haven't to get up so many sermons. It seems to me if we had more of the Word of God in our services and give up more of our own thoughts, there would be a hundred times more converted than there is.

A preacher, if he wants to give his people the Word, must have fed on the Word himself. A man must get water out of a well when there is water. He may dip his bucket in if it is empty, but he will get nothing. I think the best thing I have heard in Chicago I heard the other day, and it has fastened itself upon my mind, and I must tell it to your ministers. We had for our subject in Farwell Hall the other day the 7th chapter of John when Mr. Gibson said if a man was to come among a lot of thirsty men with an empty bucket, they wouldn't come to him to drink. He said he believed that was the trouble with most of the ministers, as that had been the trouble with himself. He didn't have a bucket of living water, and the people wouldn't come to him to drink. Just look at an audience of thirsty men, and you bring in a bucket of clear sparkling water and see how they will go for it. If you go into your Sunday schools and the children look into your buckets and see them empty, there is nothing for them there. So, my friends, if we attempt to feed others, we must first be fed ourselves.

There is another thing which has wonderfully helped me. That is to mark my Bible whenever I hear anything that strikes me. If a minister has been preaching to me a good sermon, I put his name down next to the text, and then it recalls what has been said and I can show it to others.

You know laymen have the right to take what we hear to one another. If ministers saw people doing this, they would preach better sermons. Not only that, but if we understood our Bibles better, the ministers would preach better. I think if people knew more about the Word than they do, so many of them would not be carried away with false doctrine. There is no place I have ever been where people so thoroughly understand their Bibles as in Scotland. Why, little boys could quote Scripture and take me up on a text. They have the whole nation just educated, as it were, with the Word of God. Infidelity cannot come there, as long as that is the case.

But a man got up in Glasgow at a corner and began to preach universal salvation. "Oh, sir," said an old woman, "that will never save the like of me." She had heard enough preaching to know that it would never save her. If a man comes among them with any false doctrine, these Scotchmen instantly draw their Bibles on him. I had to keep my eyes open and be careful what I said there. They knew their Bibles a good deal better than I did. And so if the preachers would get the people to read the Word of God more carefully and note what they heard, there would not be so much infidelity among us.

I want to tell you how I was blessed a few years ago, upon hearing a discourse upon the 30th chapter of Proverbs. The speaker said the children of God were like four things. The first thing was, "The ants are a people not strong," and he went on to compare the children of God to the ants. He said the people of God were like ants. They pay no attention to the things of the present but go on steadily preparing for the future. The next thing he compared them to was the conies. "The conies are but a feeble folk." It is a very weak little thing. "Well," said I, "I wouldn't like to be as a coney." But he went on to say that it built upon a rock. The children of God were very weak, but they laid their foundation upon a rock.

"Well," said I, "I will be like a coney, and build my hopes upon a rock." Like the Irishman, who said he himself trembled, but the rock upon which his house was built never did. The next thing the speaker compared them to was a locust. I didn't think much of locusts, and I thought I wouldn't care about being like one. But he went on to read, they have "no king, yet they go forth all of them by bands." There were the Congregationalist, the Presbyterian, the Methodist bands going forth without a king; but by and by our King will come back again, and these bands will fly to Him. "Well, I will be like a locust; my King's away," I thought.

The next comparison was a spider. I didn't like this at all, but he said if we went into a gilded palace filled with luxury, we might see a spider holding on to something, oblivious to all the luxury below. It was laying hold of the things above. "Well," said I, "I would like to be a spider." I heard this a good many years ago, and I just put the speaker's name to it, and it makes the sermon. But take your Bibles and mark them. Don't think of wearing it out. It is a rare thing to find a man wearing his Bible out nowadays – and Bibles are cheap, too. You are living in a land where there are plenty. Study them and mark them, and don't be afraid of wearing them. Now don't you see how much better it would be to study it? And if you are talking to a man, instead of talking about your neighbors, just talk about the Bible, and when Christian men come together just compare notes and ask one another, "What have you found new in the Word of God since I saw you last?"

Some men come to me and ask me if I have picked up anything new, and I give them what I have, and they give me what they have. An Englishman asked me some time ago, "Do you know much about Job?" "Well, I know a little," I replied. "If you've got the key of Job you've got the key to the whole Bible." "What!" I replied, "I thought it was a poetical book." "Well," said he, "I will just divide Job into seven heads. The first is the perfect man – untried – and that is Adam and Eve before they fell. The second head is tried by adversity – Adam, after the fall. The third is the wisdom of the world – the three friends who came to try to help Job out of his difficulties. They had no power to help him at all. He could stand his scolding wife, but he couldn't stand them. The fourth head takes the form of the Mediator, and in the fifth head God speaks at last. He heard Him before by the ear, but he hears Him now by the soul, and he fell down flat upon his face."

A good many men in Chicago are like Job. They think they are mighty good men, but directly they hear the voice of God they know they are sinners; they are in the dust. There isn't much talk about their goodness then. Here he was with his face down. Job learned his lesson. That was the sixth head, and in these heads were the burdens of Adam's sin. The seventh head was when God showed him His face. Well, I learned the key to the Bible. I cannot tell how this helped me. I told it to another man, and he asked me if I ever thought of how he got his property back and his sheep back. He gave Job double what he had and gave him ten children besides, so that he should have ten in heaven besides his ten on earth.

How to Study the Bible

Second Address

A great many are asking the questions, "Will this work hold out? Are these young converts going to stand?" Now I am no prophet, nor the son of a prophet, but one thing I can predict: that every one of these new converts that goes to studying his Bible and loves this book above every other book, is sure to hold out. The world will have no charm for him. He will get the world under his feet, because in this book he will find something better than the world can give him. Now what I want to say to these young converts and to old converts is to love the Word of God. Set more and more store by it. Then the troubles in your Christian life will pass away like a morning cloud. You will feed and live on the Word of God, and it will become the joy of your soul.

Now, to help some of you to a right course in studying God's word, I want to point out a number of texts that you might begin with, and then, in the same way, you can collect others. I want to call your attention first to a part of the 4th chapter of Matthew. A little boy in the seat there, while giving his experience the other day, felt so sure about his strength that he defied Satan. I trembled. Those of us who are older and know more about the devil's power know that we can only meet him with the Word of God. We can't withstand him by our feelings or by our being converted; he only laughs at such weapons. Read in this 4th chapter, from the 3rd verse on and see how Christ overcame Satan. Not by His feelings, not because He had been baptized of John in the Jordan, but by the word of the living God. Three times Satan advanced to the charge, but every time he was thrust through by the sword of the Spirit. And that must be your sword. Don't say, like the little boy in Scotland, "Old Nick, just you get behind me," but say, "O Lord, just put him behind me." You can't do anything against Satan of yourself; you can only overcome him through Christ and by the word of the living God.

Then take Romans 10:15. It shows there was a work done for you on Calvary, but that there is another work quite distinct from that. "How shall they preach except they be sent?" "Faith comes by hearing, and hearing by the word of God." How many mourning Christians there are who know little about God, and the reason is just that they do not study the Word of God. You are little acquainted with this precious book. I don't see how Christians can habitually read the newspapers on Sunday. I wouldn't advise you even to read your religious weeklies on that day. I find too many are making these take the place of the Bible. Let us have one day exclusively to study and read the Word of God. If we can't take time during the week, we will have Sunday uninterrupted. What can botanists tell you of the Lily of the Valley? You must study this book for that. What can geologists tell you of the Rock of Ages, or mere astronomers about the Bright Morning Star? In these pages we find all knowledge unto salvation; there we read of the ruin of man by nature, redemption by the blood, and regeneration by the Holy Spirit. These three things run up all through and through them.

But let us stick to the thought, how to study this Bible. A favorite way with me is just to take up one word or expression and run through the different places where they are. Take the "I ams" of John; "I am the bread of life;" "I am the water of life;" "I am the way, the truth, and the life;" "I am the resurrection;" "I am all, and in all." God gives to His children a blank, and on it they can write whatever they most want, and He will fill the bill.

And then the promises. A Scotchman found out 31,000 distinct promises in the Word of God. There is not a despondent soul in this

Tabernacle this morning, but God has a promise just to suit him. They abound even in the books of Job and Jonah.

And now let us follow on the thought, "What is God able to do?" Just get all the blessed texts on that subject to heart, and you can't help speaking for God. Then you can indeed say, "God is my Father, Jesus is my Savior, and heaven is my home." There is a blessed verse in the gospel of John. There is no more fruitful subject in the Bible than is opened up there. The conversions there and through the Bible, notice, are different from each other, though all redounding to the glory of God. Think of Nicodemus, the woman at the well, and Matthew the publican. And then the conversions in the Acts and those of the Philippian jailer and Cornelius. We make a great deal more ado about this simple act than the Bible teaches. Conversion is just to believe on Christ and follow Him and may be but the work of a moment.

Take up these texts of Peter having the word precious: "precious blood," "precious Christ," "precious faith," "precious trial of faith," "precious promises of God." Just take one word of the apostle and trace it out.

Many persons do not believe in assurance as to salvation. Turn to the 3rd chapter of the first epistle of John, "Beloved, now are we the sons of God." The 5th verse of that chapter says, "And you knew he was manifested to take away our sins," and then we come to "I know that my Redeemer lives." All the Bible puts it in that way. When it speaks of hope, it means a certain hope, not a doubtful hope. The "hope of a glorious resurrection" was a sure hope. Then the 19th verse, "Hereby we know that we are of the truth," and then, "We know that we have passed from death unto life." "You know that no murderer has eternal life," and also, "Hereby we know that he abides in us, by the spirit which he has given us." There is no reason, nay, there is no excuse, for Christians doubting that they are saved; it is presumptuous not to take God at His word. Again, the 2nd verse of the 3rd chapter of the epistle of John says, "Beloved, now are we the sons of God, and it does not yet appear what we shall be; but we know that when he shall appear we shall be like him."

So I find great comfort and advantage in just taking up the Word of God in this way and studying it with a view to some single truth. Take up in this way a single name or life or character. Thus Lazarus, in his different stages, is the type of the dead soul – the soul dead in trespasses and sins. Then he is the saved soul, then the feasting rejoicing soul, and then he testifies to the goodness of God. Galatians shows how we are first called, then justified, then sanctified; all through there is a beautiful connection, and you have only to stand right with one of these thoughts and follow the trail out.

And then take up the Christian's growth in grace; Psalm 23:2, "Lie down in green pastures," "Sitting at the feet of Jesus." Ephesians 6:13-14, "He is able to make us stand." Psalms, "Walk through the valley of the shadow of death," Hebrews 12:1, "Run with patience the race that is set before us," Psalms 18:21, and Isaiah 40:31, "They shall mount up with wings as eagles." The Christian, these verses show, goes up higher and higher, like a balloon, till the world is lost to sight; till he becomes like Christ and possessed of eyes that can gaze unblinded on the glory of the City of God. But I have spoken too long at this time and will finish my subject hereafter.

Trust

Today I am going to make the sermon an inquiry room talk. I'm not going to have anyone in the congregation go away and say they hadn't an offer of salvation. I'm going to turn the whole of the Tabernacle into an inquiry room. I call your attention to a verse in the Psalms. Some who have counted the all the verses in the Bible found that the 8th and 9th verses of Psalm 118 are the middle verses of the Bible. "It is better to trust in the Lord than to put confidence in man. It is better to trust in the Lord than to put confidence in princes." And now we read in the 3rd and 4th verses of the 26th chapter of Isaiah, "You will keep him in perfect peace, whose mind is stayed on you, because he trusts in you. Trust in the Lord forever; for in the Lord Jehovah is everlasting strength."

A boy whose mother promises him anything knows how to trust her. If she promises him a pair of skates at Christmas, he doesn't begin to analyze what trust is; he doesn't begin to ask what his feeling is. He simply says, "Mother said so, and that's enough." There was nothing miraculous about it; it was simply trust. This is the idea of trusting in God. You must trust God, even if you don't know what the result will be. In the 62nd Psalm, 8th verse it says, "Trust in Him at all times, you people; pour out your heart before him; God is a refuge for us." It is the same in the midnight darkness as in the daylight. A child in the light whose father was in the dark will still leap into his father's arms even though he can't see him. He simply trusts that his father will be there. When we can't see into the dark, we can still jump because of the simple trust that the Father is there.

When can we trust God? Trust God at all times. Trust Him as one would trust a banker whom he had tried, a doctor whom he had confidence in, or a lawyer who had been tried and had never lost a case. We have an advocate with the Father, even Jesus Christ the Righteous. Proverbs shows us how to trust Him: "with all your heart." Not a little, but with the whole heart. Don't trust the minister with the soul's salvation, but God. God wants the whole heart. God hates half-heartedness; he detests half-heartedness. Alexander, the great emperor of Greece, was once warned to beware his medicine. The emperor took the note of warning in one hand and the medicine in the other, and because he trusted in his physician, took his draught. That was perfect trust. Paul said, "I am persuaded that he is able to keep that which I have committed unto him."

The next question is, "Who will trust Him?" This is answered in the 9th Psalm at the 10th verse, "They that know Your name will put their trust in You." He must be known to be trusted; He must be believed to be trusted. No infidel can trust God because he doesn't know Him. No one could go down to hell trusting in God.

Then comes the blessing of trust: "You will keep them in perfect peace that trust You." In the 16th chapter of Proverbs, at the 20th verse was described the joy of the one who trusted God: "Whoso trusts in the Lord, happy is he." In the 32nd Psalm, at the 10th verse again it was said, "Many sorrows shall be to the wicked, but he that trusts in the Lord, mercy shall compass him about." The joy is thus described in the 5th Psalm, at the 11th verse: "But let all those that put their trust in You rejoice; let them even shout for joy, because You defend them; let them also that love Your name be joyful in You."

The inquirer might ask about feeling, "How should I feel?" Let your feelings take care of themselves, you have only to come to God. You can't be saved by your feelings, nor by your good morals, by trying to break off your sins here and there. It is like lopping off the twigs of a tree, while Christ laid the axe to the root. In the 29th chapter of Proverbs it was said, "Whoso puts his trust in the Lord shall be safe," or in the margin "set on high."

Why don't you get this trust? Is it pride or the fear of neighbors? Why don't you get this trust? The 37th Psalm tells us, "Fret not yourself because of evil doers; commit your way unto him, and he shall bring it to pass." He was the widows' God and the orphans' God. Let no one fret for the coming winter; the Lord will provide. He will be a present help. Trust in God, rest in Him. He will never leave you nor forsake you.

Sudden Conversion

I propose tonight to take a subject rather than a text, and that subject is sudden conversion – instant salvation. One reason why I am led to take up this subject is because I have received a large number of letters asking me how it is that I can teach such a pernicious doctrine that a man can be saved all at once – that salvation is instantaneous. One of the writers goes on to state that it is clearly taught in the Word of God that conversion is a gradual thing – that it is a life work – and that it is a dangerous thing to teach that a man can come into this Tabernacle a sinner and go out a saved man. Now, let us see what is taught in the Word of God, and if it doesn't teach instantaneous salvation, let us give up the idea. I hold to it as I do to my life, and I would as quickly give up my life as give up this doctrine, unless it can be proved that it is not according to the Word of God.

Now, I will admit that light is one thing and birth is another. A soul must be born before it can see light. A child must be born before it can be taught. It must be born before it can walk; it must be born before it can be educated. I think the biggest mistake among ministers is that they are talking to dead men; they are talking to men in the flesh instead of men born of God. Now, let us get them into Christ, and then educate them and build them up to the highest faith. If a man is dead in sin you may as well talk to a corpse as talk to him about spiritual things. To tell an unrenewed man, an unregenerate man, to worship, serve, and love

God is absurd. You may as well tell a man to leap over Lake Michigan as to tell a man not born of God to serve Him.

Now the first illustration I want to call your attention to is when the voice came down from heaven to Noah, "You come and all your home into the ark, for you have I seen righteous before me in this generation." Now, there was a minute when Noah was outside the ark, and another when he was inside, and by being inside he was saved. As long as he was outside of the ark, he was exposed to the wrath of God just like the rest of those living then. If he stayed out, and remained with them, he would have been swept away as they were. It was not his righteousness, it was not his faith, or his works that saved him; it was the ark. And my friends, we don't have to be like Noah, 120 years making an ark for our safety. God has provided an ark for us, and the question is: Are you inside or outside this ark? If you are inside, you are safe; if you are outside you are not safe. If you are outside, you are exposed to the wrath of God continually, and you cannot tell the day nor the hour nor the minute when you may be swept into eternity.

When I was in Manchester in one of the inquiry meetings, I went up to the gallery to speak to some people there. While we were standing in a little group, a man came up and stood near us. He was a respectable looking man, and I thought by his general appearance he was skeptical. I didn't think he had come up as an inquirer, but as I stood, I noticed tears trickling down his face, and I went to him and asked him if he wanted to seek Christ, and he answered "Yes." I went on talking to him, but he could not see what I meant. I thought I would use an illustration, and after I had put it to him, I asked him if he saw it. He said "No." I gave him another illustration, and asked him, "Do you see it now?" But he again replied "No." I used two or three more illustrations, but he could not see them. He told me, "Mr. Moody, the fact is I do not feel the evidence of God." "But" I said, "I tell you, you are not to be saved by your feelings," and I gave him this illustration: "What was it that saved Noah? Was it his ark, or was it his feelings, or his life, or his prayers?" "I see it now; it's all right," and he went away. This was Thursday night, and he had to leave on a night train.

On the Sunday afternoon, while preaching in the Free Trade Hall, a man came and tapped me on the shoulder and asked me if I knew him. I said, "No," and he said, "Do you remember when you spoke to me on Thursday and used the illustration of Noah's ark to save me?" "Yes," I answered. "Well, I got in then, and have been there ever since. The ark keeps me. Thank God for that illustration of the ark." May God help you to see this illustration tonight, and may you not be trying to save yourselves by your feelings, your tears, by your wounds. God has provided an ark, and every man who is in it is saved, and every one who is out of it is lost.

Let us take another Bible illustration. Look at those two angels coming down to Sodom. They knew that God was going to destroy it utterly, and they led Lot out. What was it that saved his life? Was it his feelings, his tears? It was by obeying the call, "Escape for your life." And now God says, escape for your life – escape to Mount Calvary. Don't delay, because He is going to destroy this world as He did Sodom. While Lot was in Sodom, he was liable to the wrath of God, but the moment he got outside of Sodom he was safe. As long as a man remains out of Christ, he is liable to the wrath of God and the fire of heaven. Look again. Look at those children of Israel when they were commanded to put the blood on the doorposts and they would be saved from the hand of death. What was it that saved them? Was it the blood or was it their feelings? The moment the blood was there they were saved, and if a man is behind the blood he is as safe as if he were walking the crystal pavement of heaven. When the blood was there, the angel of death passed over. One moment the blood was off the posts and the next moment it was on. It was instantaneous salvation.

You know Joshua received a command from God that he should erect six cities, three on each side of the Jordan, which were to be cities of refuge. There were to be great highways to these cities which were to be kept in proper repair, and the gates of the cities were to be kept open day and night. Signposts were to be placed along the road to provide for the man's guidance to these cities of refuge. The moment a man got inside one of those cities he was safe. His safety was instantaneous – the moment he stepped over the boundary line. Just look at two men out in the woods chopping wood. As one of the men brings his ax down on the tree, it splits and flies from his hand and kills his companion. He knows what the consequences will be when the killing is discovered. He knows that it will be sure death the moment the news reaches the nearest relative of the deceased. The man who will not avenge the death of his relative is not considered a true man. If a relative would not avenge the death of a kinsman, it was considered very dishonorable among the Israelites. The man knows that there is a city of refuge ten miles away, and if he can but reach it, he is safe. Thank God, our city of refuge is not ten miles away. That man just leaps upon the highway. He does not take time to argue or think; he just leaps upon the highway and makes for the city of refuge.

The news soon spreads that a man has been killed, and the murderer is making for the city of refuge. Whenever the brother learns that his kinsman has been killed, he starts after that poor fugitive. On they go – the avenger and the fugitive – flying to his haven of hope. It is a life and death struggle. Look at him! See him, as he leaps ditches and speeds along the road. Some people see him flying past. "Make haste," they cry, "because the avenger is upon you. Fly for your life." Ah, sinner, you do not know how far the avenger is behind you. Tonight he may be upon you. We do not know the day, the hour, when he will overtake us. The avenger he knows now is after him. On he goes, bounding over every obstacle, his speed at its utmost, and his face resolutely set toward the gate wherein his safety lies. He is terribly in earnest. See him leap over the highway; see his bruises. On he goes, panting and nearly exhausted. He sees the gates of the city. The officers see him from the walls, and they shout, "Hasten on, for the avenger is drawing near! He is behind you!" One moment he is outside the walls – the next moment he is inside. He is a saved man. One moment out, the next moment in. What are these illustrations in the Bible for unless to show us how we are to be saved. Don't you see from this that conversion is instantaneous. One minute you may be outside, and the next minute you are inside.

I will give you another illustration, which I think you will be able to get hold of. You will remember when we had slavery, we used to have men come up from Kentucky, Tennessee, and other slave states in order to escape from slavery. I hope if there are any Southern people here they will not think in this allusion that I am trying to wound their feelings. We all remember when these men came here how they used to be afraid lest someone should come and take them back. Why, I remember in the store we had a poor fugitive, and he used to be quaking all the time. Sometimes a customer would come in, and he would be uneasy all the time. He was afraid it was someone to take him back to slavery. But somebody tells him that if he was in Canada he would be perfectly safe, and he says, "If I could only get into Canada, if I could only get under the Union Jack, I would be free." There are no slaves under the Union Jack, he has been told – that is the flag of freedom, the moment he gets under it he is a free man.

So he starts. We'll say there are no railways. The poor fellow has gone ten miles ahead when his master comes up and hears that his slave has fled for Canada and sets off in pursuit. Someone tells the poor fugitive that his master is after him. What does the poor fugitive do? What does he do? He redoubles his exertions and presses on, on, on, on. He is a slave born, and he knows a slave belongs to his master. Faster he goes. He knows his master is after him and he will be taken if he comes up with him before he reaches the lines. He says, "If I can only hold out and get under the English flag, the English Government will protect me. The whole English army will come to protect me if need be." On he presses. He is now nearing the boundary line. One minute he is a slave and in an instant, he is a free man.

My friends, don't mistake. These men can be saved tonight if they cross the line. Your old master, Satan, may be pressing down upon you, but there is a land of liberty up there. The banner of heaven is the flag of love, and under that flag you are protected from all danger, and if an enemy comes near you God says, "If you touch him, you touch the apple of My eye." And He will hold you in His right hand and keep you for the day of redemption. Will you go out of this hall tonight and doubt sudden conversion? Will you say a man cannot be saved all at once? Look what He said to Moses. He told Him to put a brazen serpent on a pole, and whenever a man looked at that serpent he would live. If some of the preachers we have now in Chicago had lived then, they would have said a man may look 6,000 years at that and he wouldn't be saved. A man would die while they were discussing it.

A few days ago, I heard of a minister who said I was preaching a most pernicious doctrine when I preached sudden conversion. But point out to me one single conversion in this blessed Bible that was not a sudden conversion. Why, every conversion recorded in the Bible was instantaneous, and if preachers tell men conversion is a life work, they are keeping men out of the kingdom of God. We can have instant conversion. "Now is the day of salvation." I tell you, sinners, escape for your lives. Fly to the haven of safety – look, look, look, at the crucified One, and you will be saved tonight. Look and live. You will become a child of God for time and eternity. The blessing will come upon you – whenever we look we can be saved. Just go back to that camp of Israel. Everyone who looked at that brazen serpent was well. The remedy was instantaneous.

When I was in England, they were at me all the time about this sudden conversion. They said it was a life work from the cradle down to the grave. I did all I could to show them it. One day I was walking down the streets of York, when I saw a soldier coming down. You can tell a soldier in England in an instant by his coat. I stepped up to him and said, "My friend, I am a stranger in this country, and you will pardon me if I ask you a question. How long did it take you to become a soldier?" Well, he laughed in my face. I suppose he thought I was very green to ask him such a question. But he told me that he made up his mind to enlist in Queen Victoria's army, he went to a recruiting sergeant, he put an English shilling into the palm of his hand, and from that moment he was a soldier. When he had taken that shilling, from that moment he becomes one of the Queen's army. If he goes back, he becomes a deserter and if caught is put into prison. He first made up his mind to enlist, and that is the way to become a Christian. Make up your mind.

The next thing he did was to take the shilling, and from that moment he became a soldier. When we make up our mind to be a Christian the next thing we have to do is to accept His terms – take salvation as a gift. You wonder how a man can become a Christian as that man became a soldier. He was a citizen one moment; the next moment he was a soldier. He was no longer his own master when he had accepted that shilling. He belonged to the English army. So the moment you enlist in Christ's army you belong to Him. If you want to become a Christian take Christ's shilling as a gift. The minute you take that gift, that minute you are a child of God. See what He says, "To as many as receive him gave he power to become the sons and daughters of men."

When you accept Him, He becomes your way, your truth, your light, your all in all. You can have His gift if you will receive Him tonight. While I was in New York, an Irishman stood up in a young converts' meeting and told how he had been saved. He said in his broken Irish brogue that I used an illustration and that that illustration saved him. And I declare that is the only man I ever knew who was converted without being spoken to. He said I used an illustration of a wrecked vessel and said that all would perish unless some assistance came. Presently a lifeboat came alongside and the captain shouted, "Leap into the lifeboat – leap for your lives, or you will perish!" and when I came to the point I said, "Leap into the lifeboat; Christ is your lifeboat," and he just leaped into the lifeboat of salvation and was saved. If a man goes out of the Tabernacle tonight without salvation, it won't be my fault; it will be your own. It will not be because the ark is not open, but because you will not accept the invitation to enter. It will not be because the blessing is not there, but because you will not take it, for it's there. May God open your eyes to accept Him before you leave this building – to accept salvation as a gift. Let us unite in prayer.

Behold!

I want to call your attention tonight to this little word "Behold." "Behold, I was shaped in iniquity." I want to speak to you for a few minutes about this one word, and you cannot forget a simple text with only one word in it. The first thing a man has to learn in coming for salvation is that he has fallen in the sight of God; to know that none are pure in His sight. You have to learn that you are born bad, before you can even approach Him. "Behold, I was shaped in iniquity." Now, a man needn't live a great number of years before he finds that out. Whenever he comes to God, he will discover this. Everyone who has ever taken a prominent place in the Bible has found this out. They might have thought themselves good enough before they came to God, but the moment they came to Him, they discovered that they were shaped in iniquity. I suppose Isaiah thought he was as good as most men in his day, and perhaps he was a good deal better than most men, but when he saw the Lord he cried, "Woe is me, for I am undone, because I am a man of unclean lips." When he saw the Lord, he saw his own deformity, and he fell in the dust before the Lord. And that is the proper place for a sinner. As I have said before, until men realize their uncleanness, they talk of their own righteousness – but the moment they catch a sight of Him, their mouth is stopped. If we hear a man talking about himself, we may be sure that he has not seen God.

Look at that man, Daniel. Not a thing can be found against him, but see when he came within sight of God, he found that his comeliness turned to corruption. And look at Job. One would have thought he was all right. He was good to the poor, liberal to all charities – not a better man within a thousand miles. If they wanted to get $1,000 to endow a university, $1,000 to build a synagogue, if they wanted to have $1,000 for any charitable object, why, he was the man. Why, you would have liked to get him into your Presbyterian, or Methodist, or Baptist churches. If you wanted a chairman of a benevolent society, you couldn't have found a better man. Yet look at him when God came near him. It is altogether different when He comes within our sight. It is one thing to hear Him and another thing to see Him. He had heard Him with his ears, but now he saw Him with his eyes, and then he was silent. You couldn't get another word from him. Before he saw Him, he could argue and talk about Him to his friends – could argue as well as they could; but the moment Job saw God he was silent.

When God said, "Gird up your loins like a man," from that time he put no more questions to Him. He had got a lesson. No man can come into His kingdom till he knows he is vile, till he sees Him. He must come down to that. That is God's alphabet. Many men want to begin at Z, and don't want to begin at A. A man must commence at the beginning and learn there is not one thing good in the flesh. It is corrupt. As Paul said, "There is nothing good in it." We have Adam's flesh, and it is bad. God has said so. He cannot find anything good in it, and if He cannot, let us give up trying to find good spots in it. It is guilty, it is corrupt, it is false, it is at enmity with God. There is evil in it all through.

My friends, if you have learned the lesson, I have good tidings for you. You best know if you have. There are good tidings for you. The voice comes down from heaven, "Unto you is born this day, in the city of David, a Savior." That is the best news that ever came down from heaven – the best news that ever fell on the ears of man. Of course, if a man does not believe, he is ruined, and he cannot appreciate the news. But to the man who knows he is ruined, these are the best tidings that can come to him. The gospel tells you plainly that you are lost but let me tell everyone in this hall tonight that I bring you good news. It is the gospel of peace, a gospel of glad tidings. It is a gospel of joy, a gospel of reconciliation. And all a man has got to do is to believe this gospel and be saved. A great many people have got a false idea from the preaching of the gospel. Some think when we preach the gospel it means condemnation. They shout as did those men in the tombs when He came to them, "Have you come to torment us before our time?" So, men, don't believe we bring goodness.

When I was in Glasgow, I heard a story of old Dr. Arnott. He heard of a poor woman in great distress. She was poor, and her landlord was after her for the rent. He put some money in his pocket and started for her house. When he reached it, he knocked at the door but got no answer. He knocked again, but none came. He waited and waited and knocked, but he could not get anyone to come and left. A day or two afterward he met the woman on the street and said, "I heard you were in distress and could not pay your rent. I came to your door the other day, but I found no one in your house." The woman threw up both her hands. "Why, I thought it was the landlord; I had the door locked and bolted." She thought it was the landlord after her rent. And people think when Jesus Christ comes to them, He comes to demand something. "Why," said a young man, "I would like to become a Christian, but I would have to give up so much." Why, that is a ridiculous idea.

When you receive Christ, you receive everything. You are in the position of a beggar. You give up your rags and put on a brand new suit. You give up nothing and receive everything. The idea of a man being so deceived! Do you think the Lord Jesus Christ comes to you to torment you? Ask those men who have received Him if this be so. Ask those who have been deceived for forty or fifty years by Satan and who then have accepted Jesus Christ. They will tell you they have enjoyed more peace and happiness in the last few days than they have in all those years put together. I heard a Christian saying that he had enjoyed more happiness the first day he accepted Christ than he did in all the previous years of his life. Now, my friends, God doesn't want to take anything from you. He wants to give you everything that is good for your happiness.

Now, I have two little children, and I wouldn't like to give them anything but what would be good for them. So the God of heaven wants to keep nothing from us but that which will ruin us. The Son of God has come into the world to bless us. Look at that sermon on the mount. It is filled with the word "blessed," "blessed," "blessed." I think it occurs nine times. His heart was full of blessings for the people. He had to get it out before He gave His sermon. Don't believe He came to make you miserable. That is one of the devil's lies. Don't believe He has come to torment you. I heard some time ago of a little book upon a passage of Scripture – I didn't know there was such a passage – which occurred in the history of David and Mephibosheth. You know, one day Jonathan and David were together, and Jonathan said, "David, I want you to make a vow." I suppose it had been revealed to Jonathan that he was to take his place.

Instead of his heart being filled with jealousy, he loved him as a brother. "Now, I want you to make a vow that when you get my father's throne, if any of my father's house are alive, that you will show them kindness." "Why, yes, Jonathan," replies David, "I will; I would do it for your sake alone." Well, time went on. You know how Saul persecuted David and drove him into the cave of Adullam, and if he could have caught him you know how he would have slain him. News came to him that the Israelites were routed and that Saul and Jonathan were slain. David came up to Hebron and reigned for seven and a half years and came after this up to Jerusalem. I can see him in his palace in the height of his power, and the recollection of the old vow he made to Jonathan suddenly comes upon him. His conscience tells him he has made a vow to his old friend Jonathan which he has not kept. I can see him order in one of his servants. "Do you know if there are any of Saul's house alive?" "Well, I don't know, but there is an old servant of Saul's, Ziba."

David orders him in, and asks, "Are any of Saul's house alive? If there is, I want to show kindness to them." I can imagine the expression of his face. The idea of David showing kindness to any of Saul's house – to Saul, who wanted to slay him, and who persecuted him. "Well, yes," the servant answers, "there is a son of Jonathan living." "What!" he cries, "a son of my old friend Jonathan! Where is he?" "He was at Lo-debar, the last I heard of him." Now, you may have been a great traveler, and yet you have never heard of Lo-debar. You may have been all around the world and still you have not heard of Lo-debar. You may work in the post office and you have never heard of Lo-debar – never saw a letter directed to that place. Still that is the place where every one of Adam's sons have been. Everyone has been in Lo-debar. Every backslider is there.

When David heard where he was, he sent down to bring up Jonathan's son, Mephibosheth. See that chariot sweeping through the town. "Why, the king's chariot is here," the people say. "What does it mean?" We are told that this poor prince was lame, and I can see the poor, lame prince as he comes out to meet the servant. "What is it?" he inquires. "King David has sent for you," the servant replies. I can see the prince trembling from head to foot when he hears this. He thinks King David wants to slay him; he thinks he is just going to cut off his head. That's the way with sinners. They think that God stands behind them with a double-edged sword ready to annihilate them. The servant says, "I want you to come down and see the king." "But" replies the prince, "I tell you that means death to me." Just as a good many sinners in Chicago think. "But" continues the servant, "he has sent me and wants you to come." He gets him into the carriage and on to the highway, through the streets and unto the palace of the king.

Whenever he enters, he is brought into the presence of the king. The king looks upon him and sees upon his brow the image of Jonathan and says to Mephibosheth, "I will show you kindness for your father's sake, and I will restore unto you all Saul's possessions, and you shall sit at the king's table." He restores to the lame prince the inheritance he lost, and then gives him a place at the king's table. That is the gospel. God wants you to come up from Lo-debar to Jerusalem and take your inheritance. The moment you come from your Lo-debar to the city of peace, that moment you will learn the glad tidings.

Now, there is another "behold." We find it here in the 1st chapter of John, and I want to call your attention to it. "Behold the Lamb of God which takes away the sin of the world." Now, every sin which you have committed can be forgotten – every sin which has been committed during the past 1,800 years can be forgiven by Him. Now look at His life – look at Him from the manger to Calvary and see if you can find any flaw in Him. You hear people talking about the imperfections of Christians and making this an excuse for not accepting Him. They point to some of them and say they have done this and that; but my friends, it is impossible to find a perfect Christian. They will not be perfect till they arrive in the kingdom of the Master and they are washed in the blood of the Lamb.

Lift your eyes from off these puny Christians – from off these human ministers and look to Christ. He is the Savior of the world. He came from the throne to this earth; He came from the very bosom of the father. God gave Him up freely for us, and all we have to do is to accept Him as our Savior. Look at Him at Gethsemane, sweating as it were great drops of blood; look at Him on the Cross, crucified between two thieves. Hear that piercing cry, "Father, Father, forgive them, they know not what they do," and as you look into that face, as you look into those wounds on His feet or His hands, will you say He has not the power to save you? Will you say He has not the power to redeem you? Look into His face. Can you say the Lamb of God will not take away your sins? All you have to do is to accept Him and they are all forgiven. A great many people want to bring their faith, their works, their good deeds to Him for salvation. Bring your sins and He will bear them away into the wilderness of forgetfulness, and you will never see them again.

There is another "behold," and a very important one. It is a "behold" of Paul: "Behold, now is the accepted time." Now some people may listen to this carelessly. "Why, we have heard that from childhood up. 'Now is the accepted time.' We don't like that forced upon us, as if this were the only time to be saved." Suppose I say, "Behold, ten years hence will be the accepted time," wouldn't you think I had gone mad? You would say, "I might die before that time." You know that it is now. You cannot roll back the wheel of time. Every hour that passes is gone forever. You cannot look forward ten years. You may be in eternity then. You cannot say the future is yours. The only time we have is now. "Behold, now is the accepted time," and salvation is offered you tonight, and God wants you to take it. How many have been swept into eternity since we began to hold our meetings in the Tabernacle? Not less than eight or nine, to my knowledge, have been taken away. How many will go in the coming eight weeks? Think of it. They are now with the redeemed and the Redeemer. They are now singing the sweet hallelujahs of heaven – a sweeter song than they ever heard on earth.

But think of those who have gone to the dark caverns of hell – now with the fiends of darkness, now in the land where there is no hope, now listening to the wail of despair. You can accept salvation now. The idea of standing still, thinking you have time to accept Christ is a delusion of the devil. Don't be deceived by Satan. We are in the current of time that is bearing us on to eternity. While we sleep and are unconscious, we are being borne swiftly to the judgment seat, and we may be there before we know. Look at that man on the river that runs to the rapids! Look at him as he drifts with the current on to death! In a few minutes he will be in eternity, and he is not aware of it. There are thousands here sweeping on to death and judgment. "Now is the accepted time." Escape tonight, and accept the Lord Jesus Christ, and you shall be saved.

But there is another "behold." "Behold, I stand at the door and knock." He stands at the door of the sinner's heart and knocks. Do your hearts thrill tonight, my friends? That is the Son of God knocking at your heart. You don't have to go down and bring Him up, nor go up and bring Him down. He is right here tonight. Is there a skeptical one who doubts His presence here? What man could hold this immense audience during the past eight weeks but Him? Is there any political subject that could keep an audience every night for eight weeks as this has been kept? Or if a man came here to talk poetry or science, could he have such an assemblage? Surely it cannot be the singer or the preacher. There is an unseen power — a supernatural agency. It is the Son of God, my friends. He is here tonight and stands at your heart and says, "Behold, I stand at the door and knock." If anyone here hearkens to His voice and opens the door, He says with him, "I will come unto him and sup with him, and he with Me." And no man, if he only enters to Him, will go down to the caverns of death and damnation; but if you reject Him, and shut and lock and bolt the door of your heart, He cannot come in, and of course, you must perish.

In one part of Scripture, He says He "stands with his locks wet with the dew of the night." He stands now. A man in the inquiry room said he made a vow some years ago to come to Christ. He was knocking at his heart then, but for thirty years he kept Him out. This week he let Him in. Think how merciful God is. He might have called that man away to eternity during those thirty years. Listen, sinners, perhaps He is making His last call to you.

A friend of mine once said when Christ came first he knocked pretty loud. The second time conscience was not so keen, and it was not so loud. When he came a third time, His knock was fainter, and the fourth time fainter still, and the fifth time almost inaudible, till by and by He could not be heard at all. Is not that the case with some here? Christ stands knocking now. You may put Christ off – that is man's free will – but you cannot put death off. When he comes and puts his cold hand upon you, feeling for the cords of life, you cannot put him off. The question will then be settled for time and eternity, and then you must answer at the judgment seat. "Behold, I stand at the door and knock." Sinner, what will you do tonight? Young man, don't laugh! Don't make light of this question. One of two things you must do – either reject Him or receive Him. Either keep Him out of your heart or take Him in.

And there is another "Behold." It is a behold they heard of in the days of Paul. You know, when they heard that Paul was praying, it did not come from Damascus, or Rome, or Jerusalem; it came from heaven. "Behold, he is praying." I hope some are praying here tonight. Let the news go up to heaven, "Behold, he prays," and "Behold, she prays," and an answer will come. If you pray from the depths of your soul, an answer will come tonight. If you want to accept on this, the last night of our meetings this week, the waters of life, you can. Just lift up your heart, and the message will go up, "Behold, he prays." Let all Christians here pray. Let there be a silent wave of prayer go up to heaven and let those who have never prayed ask God for mercy. Let these little children pray. I like to hear children praying. Sometimes a child's prayers have more effect than any others. How many infidel fathers and mothers have been brought to Christ by their praying children.

I remember while out in Kansas, while holding a meeting, I saw a little boy who came to the window crying. I went to him and said, "My little boy, what is your trouble?" "Why, Mr. Moody, my mother's dying, and my father drinks, and they don't love me, and the Lord won't have anything to do with me because I am a poor drunkard's boy." "You have got a wrong idea, my boy; Jesus will love you and save you and your father too," and I told him a story of a little boy in an eastern city. The boy said his father would never allow the canting hypocrites of Christians to come into his house and would never allow his child to go to Sunday school. A kind-hearted man got his little boy and brought him to Christ.

When Christ gets into a man's heart he cannot help to pray. This father had been drinking one day and coming home, he heard the boy praying. He went to him and said, "I don't want you to pray any more. You've been along with some of those Christians. If I catch you praying again, I'll flog you." But the boy was filled with God and he couldn't help praying. The door of communication was opened between him and Christ, and his father caught him praying again. He went to him. "Didn't I tell you never to pray again? If I catch you at it once more, you leave my house." He thought he would stop him.

One day a temper came upon the boy, and he did something wrong and got flogged. When he got over his mad fit, he forgot the threats of his father and went to pray. His father had been drinking more than usual and coming in found the boy offering a prayer. He caught the boy with a push and said, "Didn't I tell you never to pray again? Leave this house. Get your things packed up and go." The little fellow hadn't many things to get together – a drunkard's boy never has, and he went up to his mother's room. "Goodbye, mother." "Where are you going?" "I don't know where I'll go, but father says I cannot stay here any longer. I've been praying again," he said. The mother knew it wouldn't do to try to keep the boy when her husband had ordered him away, so she drew him to her bosom and kissed him and bid him goodbye. He went to his brothers and sisters and kissed them goodbye.

When he came to the door, his father was there, and the little fellow reached out his hand – "Goodbye, father. As long as I live I will pray for you," and left the house. He hadn't been gone many minutes when that father rushed after him. "My boy, if that is religion, if it can drive you away from father and mother and home, I want it." Yes, maybe some little boy here tonight has got a drinking father and mother. Lift your voice to heaven, and the news will be carried up to heaven, "He prays." Yes, Paul prayed, and the news went, "He prays." Let all Christians lift their voices up to heaven, and let all who have not accepted Christ cry, and he will hear you, "God be merciful to me a sinner." Let us unite in silent prayer.

How to Conduct Inquiry Meetings

I've chosen as my subject this morning, "How to Hold an Inquiry Meeting or what are best-adapted texts of Scripture to be dwelt upon at these meetings?" Of course, I am not going to quote all the texts that could be used and to good advantage. I am just going to bring to mind some few of the best ones. And what I want first to call your attention to, if you are going to be successful in winning souls to Christ, is the need for discrimination in finding out people's differences. People are not the same in their wants, spiritual any more than temporal. What is good for one is rank poison for another. You can't treat all alike.

I've a friend that, when he is sick, drinks a lot of hot water, and goes to bed. Another says to me, just take this dose and you will get well. It doesn't make any difference what's the matter with you, this friend has one single remedy. So many have just one verse of Scripture. He's always quoting it. It fits his case, and he thinks it does everybody else's.

A man I knew up in Wisconsin was converted under a railway bridge, and to this day he keeps urging people to go right down under that bridge if they want to get converted for sure. But God never repeats Himself. No two thoughts are just alike, no two needs are just alike, no two sinners are going to come to Christ in the same precise way. Instead of looking for others' experiences, look for one for yourself. So when talking to persons in the inquiry room, you must find out just these differences.

Now, I am going to divide inquirers into classes or divisions this morning and point out a few passages suitable for each. The first class, I think, in point of numbers, is that of the doubters – those who are always in Doubting Castle. And these generally are among professing Christians. Oh, I think we shall make a different start with these when we get to Boston from what we did here. I'm convinced we made a mistake here in not opening the inquiry rooms for professing Christians first. For twenty or thirty years they have been living on making empty professions. Now, they just want to get off their crutches and get to walking and running for Christ. I don't believe they can accomplish much; I know they can't, if they continue in this half-dead state. If Christians haven't assurance, they are just stumbling blocks – they are in the way of the work. How many hurts these professing Christians give, who show no sign of their faith! They have no joy in serving the Lord, and their children, with reason, say, "I don't want that kind of a religion."

And here I want to call your attention to a proper remedy for this class, to be found in the book of John. That whole book was written for this one thing, to help people out of Doubting Castle and teach them that they may know they are saved. Only last Friday I met a woman, a prominent member of a prominent church, who said it was presumption to say with certainty that we are saved. I said it was presumption to say that we are not saved when we have the very word of the Lord Jesus Christ for it. Oh, if you will just read those precious words, "He that hears my words and believes on Him that sent Me has everlasting life, and shall not come into condemnation, but is passed from death unto life." Then turn to those other divine words: "These things have I written unto you that believe on the name of the Son of God, that you may know that you have eternal life, and that you may believe on the name of the Son of God." If you will just read these sure words of God, you will not talk about having no assurance as to your salvation. Just believe in the words of the Son of God, and you know right now that you are saved. You know right now, I say, and don't have to put it off till you are going to die. Therefore, I would talk to these doubting citizens about the epistle of John. I would say to you, persuade them to take these words of Jesus, "They have passed from death to life." Oh, yes, it is the privilege of every child of God to know that he is saved.

The next class are the backsliding. They do not want so much assurance as reviving. I know a lady who has a homeopathic doctor's book, and whenever she is at all out of sorts, she goes right to it. In spiritual things there is a good remedy for all sorts and for the backsliders as well. Though they have left God, He makes a way for them to return. I have just turned down the leaves of my Bible at the 2nd and 3rd chapters of Jeremiah. I don't think anyone can feel this way with that Bible in hand. "Thus says the Lord, What iniquity have your fathers found in me that they are gone far from me, and have walked after vanity and are become vain?" Now, what did Christ ever do against you? Did He ever lie to you? Did He ever abuse you? Did He ever deceive you? Only one man I know of ever said that, and he was out of his head, and anyone would know he was. No man can accuse Christ of any bias or offence. "What iniquity have you found in Me?" None at all. The trouble has been with us. It was He that brought the early church through the wilderness, through all the dangers of the way, and into the promised land. It is He that gives you power and lifts you up. Oh say, then, what evil or iniquity have you found in Him?

The trouble is with you, O backsliders, who "have forsaken the fountains of living waters, and hewed out cisterns, broken cisterns that can hold no water." The 19th verse says, "Your own wickedness shall convict you, and your backslidings shall reprove you; know, therefore, and see that it is an evil thing and bitter, that you have forsaken the Lord your God, and that my fear is not in you, says the Lord of Hosts." Enforce the miseries of this text, and then use the exhortation of the 3rd chapter, 22nd verse: "Return, you backsliding children, and I will heal your backsliding. Behold, we come unto you, for you are the Lord our God." And then the 14th verse: "Only acknowledge your iniquity that you have transgressed against the Lord your God."

I remember repeating these promises to a backslider, and he couldn't believe them at first for joy. How tender these words of Scripture to the backslider! Bring these words right to bear on them and tell how God pleads with them. Read to them the opening words of Hosea, 14th chapter: "Return unto the Lord your God, for you have fallen by your iniquity; say unto him, take away all iniquity and receive us graciously. . . I (God) will heal their backsliding, I will love them freely; for mine anger is turned away." Then bring up the story of the prodigal for illustration and the Apostle Peter, how he was drawn to God after grievously backsliding, and how he was even admitted to the blessings of Pentecost. Then say, "You, too, can be restored if you only believe, and God will yet make you a blessing to believers."

The third class are those who are not stricken by their sins, who have no deep conviction of guilt. Just bring the law of God to bear on these and show them themselves in their true light. Repeat Romans, 3rd chapter, 10th verse, "There is none righteous, no, not one," and also the succeeding verses. Then repeat from Isaiah, "The whole head is sick and the whole heart faint; from the sole of the foot even unto the head there is no soundness, but wounds and bruises and putrefying sores," And then bring in that verse, "The heart is deceitful above all things and desperately wicked." Don't try to heal the wound before the hurt is felt. You may, perhaps, get but few satisfactory inquirers in this way, but what you do get are worth something.

If a man doesn't see his guilt, he won't be a valuable or true convert. Read him the 1st chapter of First John, 10th verse: "If we say that we have not sinned, we make him a liar, and his word is not in us," and hold him right to it. Don't attempt to give the consolations of the gospel until your converts see they have sinned – see it and feel it. I met a man who expressed doubts about his being much of a sinner. "Well," said I, "let's find out if you have sinned. Do you swear?" "Well, as a general rule, I only swear when I get mad." "Yes, yes. But what does the Lord say about not holding a man guiltless that swears? Believe me, He will hold you responsible for that. Bear that in mind; you must be able to hold your temper, but if not, beware to take the name of God in vain. Are you not now a sinner?" And the man was convinced. Sometimes, too, I've found a merchant this way, and yet one openly confesses to me that he did cheat sometimes. "You lie, then, don't you?" said I. He didn't want to put it quite so plainly, but pretty soon he saw it in my light. Oh yes. Enforce this truth kindly but firmly, that our natural hearts are as black and deceitful as hell. Man must say from his heart, "I have sinned and come short of the glory of God."

The fourth class are those completely broken down by a sense of sin, those who have too much conviction of sin distinguished from the preceding inquirers who haven't enough. One of these tells you that God can't save such as he. Then you have to prove his mistake and show that God can save to the uttermost. Take the 1st chapter of Isaiah, 18th verse: "Come now, and let us reason together, says the Lord; though your sins be as scarlet, they shall be as white as snow; though they be red like crimson, they shall be as wool." Just turn your Bible right over to that passage and many such passages in Isaiah: they will all help in the inquiry room.

The 43rd chapter, 25th verse says, "I, even I, am He that blots out your transgressions for My own sake and will not remember your sins." And the 22nd verse of the next chapter is stronger: "I have blotted out, as a thick cloud, your transgressions, and as a cloud, your sins: return unto Me, for I have redeemed you." Make the anxious soul believe that God has blotted out his sins as a thick cloud; make him see the dense cloud vanishing, as it were, from the face of the sun, vanishing forever. That cloud can never come up again; others may, but that old cloud of the past guilt is dissolved forever. The Lord Himself has blotted it out.

Use the two verses, John 1:11 12: "He came unto His own, and His own received Him not. But as many as received Him, to them gave He power to become the sons of God, even to them that believe on His name." The idea is that those fearing ones cannot serve God until they receive Christ fully as their salvation. It won't do for them to merely take up with some minister or church or creed. The minister dies or moves away; the only lasting resource is in Christ at the right hand of God, where He will never forsake His own. Yes, press Jesus upon these anxious souls. Tell them, "God so loved the world that He gave His only begotten Son." "So loved the world." That includes them. If they inhabited some other land they might tremble, but they are on this earth, for all the sons and daughters of which Christ died, the just for the unjust.

Use also the text: "Verily, verily, I say unto you, he that hears my words and believes on Him that sent Me shall not come into condemnation but has passed from death unto life." Now, some people do not just understand believing in Christ. They believe Christ came as an historical being, as Moses and Elijah came. They believe the Cunard line of steamers will take them to Liverpool in twelve or fourteen days. But these beliefs don't make men good; they are head beliefs only. They are not what your inquirers want. What you and they want is heart belief, or, in other words, to just trust Christ to save you. Sometimes people can't digest the word "belief;" then let them take this sweet word "trust."

From Isaiah 26:3-4, read to them, "You will keep him in perfect peace whose mind is stayed on You; because he trusts in You. Trust in the Lord forever; for in the Lord Jehovah is everlasting strength." By trusting in Him, you see we have everlasting strength. You must get them to trust and believe entirely in Christ and not try to save themselves. They cannot save themselves by their feelings; assure them of that. There is not a word of warrant for such a thought from the first of Genesis to the last of Revelation. Oh, it is much better to trust in the precious, changeless Word of God than in our own changing feelings. Thank God that this is also our duty!

Then you hear some inquirers say, "I haven't got strength sufficient." But Christ died to be their strength. A loving hand will support them in the Christian journey, and "His strength will be made perfect in weakness." Bid such be strong in the Lord and in the power of His might.

And then another class that cannot be saved in this way, they think, because of doubting instantaneous conversion. Read to such from Romans 6:23, "The wages of sin is death, but the gift of God is eternal life." Salvation is a gift and so must have a definite point in time. I say, "Will you take this Bible?" You must first make up your mind to take it and then reach out and – the work of an instant – grasp the gift. Just so with God's best gift, salvation; to take it is the work of an instant, and your inquirer may have it for the asking. "Let him that hear say come;" "whosoever will, let him come and drink of the water of life freely." With the gift God gives the power to take it. When we get before the tribunal of the great white throne, we will have to answer for it if we refuse to take it. This is the richest jewel that heaven has; God gives up His Son for our Savior.

Another class say to you and me when, in the inquiry room, we press them to openly confess Christ, "We're afraid we won't hold out." Say to these repeatedly that blessed text, "Now unto Him that is able to keep you from falling." Think, and tell them to think of the thousands who never fall. The idea that it is necessary to fall into sin is wrong. Then take those passages: "I, the Lord your God, will take your right hand,"

"Fear not, I will lead you," and "I am persuaded that I will be able to keep them that are committed unto me against that day." Let a man just trust the Lord to keep him from falling and He will do it.

Suppose I have a hundred thousand dollars with me; it's all I have in the world. Thieves are after it, and I'm quaking every minute lest they get it. I find my banker here, and I say, "Here, take it quick; I can't keep my money but by your help. I wish you would hurry and put it in the vault. When it's deposited there, and not before, I shall be safe." Is not this the way to give our all into God's keeping? Is not this the way to live secure from temptation and backsliding? In God's keeping we are safe. "Our life is hid with Christ in God." Oh, let us each make this deposit of our personal trust this morning; trust him entirely, and then we can the better lead inquirers in the same way. Jesus can hold us close to Himself. "Nor height, nor depth, nor any other creature shall be able to separate us from the love of God, which is in Christ Jesus our Lord."

If you just take up the words of Christ in the book of Romans, love and peace and joy flow out. One verse tells of love, the next of joy, the next and next of the peace that comes from believing Romans, 4th chapter and 28th verse, and all those verses along there might be read. The result of believing is joy, rest, and peace. John 15:11 – that is joy. Matthew 11:28 – that is rest. John 14:27 – that is peace. Never, however, tell a man he is converted. Never tell him he is saved. Let him find that out from heaven. You can't afford to deceive one about this great question. But you can help his faith and trust and lead him right.

I find that those in the inquiry room do best who do not run about from one to another, offering words of encouragement everywhere. They would better go to but one or two of an afternoon or evening. We are building for eternity and can take time. The work will not then be superficial. If it is so, it will not be the fault of the workers or preachers. And then, to do all our duty, we must talk more of restitution. I don't think we preach enough the need of our making good to one another injuries to person, property, or feeling. If you have done one a detriment, you must go and pay it back or make it up if it is a tangible loss, and if it is a wound to the feelings, fully apologize. It is a good deal better to go up and do the fair thing, whatever the result. It may be that some will refuse such amends, but it is our duty to offer them. But in the end a complete reconciliation from such a course is almost sure to result.

The antipathy supposed to exist on the other side is often only imagined. You need not expect that God is going to forgive you if you don't forgive others. We say daily, "Forgive, us our debts as we forgive our debtors," and we must show that we understand this conditional request. What if God should take us at our word and just forgive us to the extent to which our small grievances are forgiven! And this He surely will do, so let us be wise.

A young lady in Michigan, at a recent revival service, was troubled greatly, and to kind inquiries at last confessed that her unwillingness to confess Christ resulted from a schoolroom quarrel which was still unsettled. She felt she couldn't forgive her enemy, but at last told her trouble and asked for advice. "Must she forgive her mate?" "Certainly, if you want God's forgiveness," was the answer of the minister, and immediately she ran with all her might to her old friend, and instead of meeting a cold reception, they were soon crying on each other's necks. And so it always should be, and most always there will be the same prompt half-way meeting between those aggrieved.

My wife was laboring in the inquiry room the other evening with a lady who was in just this state of mind, and very soon reparation and complete reconciliation were effected, and two old friends walked off arm in arm, happier than ever before this little misunderstanding. And one of those ladies felt so strong in her new-found charity for all, that she won over her husband, and last Sunday he openly in the Tabernacle confessed Christ, remembering that "with the mouth confession is made unto salvation." Many more texts, did time allow, might be cited, all applicable to anxious inquirers.

But one word more. Do not let a man go out of the inquiry room without praying with him. Fear not you but do the work boldly. There was a man the other day who said, "I don't believe there's any God." The resolute Christian worker, to whom he spoke answered impetuously, "I will just ask God to shake you – to just shake this demon out of you." And down he fell on his knees by the poor infidel and prayed with loud earnestness. The man began to shake from head to foot. It was God shaking him. And by just these means, more than any others, skeptics and infidels will know there is a God.

Let me say a word to those ministers that have not and do not go into the Inquiry room. Many in your flocks, never seeing you there, think you are not in sympathy with this work, and then begin to think you don't care anything about their salvation. They feel in bondage, and you do not go to help them. Well, there was a minister in a city we visited who did not "condescend" to be seen in our humble Tabernacle. He would have nothing to do with us. One day he was at a dinner party where they were discussing our work. Said he, "That sort of thing is good enough for those people, but it would never do for me." "Well," said another clergyman of the same belief, "fifty-seven of your congregation stood up in the Tabernacle for prayers today, and all of them afterward went into the inquiry room."

The cultured and popular pastor of those Christians could not kill the humane promptings to be charitable to all professing the name of Christ, and to worship along with such even in perhaps irregular modes. But with the cordial cooperation of every Christian pastor in the Tabernacle and inquiry room, what limit would there be to the Christian inroads on the citadels of sin? Oh, make it a duty, all of you, to talk to some soul at every meeting in these blessed inquiry rooms. Don't take those in a position in life above your own but take those on the same footing. Bend all your endeavors to answer for poor, struggling souls that question of all importance to them, "What must I do to be saved?" Yes, this is the question. What else but to answer it brought out these thousands at this early hour! My friends, God is with you in this work. Go on more diligently and implicitly trusting in Him; go on to a more and more glorious harvest. Let us pray.

The Penitent Thief

I want to call attention this evening to the conversion of the thief on the cross. I have spoken two or three times about sudden conversions and have been approached by several people upon the subject. This morning two ladies came to me after the meeting and said they were in darkness, because I had been preaching that people could be converted suddenly. I thought we had got beyond that question. I thought I had got beyond that last Thursday night when trying to prove that conversion was instantaneous, but it seems we have not, and I want to call attention to it tonight. Well, we are told, by both Matthew and Mark, that these two thieves, who were hung up on either side of Him, reviled Him and scoffed at Him, as did the crowd. They cast His title in His teeth. We are told there was no difference between those men. Both had been in rebellion against God all their lives. Both were led out to execution as thieves and malefactors on the same day, but one of them was converted during the day, and the other was not.

Over one of them came a wonderful change. What was it? How was it? What brought him under conviction? I don't know, but one thing I do know – he was convicted of sin and confessed, and Christ saved him and snatched him from the very borders of hell. It says in Isaiah that Jesus came to take the power from the mighty. Here was one who had been brought to the very borders of the pit by Satan, and yet Christ, whenever he called upon Him, was ready to help him. The thief had only to cry to Him and he was pardoned. You would think He had all He could do in attending to His own sufferings when nailed to that tree, but the first cry from that thief was heard and answered.

My friends, the Son of God was never in a position where He could not hear a sinner's prayers. No sinner ever uttered a cry that was not heard by Him. This man had no works to offer Him, no deeds of righteousness to bring before Him. He was a lost, ruined sinner. He had nothing to commend himself – nothing to offer. There he was, all mangled and bruised in consequence of his own sin. He had not only been a thief, but the very worst kind of a thief. I suppose he was a companion of Barabbas and of the most notorious thieves in the country. I have no doubt he was a highwayman, and guilty of murder. He had been tried, but his trial had not broken his heart; the scourge had not softened him; imprisonment had not brought repentance.

There he was on the cross, his heart as hard as ever, nailed hand and foot, and reviling the Son of God. I can just imagine what came over him when he heard the Son of God exclaim. "Father, forgive them, for they know not what they do." I can imagine this thief saying, when he heard this, "That is a strange thing to say. If I had the power, I couldn't forgive them, but would call down fire from heaven to consume these wretches who are making jests about me." Perhaps it was the very cry of Christ on the cross while all those people were reviling Him and wagging their heads that convicted him and that saved him. When He had uttered this prayer one of the malefactors reviled Him, and we find his companion rebuking him, saying, "Do you fear God?" We are told in Proverbs that, "The fear of the Lord is the beginning of knowledge," and there is no hope for a sinner till the fear of God comes upon him. Sometimes in an audience like this a text similar to this one strikes into the heart of the people, and the fear of God comes upon them and they begin to see knowledge. I hope that may be the case tonight.

This thief had been tried and scourged, the nails had been driven into his hands and feet, and he was suffering the agonies of the terrible death of the crucifixion, yet we find that then the fear of the Lord came upon him, and the moment the fear of God came upon him he confessed Christ. Not only did he confess Christ, but he confessed his own sins and turned and rebuked the thief on the other side of the cross, for we read that he said, "We receive the due reward of our deeds, but this man has done nothing amiss." He confessed that he had been a sinner, and he was getting his just reward – death; then there was hope for the man to be saved. This was the first step. There is no hope for a man being saved till he knows he is a sinner; there is no hope for a man who folds his arms and says, "I am willing to take the consequences if I am a sinner. I don't think God will condemn me." This thief stood, when he confessed, where every sinner ought to stand. He took his place as a sinner. He confessed his sins. And if you are to be saved tonight you must take your place before God as a sinner. If a man does not admit that he is a sinner, and that he has gone astray, there is no chance for God to forgive him.

Suppose my boy has disobeyed me; suppose he has told me a falsehood, and he won't ask my forgiveness and won't acknowledge that he has told a falsehood. I can't forgive him. I must first get him to admit that he has told a lie, and when he does that, then I can forgive him. So we must confess our sins, acknowledge that we have committed sin in God's sight before He can forgive us. This thief confessed his sins and confessed Christ. "We receive the due reward of our deeds, but this man has done nothing amiss." A great many men in Chicago think that Christ did many things amiss, but the poor thief, who probably never heard the gospel in his life, who had perhaps lived in an atmosphere of crime said, "This man has done nothing amiss." He confessed him. That must have been a sweet moment in this, the darkest hour of His life. Judas had betrayed Him for thirty pieces of silver. Peter had denied Him. He had been brought before Caiaphas and had been tried and found guilty by the Sanhedrim. There was a howling multitude around Him jeering at His sufferings and wagging their heads saying, "If you are Christ, save Yourself." How pleasant it must have been to the Son of Man to hear the confession of this thief in those moments of bitterness.

We read of Abraham in the promised land twenty-five years with abundant proofs of God's love to build up his faith, and yet he did not seem to have as much faith as this man. We read of Moses in the wilderness for forty years. He saw God's mighty hand leading the children through the Red Sea. He saw the water coming from the rock. He had everything to give him faith in his God, and yet he had not as much faith as this poor thief who, during his life, had nothing to school him in the faith of God. Look at Elijah. How much God gave him, how much He did for him, how miraculously He took care of him. He had everything to build up his faith. But here is a man who had never heard the gospel, who had never met Him before, who had mingled with the blasphemers, who had associated with the revilers and consorted with the worst classes of thieves.

Why, if he had lived in Chicago today, and we had looked over the annals of crime, we would have found that he had been familiar with the penitentiary, and yet this man as black as sin and standing on the borders of hell, confessed Him and was saved. Peter had seen Him when raised from the dead, had witnessed the transfiguration, and he hadn't the faith of this man. I consider this one of the most remarkable evidences of conversion suddenly – the faith of this man on Calvary. He had heard none of His sermons, he had none of His miracles, and yet the very day he met Christ, he was convicted and confessed and took his place before Him as a sinner. He owned himself a sinner, and I tell you a man can never be saved till he has owned himself a sinner. If he tries to put before Christ his own deeds and justify himself, there is no hope for his salvation. This man merely took his place before Christ among the sinners, and his faith saved Him.

When I was a boy, I used to be a pretty bad speller – I haven't improved much since – and I remember one day a word was given in the class. All passed the word, but when it came to me, I was able to spell it and got clear up to the head of the class, and I was very proud of my promotion. If you will allow me the expression, this thief by his faith got clear up from the bottom to the head of the class. He passed by all the men of God and took his lead at the top of the class. He surpassed Peter, he surpassed Abraham, Noah, Elijah, Moses, and all of them when he said, "Why, this man has done nothing amiss." Thank God for faith, thank God for this testimony, thank God for this confession. But what did he next do? He called Him, "Lord." That is the marvelous thing. He was suffering upon that cross, his hands and feet nailed to it, and he called Him, "Lord." Why, there was no scepter in His hand. There was no crown on His head, except a crown of thorns, which sent the blood trickling down His face, causing Him to look hideous. He was a sorry sight, and amid the jeers of the multitude, he called Him, "Lord." Thank God for such faith.

My friends, call Him Lord tonight. His prayer was short. He put it into three words, "Lord, remember me." It was short, but it was a chain of golden leaves. He owned Him. "Lord, remember me when You come into Your kingdom." What was it that induced this man to call Him Lord, and ask Him to remember him when He came into His Kingdom? The idea of the Man nailed to that cross and bleeding from His wounds having a kingdom! If He had a kingdom, where were his subjects? See that howling crowd wagging their heads and reviling Him, and when He asked for a drink of water, they brought Him vinegar. They were not His subjects. Where was the kingdom? His faith went beyond that, and that is what faith does. He didn't look upon his surroundings but trusted Him and cried to Him, "Lord, remember me." And how quick the answer came. "Lord, remember me when You come into Your kingdom," and back came the answer, "Today you shall be with Me in Paradise."

He got more than he asked for, and my friends, when a man comes to Christ in faith, he receives more than he asks. "Today you shall be with Me in Paradise." Here was, without conversation, sudden salvation, and I think that this is a proof which, if we are honest, ought to forever settle the question. How we linger around the deathbed of a man and hesitate about believing him accepted if he has not partaken of the Sacrament? If he hasn't, people are in great distress. Now this man never partook of the Sacrament. Remember, I am saying nothing against the ordinance. May my tongue cleave to the roof of my mouth if I say anything against the ordinance commemorating the death of our Savior. I am saying nothing against the blessed ordinance when I say it has nothing to do with salvation. It is distinct. This man's conversion was instantaneous. He had never been a Christian; he had never accepted a single Christian ordinance; he had never worked for Him, and yet when he called upon Him, he was saved. The man had been a thief – a highway robber. His feet were nailed to that cross, and he could not have worked for Him if he'd wanted. But they could not nail his heart, and with his heart that man believed, and the blessed Lord gave him salvation.

If you but believe on Him tonight with your heart you will be saved. Christ did not look at his works. My friends, let us keep salvation in its place. It is distinct from works, and any man or woman can be saved before leaving this Tabernacle tonight; can be saved without lifting their hands, without moving an eyelash. If this thief had lived fifty years, he could not have done Him better service than by testifying his faith on that cross. His prayer has come down these 1,800 years, and its answer is a testimony of His love and forgiveness to the sinner. In the morning he was led out from that prison a blasphemer reviling Christ, and in the evening, he was walking the crystal pavements of heaven. He only asked to be remembered and the answer came, "Today you shall be with Me in Paradise." Thanks be to God; He was not ashamed of the poor thief. The moment the cry came from his lips a welcome was given him.

Now, my friends, why not make the prayer of this thief tonight. If we make it from the heart we can be saved tonight. Thank God, we have communication from the Tabernacle to the throne, and an earnest prayer can go from this building and will be answered. Suppose you make it now, "Lord, remember me." Who cannot say that? Who cannot say from their heart, "Lord, remember me." Make it a personal prayer. It is a very short one. Every prayer in the Bible that brought salvation is very short. Peter's prayer was only, "Lord, save me." Someone has said if he had made a long preamble he would have been forty feet under water. It was simply, "Lord, save me." Just say, "Lord, remember me," and He will remember you. Simply do as the thief did, and you will be saved. That is what I call instantaneous conversion.

Now this thief, as I said before, when led out from the prison that morning had no thought of being saved. His heart was not touched by the trial, he did not feel sorry for what he had done. He was hung up on one side of Christ and reviled Him, and the moment he asked Him to be remembered he got His forgiveness. He might have replied, "You miserable thief. You have scoffed at religion all your life; you were reviling me just now. Why should I forgive you?" but instead of that came the answer, "Today you shall be with me in Paradise."

It is said of Whitfield that he once exclaimed, "Why, the Lord is so anxious to save sinners that He is willing to take the devil's castaways." Lady Huntly heard him, and took exception to his utterance. "The idea," she said, "of the Lord being willing to take the devil's castaways." She wouldn't believe him. But shortly after, a poor fallen woman came to him and said, "You told us the other night that the Lord was willing to take the devil's castaways." She admitted her sin and accepted Him. My friends, the Son will save the vilest in Chicago tonight if they will only admit their guilt. I was greatly cheered this afternoon when two men went into the inquiry room, and I got down to pray with them. After I had prayed with them, they did not spring up on their feet as inquirers very often do. One of them cried, "God be merciful to me a sinner; that's all I can say." "That's enough," I said. "That was all the publican could say, and he went down to his house saved because it came from his heart." The other man could only say, "Lord save me," and that is enough. He will save you if you only cry from your heart. Thank God, you can be saved if you will.

I can imagine when they came to take down the body of Christ, and when they came to break the bones of those two thieves. I can imagine Him saying to the officer, "Hurry up, for I will soon be with my Master." Christ went up before him to give him a warm welcome, and that thief rejoices that he will soon be in the kingdom. Whenever he put his trust in Him, he was changed in the twinkling of an eye, because he had got salvation. But let me say here that Christ drew the dividing line while upon that cross. On one side of Him was unbelief, and the unbeliever died reviling Him. On the other side was belief, and the believer went up to Paradise. He believed in a moment, and yet there are men who cannot understand sudden conversion.

There are two classes in Chicago – as they were represented by those two thieves – those for and those against Him. They must either accept Him or reject Him. One of them would not receive salvation and went down to death; the other accepted salvation as a gift and went up to His kingdom. I can imagine him now singing the sweet songs of Moses and the Lamb. No one sings those sweet songs any louder than does that thief. Ask that poor thief who, when down here, was a reveler, who was a blasphemer, and lived at enmity with God, how he came into that world of light? Ask him how he got that scepter in his hand, that crown on his brow, how he was permitted to sing the high hallelujahs of the redeemed, and his voice will come back telling you, "I took salvation as the gift of God."

Ah, my friends, there is salvation for all who will have it, and damnation for those who won't accept the gift. He commanded His disciples to preach the gospel as a gift before He left the earth. "Go into all the world and preach the gospel to every creature; he that believes and is baptized shall be saved, but he that believes not shall be damned." One of those thieves believed and was saved, the other rejected Him and was damned. What will you do? Will you believe and be saved? Will you accept this gift of eternal life or trample the gift under your feet? Will you take His offer tonight or reject it? May God open your eyes too and bring you to Himself on this, the last Sunday in November, one of the sweetest months of my life. May this be the Sabbath night of your salvation, and it will be an evening full of sweetness.

Address to Parents

First Address

I want to call your attention to Deuteronomy 5:29. "O that there were such a heart in them that they would fear Me, and keep all My commandments always, that it might be well with them, and with their children forever." And also the 6th chapter and 7th verse, "And you shall teach them diligently unto your children, and shall talk of them when you sit in your house and when you walk by the way, and when you lie down, and when you rise up." I used to think when I was superintendent on the North Side, when I was laboring among the children and trying to get the parents interested to save their children, that if I ever did become a preacher, I would have but one text and one sermon, and that should be addressed to parents, because when we get them interested, their interest will be apparent in the children.

We used to say, if we get the lambs in, the old sheep will follow, but I didn't find that to be the case. When we got the children interested in one Sunday, the parents would be sometimes pulling the other way all the week, and before Sunday came again the impression that had been made would be gone, and I came to the conclusion that, unless we could get the parents interested, or could get some kind Christian to look after those children, it would almost be a sin to bring them to

Christ. If there is no one to nurse them, to care for them, and just to water the seed, why they are liable to be drawn away, and when they grow up, to be far more difficult to reach.

I wish to say tonight that I am as strong as ever upon sudden conversion, and there are a great many ministers, a great many parents, who scoff and laugh when they hear of children who have been brought unto Christ at these meetings. Now, in many of the churches the sermons go over their heads. They don't do the young any good; they don't understand the preaching. And if they are impressed here we ought not to discourage them. My friends, the best thing we can do is to bring them early to Christ. These earliest impressions never, never leave them, and I do not know why they should not grow up in the service of Christ.

I contend that those who are converted early are the best Christians. Take the man who is converted at fifty. He has continually to fight against his old habits. But take a young man or a young girl and they get a character to form and a whole long life to give to Christ. An old man, unconverted, got up in an inquiry meeting recently, and said he thought we were very hard-hearted down in the Tabernacle; we went right by when we saw some young person. He thought, as he was old, he might be snatched away before these young people; but with us it seemed as if Christ was of more importance to the young than the old. I confess truly that I have that feeling. If a young man is converted, he perhaps has a long life of fifty years to devote to Christ, but an old man is not worth much. Of course, his soul is worth much, but he is not worth much for labor.

While down at a convention in Illinois an old man got up, past seventy years. He said he remembered but one thing about his father, and that one thing followed him all through life. He could not remember his death, he had no recollection of his funeral, but he recollected his father one winter night, taking a little chip, and with his pocketknife whittling out a cross. With the tears in his eyes he held up that cross and told how God in His infinite love sent His Son down here to redeem us, how He had died on the cross for us. The story of the cross followed him through life, and I tell you if you teach these children truths they will follow them through life.

We have got so much unbelief among us, like those disciples when they rebuked the people for bringing the children to Christ, but He said, "Suffer little children to come unto Me, and forbid them not, for of such is the kingdom of heaven."

I heard of a Sunday school concert at which a little child of eight was going to recite. Her mother had taught her, and when the night came the little thing was trembling so she could hardly speak. She commenced, "Jesus said," and completely broke down. Again she tried it, "Jesus said, suffer," but she stopped once more. A third attempt was made by her, "Suffer little children – and don't anybody stop them, for He wants them all to come," and that is the truth. There is not a child who has parents in the Tabernacle but He wants. If you bring them in the arms of your faith and ask the Son of God to bless them and train them in the knowledge of God, and teach them as you walk your way, as you lie down at night, as you rise up in the morning, they will be blessed. But I can imagine some skeptic in yonder gallery saying, "That's well enough, but it's all talk. Why, I have known children of ministers and Christian people who have turned out worse than others." I've heard that all my life, but I tell you that is one of the devil's lies. I will admit I've heard of many Christian people having bad children, but they are not the worst children. That was tested once.

A whole territory was taken in which fathers and mothers were Christians, and it was found that two-thirds of the children were members of churches, but they took a portion of country where all the fathers and mothers were not Christians, and it was found that not one in twelve of the children attended churches. That was the proportion. Look at a good man who has a bad son. Do you want to know the reason? In the first place, children do not inherit grace. Because fathers and mothers are good is no reason why their children should be good. Children are not born good. Men may talk of natural goodness, but I don't find it. Goodness must come down from the Father of Light. To have a good nature a man must be born of God. There is another reason – a father may be a very good man, but the mother may be pulling in another way. She may be ambitious and may want her children to occupy a high worldly position. She has some high ambition and trains the child for the world.

Again, it may be the reverse – a holy, pious mother and a worldly father, and it is pretty hard when father and mother do not pull together. Another reason is, and you will excuse me the expression, but a great many people have got very little sense about bringing up children. Now, I've known mothers punish their children by making them read the Bible. Do not be guilty of such a thing. If you want children not to hate the Bible do not punish them by making them read it. It is the most attractive book in the world. But that is the way to spoil its attractiveness and make them hate it with a perfect hate. There is another reason. A great many people are engaged in looking after other people's children and neglecting their own. No father or mother has a right to do this, whatever may be the position they hold in the world. The father may be a statesman or a great businessman, but he is responsible for his children. If they do not look after their children, they will have to answer for it someday. There will be a blight in their paths, and their last days will be very bitter.

There are a great many reasons which I might bring forward if I had time why good people's children turn out bad. But let me say one word about bringing up these children, how to train them in Christian ways. The word is very plain: "Teach them diligently." In the street cars, as we go about our business night and morning, talk of Christ and heavenly things. It seems to me as if these things were the last things many of us think about and as if Christ was banished from our homes. A great many people have a good name as Christians. They talk about ministers and Sunday schools and will come down and give a dinner to the bootblacks and seem to be strong patrons of the cause of Christ, but when it comes to talking to children personally about Christ, that is another thing. The word is very plain, "Teach them diligently," and if we want them to grow up a blessing to the church of God and to the world, we must teach them. I can imagine some of you saying, "It may be very well for Mr. Moody to lay down theories, but there are a great many difficulties in the way."

I heard of a minister who said he had the grandest theory upon the bringing up of children. God gave him seven children, and he found that his theory was all wrong. They were all differently constituted. I will admit that this is one difficulty, but if our heart is set upon this one thing – to have our children in glory – God will give us all the light we need. He is not going to leave us in darkness. If that is not the aim of your heart, make it this very night. I would rather, if I went tonight, leave my children in the hope of Christ than leave them millions of money. It seems to me as if we were too ambitious to have them make a name, instead of to train them up for the life they are to lead forever.

And another thing about government. Never teach them revenge. If a baby falls down on the floor, don't give it a book with which to strike the floor. They have enough of revenge in them without being taught it. Then don't teach them to lie. You don't like that, but how many parents have told their children to go to the door, when they did not want to see the visitor, and say, "Mother is not in." That is a lie. Children are very keen to detect. They very soon see those lies, and this lays the foundation for a good deal of trouble afterward. "Ah," some of you say, "I never do this." Well, suppose some person comes in that you don't want to see. You give him a welcome, and when he goes, you entreat him to stay, but the moment he is out of the door you say, "What a bore!" The children wonder at first, but they very soon begin to imitate the father and mother. Children are very good imitators. A father and mother never ought to do a thing that they don't want their children to do. If you don't want them to smoke, don't you smoke. If you don't want them to chew, don't you chew. If you don't want them to play billiards, don't you play billiards. If you don't want them to drink, don't you drink, because children are grand imitators.

A lady once told me she was in her pantry on one occasion, and she was surprised by the ringing of the bell. As she whirled round to see who it was, she broke a tumbler. Her little child was standing there, and she thought her mother was doing a correct thing. The moment the lady left the pantry, the child commenced to break all the tumblers she could get hold of. You may laugh, but children are very good imitators. If you don't want them to break the Sabbath day, keep it holy yourself; if you want them to go to church, go to church yourself. It is very often by imitation that they utter their first oath, that they tell their first lie, and then they grow upon them, and when they try to quit the habit, it has grown so strong upon them that they cannot do it. "Ah," some say, "we do not believe in children being converted. Let them grow up to manhood and womanhood and then talk of converting them." They forget that in the meantime their characters are formed, and perhaps have commenced to enter those dens of infamy. When they have arrived at manhood and womanhood, we find it is too late to alter their character.

How unfaithful we are. "Teach them diligently." How many parents in this vast assembly know where their sons are? Their sons may be in the halls of vice. Where does your son spend his evenings? You don't care enough for him to ascertain what kind of company he keeps, what kind of books he reads; don't care whether or not he is reading those miserable, trashy novels and getting false ideas of life. You don't know till it is too late. Oh, may God wake us up and teach us the responsibility devolving upon us in training our children.

While in London, an officer in the Indian army, hearing of us being over there said, "Lord, now is the time for my son to be saved." He got a furlough and left India and came to London. When he came there for that purpose, of course God was not going to let him go away without the blessing. How many men are interested in their sons who would do as this man did. How many men are sufficiently interested in them to bring them here. How many parents stand in the way of the salvation of their children. I don't know anything that discouraged me more when I was superintendent on the North Side than when, after begging with parents to allow their children to come to Sunday school – and how few of them came – whenever spring arrived those parents would take their children from the school and lead them into those German gardens. And how a great many are reaping the consequences.

I remember one mother who heard that her boy was impressed at our meeting. She said her son was a good enough boy, and he didn't need to be converted. I pleaded with that mother, but all my pleading was of no account. I tried my influence with the boy; but while I was pulling one way, she was pulling the other. Her influence prevailed. Naturally it would. Well, to make a long story short, some time after I happened to be in the county jail, and I saw him there. "How did you come here?" I asked. "Does your mother know where you are?" "No, don't tell her. I came in under an assumed name, and I am going to Joliet for four years. Do not let my mother know of this," he pleaded. "She thinks I am in the army."

I used to call on that mother, but I had promised her boy I would not tell her, and for four years she mourned over that boy. She thought he had died on the battlefield or in a southern hospital. What a blessing he might have been to that mother if she had only helped us to bring him to Christ. But that mother is only a specimen of hundreds and thousands of parents in Chicago. If we would have more family altars in our homes and train them to follow Christ, why the Son of God would lead them into "green pastures," and instead of having sons who curse the mothers who gave them birth, they would bless their fathers and mothers.

In the Indiana Penitentiary I was told of a man who had come there under an assumed name. His mother heard where he was. She was too poor to ride there, so she footed it. Upon her arrival at the prison, she at first did not recognize her son in his prison suit and short hair, but when she did see who it was, that mother threw her arms about that boy and said, "I am to blame for this; if I had only taught you to obey God and keep the Sabbath you would not have been here." How many mothers, if they were honest, could attribute the ruination of their children to the early training. God has said if we don't teach them those blessed commandments, He will destroy us, and the law of God never changes. It does not only apply to those callous men who make no profession of religion, but to those who stand high in the church if they make the same mistake.

Look at that high priest Eli. He was a good man and a kind one, but one thing he neglected to do – to train his children for God. The Lord gave him warning, and at last, destruction came upon his house. Look at that old man, 98 years old, with his white hair, like some of the men on the platform, sitting in the town of Shiloh waiting to hear the result of the battle. The people of Israel came into the town and took out the ark of God, and when it came into the camp, a great shout went up to heaven, for they had the ark of their God among them. They thought they were going to succeed, but they had disobeyed God. When the battle came on, they fought manfully, but no less than 30,000 of the Israelites fell by the swords of their enemies, and a messenger came running from the field through the streets of Shiloh to where Eli was, crying, "Israel is defeated, the ark is taken, and Hophni and Phineas have been slain in battle!" and where the old priest, when he heard it, fell backward by the side of the gate, and his neck broke and he died. Oh, what a sad ending to that man, and when his daughter-in-law heard the news, there was another death in that family recorded. In that house, destruction was complete.

My friends, God is true, and if we do not obey Him in this respect, He will punish us. It is only a question of time. Look at King David. See him waiting for the tidings of the battle. He had been driven from his throne by his own son, whom he loved, but when the news came that he was slain, see how he cried, "Oh, my son Absalom, would to God I had died for thee!" It was worse than death to him, but God had to punish him because he did not train his son to love the Lord. My friends, if He punished Eli and David, He will punish you and me. May God forgive us for the past, and may we commence a new record tonight. My friends, if you have not a family altar, erect one tonight. Let us labor that our children may be brought to glory. Don't say children are too young. Mothers and fathers, if you hear your children have been impressed with religion, don't stand in the way of their conversion, but encourage them all you can.

While I was attending a meeting in a certain city some time ago, a lady came to me and said, "I want you to go home with me; I have something to say to you." When we reached her home, there were some friends there. After they had retired, she put her arms on the table and tears began to come into her eyes, but with an effort she repressed her emotion. After a struggle she went on to say that she was going to tell me something which she had never told any other living person. I should not tell it now, but she has gone to another world. She said she had a son in Chicago, and she was very anxious about him. When he was young, he got interested in religion at the rooms of the Young Men's Christian Association. He used to go out in the street and circulate tracts. He was her only son, and she was very ambitious he should make a name in the world and wanted to get him into the very highest circles. Oh, what a mistake people make about these highest circles.

Society is false; it is a sham. She was deceived like a good many more votaries of fashion and hunters after wealth at the present time. She thought it was beneath her son to go down and associate with those young men who hadn't much money. She tried to get him away from them, but they had more influence than she had, and finally, to break his whole association, she packed him off to a boarding school. He went soon to Yale College, and she supposed he got into one of those miserable secret societies there that have ruined so many young men, and the next thing she heard was that the boy had gone astray.

She began to write letters urging him to come into the kingdom of God, but she heard that he tore the letters up without reading them. She went to him to try and regain whatever influence she possessed over him, but her efforts were useless, and she came home with a broken heart. He left New Haven, and for two years they heard nothing of him. At last, they heard he was in Chicago, and his father found him and gave him thirty thousand dollars to start in business. They thought it would change him, but it didn't. They asked me when I went back to Chicago to try and use my influence with him. I got a friend to invite him to his house one night, where I intended to meet him, but he heard I was to be there and did not come near. Like a good many other young men who seem to be afraid of me, I tried many times to reach him but could not.

While I was traveling one day on the New Haven Railroad, I bought a New York paper, and in it I saw a dispatch saying he had been drowned in Lake Michigan. His father came on to find his body, and after considerable searching, he discovered it. All the clothes and his body were covered with sand. The body was taken home to that broken-hearted mother. She said, "If I thought he was in heaven, I would have peace." Her disobedience of God's law came back upon her. So, my friends, if you have a boy impressed with the gospel, help him to come to Christ. Bring him in the arms of your faith, and He will unite you closer to Him. Let us have faith in Him and let us pray day and night that our children may be born of the Spirit. Let us pray.

Address to Young Men

First Address

I want to call your attention tonight to a text which you will find in the 18th chapter of First Kings, 21st verse: *"And Elijah came unto all the people, and said, 'How long will you waver between two opinions? if the Lord be God follow Him, but if Baal then follow him.' And the people answered him not a word."* We find in this portion of the Word of God that Elijah was calling the people of Israel back, or he was calling them to a decision as to whether they were for God or Baal, and a great many were wavering, just halting between two opinions, like the people of Chicago at the present time. During the last eight weeks a great deal has been said upon the subject of religion. Men have talked about it all over the city. A great many are talking, a great many are taking their stand for, and a great many against Him. Now, what will you do tonight? I will just divide this audience into two portions – one against and one for Him.

It seems to me a practical question to ask an audience like this, "How long will you waver between two opinions? If the Lord be God follow Him, but if Baal, then follow him." A man who is undecided about any question of any magnitude never has any comfort; never has any peace. Not only that, but we don't like a man who cannot decide upon a question. I like men of decision, and firmly believe that more men are lost by indecision than by anything else. It is a question whether I am not talking to many men tonight who intend some day to settle this question. Probably everyone here intends to make heaven his home, but Satan is trying to get you to put off the settlement of the question till it will be too late. If he can only get men to put off till the tomorrow, which never comes, he has accomplished all he wants. How many in this audience have promised some friend years ago that they would settle this question? Maybe you said you would do it when you came of age. That time has gone with some of you, and it has not been settled yet. Some have reached thirty, some forty, and others have reached fifty years; their eyes are growing dim, and they are hastening toward eternity, and this is not settled with them yet.

Some of you have promised dying brothers that you would meet them in that world, some have promised dying wives that you would see them in that land of light, and again, others have given their word to dying children that you would meet them in heaven. Years have rolled away, and still you have not decided. You have kept putting it off week by week and year by year. My friends, why not decide tonight? "How long will you waver between two opinions?" If the Lord be God serve Him; if not, turn your back upon Him. It seems to me a question every man can settle if he will.

You like those grand old characters in the Bible who have made a decisive stand. Look at Moses! The turning point in his life was when he decided to give up the gilded court of Pharaoh and cast his lot with God's people. You will find that every man who has left a record in the Bible has been a man of decision. What made Daniel so great? It was because he was a man of decision. What saved the prodigal? It was not that he got into his father's arms, it was not his coming home. The turning point was when he decided the question: "I will arise and go to my father." It was the decision of the young man that saved him.

Many a man has been lost because of indecision. Look at Felix, look at Agrippa. Felix said, "Go your way for this time; when I have a convenient season, I will call for you." See what Agrippa said, "Almost you persuade me to be a Christian." Look at Pilate – all lost; lost because of his indecision. His mind was thoroughly convinced that Jesus was the true Christ. He said, "I find no fault in Him," but he hadn't the courage to take his stand for Him. Thousands have gone down to the caverns of death for want of courage.

My friends, let us look this question in the face. If there is anything at all in the religion of Christ, give everything for it. If there is nothing in it – if it is a myth, if our mothers who have prayed over us have been deceived, if the praying people of the last 1,800 years have been deluded, let us find it out. The quicker the better. If there is nothing in the religion of Christ, let us throw it over, and eat, drink, and be merry for time will soon be gone. If there is no devil to deceive us, no hell to receive us; if Christianity is a sham, let us come out like men and say so. I hope to live to see the time when there will only be two classes in this world – Christians and infidels – those who take their stand bravely for Him, and those who take their stand against Him. This idea of men standing still and saying, "Well, I don't know, but I think there must be something in it," is absurd. If there is anything in it there is everything in it. If the Bible of our mothers is not true, let us burn it. Is there one in this audience willing to say and do this? If it is a myth, why spend so much money in publishing it? Why send out millions of Bibles to the nations of the earth? Let us destroy it if it is false and all those institutions giving the gospel to the world. What is the use of all this waste of money? Are we mad, are we lunatics who have been deluded? Let us burn the book and send up a shout over its ashes. "There is no God. There is no hell. There is no heaven. There is no hereafter. When men die, they die like dogs in the street!" But my friends, if it is true – if heaven, if a hereafter in the Bible is true, let us come out boldly, like men, for Christ.

Let us take our stand and not be ashamed of the gospel of Jesus Christ. Why, it seems to me a question that ought to be settled in this nineteenth century easy enough, whether you are for or against Him or not. Why, if Baal be God, follow him, but if the Lord be God follow Him. If there is no truth in the religion of Jesus Christ, you may as well tear down all your churches, destroy your hospitals, your blind asylums. It's a waste of money to build them. Baalites don't build blind asylums, don't build hospitals, or orphan asylums. If there hadn't been any Christians in the world, there would have been no charitable institutions. If it hadn't been for Christianity, you would have had no praying mothers. Is it true that their prayers have exercised a pernicious influence? Is it true that a boy who had a praying father and mother, or a good teacher, is no better off than a boy who has been brought up amid blasphemy and infamy? Is it true? It must be either one way or the other. Did bad men write that Bible? Certainly not, or they wouldn't have consigned themselves to eternal perdition.

The very fact that the Bible has lived and grown during these 1,800 years is a strong proof that it came from God. Men have tried to put it out of the world; they have tried to burn it out of the world, but they have failed. It has come down to us – down these 1,800 years amid persecution, and now we are in a land where it is open to all, and no man need be without one. What put it into the minds of those men to give money liberally to print and circulate this book? Bad men wouldn't do this. This is a question that, it seems to me, couldn't be decided tonight. If it is not good, then take your stand. If the Lord be God, follow Him, but if God be Baal, then follow Him. Someone asked Alexander how he conquered the world, and he replied that he conquered it by not delaying. If you want to conquer the devil you must not delay – accept eternal life as a gift tonight.

Let us take the surroundings of this text. We are told that Elijah stood before Ahab and told him because of the evil deeds of Israel and the king, there would no rain come upon the land for three years and a half. After that, Elijah went to the brook Cherith, where he was fed by the ravens, after which he went to Zarephath, and there dwelt with a poor widow for months and months. Three years and a half rolled away, and not one drop of rain or dew had come from heaven. Probably when Elijah told the king there would be no rain, he laughed at him. The idea that he should have the key of heaven! He scouted the very idea at first. But after a little it became a very serious matter. The brooks began to dry up, and the cattle could not get water. The crops failed the first year, the next year they were worse, the third year they were even a worse failure, and the people began to flee out of his kingdom to get food, yet they did not call upon Elijah's God. They had four hundred and fifty prophets of Baal and four hundred prophets of the groves, and yet all their prayers did not bring rain.

Why did they ask God for rain? Baal was not an answerer of prayer. The devil never answers prayer. If prayer has ever been answered, it has been answered by the God of our fathers, by the God of our mothers. After Elijah had been gone three and a half years he returns and meets Obadiah, the governor of the king's house, and Ahab says, "You go down that way, and I'll go down this way and see if we can't discover water." They hadn't been separated long when Obadiah meets Elijah and asks him to come to the king. The prophet tells him to go and say to Ahab, "Elijah is here." But Obadiah doesn't want to leave him. "If I lose sight of you this time, when the king knows you have stepped through my lands, it may cost me my life. Don't you know I've been a servant of the true God all the time, and I've had a hundred of the prophets of the Lord in a cave. If you don't come, I will lose my life."

Elijah tells him to go and bring Ahab, and instead of Elijah going to Ahab, Ahab comes to him. When the king comes, he say,: "Are you he that troubles Israel?" That is the way with men. They bring down the wrath of God upon themselves, and then blame God's people. A great many people are blaming God for these hard times. Look on the millions and millions of dollars spent for whiskey. Why, it is about time for famine to strike the land. If men had millions of dollars, it wouldn't be long before all the manhood would be struck out of them. Now, the people of Israel had gone over to Baal, they had forgotten the God that brought them out of Egypt – the God of Jacob and Abraham and of their fathers. "Now," says Elijah, "let's have this settled. Let some of your people make an offering to their god on Mount Carmel, and I will make an offering to my God, and the God that answers by fire will be the God."

The king agrees, and the day arrives. You can see a great stir among the people that day. They are moving up to Mount Carmel. By and by Ahab comes up in his royal carriage, and those four hundred and fifty prophets of Baal and four hundred prophets of the groves made a great impression. Dressed in priestly robes, they moved solemnly up that mountain. The king has swept along in his chariot, and perhaps, passed by the poor priest Elijah, who comes slowly up, leaning upon his staff, his long white hair streaming about his shoulders. People don't believe in sensations. That was one of the greatest sensations of their age. What is going to happen? No doubt the whole nation had been talking about this Elijah, and when he came to that mountain, the crowd looked upon him as the man who held the key of heaven.

When he came up, he addressed the children of Israel. Perhaps there were hundreds of thousands. "How long will you waver between two opinions? If the Lord be God follow him, but if he be Baal then follow him; and the people answered not a word." Their eight hundred and fifty prophets had made a great impression upon them, and the king was afraid too. These people are just like a great many people now. They are afraid to go into the inquiry room because of what people will say. If they do go in, they get behind a post, so that they can't be seen. They are afraid the people in the store will find it out and make fun of them. Moral courage is wanted by them, as it was wanted by those people. How many among us have not the moral courage to come out for the God of their mothers! They know these black-hearted hypocrites around them are not to be believed. They know these men who scoff at their religion are not their friends, while their mothers will do everything for them.

The truest friends we can have are those who believe in Christ. "And the people answered not a word. Then said Elijah unto the people, 'I, even I only, remain a prophet of the Lord; but Baal's prophets are four hundred and fifty men. Let them, therefore, give us two bullocks; and let them choose one bullock for themselves, and cut it in pieces, and lay it on wood, and put no fire under; and I will dress the other bullock, and lay it on wood, and put no fire under it. And you call on the name of your gods, and I will call on the name of the Lord, and the God that answers by fire let him be God.' And all the people answered and said, 'It is well spoken.'" "Yes, sir, that's right. We'll stand by that decision." They built an altar and laid their bullock on it, and began to cry to Baal, "O Baal! O Baal! Baal! Baal!" No answer.

They cried louder and louder, but no answer came. They prayed from morning till noon, but not a sound. Elijah said, "Louder; you must pray louder. He must be on a journey; he must be asleep. He must be on a journey or asleep." They cried louder and louder. Some people say it doesn't matter what a man believes, so long as he is earnest. These men were terribly in earnest. No Methodists shout as they did. They cried as loud as their voices will let them, but no answer. They took their knives and cut themselves in their earnestness. Look at those four hundred and fifty prophets of Baal and four hundred prophets of the grove, all covered with blood, as they cry out in their agony. They have no God. Young man, who is your master? Whom do you serve? If you are serving Baal, I tell you if ever you get into trouble, he will not answer you. No answer came.

Three o'clock came, the hour for the evening sacrifice, and Elijah prepared his altar. He would have nothing to do with the altar of Baal. He merely took twelve stones, representing the twelve tribes of Israel, and built his altar and laid his bullock on. No doubt some skeptic said he had some fire concealed in his garment, for he dug a trench all around it to hold water. Then he told them to bring four barrels of water and emptied them over his sacrifice. Four more barrels were brought and thrown on the bullock, making eight, and then four barrels more are added, making twelve in all. Then, there lies that bullock, dripping with water, and Elijah comes forward. Every ear and eye is open. Those bleeding Baalites look at him. What is going to be the end of it? He comes forward, calm as a summer evening. He prays to the God of Isaac and Abraham – when, behold, look! Look! Down it comes – fire from the very throne of God and consumes the wood and the stones and the sacrifice, and the people cry, "The Lord is the God!" The question is decided. The God that answers by fire is the God of man. My friends, who is your God now? The God who answers prayer? Or have you no God?

I can imagine some of you saying, "If I had been on Mount Carmel and seen that, I would have believed it." But I will tell you of a mount on which occurred another scene. That was a wonderful scene, but it does not compare with the scene on Calvary. Look there! God's own beloved Son hanging between two thieves and crying, "Father, forgive them, for they know not what they do." Talk about wonderful things. This has been the wonder of ages. A man once gave me a book of wonderful things. I saw a good many wonders in it, but I did not see anything so wonderful in it as the story of the cross. My friends, see his expiring look. See what happened.

The very rocks were rent, the walls of the temple were rent, and all nature owned its God. The sun veiled its face and darkness fell over the earth when the Son of Man expired on Mount Calvary. Where can you find a more wonderful sight than this? Those Israelites lived on the other side of the cross; we live on this side of it. If a man wants proof of His gospel look around this assembly. See men who thirty days ago were slaves, bound hand and foot to some hellish passion which was drawing them to hell. What a transformation there is. All things seem changed to them. They have got a new nature. "Is not this the power of God?" said a young convert to me today. "It seems as if we were living in the days of miracles, and the Son of God is coming down and giving men complete victory over lusts and passions." That is what the Son of God does for men, and yet, with all the proofs before their eyes, men are undecided.

What it is that keeps you from your decision? I wish I had time to tell you many of the reasons. Hundreds of thousands of men are thoroughly convinced, but they lack moral courage to come out and confess their sins. Others are being led captive by some sin. They have got some darling sin, and as long as they hold on to it, there is no hope. A man the other day said he would like to become a Christian, but he had a bet upon the election, and he wanted that settled first. He did not think that he might die before that was decided. Eternity is drawing on. Suppose we die without God, without hope, without everlasting life; it seems to me it would have been better never to have been born. My friends, I ask you tonight, why not come out like men? Say, "Cost what it will, I will accept Jesus tonight." Now, have moral courage. Come. How many of you are thoroughly convinced in your minds that you ought to be Christians tonight? Now just ask yourselves the question, "What hinders me, what stands in my way?"

I can imagine some of you looking behind you to see how the one sitting there looks. If he seems serious, you look serious; if he laughs, you will laugh, and come to the conclusion that you'll not accept Him tonight. You think of your companions, and you say you cannot stand their jeers. Is not that so? Come. Trample the world under your feet and take the Lord tonight, cost what it will. Say, "By the grace of God I will serve Him from this hour." Turn your backs upon hell, and set your faces toward heaven, and it will be the best night of your lives. Have you ever seen a man who accepted Christ regret it? You cannot find a man who has changed masters and gone over to Christ who has regretted it. This is one of the strongest proofs of Christianity. Those who have never followed Him only regret it.

I have seen hundreds dying when in the army and when a missionary, and I never saw a man who died conscious but who regretted that he had not lived a Christian life. My friends, if you accept Him tonight it will be the best hour of your life. Let this night be the best night of your lives. Let me bring this to your mind, if you are lost it will be because you do not decide. "How long will you waver between two opinions; If the Lord be God, follow Him, but, if Baal, then follow him." How many men in this assembly want to be on the Lord's side? Those who want to take their stand on the side of the true God rise.

Upon this request by Mr. Moody, nearly 2,000 men instantly arose.

Praise

I want to take for my subject tonight "praise." We spoke at the noonday meeting upon the subject of "thanksgiving." Now, praise is a step in advance of thanksgiving. If you receive blessings from a man you may thank him, yet you may not praise him. Now, praise is not only speaking to the Lord on our own account, but it is praising Him for what He has done for others. We have had a great many prayers going up in this Tabernacle during the past eight weeks for others, and hundreds – I may say thousands – of them have been answered. We should give praise for this. We have in our churches a great deal of prayer, but I think it would be a good thing if we had a praise meeting occasionally. If we could only get people to praise God for what He has done it would be a good deal better than asking Him continually for something.

We like to have our children ask us for things, but if they keep on asking without ever giving thanks, we become discouraged. Bear this in mind: God expects us to praise Him for what He has done, and if our heart is full of gratitude, and we will praise the Lord, He will do a great deal more for us. And I want to say here a church full of praise is what the Lord wants now. A cold church – a church that is full of formalism – will never be full of praise, but a church that is full of joy, full of gladness, is praising God all the time. "Restore unto me the joy of Your salvation, and uphold me with Your free spirit, then I will teach transgressors Your ways." It seems to me that if we had that text all over Christendom at the present time, the ministers holding it up to the people till the church is filled with peace, till it is filled with rest, till it is filled with gladness, with promise – it seems to me that we would then see a revival as lasting as eternity itself. Now, as I said one night here before, the world is after the best thing. If a man wants to buy a horse, he goes where he can get the best horse for his money.

If a woman wants to get a dress, she'll hunt till she gets the very best she can. Why, I have heard of a woman going for half a day from store to store to get the best piece of ribbon she could. It's a universal law – the world wants to get the very best thing it can. Now, if we can show the world that the religion of Jesus Christ is the best thing in it, the world will take it, but if we are despondent or cast down, look gloomy, are not full of praise, if we are not full of joy, the world will not want it. We will only drive men out of the kingdom of God. If we have a church full of praise, we will have people converted. I don't care where it is, what part of the world it's in, if we have a church full of praise we'll have successful Christianity.

A young man went down to a church in the East, the pastor of which had become an old man. The people got asleep. The new man came and tried to rouse them, but it was no use. He preached and preached and tried to get them aroused and go into the prayer meetings, but he could not. One night he said, "Tonight we'll have no prayer meeting." They wondered what it meant, the idea that this young minister should do away with this prayer meeting which they had had for fifty years. They were astonished. "But" said he, "we will have a praise meeting." At the close of the meeting one elder came to another one, "What's he going to give up the prayer meeting for? Has he consulted you about it?" "No." "Well," replied the former, "that's a very serious matter. What is the meaning of a praise meeting?" They had been going along without any praise meeting, and they did not know what a praise meeting meant. They went to ask him, but he wouldn't tell them but said to wait till Friday night, and then they would see.

They began to talk about it, and out of curiosity a great many came to see what it was. The young minister read some of those good old psalms. "Now," said he "if you can think of anything in your past life that you have received from God, praise God for it. You have been asking God for everything, and it chills the church through. Now if you can think of any benefits you have received, praise God for them." They began to think, and they found they had a good many things to praise God for. One man got up and praised God for a praying mother who had led him to Christ. Another man got up and praised God for the Bible. Another praised God for this and that, and the result was that when the meeting was over, instead of getting up and walking out, they stopped and shook hands with one another and spoke to one another and said, "I believe we are going to have a revival."

My friends, if we don't thank God for what He has done for us, and be full of joy and gladness, the world will not come to Christ. Would to God that we had churches filled with praise all over Christendom. Let Christ's name be in the churches. Let them praise Him for what He has done, and the world will come. Let the world know that this is the name in which we trust, that this is the name we speak well of. When His disciples begin to do this, then the world will realize the goodness of His gospel. Thank God, the people of Chicago begin to talk about Christ,and if we can get men to talk about Christ in the steam cars, in the places of business, in the horse cars, in the streets – if we can get them to talk about Christ and His loveliness, it won't be long before thousands are converted in a day. May God awaken the Christians to praise Him for what He has done. Did you ever stop to think that the heart of man is the only thing that does not praise the Lord?

The heavens declare His glory; the sun praises Him; the moon and stars praise Him. As the rain falls from heaven it praises God. All nature praises God. The very dumb creatures give Him praise, and it is only the heart of man that won't praise Him. Oh, how deceitful is the heart of man. He who gets the most temporal blessings is the man that praises God least. A man may be thankful for those blessings, yet he does not praise Him. In fact, I don't believe that any man can praise God till he is born of God. You may be thankful for His blessings but praising Him is another thing; praise is the occupation of heaven. Those people who do not praise God here, I don't know what they will do when they get into heaven. They will be strangely out of place there, because that is the occupation of heaven. The redeemed praise Him all the time.

There was a little boy converted, and he was full of praise. When God converts man or boy his heart is full of joy – he can't help praising. His father was a professed Christian. The boy wondered why he didn't talk about Christ and didn't go down to the special meetings. One day, as the father was reading the papers, the boy came to him and put his hand on his shoulder and said, "Why don't you praise God? Why don't you sing about Christ? Why don't you go down to these meetings that are being held?" The father opened his eyes and looked at him and said gruffly, "I am not carried away with any of those doctrines, I am established."

A few days after, they were out getting a load of wood. They put it on the cart. The father and the boy got on top of the load and tried to get the horse to go. They used the whip, but the horse wouldn't move. They got off and tried to roll the wagon along, but they could neither move wagon or horse. "I wonder what's the matter?" said the father. "He's established," replied the boy. You may laugh at that, but this is the way with a good many Christians. The reason is that they are not born of God, or else they have got so far away that they don't exactly know where they are. Now, if we are really born of God, if our heart is really filled with the Spirit of God, we cannot help praising Him. I pity the Christian that has no praise in his heart. You are living a life of formalism – you are living on doctrines. You haven't got Christ in your soul if you don't praise Him. Now, that ought to be the text. Ask yourself, have you praised God on this peaceful day of thanksgiving? You say, "Oh, yes, I've thanked Him." But have you spoken well of Christ? Have you spoken well of what He has done? Have you sung, "Hallelujah! Hallelujah!" for these six months or a year, for this is what they sing in Heaven.

If a man is born of God, he can't help praising God. Fill this building with young converts and see how they will sing, "Oh! happy day, happy day, When Jesus washed my sins away." They cannot hear such songs without praising God. The first impulse of a young convert is to praise, and if he doesn't feel like praising the God who saved him, it is a true sign that he hasn't been converted by the grace of God; he has been born to some creed or profession, some man or some church, and not to the loving Son of God, because when Christ comes into the heart, He brings joy. Now, take a servant of the devil, he doesn't praise. Fill this building full of unregenerate men and try to get them to sing praises. You can't do it; their mouths are sealed. There is no praise in their heart. But you get this building filled with men with the Lord Jesus Christ in their hearts, they cannot help praising Him. How can a man, whose master is the devil, praise him? Have you ever heard a man rejoice in his service? I never heard one.

Now a great many of you say, "It is all very well for him to stand up there and talk about praise. If I was in a comfortable condition, good health, and everything I wanted, like a good many others I see, I would praise God." It is circumstances with a good many, but I have found people who were poor in this world's goods, in bad health, and yet continually praising God. I can take you to a poor burdened one, who has not been off her bed for ten years, and yet she praises Him more than hundreds of thousands of Christians. Her chamber seems to be just the anteroom of heaven. It seems as if that woman had just all the secrets of heaven. Her soul is full of the love of God, full of gladness, and she is poor. Like Elijah at the brook of Cherith, she is just fed by the Almighty; God provides for all her wants.

Any man who knows God can trust Him and praise Him. He knows that the Word of God is true, for he knows that He will care for him. He who cares for the lilies of the field, He, without whose knowledge not a sparrow can fall to the ground, He who knows every hair of our heads. Any man who knows this, cannot he rejoice? Is there anyone here, who, although he is poor, can find no reason to praise God? Some of those Christians who are so poor, but who have the love of God, would not give up their place for that of princes. Now my experience is that a man who lives nearest to God praises Him most, whether he is rich or poor. The nearer he gets to heaven, the more he praises Him.

The man who is furthest from God praises Him least. Now, if there is any Christian here who cannot praise God, there is something between him and God. Take my advice and have it removed before you go to bed tonight. What the world wants is joyful Christianity, and if we have not that, we are not going to see a saved world. A backslider cannot see God. Fill this building with backsliders and see if they will sing praises. That prodigal off there in that foreign land would sing strangely, "Rock of ages, cleft for me." Men astray from God cannot praise. Do you think that Peter when he had denied Christ, could sing a song of praise to Him? The moment a man turns his back on God there is no praise.

I think that is the reason there are so many quartet choirs in the churches. The people cannot sing themselves, and they have to hire people to sing for them, give them $4,000 or $5,000 per year to sing the songs of praises. Look at a church filled with the children of God. The moment a minister gives out the song, their hearts burst with praise; they don't want anybody to sing for them. If they can't sing with their mouths, songs will bubble out of their hearts, but when a man is backslidden he wants artistic sounds, wants fine music to touch his ears, doesn't want it to affect his heart.

Now, Israel could not sing there in Egypt when they were making bricks with straw; they could not sing with the crack of the slave driver's whip in their ears, but when they got through the Red Sea, they struck up the song of redemption, and when a man is redeemed by the precious blood of Jesus Christ, he cannot help praising God. Do you know, I believe the devil is very wise in this? He doesn't want a singing church. He doesn't want a church full of praise. If we have a church full of praise, a singing church, he knows there will be a good many joining us. He knows that is the native air of heaven, and the moment a child is born in heaven, he catches the enthusiasm. I am told that once during a campaign, the general of an army forbade the playing of the soldiers' native airs, because it made them so homesick and despondent that they could not fight. So when we hear the songs of Zion we are weaned from this world and want to go home. We feel that we are pilgrims and strangers here and we have a better world yonder.

Now, how is it that the church does not praise God more? I tell you I think it is very plain. The trouble is we have got settled down and gone to sleep. I never heard of a bird that sung in its nest; I don't believe that any man ever did, and when a church gets settled down it goes to sleep. It is when the bird is on the wing that it sings; and so it is when the church is up, it sings songs of praise. And it can sing in the dark; a nightingale can sing in the dark. Paul and Silas in the darkness of that Philippian jail sung songs of praise. When they put them into that jail, Almighty God was with them. You know when Joseph went down to

Egypt how God was with him. When they put him in prison, they had to lock God Almighty up with him, and Joseph sung songs of praise.

But, my friends, if we are down in Egypt and have turned our backs on God and been taken captive, we are dumb. It is only when we have been true to God that we can sing in the darkness. Now, I am told that an English lark never sings when coming down; only when mounting up. That may be true or not, but when a church is coming down, it is not a church full of praise. When mounting up, and it knows it is coming nearer and nearer to God, it is full of praise. It cannot help it. When the lark is mounting up, up, up, when it is nearly out of sight so that you can scarcely see it, it sings sweetest. And so when the Christian is rising up near to Christ, so that you cannot see him, he gives out the sweetest notes of praise from his heart.

Now, I can imagine some of you saying. "I have got a good many things going against me: I've got a good many reasons for not praising God." I find there is no reason in the world why you should not praise God. If we have troubles, if we have sorrows or afflictions, we have brought them upon ourselves. They are only to wean us to God. Every good gift that we have had from the cradle up has come from God. If a man just stops to think what he has to praise God for, he will find there is enough to keep him singing praises for a week. As the flakes of snow come down from the heavens, He showers His blessings upon us, and if we praise Him for them, He will bless us more abundantly.

Now, there are people always praising. If you are sick it is like good medicine to see them. Then there are other people always looking on the dark side. There was a man converted here some years ago, and he was just full of praise. He was living in the light all the time. We might be in the darkness, but he was always in the light. He used to preface everything he said in the meeting with, "Praise God." One night he came to the meeting with his finger all bound up. He had cut it and cut it pretty bad, too. Well, I wondered how he would praise God for this; but he got up and said, "I have cut my finger, but praise God, I didn't cut it off." And so, if things go against you, just think they might be a good deal worse.

A soldier who came from the war always used to say he could tell when a Christian addressed a soldier. One man would say, "You lost your leg. Where did you lose it?" "In the army." "What a pity you ever went into the war," he would reply. "I feel sorry for you." Another would come along. "You've lost an arm; have you been in the army?" "Yes." "Well, that is a pity; but, bless God, you didn't lose the other arm." There was a man on the North Side, and I never came out of his house without praising God. He was deaf, dumb, blind, and had the lockjaw. He had a hole in his tooth, and all the food he took was put through that hole. My friend, do you ever thank God for your senses? Do you ever thank God for your eyes, by which you can read His Word?

Think of the three million people in this world who haven't any sight at all. Hundreds of thousands of them never saw the mother that gave them birth; never saw their own offspring; never saw nature in all its glory; never saw that beautiful sun and all the stars. Do you ever praise God for the ears by which you can hear the voice of man, by which you hear the gospel preached, by which you hear the songs of Zion? Did you ever praise Him for your hearing and for your reason? Go down to yonder madhouse. I never come out of it without feeling full of praise to God. There you will find fathers and mothers and children without the light of reason. Now, my friends, let us praise God we have a home in this gospel land. Let us praise God for this blessed Bible. Let us praise God for the gift of His only Son. Let us praise Him that He gave up that Son freely for us all. Let us praise Him tonight for the love of His Son and let us go out of this building with our hearts full of joy.

Weighed in the Balance

You will find my text tonight in one short word, "Tekel," meaning: "You are weighed in the balance and are found wanting." In the 5th chapter of Daniel we read the history of King Belshazzar. It is very short. Only one chapter tells us all we know about him. One short sight of his career is all we see. He just seems to burst upon the stage and then disappears. We are told that he gave a great feast, and at this feast he had one thousand of his lords, and they were drinking and praising the gods of silver, of gold, of brass, of iron, and of wood out of the vessels which had been brought from the temple at Jerusalem. As they were drinking out of these vessels of gold and silver from the house of God – I don't know but what it was at the midnight hour, all at once came forth the fingers of a man's hand and began to write upon the wall of the hall. The king turns deathly pale, his knees shake together, and he trembles from head to foot. Perhaps if someone had told him the time was coming when he would be put into the balance and weighed, he would have laughed at him. But he knows the vital hour has come, and that hand has written his doom in the words, "Mene, mene, tekel, upharsin." He calls the wise men of his kingdom, and the man who can interpret this will be made the third ruler of his kingdom, be clothed in scarlet, and have a chain about his neck. One after another tried, but no uncircumcised eye could make it out. He was greatly troubled. At last, one was spoken of who had been able to interpret the dream of his father Nebuchadnezzar. He was told if he would send for Daniel he might interpret the writing. And now the prophet came in and looked upon the handwriting and told him how his father had gone against God, and how he, Belshazzar, had gone against the Lord of Heaven, and how his reign was finished. And this was the writing: "Mene: God has numbered your kingdom and finished it. Tekel: You are weighed in the balance and are found wanting. Peres: Your kingdom is divided and given to the Medes and Persians." The trial is over, the verdict is rendered, and the sentence brought out. That very night the king was hurled from his throne. That very night the army of Darius came tearing down the streets, and you might have heard the clash of arms, shouts of war, and have seen the king's blood mingling with the wine in that banquet hall.

Now I want to call your attention to that word "tekel." We are weighed in the balance. Now you cavil at the Word of God; you make light when all is going well in the hour of your prosperity. But when the time of trial comes, and we are called into judgment, it will be altogether different. Suppose the sentence should come down from heaven upon every man and woman in this Tabernacle to be weighed in the balance tonight, how would it be with you? Come, my friends, are you ready to be weighed tonight? Not in our own scales, but in God's balance. Suppose the scales were dropped now from the kingdom of God; are you ready to step into the balance and be weighed. Are you willing to be weighed by the law? I can imagine some of you saying, "I wouldn't be weighed by that law (meaning the decalogue); I don't believe it." Some men think we are away beyond the Mosaic law; we have got out of it. Why, Christ said in the 5th chapter of Matthew, "Think not that I am come to destroy the law, or the prophets; I am not come to destroy but to fulfil. Heaven and earth may pass away, but my law shall never pass away." But not until heaven and earth shall be removed will the Word of God be removed. Now the commandments that I read to you tonight are as binding as ever they have been. Many men say that we have no need of the commandments, only the sermon on the mount. "Think not that I am come to destroy the law or the prophets; I am not come to destroy but to fulfil." Now, my friends, are you ready to be weighed by the law of God – by that magic law? What is the first commandment?

"You shall have no other Gods but me." Are you ready to be weighed by this commandment? Now, the question is, have you fulfilled, or are you ready to fulfil, all the requirements of this law? A great many people say if they keep the commandments, they don't need Christ. But have you kept them? I will admit if you keep the commandments you can be saved by them, but is there a man in this audience who can truly say that he has done this? Young lady, can you say, "I am ready to be weighed by the law tonight?" Can you, young man? Now, suppose we have these commandments written upon pieces of iron. You know when you go into a grocery store you see them taking a weight and putting it into the scales against what you have bought. Now, suppose the pieces of iron as weights and the law of God written on them. Take this first commandment, "You shall have no other God but me" upon one of the weights. Put it in one of the scales and just step on the other. "You are weighed in the balance." Is your heart set upon God tonight? Have you no other idol? Do you love Him above father or mother, the wife of your bosom, your children, home or land, wealth or pleasure? Have you got another god before Him? If you have, surely you are not ready to step in and be weighed against that commandment, "You shall have no other God before me." That is the commandment of God, and it is binding tonight. Then take another. You will say there is no trouble about this one. We might go off to other ages or other lands, and we can find people who worship idols, but we have none here. But how many idols have we in our hearts? Many a man says, "Give me money and I will give you heaven; what care I for all the glories and treasures of heaven; give me treasures here. I don't care for heaven. I want to be a successful businessman." They make money and business their god. Although they don't make gods of silver and gold, they bow before them. There are more men who worship silver and gold in Chicago than any other god. But take another one: "You shall not take the name of the Lord your God in vain." Is there a swearing man ready to put the weight into the scales and step in? Young man, have you been taking the name of the Lord in vain today? What does He say? "The Lord will not hold him guiltless that takes His name in vain." I don't believe men would ever have been guilty of swearing unless God had told them not to. They don't swear by their friends, by their fathers and mothers, by their wives, by their children. But because God has forbidden it, man wants to show how he despises His law. "You shall not take the name of the Lord your God in vain." Blasphemer, go into the scales, and see how quick you will fly out. You will be like a feather in the balance. A great many men think there is nothing very serious in swearing; they don't think there's much wrong in it. Bear in mind that He sees something in it when He says, "You shall not take the name of the Lord your God in vain." You cannot trifle with God. Some men say they never swear except when they get angry. Suppose you swear only once in six months, or a year – suppose you swear once in ten years, do you think God will hold you guiltless for that one act? A man that swears once shows that his heart is rebellious to God. What are you going to do, blasphemer? If the balances were here tonight, and God told you to step in, what would you do?

But take the fourth commandment: "Remember the Sabbath day to keep it holy." Suppose you could see the law written over those walls, "Remember to keep the Sabbath day to keep it holy," could you say that you had observed it? Are you ready to be weighed by the weight, "Remember the Sabbath day to keep it holy?" Some of us may be professed Christians, but do we observe the Sabbath? If this country falls into neglect of the observance of the Sabbath, it will go the way of France, Mexico and Spain. Every nation that gives up the Sabbath must go down. It is only a question of time with them. Look when the children of Israel refused to obey the injunctions of the Lord in regard to the cultivation of their land, how He took them into bondage and kept them for seventy years to let them know that God's land was not to be trampled under their feet. Are you guilty or not guilty in regard to this law: "You shall keep the Sabbath day holy?" When I was in France in 1867, I could not tell one day from another. On Sunday stores were open, buildings were being erected, the same as on other days. See how quick that country went down. Only a few years ago it stood breast to breast with other nations, it stood side by side almost with England. But it didn't have any respect for the Sabbath: it trampled God's message under foot, and when the hour of battle came, God left them alone. My friends, every nation that tramples the Sabbath under its feet must go to ruin. Are you innocent or guilty? Do you keep the Sabbath day holy or not? I have been talking to those car conductors – and if there's any class of men I pity more than another it is them – and they have to work on the Sabbath. Some of you are breaking this law by coming down here on Sunday in the cars. What will you do? Foot it. It will be better for you. I make a point of never allowing myself to break the Sabbath of any man. When I was in London, and it's a pretty big city, you know, but in my ignorance, I made arrangements to preach four times at different places on one Sunday. After I had made the appointments, I found I had to walk sixteen miles, and I walked it, and I slept that night with a clear conscience. I want no hackman to rise up in judgment against me. My friends, if we want to help the Sabbath, let businessmen and Christians never patronize cars on the Sabbath. I would hate to own stock in those horse-car companies, to be the means of taking the Sabbath from these men and have to answer for it at the day of judgment. No man can work seven days a week and save his soul. And the very best thing we have is being taken from these men by us Christians. Are you willing to step into the balance and be weighed against "You shall keep the Sabbath day holy?"

Well, there is the fifth: "Honor your father and mother." Are you ready to be weighed against this? Have you honored them? Is there anyone here tonight who is dishonoring father or mother? Now, I've lived nearly forty years, and I've learned one thing if I've learned nothing else, that no man or woman who treats disrespectfully father or mother ever prospers. How many young ladies have married against their father's wishes and gone off and just made their own ruin. I never knew one case that did not turn out bad. They brought ruin upon themselves. This is a commandment from heaven: "Honor your father and mother." In the last days men shall be disobedient to parents, void of natural affection, and it seems as if we were living in those days now. How many sons treat their mothers with contempt, make light of their entreaties. God says, "Honor your father and mother." If the balances were placed in this hall would you be ready to step into them against this commandment? You may make light of it and laugh at it, but young men, remember that God will hedge your way. No man shall succeed that disobeys this commandment. But bear in mind you are not going to be weighed only against this solitary commandment – every weight will be put in.

"You shall not kill." Most of you say, "That doesn't touch me at all; I never killed anyone. I'm no murderer." Look at that sermon on the mount which men think so much of. Look at it. Did you never in your heart wish a man dead who had done you an injury? That's murder. How are you? Innocent or guilty? If you have, you are a murderer at heart. Now, come, my friends, are you ready to be weighed against the law? Ah, if most of us were weighed tonight we would find this word written against us: "Tekel," you are weighed in the balance and found wanting.

But let us take another: "You shall not commit adultery." I don't know any sin that afflicts us like this. It is a very delicate subject to approach, but I never preach without being compelled to touch upon it. Young men among us are being bound hand and foot with this evil. Young men, hear this law tonight: "You shall not commit adultery." Are you guilty even in thought? How many would come into the Tabernacle but that they are tied hand and foot, as one has been in the halls of vice, and some harlot, whose feet are fastened in hell, clings to him and says, "If you give me up, I will expose you." Can you step on the scales and take that harlot with you? "You shall not commit adultery." You may think that no one knows your doings; you may think that they are all concealed, but God knows it. He that covers his sins shall not prosper. Out with it tonight. Confess it to your God. Ask Him to snap the fetters that bind you to this sin; ask Him to give you victory over your passions, and shake yourself like Samson and say, "By the grace of God, I will not go down to hell with a harlot," and God will give you power. "You shall not commit adultery." As I said the other night, I don't know a quicker way to hell. How many men have by their lecherous life broken their mother's heart and gone down to their grave rotten, leaving the effect of their sin to their posterity?

Well, let us take up the next. "You shall not steal." How many have been stealing today? I may be speaking to some clerk, who perhaps today took five cents out of his employer's drawer to buy a cigar, perhaps he took ten cents to get a shave, and thinks he will put it back tomorrow; no one will ever know it. If you have taken a penny, you are a thief. Do you ever think how those little steals may bring you to ruin? Let an employer find it out. If he doesn't take you into the courts, he will discharge you. Your hopes will be blasted, and it will be hard work to get up again. Whatever condition you are in do not take a cent that does not belong to you. Rather than steal, go up to heaven in poverty – go up to heaven from the poor house – and be honest rather than go through the world in a gilded chariot of stolen riches. A man who takes money that does not belong to him never gets any comfort. He never has any pleasure, for he has a guilty conscience. "You shall not steal." Are you ready to be weighed tonight in the balances?

Then let us take the ninth commandment: "You shall not bear false witness against your neighbor," or in other words, you shall not be guilty of lying. If you had a chance to make $200 or $300 are you not willing to go into a court and lie to get it? "You shall not bear false witness against your neighbor." Are you ready to step into the balances against this? Then take another. "You shall not covet your neighbor's goods." Are you innocent or guilty? How many times I used to covet that which belonged to other people before I was converted. I believe that is one of the greatest sins among us. My friends, how is it? Innocent or guilty? But suppose you are innocent of all these ten commandments, let us take that eleventh commandment of Christ's: "A new commandment I give unto you; you shall love one another." My friends, how is it tonight? Is love reigning in your hearts? Do you love your neighbors? Do you try to do them good, or are you living a life of selfishness, merely for yourself?

Now I can imagine that nearly every man or woman is saying to himself or herself, "If we are to be judged by these laws, how are we going to be saved?" Every one of them has been broken by all people. The moral man is just as guilty as the rest. There is not a moralist in Chicago who, if he steps into those scales, can be saved; "Except a man be born again he cannot see the kingdom of God." "Except you repent, you shall all perish." That is on one side of the scales, and He will see on the other. "Except you be converted you shall not enter the kingdom of God." I have heard a good many pharisees saying, "These meetings are reaching the drunkards and gamblers and harlots; they are doing good," but they don't think they need these meetings. They are all right: they are moral men. "Except a man be born again he cannot see the kingdom of God." I don't care how moral he is. Nicodemus was probably one of the most moral men of his day. He was a teacher of the law, yet Christ said, "Except a man be born again he cannot see the kingdom of God." I would a good deal rather preach to thieves and drunkards and vagabonds, than preach to self-righteous pharisees. You don't have to preach to those men weeks and months to convince them that they are sinners. When a man learns that he has need of God, and that he is a sinner, it is very easy to reach him. But, my friends, the self-righteous pharisee needs salvation as much as any drunkard that walks the streets of Chicago. There is another class I want to speak of. If I had time, I would just like to take up the different classes in the city. That class is the rum sellers. Put the rum sellers in the balances. They ignore God's laws, but by and by He will say to them, "Tekel," "Woe be to the man that put the bottle to his neighbor's lips." My friends, I would rather have that right hand cut off before I would give the bottle to a man. I would rather have my right arm cut off than deal out death and damnation to my fellowmen. If any poor drunkard here should be summoned into eternity tonight – weighed in the balances, what would he hear? "No drunkard shall inherit the kingdom of God." I can see how he would reel and stagger when he heard that. "No drunkard shall inherit the kingdom of heaven."

My friends, if you don't repent of your sins and ask Him for mercy, there is no hope for you. Let me ask you tonight to take this question home to yourself. If a summons should come at midnight to be weighed in the balances, what will become of your souls? The law of God must be kept. Now there are many of you only making professions. You belong to the First Methodist church, or you may be a member of a Baptist church, but are you ready to be weighed – ready to step into these scales tonight? I think a great many would be found like those five foolish virgins. When the hour came, they would be found with no oil in their lamps. If there is a person here tonight who has only an empty lamp or is living on mere formalism, I beg of you to give it up. Give up that dead, cold, miserable lukewarmness. God will spit it out of His mouth. He will have none of it. Wake up. Some of you have gone almost to sleep while I have been trying to weigh you in the balances. God will weigh you, and then if you have not Christ it will be "Tekel."

I can imagine some of you saying, "I would just like Moody to put those tests to himself. I wonder what would become of him." My dear friends, if God were to ask me tonight, I would tell Him, "I am ready." I don't say this in any spirit of egotism or of self-righteousness, remember. If you ask me if I have broken the law of Moses, I would answer, "Yes, sir." Ask me if I have broken the commandments, "Yes, sir." You may ask me then how I am ready to be weighed. If I step into the scales tonight, the Son of God will step into the scales with me. I would not dare to go into them without Him. If I did how quick the scales would go up. If a man has not got Christ, when the hour comes for him to be weighed, it will be "Tekel, tekel, tekel. How are you tonight, my friend – ready to be weighed? (pointing to one of the audience).

Answer – Yes, sir.

Mr. Moody – Have you got Christ?

Answer – Yes, sir.

Mr. Moody – That's right. Suppose I put the question to every man and woman in this audience. How quick many of them would begin to color up. Oh, my friends, if you haven't got Him, get Him tonight. May God open your eyes and your minds to receive Him before you leave this Tabernacle tonight. Christ kept the law; Christ was the end of the law. If He had broken the law, He would have had to die for Himself. But He kept it, and we are enabled to be clothed in righteousness. My friends, it is the height of madness to go out of this hall tonight and run the risk of being called by God and have to answer without Him. Now is the day and hour to accept salvation, and then He will be with us. Then there will be no alarm with us. I pity those Christian people who are afraid of death. They need not be afraid of death if they have Him. When He is with us, it is only a translation. We are absent from the body to be present with the Lord. Here is the gospel of Jesus Christ. Will you be saved tonight? If you do not, when by and by God summons you into these scales, it will be written over you: "Tekel, tekel; you are weighed in the balances and are found wanting." My friends, what will you do tonight? Remain as you are and be lost or accept salvation and be saved? Let us pray.

The "I Wills" of Christ

I want to call your attention tonight to the eight "I wills" of Christ. Now, when we say, "I will," very often it doesn't mean much. My friends, I want you to pay attention to the text. I see some of you looking after Mr. Sankey. You may forget the songs which have been sung tonight, you may forget the sermon, but if the text gets down to your heart, you will never forget it. The eight "I wills" of Christ. I was going to say that a man, when he says "I will," may not mean much. We very often say "I will" when we don't mean to fulfil what we say, but when we come to the "I will" of Christ, He means to fulfil it; everything He has promised to do He is able and willing to accomplish, and He is going to do it. I cannot find any passage in Scripture in which He says "I will" do this, or "I will" do that, but it will be done.

The first "I will" I want to call your attention to occurs in Matthew 11:28: "Come unto me all you that labor, and I will give you rest. Take my yoke upon you and learn of me, for I am meek and lowly in heart, and you shall find rest unto your souls. For my yoke is easy and my burden is light." Now, what is it that man wants more than rest? What is it that the world is in pursuit of? What are all the men in Chicago after if it isn't rest? What do businessmen toil for if it isn't for rest? Why do men spend their lives in hunting for wealth if it is not for rest? But my friends, that is not the way to get rest. A man cannot find it in wealth: he cannot find it in pleasure. Take the pleasure-seekers of Chicago, and ask them if they have rest. They are like the waves of the sea, perpetually troubled. My friends, the man who is away from God never knows what rest is. You can see this in their faces – in the wrinkles of their brow. They don't know what rest is. What does Christ say, "Come unto Me, all you that labor and are heavy laden, and I will give you rest." It isn't in the market for sale. How many men in Chicago would not gladly go up to the Board of Trade tomorrow morning, and give thousands for it if it were for sale? They would give thousands of dollars for it if they could buy it. But salvation isn't for sale. If you get it, you must take it as a gift from Him who came from heaven to give it. The moment a man is willing to take it as a gift, it is his. There is one thing I notice: that a man goes in every direction, seeks every means, tries every person for rest before he comes to the true source. He will try to get rest in the world; he will try to find honor in pleasure, in politics, but he doesn't get it. You cannot find one of these politicians who know what rest is; you cannot find one of those businessmen who knows what rest is unless he has Christ. Ask any man who is after the things of the world if he really knows what rest is, and he will answer you, "No." If you come to Christ, He tells you, "I will" give it. I like this "I will." He means it, and if you want rest, go tonight and say you are weary and your soul is seeking rest, and He will give it. He will give it without price. Take it. "O man, you have destroyed yourself, but in Me is your help." In Him is your help and in Him will you find rest. If there is a poor, mangled one here, come to Christ tonight and confess to Him. Come to Christ and He will take your burden away and put it behind His back, and He will give that weary soul rest. Now, just test it tonight. Let everyone who is weary and heavy-laden come to Him tonight.

The next "I will" is in John, 6th chapter: "Him that comes to me I will in nowise cast out." That is as broad as the world itself. It takes that man in the gallery yonder. It may be there is a poor, afflicted one hidden behind that post, it takes him. It just sweeps around this building, taking rich and poor alike – "He that comes to me I will in nowise cast out." He is so anxious to save sinners He will take everyone who comes. He will take those who are so full of sin that they are despised by all who know them, who have been rejected by their fathers and mothers, who have been cast off by the wives of their bosoms. He will take those who have sunk so low that upon them no eye of pity is cast. "Him that comes to me I will in nowise cast out." Now, why not take Him at His word? I remember a few years ago a man in Farwell Hall was greatly troubled about his soul. "Now," said I, "take that verse; what does the Lord mean when He says, 'Him that comes to me I will in nowise cast out.' When He says that He means it." The man replied, "I will just take Him at His word." He started home, and while going over the Clark Street bridge something whispered to him, "How do you know but that is a wrong translation?" He was just laying right hold of it when this was whispered to him. The poor fellow didn't sleep at all that night. He was greatly troubled, but at last he made up his mind that he would just believe it, and when he got to the Lamb of God he would tell Him of it, and the devil left him. Now, my friends, just take it. Some men say, "I am not worthy to come." I never knew a man yet to go to church who was worthy. Why, He does not profess to save worthy men; He saves sinners. As a man said in the inquiry room, "He didn't come to save make-believe sinners – painted sinners, but real sinners." A man doesn't want to draw his filthy rags of self-righteousness about him when he comes to Him. The only thing a sinner has that God wants is his sin. You need not bring your tears, your prayers, your good works, or deeds; you must come to Him as a sinner, and He will clothe you in a garment fit to come before Him. Now the kings of this earth call around them the wealthy and influential men of their kingdom, but when Christ came down here, He called the outcasts, the publicans, and sinners around Him. And that was the principal fault the people found with Him. Those self-righteous Pharisees were not going to associate with harlots and publicans. The principal charge against him was: "This man receives sinners and eats with them." Who would have such a man around him as John Bunyan in his time? He, a Bedford tinker, why he couldn't get inside one of the princely castles. I was very much amused when I was over on the other side. They had erected a monument to John Bunyan, and it was unveiled by lords and dukes and great men. Why, while he was on earth, they wouldn't allow him inside the walls of their castles. Yet he was made one of the mightiest instruments in the spread of the gospel; no book that has ever been written comes so near the Bible as John Bunyan's "Pilgrim's Progress." And he was a poor Bedford tinker.

So it is with God. He picks up some poor, lost tramp, and makes him an instrument to turn hundreds and thousands to Christ. It is a question whether in all Chicago there is a man who is exercising such an influence for good as this man Sawyer. Four years ago, he was a tramp; he had been cast off by his own mother, by his own sisters, by his wife, and he hadn't seen his own son for fifteen years. Then he was a lost man. Cast off by everyone, but the Son of God stooped low enough to save him. I doubt, as I said before, whether there is a man who has so much influence as that man has today. "Him that comes to Me I will in nowise cast out." Is there some poor outcast, some poor tramp here tonight? I've got a good message for you. Maybe you are hiding away behind that post – I've got a good message for you, the best message you ever heard: "Him that comes to Me I will in nowise cast out." Come all – just as you are. Don't wait. He will take you as you sit into His loving bosom; He will make you a champion of the cross, and you will become an instrument in His hand to build up His kingdom. Thank God for such a book; thank God for such a gospel – thank the God of heaven for such a text: "Him that comes to Me I will in nowise cast out."

The next "I will" is found in Luke. We are told of a man who was full of leprosy; he was just rotten with it. Perhaps his fingers had rotted off. It might have been that his nose was eaten off. That is the way leprosy affects a man. Well, there is a man full of leprosy, and he comes to Christ just as he was. A good many people, if they had been in his place, would have waited till they got a little better before they came before Him, but this man wanted to get the leprosy away. If he had waited to see if he got better there would have been no sense in it. A man might as well, if he had a sick child say, "When it gets better, I will send for the doctor." It is because your child is sick that you want the doctor. It is because this man had the leprosy that he wanted Christ. The leper came to Him and said, "Lord, if You will, You can make me clean." There is faith for you, and the Lord touched him saying, "I will; be clean," and away went the leprosy as if it had been struck by lightning. I have often wondered if he ever turned around to see where it had gone, no doubt, like Naaman, his flesh became as the flesh of a little child. He didn't wait to see whether the leprosy would improve, because he was convinced it was growing worse and worse every day. So it is with you. You will never have a night so favorable for coming to Christ as this one. If you put off till tomorrow, your sins will have become more numerous. If you wait till Sunday next, a whole week's sins will be built upon those you have already. Therefore, the sooner you come, the fewer sins you will have to be forgiven. Come to Him tonight. If you say to Him, "Lord, I am full of sin. You can make me clean;" "Lord, I have a terrible temper – You can make me clean;" "Lord, I have a deceitful heart – cleanse me, O God; give me a new heart. O God, give me the power to overcome the flesh and the snares of the devil!" – if you come to Him with a sincere spirit you will hear the voice, "I will; be clean." It will be done. Do you think that the God who created the world out of nothing, Who by a breath put life into the world – do you think that if He says, "You will be clean," you will not? A great many people say, "If I become converted, I am afraid I will not hold out." Why, don't you see that we cannot serve God with our own strength. When we accept Him, He gives us strength to serve Him. When He has taken away the leprosy of sin, it is easy to live for Him. And I want to call your attention to the fact that even if you are bad, He doesn't care. It may be that someone here has disgraced his or her father or mother; it may be that they have disgraced every friend they ever had, and that they just despise themselves. Come to Him and He will cleanse you. It is to you I am speaking tonight. He can save you to the uttermost.

The next "I will" I want to call your attention to is the "I will" of confession in Matthew. "Whosoever, therefore, shall confess me before men, him will I confess also before my Father which is in Heaven." Let me say right here that this is the very verse up to which men in Chicago have come. Men come to me and say, "Do you mean to affirm, Mr. Moody, that I've got to make a public confession when I accept Christ; do you mean to say I've got to confess Him in my place of business, in my family? Am I to let the whole world know that I am on His side?" A great many are willing to accept Christ, but they are not willing to publish it, to confess it. A great many are looking at the lions and the bears in the mountains. Now, my friends, the devil's mountains are only made of smoke. Why, he can throw a straw into your path and make a mountain of it. He says to you, "You cannot confess and pray to your family; why, you'll break down. You cannot tell it to your shop mate; he will laugh at you." But when you accept Him, you will have power to confess Him. He has said, "If any man will come after Me let him deny himself, and take up his cross and follow Me." It is the way to heaven – by the way of the cross, and I believe in my soul that more men are stumbling upon this verse than upon any other. They are willing to do everything necessary except take up the cross and follow Him. Now, let me read this verse again: "Whosoever, therefore, shall confess Me before men, him will I confess also before My Father, which is in heaven." When I was in London, a leading doctor in that city, upwards of seventy years of age, wrote me a note to come and see him privately about his soul. He was living at a country seat a little way out of London, and he only came into town two or three times a week. He was wealthy and was nearly retired. I received the note right in the midst of the London work and told him I could not see him. I received a note a day or two after from a member of his family urging me to come. The letter said his wife had been praying for him for fifty years, and all the children had become Christians by her prayers. She had prayed for him all those years, but no impression had been made upon him. Upon his desk they had found the letter from me, and they came up to London to see what it meant, and I said I would see him. When we met, I asked him if he wanted to become a Christian, and he seemed every way willing, but when it came to confession to his family he halted. "I tell you," said he, "I cannot do that; my life has been such that I would not like to confess before my family." "Now there is the point; if you are not willing to confess Christ, He will not confess you. You cannot be His disciple." We talked for some time, and he accepted. I found that while I had been in one room, the daughter and some friends, anxious for the salvation of that aged parent, were in the other room praying to God, and when he started out, willing to go home and confess Christ, I opened the door of the other room not knowing the daughter was there, and the first words she said were, "Is my father saved?" "Yes, I think he is," I answered and ran down to the front door and called him back. "Your daughter is here," I said. "This is the time to commence your confession." The father, with tears trickling down his cheeks, embraced his child. "My dear daughter, I have accepted Christ," and a great flood of light broke upon him at that confession.

A great many here in Chicago are ashamed to come out and take their stand for Christ. If you want peace and joy, my friends, you must be willing to confess. I am told that in China the height of a Chinaman's ambition is to have his name put in the house of Confucius. He must have performed some great act of valor or done the State some great service before he can have his name there. That is the highest point of a Chinaman's ambition. It ought to be the height of our ambition to have our name registered in heaven and have Christ to confess us in the courts of heaven. How excited we used to be during the war when some general did something extraordinary, and someone got up in Congress to confess his exploits. How the papers used to talk about it. If we come out for Christ down here, He will confess us in heaven before the throne and the angels. May God help you to confess Him tonight.

Another "I will" – to me a very precious "I will" – was given to those early fishermen. He said, "If you will follow Me, I will make you fishers of men." That is the "I will" of service. I pity those Christians from the very depth of my heart, who have only made a profession of religion and stopped there. My friends, they don't have the joy of salvation. I tell you the only happy Christians are those who are fishers of men. If a man be a true Christian, he wins souls. He cannot help it, for He says, "If you will follow Me, I will make you fishers of men." Peter caught more men at Pentecost than he ever caught fish in his nets. I have often thought of the remark one of the disciples made to Him as they were standing together one day, "Lord, we have left all to follow You." What did they leave? A few old fishing boats and broken nets. They were looking to those they had left behind, and a great many people here are looking to what they will leave if they serve Him. It is not necessary to leave the things of this life when you follow Him. It is not necessary to give up your business, if it's a legitimate one, in order to accept Christ. But you mustn't set your heart on the old nets by a good deal. Now, my friend, if you want to be a religious Christian, follow Christ fully. No man follows Christ and ever regrets it, and the nearer we get to Him, the more useful we become. Then we will save men. It seems to me after I am dead and gone, I would rather have a man to come to my grave and drop a tear and say, "Here lies the man who converted me, who brought me to the cross of Christ" – it seems to me I would rather have this than a column of pure gold reaching to the skies built in my honor. If a man wants to be useful, follow Christ. You will succeed if you follow Him. Whenever you find a man who follows Christ you will find that man a successful one. He doesn't need to be a preacher. He doesn't need to be an evangelist to be useful. They may be useful in business. See what power an employer has if he likes. How he could labor with his employees and in his business relations. Often a man can be far more useful in a business sphere than he could in another. If we want to spend a life of usefulness, accept Him, and He will make you fishers of men. Young man, don't you want to win souls to Christ? Well, then, just follow Him. "You follow Me, and I will make you fishers of men."

The next "I will," a very precious one is, "I will not leave you comfortless" down here in this dark world. Now some people think they have a very hard battle before them when they accept Him. A lady came to me lately and said, "I am the only one of my family who is a Christian, and I feel lonely. "Why," said I, "Christ is with you; if you have got an elder sitting at the right hand of God, what more do you want?" Oh, this precious "I will." This comfort and joy. "I will be with you to the end of the world." "I will never forsake you." You may take comfort tonight. He will be with you always. You may not see Him with the eye of flesh, but you will see Him by the eye of faith.

The next "I will" is found in the 4th chapter of John: "I will raise him up at the last day." These bodies of ours are going down to the grave, but they are not going to lie there long. The Son of God will wake it up. When He was here, He raised up three bodies, and let me say to you, young children, that the first one He raised was a little child. Ah, there will be many little children there, "For of such is the kingdom of heaven." He gave us three instances. The first was the little girl. When the people heard He had raised up someone from the dead they thought it was a mistake. She wasn't dead, only asleep; it wasn't a real miracle.

The next one was a young man. "Oh no," they thought, "That's no miracle. If they had left him alone, he'd have awoken; he was only asleep." But the next case that came along was that of Lazarus, and Matthew tells us he had been dead four days – had been laid away in the sepulcher, and the Son of God merely said, "Lazarus, come forth."

Now, I like a religion that gives me such comfort, that when I lay away any loved one in the grave, I know they will by and by hear the voice of the Son of God calling them forth. I used to wonder how Christians had so much comfort in affliction and used to question whether I could have as much. But I have learned that God gives us comfort when we need it. A few weeks ago, I stood at the grave of a man I loved more than any one on earth, except my wife and family. As he was laid down in the narrow bed, and the earth dropped upon the coffin lid, it seemed as if a voice came to me saying, "He will rise again." I like a religion by which we can go to the grave of our loved ones and feel that they will rise again. I like a religion that tells us although we sow them in corruption, they will rise incorruptible; that although we sow them in weakness, they will rise in power and glory and ascend to the kingdom of light. This is the comfort for Christians. Thank God for this, "I will not leave you comfortless."

"I will that they may be with Me" is the sweetest of all. The thought that I will see Him in His beauty. The thought that I will meet Him there, that I will spend eternity with Him, is the sweetest of them all. This last week we had Thanksgiving Day. How many families gathered together, perhaps the first time in many years, and the thought would come stealing over some of them, "Who will be the first to break the circle?" Perhaps many of these circles of friends will never meet again. Thank God yonder the circles shall never be broken – when the fathers and mothers and children gather around Him in those mansions into which death never enters, where sickness and sorrow never enter through yon pearly gates. Oh, thank God for this blessed religion – thank God for the blessed Christ. Thank God for those blessed eight "I wills" – "Come unto Me all you that labor and are heavy laden, and I will give you rest" "Him that comes unto Me I will in no wise cast out;" "Whosoever therefore shall confess Me before men, him will I confess also before My Father which is in heaven" "If you will follow Me I will make you fishers of men;" "I will, be clean;" "I will not leave you comfortless;" "I will that you may be with Me." May God bless every soul in this building tonight and bring you to the cross.

Mission of Christ

I am going to ask our friends if they will please turn in their Bibles to the 4th chapter of John, and the 17th verse: *"And there was delivered unto Him the book of the prophet Isaiah, and when He had opened the book He found the place where it was written: 'The Spirit of the Lord is upon me, because he has anointed me to preach the gospel to the poor; He has sent me to heal the brokenhearted, to preach deliverance to the captives, and recovery of sight to the blind, to set at liberty them that are bound; to preach the acceptable year of the Lord.' And He closed the book, and He gave it again to the minister and sat down. And the eyes of all of them that were in the synagogue were fastened on Him. And He began to say unto them, 'This day is the Scripture fulfilled in your ears.'"* I suppose our friends have noticed in reading the life of the Lord Jesus Christ that never when He was down on earth do we read about Him taking a copy of the Scriptures in His hands except in this synagogue. I have no doubt that the Lord Jesus Christ knew the Scriptures from beginning to end, so that He did not require to take them up to find a passage. Here for the first and for the last time do we read about Him taking them in His hands. It was a prophecy He took up, and that prophecy was the book of Isaiah. We are told in Luke that the Lord Jesus Christ found a certain place. I suppose that means that He searched for a certain passage of Scripture which declared His mission to the children of men. He might have preached from any single text in that wonderful book. If He had liked, He could have told His message without any reference to that wonderful book, but He turned to the place and read, "The Spirit of the Lord is upon me, because he has anointed me to preach the gospel; He has sent me to heal the brokenhearted, to preach deliverance to the captives and recovering of sight to the blind, to set at liberty them that are bruised." You know that 1,800 years ago books were not printed as they are today. These books were written on parchment and put on rollers, and the Lord Jesus Christ had to unroll these parchments before He came to the passage saying, "The Spirit of the Lord is upon Me." I have often tried to imagine what thoughts passed through His mind as His blessed eye rested upon passage after passage of that book. He might have pointed to that passage: "I have nourished and brought up children and they have rebelled against me. The ox knows his owner, and the ass his master's crib, but Israel does not know," but the Lord passed that by. He might have turned to a passage in the same chapter: "From the sole of the foot even unto the head there is no soundness in it, but wounds and bruises and putrefying sores; they have been closed, neither bound up, neither mollified with ointment," but He passed that by. He might have turned to that wonderful passage in the 9th chapter: "For unto us a child is born, unto us a son is given, and the government shall be upon his shoulder, and his name shall be called wonderful Counsellor, the mighty God, the Everlasting Father, the Prince of Peace," but Jesus passed that by. He did not want to read about the divinity; He came into that synagogue to read about the mission to sinners: "The Spirit of the Lord is upon me." He might have read that sweet passage, "Though You were angry with me Your anger is turned away, and You comfort me." Jesus didn't need that – the cross had not yet had its victim. He might have turned to that sweet 32nd chapter: "And a man shall be as a hiding place from the wind, and a covert from the tempest, as rivers of water in a dry place, as the shadow of a great rock in a weary land," but he just passed that by. He ought to have opened the book at that 35th chapter, where it speaks about water breaking out in the wilderness and the desert blooming, but the millennium had not come yet. Without Calvary there could be no millennium. So He turned to the passage which says, "The Spirit of the Lord is upon me." I wonder how those men would have felt had

He read, "He was despised and rejected of men – a man of sorrows." He did not tell them how they treated Him; He merely turned to the passage which spoke of His mission.

And in that synagogue, on that Sabbath day, beloved friends, there was not a human heart any different from yours. They loved to hear good news or glad tidings, and I am sure there is not one here tonight, rich or poor, high or low, but likes to hear glad tidings. In Ireland, a man used to live opposite to where I was living, and when a man would come from the market with something that had been ordered he would ring the bell and stand waiting for five or six minutes before any servant would come to the door. Sometimes ladies and gentlemen would come up and stand waiting for the door to be opened, but I always noticed one thing. Whenever the postman would come and give his double knock, that moment three or four of them would come to the door. Sometimes the master and mistress of the house themselves would run to the door to get what they thought good news. You know you never keep the postman at the door. Everybody is fond of good news – of glad tidings. Previous to my coming across to this great country of yours, I was holding meetings in London. I took my ticket from there to Manchester to bid some friends goodbye. When I got to the railway carriage, I saw little groups of boys around two little fellows. Their coats were threadbare, with patches here and there carefully covering up the holes. Some good mother, it was evident, too poor to send them away in fine style, was trying to make them as neat as she could. The boys belonged to a Sunday school in London, and the group around them was their schoolmates, who had come down to bid them goodbye. They shook hands, and then their Sunday school teacher did the same and wished them Godspeed. After that, their minister came and took them by the hand and breathed a prayer that they would be blessed. When they all had bade the boys goodbye, a poor widow came up and put her arms around the companion of her son. Perhaps he had no mother, and she kissed him for his mother and wished him goodbye. Then she put her arms around the neck of the other boy, and put his arms around her, and she began to weep. "Don't cry, mother," said the boy. "Don't cry; I'll soon be in America, and I'll save money, and soon send for you to come out to me. I'll have you out with me.

Don't cry." He stepped into the carriage, the steam was turned on, and the train was in motion when he put his head out of the window and cried, "Farewell, dear mother!" and the mother's prayer went out, "God bless my boy; God bless my boy." Don't you think that when they came to America and sent the first letter to England that mother would run quickly to the door when the postman came with that letter? How quick that mother would take that letter and break the seal. She wants to hear good news. There is not one here tonight who has not a message of good news, of glad tidings – better news than was ever received by a mother in England from a son in America. It is glad tidings from a loving Savior – glad tidings of great joy. He says, "The Spirit of the Lord is upon me" to preach good news. That is what brought the Savior down from glory – to preach glad tidings.

But mark you, it is to the poor – but not the poor in pocket. God never looks into a bankbook; He never looks into your purse to see whether you are rich or poor. He looks into the sinner's heart, and if that sinner has nothing – no deeds, no prayers, no tears, then the Son of God comes from heaven to that poor soul: "The Spirit of the Lord is upon me, because he has anointed me to preach the gospel to the poor." On Friday night, in a certain place where I was, two or three ladies were talking about the Bible. One lady said to another, "I saw some of my friends reading the Bible, and they were looking so glum and melancholy." Turning 'round to me she said, "I don't think people should be melancholy when they read the Bible; do you, Mr. Moody?" "Well," I replied, "it depends upon the kind of people who read the Bible; if they are unsaved sinners, they will." "But" she asked, "tell me why." "Because that book is the death warrant of an unsaved sinner; but if a man knows that he is lost, that he is guilty and condemned, and he comes to the Savior, then the Bible is not a death warrant." It is a reprieve – it is a pardon – it is good news, glad tidings, and every man here tonight who is unsaved, ought to be sad when he reads his death warrant. That is the reason why people unsaved do not like to read this book. When we believe, we hear the good news that comes to us in the cry from Calvary, "It is finished!" That is the news. "It is finished!" That is not bad news – that is not our death warrant – that is my pardon – that is my peace – my justification. Jesus finished that work, and He finished that work for me. It is good news and glad tidings to the sinner, and there is not a little child in this hall tonight but can understand it, if they take it as God gives it in this book. It is not long ago, it just seems the other day, when my dear friend Dr. Mathieson, now in heaven, told me he was preaching the gospel in Scotland, and a minister told him he had in his congregation a little idiot boy. He did not know what to do with him, he had spoken to him many times, but the boy always said: "Ye maun wait till a'come to ye, and when a'come I'll sing ye a sang an'tell ye a story; but ye maun wait till a'come to ye." The minister heard that the boy was dying, and he went to him and said: "Sandy, you promised me that you would sing me a song and tell me a story before you died; will you tell it now?" "Yes, minister," replied the boy, "Three in ane an' ane in three, an' Jesus Christ He died for me; that's a'." ("Three in one and one in three, and Jesus Christ He died for me.")

I tell you, I would rather be a poor idiot and know that than be one of the mightiest and so-called wisest men in the city of Chicago and not believe that Jesus took my place and died for me on Calvary's cross. That gospel's very simple; it is very easy to understand. Here am I, a poor sinner, and God has said, "The soul that sins shall die." But God so loved that sinner that He doesn't want him to die. He had a Son Whom He sent from heaven to Calvary to die on that cross on purpose to put away our sin. Now I believe, and my sins are put away, and I am saved. Do you want to be saved tonight? Jesus's blood was shed for you; He put away sin by the sacrifice of Himself. What must I do to be saved? Believe. How can believing save me? Jesus died to save. It is not my believing that puts away my sin; it is my belief that accepts Christ as my Savior, and the moment I believe on Him, I know that 1,800 years ago He bled and died on purpose to give me everlasting life. How can I know that I can be saved tonight? That dear young man in the gallery yonder – "Can I know I can be saved tonight?" Yes. That dear mother over there – "Can I know I can be saved tonight?" Yes. That dear father here – "Can I know I can be saved tonight?" Yes, before you leave your seat and go into the inquiry room, if you believe He took your place and sent the message to you.

On Thanksgiving night, there was a young lady in the inquiry room who came to me.

"Oh," said she, "will you tell me what you mean by knowing that you are saved?" She said she was a member of a church and loved the Savior but didn't know that she was saved. "Will you come and sit down here, and open your Bible at the 5th chapter of St. John and read the 24th verse?" She turned and read, "Verily, verily, I say unto you, he that hears my word and believes in Him that sent me" – "Now, I spell the next word, 'H-a-t-h.'" "That's not hope," I said, "That's hath." She turned to me, a smile lighting up her face through her tears and said, "That is to have everlasting life." "Are you saved now?" I asked. "Yes." "How do you know?" "Because" she replied, "I said so; that is how I know." We tell you tonight, in the Master's name, you can be saved here if you are guilty – if you have nothing to give to God – for He came to preach the gospel to the poor. Some of you say, "Mustn't I repent for a week or two – must I not try and get some of the sin taken from me, and then go to the Lord, and when He sees I desire to be better it will be easier?" My friends, you can't improve yourselves. He wants to take you just as you are now.

When I was holding meetings a little time ago at Wharncliffe, England, a coal district, a great burly collier came up to me and said in his Yorkshire dialect, "Dost know wha was at meetin' t'night?" "No," I answered. "Why," said he, "So-and-so" (mentioning name). The name was a familiar one. He was a very bad man, one of the wildest, wickedest men in Yorkshire, according to his own confession and according to the confession of everybody who knew him. "Weel," said the man, "he cam' into meetin' an' said you didn't preach right; he said thou preached nothin' but love o' Christ, an'that won't do for drunken colliers; ye want t' shake 'em over a pit, an he says he'll ne'er come again." He thought I didn't preach about hell.

Mark you, my friends, I believe in eternal damnation; I believe in the pit that burns, in the fire that's never quenched, in the worm that never dies, but I believe that the magnet that goes down to the bottom of the pit is the love of Jesus. I didn't expect to see him again, but he came the next night, without washing his face, right from the pit, with all his working clothes upon him. This drunken collier sat down on one of the seats that were used for the children and got as near to me as possible. The sermon was love from first to last. He listened at first attentively, but by and by I saw him with the sleeve of his rough coat, wiping his eyes. Soon after we had an inquiry meeting, when some of those praying colliers got around him, and it wasn't long before he was crying, "O, Lord, save me; I am lost. Jesus have mercy upon me." That night he left the meeting a new creature. His wife told me, herself, what occurred when he came home. His little children heard him coming along – they knew the step of his heavy clogs – and ran to their mother in terror, clinging to her skirts. He opened the door as gently as could be. He had had a habit of banging the door. My friends, if a man becomes converted, it will even make a difference in the slamming of doors. When he came into the house and saw the children clinging to their mother, frightened, he just stooped down and picked up the youngest girl in his arms, and looked at her, the tears rolling down his cheeks. "Mary, Mary, God has sent thy father home to thee," and kissed her. He picked up another, "God has sent thy father home," and from one to another he went, and kissed them all, and then came to his wife and put his arms around her neck, "Don't cry, lass; don't cry. God has sent thy husband home at last; don't cry," and all she could do was to put her arms around his neck and sob. And then he said, "Have you got a Bible in the house, lass?" They hadn't such a thing. "Well, lass, if we haven't, we must pray." They got down on their knees, and all he could say was,

> "Gentle Jesus, meek and mild,
>   Look upon a little child;
> Pity my simplicity –
>   for Jesus Christ's sake, amen."

It was a simple prayer, but God answered it. While I was at Barnet some time after that, a friend came to me and said, "I've got good news for you. So-and-so (mentioning the collier's name) is preaching the gospel everywhere he goes – in the pit and out of the pit, and tries to win everybody to the Lord Jesus Christ." O, brother and sister, won't you trust the Savior tonight? Dear mother and father, won't you believe the gospel – won't you rest upon that finished work; won't you give up your doings and strivings, and just like a little child rest upon that Savior?

Believe the glorious gospel and have everlasting life. May God bless you all, for Jesus Christ's sake. Amen.

The Life of Lot

I am going to select for my subject tonight, "The Life of Lot." One reason why I take up this character is because I believe he is a representative man, and perhaps there is no Bible character that represents so many Chicago men at the present day as Lot of Sodom. Where you can find one Abraham, or one Daniel, or one Joshua, you can find a thousand Lots. He started very well; he got rich, and that was the beginning of his troubles. He and Abraham, his uncle, went down to Egypt, and they came out of Egypt with great wealth, and the next thing we hear of is strife among their herdsmen. He could not get up a quarrel with Abraham. Abraham said to him, "You are my nephew, and I cannot quarrel with you; but take your goods and go to the right, and I will go to the left, or I will go to the right and you go to the left," and they separated.

Right here Lot made his mistake. He should have said, "No, I don't want to leave you. The Lord has blessed me with you, and I don't want to leave you." Or, if he had been determined to leave his uncle, he should have asked Abraham to choose for him. Instead, he lifted up his eyes and saw the well-watered plains of Sodom, and that decided him. No doubt he was very ambitious; he probably wanted to become richer. Perhaps there was a little spirit of rivalry toward his uncle. He wanted to excel Abraham in worldly goods, to become rich faster. So he saw and determined upon the well-watered plains of Sodom. If he had asked Abraham, he would not have gone there. If he had asked God, Lot would never have entered Sodom; no man ever goes into Sodom by God's advice. He determined himself and pitched his tent toward Sodom.

I don't know how long he lived on these well-watered plains, but no doubt the men of those days said of him when he had settled down, "There is a shrewd man; he's a smart man. Why, I can predict that in a very short time he will be a wealthier man than his uncle Abraham. Look at these well-watered plains. Why, he is a great deal better off than Abraham now." He is in a position in which he can soon become rich. How long he remained on these plains I don't know, but the next thing we know is that he got into Sodom. We are told that Sodom was very wicked. He lived near it, and went into it with his eyes open, and he knew all about it. The wickedness of Sodom was coming up to God. He was going to destroy it soon. And do you think, if Lot had asked Him, He would have allowed Lot to enter that city?

I think one of the greatest mistakes the people of the present day make is that they won't let God choose for them; He wouldn't choose ruin for them. All the years that Lot was in Sodom we don't read that he had any family altar. He thought it would be ruin for his family to take them in there. He did not look at that, however. It was business or something, that took him there. He might have said, "Well, I've got a large family; I've got a great many dependent upon me, and I must get rich faster, so I will go into Sodom. Business is the first consideration, and it must be attended to."

So he goes to Sodom, and the next thing we hear he is in trouble. Sodom had got a war on hand, and when he went into the city, he had to take its side. In the war he was taken captive. It is a great mercy he wasn't killed in the battle. The first thing his uncle did when he heard of his nephew's trouble was to set out after him. When he was taken in battle, he was liable to be taken into slavery and his children also. He might have died in slavery if Abraham hadn't gone after him. But Abraham takes his servants and sets out and overtakes the warriors who had taken Lot captive and brought him and all the property back that had been taken.

Now, you would have thought that he would have kept out of Sodom. You'd have thought that he would have said, "I've had enough of Sodom;

I won't go near it again." You would think that men, when they get into this and that difficulty and affliction, would strike out of Sodom, but they won't. It is one of the greatest mysteries to me why men will remain in their Sodom when they have continual trouble. So he went back. Probably he said, "I've lost a good deal, and I must go back and try and recover it; I must go back and make it up for my children." And he prospered in Sodom. If you had gone into Sodom before these angels came down, you would probably have found that no man had got on so well. If they had a Congress, perhaps they sent him to represent Sodom because no man had done better in business. That is the way of the world. Perhaps they might have made him Mayor of Sodom. If you could have seen his "turn out" it would have been one of the very best. Mrs. Lot must have moved in the very best society of the city. The Misses Lot were looked upon as the most fashionable people there. They got on well. Oh yes, that is the way the men talk now. Men thousands of miles from God take their children right into the whirlpool that takes them to sure ruin. Perhaps he was a judge and had great influence.

When the angels got to the gate, they might have heard of the honorable Judge Lot. It sounded pretty well. He might have owned a good many corner lots; he might have owned a good many buildings with "Lot, Lot," printed all over them, and on account of his property he might have been a very high man in Sodom. That is the way the world looks at it. No doubt the dispositions of the people were exactly as they are today; human nature has been pretty much the same always.

But time rolls on, and Lot, while sitting at the gate one evening, saw two strangers upon the highway. They are coming toward Sodom. Likely these Sodomites did not know them, but twenty years before Lot had been in the company of Abraham, and he had seen these men at his uncle's home, had seen them sitting at his uncle's table. He knew these angels when they approached and bowed down and worshipped them, bowed down to the ground and invited them into his house. But it was a sink of iniquity and they would not go in: they preferred to walk about the streets. But he pressed his invitation upon them, and they accepted. It soon got noised around the streets that he had two strangers there, and it wasn't long before a crowd was around the door and wanted to know who he had inside. And he came out to try to pacify them, but they received him with cries of "Who made this fellow a judge over us?" and Lot was dragged into the house and the door was shut against the mob. His influence was gone. He had been in the city twenty years and hadn't made a convert.

My friends, no man ever goes down to Sodom and retains his influence. Talk about men of influence whose heart is not with God. What is their influence? Someone said to me tonight, "You have been preaching to drunkards and vagabonds; why don't you preach to those sinners who live in marble-front houses and have influence?" Why, I would rather preach to harlots and drunkards because it is easier to get them into the kingdom of God than those sinners who live in marble-front houses. We can reach them sooner; it doesn't take so long to convince them they are sinners. I suppose Lot lived in a marble-front house there, and his heart was away from God.

Then these men said to Lot, "Who have you got here beside yourself? What is your family? Have you got any others beside yourself in this town?" Well, the father and mother had to own up that they had married their children to some of the Sodomites; that was the result of his going into the city. You go into the world and live like the world and see what the result will be. How many mothers and fathers are now mourning on account of marrying their sons and daughters to Sodomites, marrying them to death and ruin. "Now," they say, "if you have got any, get them out of this place, for God is going to burn it up. Tell them this, and if they won't come, escape for your lives and leave them, for He will destroy the city." People say, "Why are we so afflicted; why have we so many sorrows?" I believe it is because our hearts are far from God. They have gone down to Sodom and left the God of their fathers.

Now, all these twenty years we do not know that he had ever a family altar. He could not call his children around him and pray to his God. They had become identified with Sodom and its people. Look at that scene. There are the men at the outside of the door groping about to find it, and the door opens, and Lot starts out to tell his son-in-law of the coming destruction. I can see the old man's head bowed down passing through the streets of Sodom at midnight. He goes to a house and knocks. No sound, all are asleep. He knocks again, and perhaps, too, shouts at the top of his voice, and the man gets up and opens the window. He puts his head out. "Who's there?" "Your father-in-law," answers the old man. "What has brought you out of bed at this hour? What's up?" "Why," says Lot, "two angels are at my house, who say that God is going to destroy Sodom and everyone who remains." "Why, you go home and go to bed," replies the son-in-law and mocks him. They mock him. He had lost his testimony, my friends. They think he is deluded. I can see him now going off to another daughter's house. I don't know how many daughters he had. He might have had as many daughters as Job; he goes to them and they mock him too.

I tell you, my friends, if we have got into Sodom, our children will mock us. There is that old man in that midnight hour, plodding along those streets of Sodom to urge them to flee from the city, and they mock him. He had been long enough with Abraham to know that everything that came from God could be relied upon. Now he starts back home. You can see him, his head bowed down, his long white hair flowing over his bosom, and the tears flowing from those aged eyes. The world calls him a successful man, but what a miserable end is his. Look at him tonight. He had got wealth; that's what he was after. He obtained what he wanted, but he got leanness of soul. You can see him go back bowed down with grief. Next morning the angels take him by the hand; he, his wife, and two daughters are led out of the city. And they lingered. How could they do otherwise than linger, when they had left their sons and daughters in the city and knew they would be destroyed.

Where are your sons and daughters now? Have you taken them down to Sodom, saying they must live in the pleasures of society – they must get on in the world? Where are they now? Have you got them into some store or some office where they will hear nothing but infidelity? If you have, these gray hairs will come down to an untimely grave. You will learn the folly of your own course when it is too late. Take your children from that city; urge them to come from the Sodom in which they are living; tell them to flee before it is too late, for the city will be destroyed. Yes, they linger. I don't blame them. They probably had a lingering hope that the storm might be stayed and they could get their children out. But the angels took them by the hand and hastened them out of the city. Poor mother! Ah! How sad when God came in judgment! I can see that mother hesitating, but God orders her not to look back.

"Flee for your life! Escape or you will be destroyed." "No man having put his hand to the plow, and looking back, is fit for the kingdom of God." She gets out of Sodom, but she looks back, and judgment falls upon her. And I believe that the condition of Lot's wife is the condition of hundreds in Chicago. They have come out of Sodom, but their heart is in the world. They say, "Have I to give up the world; have I to give all and follow Christ?" They linger and look back, and judgment will fall upon them.

We are told in that portion of Scripture which was read tonight, that they were eating, drinking, buying and selling, planting and building until the very moment Lot went out of Sodom. Perhaps not a man in all Sodom took any account of his going out. It might have got rumored around that he was going because he believed the city was to be destroyed, but no man believed it. His sons and daughters didn't believe what their father said to them, and so destruction fell upon them, and the Son of God says they were all destroyed – great and small, learned and unlearned, rich and poor, all perished alike. Bear in mind that if you live in Sodom, destruction will come upon you. The world may call you successful, but the only way to test success is to take a man's whole life, not the beginning or the middle, but the whole of it. If a man is in Sodom, as Mr. Sankey sang tonight, he will find at last the fruits of his life to be –

"Nothing but leaves, nothing but leaves."

Lot spent his life in gaining worldly goods for his children, and he lost all and his children besides. How many men in Chicago are there who can only say they have the same object in view that Lot had? They have come to this city to make money. They haven't any family altar. They recognize only two things – money, money; business, business. "My sons," they say, "may become gamblers and drunkards; my daughters may go off into ungodly society and marry drunkards and make their lives miserable, but I want money, and I'll have all I want if I get it." That is the condition of thousands of people here.

My friends, was Lot's life a successful one? It was a stupendous failure. He lost his sons and daughters, he lost his property, his wealth, his hold on the society and friendship of his uncle Abraham. Is not that the condition of hundreds here tonight? Let us strike for a higher plane; let us go up to Bethel. Let us call upon God to save our children before it is too late. If your children have wandered off and got among the Sodomites, let one piercing cry go up, "O God, save my children! Forgive me, O Lord, for taking them into Sodom." Let us turn from our lukewarmness, our worldly-mindedness, and seek His face. O may the Spirit of God come upon you, and may you flee from the doomed city before it is too late.

A mother came to me a few days ago and said, "Mr. Moody, I want you to pray for me." "Well," I asked, "Why do you want to be prayed for?" She said, "I feel I am to blame. I've got three sons, and they have all gone astray, and I am the most wretched woman living. I feel I haven't been true to the charge God gave me, and the thought is killing me. I want you to pray for me, and if God will forgive me, and if I get right in His sight, with His grace by my prayers and faith they may be brought back."

Are there not hundreds here in the same condition as this poor woman? You have been ambitious for your children; you were after great things for them, and you have led them into Sodom. Now ruin has come upon them; darkness and misery cover them. Let us humble ourselves before God tonight that He may forgive us in our lukewarmness for His cause, in our ambition to obtain great things in this world. Let us not follow in the footsteps of this man Lot. Look at a representative Lot here. I can imagine him starting as a moderate drinker, but the passion grows and his children are infected, and he becomes, as it were, the father of a whole army of backsliders. He becomes the father of backsliding and worldly-mindedness by turning away from God himself. If you are in the city of Sodom, flee from it at once – escape with your lives, for destruction will come. May God bring everyone in this hall out of Sodom tonight is the prayer of my heart. Let us unite in prayer.

Their Rock Is Not as Our Rock

I want to call your attention tonight to a text which you will find in the 32nd chapter of Deuteronomy and 31st verse: *"For their rock is not as our rock, even our enemies themselves being judges."* I wish that this audience for about thirty minutes would just imagine they are sitting in judgment – that each one is sitting upon the case brought up. We want every man, woman, and child in this building to decide the question brought before them. "For their rock is not as our rock, even our enemies themselves being judges." This was uttered by Moses in his farewell address to Israel. He had been with them forty years, day and night. He had been the king, or president, or judge, or whatever you may call it; he had been their leader or instructor. In other words, he had been a god to them, for all the blessings of heaven came through him. And the old man was about to leave them. He had taken them to the borders of the promised land, and all who had left Egypt with him, but Joshua and Caleb, had been laid in that wilderness.

Now he is making his farewell address; and, young man, if you have never read it, read it tonight. It is the best sermon in print. I do not know any other sermon in the New or Old Testament that compares with it. His natural activity hadn't abated – he had still the vigor of youth. I can see him as he delivers it: his long white hair flowing over his shoulders, and his venerable beard covering his breast as he gives them the wholesome instruction. Now, I want everyone to wake up here. I see one young man over there who has just gone to sleep. All you young men will help me if you see any one next you going to sleep by pinching his elbow. We don't want anyone here to sleep.

I remember when I was in Boston, I fell asleep in church, and a man just pinched me, and I rubbed my eyes and woke up. I looked at the minister, and lo and behold, I thought he was preaching directly at me. It seemed as if he knew all about my faults, and my disposition, and everything about me. I never felt so cheap in my life. All his remarks seemed to be directed to me, and I wondered who had been telling that minister about me. At the conclusion of the sermon, I pulled my coat collar up and got out as quick as I could. Now bear in mind, you men who have gone to sleep are the very men I want to speak to. But let us go back to the subject.

The old man was giving his farewell address in which he said, "This rock is not as our rock, even our enemies themselves being judges." Now I am not going to call upon Christians to settle this question. The ungodly, the unconverted, must decide this question, and if you be fair with the argument, you will have to admit that, "Your rock is not as our rock;" your peace is not as our peace, because we have got our feet on the rock of Jesus.

You know, in the first place, that the atheist does not believe in any God. He denies the existence of a God. Now, I contend that his rock is not as our rock and will let those atheists be the judges. What does an atheist look forward to? Nothing. He is taking a very crooked path in this world. His life has been dark; it has been full of disappointments. When he was a young man, ambition beckoned him on to a certain height. He has attained to that height, but he is not satisfied. He climbs a little higher, and perhaps he has got as far as he can get, but he is not contented. He is dissatisfied, and if he takes a look into the future, he sees nothing.

Man's life is full of trouble. Afflictions are as numerous as the hairs of our head, but when the billows of affliction are rising and rolling over him, he has no God to call upon. Therefore, I contend his "rock is not as our rock." Look at him. He has a child. That atheist has all the natural affection for that child possible. He has a son – a noble young man – who starts out in life full of promise, but he goes astray. He has not the will power of his father and cannot resist the temptation of the world. That father cannot call upon God to save his son. He sees that son go down to ruin step by step, and by and by he plunges into a hopeless, godless, Christless grave. And as that father looks into that grave, he has no hope. His "rock is not as our rock."

Look at him again. He has a child laid low with fever, racked with pain and torture, but the poor atheist cannot offer any consolation to that child. As he stands by the bedside of that child she says, "Father, I am dying. In a little while I will go into another world. What is going to become of me? Am I going to die like a dumb beast?" "Yes," the poor atheist says, "I love you, my daughter, but you will soon be in the grave and eaten up with the worms and that will be all. There is no heaven, no hereafter; it is all a myth. People have been telling you there is a hereafter, but they have been deluding you." Did you ever hear an atheist going to his dying children and telling them this?

My friends, when the hour of affliction comes, they call in a minister to give consolation. Why doesn't the atheist preach no hereafter, no heaven, no God, in the hour of affliction? This very fact is an admission that "their rock is not as our rock, even our enemies themselves being the judges." But look again. That little child dies, and that atheist father follows the body to the grave and lays it down in its resting place and says, "All that is left of my child is there; it will soon become the companion of worms, which will feed upon it. That is all there is." Why, the poor man's heart is broken, and he will admit his "rock is not as our rock." A prominent atheist went to the grave with the body of his friend. He pronounced a eulogy and committed all that was left of his friend to the winds – to nature – and bade the remains farewell forever. Oh, my friends, had he any consolation then? His rock was not as our rock.

A good many years ago there was a convention held in France, and those who held it wanted to get the country to deny a God and to burn the Bible. They wanted to say that a man passed away like a dog – like a dumb animal. What was the result? Not long after, that country was filled with blood. Did you ever think what would take place if we could vote the Bible and the ministers of the gospel and God out from among the people? My friends, the country would be deluged with blood. Your life and mine would not be safe in this city tonight. We could not walk through those streets with safety. We don't know how much we owe God and the influence of His gospel among even ungodly men. I can imagine some of you saying, "Why this talk about atheists? There are none here." Well, I hope there isn't but I find a great number who come into the inquiry rooms just to look on, who confess they don't believe in any God or any hereafter.

But there is another class called deists, who, you know, don't believe in revelation – who don't believe in Jesus Christ. Ask a deist who is his God. "Well," he will say, "He is the beginning – He who caused all things." These deists say there is no use to pray, because nothing can change the decrees of their deity; God never answers prayer. "Their rock is not as our rock." In the hour of affliction, they, too, send off for some Christian to administer consolation.

But there is another class. They say, "I am no deist; I am a pantheist. I believe that God is in the air. He is in the sun, in the stars, in the rain, in the water." They say God is in this wood. Why, a pantheist the other night told me God was in that post; He was in the floor. When we come to talk to those pantheists, we find them no better than the deists and atheists. There was one of that sort that Sir Isaac Newton went to talk to. He used to argue with him and try to get the pantheist into his belief, but he couldn't. In the hour of his distress, however, he cried out to the God of Sir Isaac Newton. Why don't they cry to their god in the hour of their trouble? When I used to be in this city, I used to be called on to attend a good many funerals. I would inquire what the man was in his belief. If I found out he was an atheist, or a deist, or a pantheist, when I would go to the funeral and in the presence of his friends said one word about that man's doctrine, they would feel insulted. Why is it that, in a trying hour, when they have been talking all the time against God – why is it that in the darkness of affliction they call in believers in that God to administer consolation?

The next class I want to call attention to is the infidel. I contend his "rock" is not as our "rock." Look at an infidel. An infidel is one who doesn't believe in the inspiration of Scripture. These men are very numerous, and they feel insulted when we call them infidels, but the man who doesn't believe in the inspirations of Scripture is an infidel. A good many of them are in the church, and not a few of them have crept into the pulpit. These men would feel insulted if we called them infidels, but if a man says – I don't care who he is or where he preaches – if he tries to say that the Bible is not inspired from back to back, he is an infidel. That is their true name, although they don't like to be called that.

Now in that blessed book there are five hundred or six hundred prophecies, and every one of them has been fulfilled to the letter, and yet men say they cannot believe the Bible is inspired. As I said the other night, those who cannot believe it have never read it. I hear a great many infidels talk against the Bible, but I haven't found the first man who ever read the Bible from back to back carefully and remained an infidel. My friends, the Bible of our mothers and fathers is true. How many men have said to me, "Mr. Moody, I would give the world if I had your faith, your consolation, the hope you have from your religion." Is not that a proof that "their rock is not as our rock?"

Now look at these prophecies in regard to Nineveh, in regard to Babylon, to Egypt, to the Jewish nation, and see how literally they have been fulfilled to the letter. Every promise God makes He carries out. But although infidels prefer their disbelief in the inspiration of Scripture, they do not believe in their hearts what they declare, else why when we talk with them, if they have any children, do they send them out of the room?

Now, not long ago, I went into a man's house, and when I commenced to talk about religion, he turned to his daughter and said, "You had better go out of the room; I want to say a few words to Mr. Moody." When she had gone, he opened a perfect torrent of infidelity upon me. "Why," said I, "did you send your daughter out of the room before you said this?" "Well," he replied, "I did not think it would do her any good to hear what I said." My friends, his "rock is not as our rock." Why did he send his daughter out of the room if he believed what he said? It was because he did not believe it. Why, if I believed in infidelity, I would wish my daughters and my sons, my wife, and all belonging to me to share the same belief. I would preach it wherever I went. But they doubt what they advocate. If they believed it down in their souls why when their daughters die, do they send for a true Christian to administer consolation? Why don't they send for some follower of Voltaire, or Hume, or Paine? Why when they make their last will do they send for some Christian to carry it out? My friends, it is because their rock has no foundation; it is because in the hour of adversity, in spite of all their boasts of the grandeur of infidelity, they cannot trust their infidel friends. "Their rock is not as our rock, even our enemies themselves being judges."

Now, did you ever hear of a Christian in his dying hour recanting? You never did. Did you ever hear of Christians regretting that they had accepted Christianity and in their dying hour embracing infidelity? I would like to see the man who could stand and say he had. But how many times have Christians been called to the bedside of an atheist, or deist, or infidel in his dying hours and heard him crying for mercy? In that hour, infidelity is gone, and he wants the God of his father and mother to take the place of his black infidelity.

It is said of West, an eminent man, that he was going to take up the doctrine of the resurrection and show the world what a fraud it was, while Lord Lyttelton was going to take up the conversion of Saul and just show the folly of it. These men were going to annihilate that doctrine and that incident of the gospel. They were going to emulate the Frenchman, who said it took twelve fishermen to build up Christ's religion, but one Frenchman pulled it down. From Calvary this doctrine rolled along the stream of time, through the 1,800 years, down to us, and West got at it and began to look at the evidence; but instead of being able to cope with it he found it perfectly overwhelming – the proof that Christ had risen, that He had come out of the sepulcher and ascended to heaven and led captivity captive.

The light dawned upon him, and he became an expounder of the Word of God and a champion of Christianity. And Lord Lyttelton, that infidel and skeptic, hadn't been long at the conversion of Saul before the God of Saul broke upon his sight, and he too began to preach. I don't believe there is a man in the audience who, if he will take his Bible and read it, will not be convinced of its truth. What does infidelity do for a man? "Why," said a dying infidel, "my principles have lost me my friends, my principles have sent my wife to her grave with a broken heart, they have made my children beggars, and I go down to my grave without peace or consolation." I never heard of an infidel going down to his grave happily. But not only do they go on without

THEIR ROCK IS NOT AS OUR ROCK

peace, but how many youths do they turn away from God? How many young men are turned away from Christ by these infidels and devils? Let them remember that God will hold them responsible if they are guilty of turning men away from heaven.

A few infidels gathered around a dying friend lately, and they wanted him to hold on to the end, to die like a man. They were trying to cheer him, but the poor infidel turned to them. "Ah," said he, "what have I got to hold on to?" My friends, let me ask you, what you have got to hold on to? Every Christian has Christ to hold on to – the resurrected man. "I am He that lives and was dead; and behold, I am alive for evermore." Thank God, we have someone to carry us through all our trials. But what has the infidel got to hold on to? What hope has the atheist, deist, or pantheist? His gods are false gods.

They are like the false gods of the Hebrews; they never hear their cry. Whereas, if we have the God of Daniel, of Abraham, He is always ready to succor us when in distress. We can make Him our fortress, and we have a refuge in the storm of adversity. There we can anchor safely, free from danger and disaster. I was reading tonight almost the last words of Lord Byron, and I want to draw a comparison between the sorrowful words of Byron and those of Saint Paul. He died very young – he was only thirty-six – after leading an ungodly life.

> "My days are in the yellow leaf,
>   The flower and fruit of life are gone;
> The worm, the canker and the grief
>   Are mine alone."

Compare those words with the words of St. Paul. "I have fought a good fight, I have finished my course, I have kept the faith. Henceforth there is laid up for me a crown of righteousness, which the Lord, the righteous Judge shall give me at that day." What a contrast! What a difference! My friends, there is as much difference between them as there is between heaven and hell, between death and life. Be judges. Which is the most glorious – atheism, deism, infidelity, or the Christianity of St. Paul? May God take all these "isms" and sweep them from the world.

I want to read to you a letter which I received some time ago. I read this to you because I am getting letters from infidels who say that not an infidel has repented during our meetings. Only about ten days ago I got a letter from an infidel who accused me of being a liar. He said there had not been an infidel converted during our meetings. My friends, go up to the young converts' meeting any Monday night, and you will see there ten or twelve every night who have accepted Christ. Why, nearly every night we meet with a poor infidel who accepts Christ. But let me read this letter. We get many letters every day for prayer, and my friends, you don't know the stories that lie behind those letters. The letter I am about to read was not received here, but while we were in Philadelphia. When I received it, I put it away, intending to use it at a future day.

"Dear Sir: – Allow me the privilege of addressing you with a few words. The cause of writing is indeed a serious one. I am the son of an aristocratic family of Germany – was expensively educated, and at college at Leipsic was ruined by drinking, etc.; was expelled for gambling and dishonesty. My parents were greatly grieved at my conduct, and I did not dare return home, but sailed for America. I went to St. Louis and remained there for want of money to get away. I finally obtained a situation as bookkeeper in a dry goods house; heard from home and the death of my parents. This made me more sinful than ever before. I heard one of your sermons, which made a deep impression on me. I was taken sick, and the words of your text came to me and troubled me. I have tried to find peace of God but have not succeeded. My friends, by reasoning with me that there was no God, endeavored to comfort me. The thought of my sinfulness and approaching the grave, my blasphemy, my bad example, caused me to mourn and weep. I think God is too just to forgive me my sins. My life is drawing to a close. I have not yet received God's favor. Will you not remember me in your prayer and beseech God to save my soul from eternal destruction? Excuse me for writing this, but it will be the last I shall write this side of the grave."

Ah, my friends, his "rock was not as our rock, even our enemies themselves being judges." I have two more letters I would like to read. I am not accustomed to read so many letters, but on this occasion, I will read them to you. Some of you remember me speaking of a man who came in here who was a fugitive from justice. The governor of the state from which he came had offered a reward for him. He came into this Tabernacle and he received Christ and returned to his State. This morning I received the following letter:

"Dear Sir and Brother: – Owing to the law's slow delay, I am yet a prisoner of hope. By Thursday or Friday my case will be reached, and I'll be committed to the penitentiary, how long I do not know. This condition is voluntary, or of my own seeking, because I feel it due the cause of God, or the only evidence I can give of my repentance and desire to do better. My family and friends hope ultimately to obtain a pardon. I desire to thank you for the interest you have taken in me, and I ask your prayers, and those of God's people in Chicago, that I may have strength and grace to live under these calamities, that my poor, heart-broken wife and children may be sustained, and further, that God's blessing may rest on all efforts being made for my future.

After it is all over, and I am in a felon's cell, I'll write you. In your efforts to warn men to do better and lead a new life, bid them beware of ambition to accomplish an undertaking at all hazards. Such is my condition. Had I left off speculation in an invention I might now be happy. Step by step I yielded until my forgeries reached over $30,000. My aim was not to defraud, but to succeed, and pay it all back. Oh, pray for me – for all who suffer with me. While in Chicago I was under an assumed name. Here I am, in my native village, in my father's home, a prisoner, not daring to go out, or even to see my children (we have three, two boys and one girl). I hear their voices, and when they sleep, I silently go in their little room and look at them in innocent slumber. My crimes are in another county whither I go Thursday. May our heavenly Father bless your labors. Humbly and repentant I am, _____"

Tomorrow, probably, he will go into the penitentiary to suffer for his crime, but now his rock is our rock.

Last week a handsome young man came into the inquiry room. He had been brought up in a happy home with a good father and mother, but he had gone astray. When he came into the inquiry room, he said he intended to become a Christian, but he could not because he knew what it would make him do. He had robbed an express company and that sin came between him and God. He had been heard and received a verdict in his favor, but he knew he was guilty. He had gone into the witness box and committed perjury. He turned away and left the building. Last

Friday, however, he was at the noonday meeting. He was in my private room for a while, and I never felt so much pity for a man in my life. He wanted to become a Christian, but he thought of having to go back and tell his father that he was guilty after his father had paid $2,000 to conduct his trial. After a great struggle he got down on his knees and cried out, "O God, help me; forgive me my sins!" And at last he got up and straightened himself and said, "Well, sir, I will go back." A friend went down to the railway station and saw him off, and shortly after, I got this dispatch from him:

"Mr. Moody – God has told me what to do. The future is as clear as crystal. I am happier than ever before."

He went on his way, reached his native village, and I received this letter from him this morning, and I have felt my soul filled with sorrow ever since it came. Let me say here, if there is anyone in this hall who has taken money from his employer, go and tell him of it at once. It is a good deal better for you to confess it than have it on your mind – than to try to cover it up. "He that covers his sins shall not prosper." If you have taken any money that doesn't belong to you, make restitution by confession at least. If anyone here is being tempted to commit a forgery or any crime, let this be a warning to them:

"My Beloved Friend and Brother: I am firm in the cause. I have started and feel that God is with me in it. And, oh, dear brother, do never cease praying for my dear father and praying mother, and I wish you would someday write them and tell them that God will make this all for the best. If I live for ages, I will never cease praying for them, and I never can forgive myself for my ungratefulness to my dear broken-hearted sisters and brothers and dear good parents. Oh, that link that held the once happy home is severed. O God! May it not be forever. Would that I had been a Christian for life; that I had taken my mother's hand when a child and walked from there, hand in hand, straight to heaven, and then the stains would not have been. But we know, O God, that they can't follow me into heaven, for then I will be washed of all my sins, and the things that are on this earth will stay here.

"Oh, my dear Christian brothers, my heart almost failed me when I was approaching my dear, happy home, and the thought that I was the one out of eight brothers and sisters to break the chain of happiness that surrounded that once happy and beautiful home, which is now shaded with misery, and the beautiful sunshine that once lit that happy, that dearest of homes, is now overshadowed with darkness. Oh, I fear it will take my dear parents; it is more than they can bear. When I reached home, and they all greeted me with a kiss, and I told them I had started for heaven, and God sent me home to tell them, my mother shed tears of happiness, and when I was forced to bring the death stroke upon her, the tears ceased to flow, and God only can describe the scene that took place. I called them all around me, and I thought I could not pray if I were to attempt it. But when I knelt with them in prayer, God just told me what to say, and I found it the will of God. After I had prayed, I kissed them all and asked their pardon for my ungratefulness, which I received from them all.

Then I made my preparation to leave home, for how long God only knows, but I got grace to leave in a cheerful way, and it appeared for a short time. If God lets me live to return home, I will join my mother's side, take her to church, and bring my brothers and sisters and father to God. We will all go to heaven together. My beloved brother, I must see you some day and just tell you what God has done for me, and I know He will never forsake me when I am shut up in those prison walls receiving the punishment I justly deserve for my crime. When I can't communicate with anyone else I know I will not be shut off from God. Oh, glory!

"I came to Cleveland last night and was going to get that money and return it to the General Superintendent, but my attorney had made that arrangement already. I find there is an indictment at Akron against me now for perjury, and I am going to take the morning train and go to Akron. Court is in progress now, and I am going to ask the court if there is an indictment against me, and if there is, I will hear it and then plead guilty. I will write you again soon and give you all the particulars and the length of my sentence."

I want to urge this letter upon your consideration as a warning. Think of the punishment that young man has brought upon himself; think of the agony of that father and mother when he broke the news to them – when he told them of his guilt. His "rock was not as our rock." May God bless every young man here tonight, and may they be brought to the acceptation of salvation. May they turn to You, God of their fathers and of their mothers, so that they can say, "Your rock is our rock – we are servants of God."

The Pharisee and the Publican

In this first parable we are told that men ought to pray always and everywhere; that prayer should not be left to a few in the churches, but all men ought to pray. He gives us a picture, so that we may understand in what spirit we ought to pray. Two men went up to the temple – one to pray to himself and the other to pray to God, and I think it will be safe to divide the audience into two bodies and put them under these two heads. I think, however, whether we divide the audience or not, we come under these two heads – those who have the spirit of the publican and those who have the spirit of the Pharisee. You can find that the whole community may be divided into these two classes. The spirit of the prodigal and the spirit of an elder brother are still in the world; the spirits of Cain and Abel are still in the world, and these two are representative men.

One of them trusted in his own righteousness and the other didn't have any trust in it, and I say I think all men will come under these two heads. They have either given up all their self-righteousness – renounced it all and turned their back upon it – or else they are clinging to their own righteousness. And you will find that these self-righteous men who are always clinging to their own righteousness are continually measuring themselves by their neighbors. "I thank God that I am not as other men are." That was the spirit of that Pharisee, and that is the spirit today of one class in this community, and the other class comes under the head of this other man.

Now let us look at the man Christ pictured first. It is evident that he was full of egotism, full of conceit, full of pride, and I believe, as I have said before on this platform, that is one of the greatest enemies the Son of God has today. I believe it keeps more men from the kingdom of God than anything else. Pride can grow on any soil, in any climate – no place is too hot for it, and no place is too cold for its growth. How much misery has it caused in this world! How many men here are kept from salvation by pride! Why, it sprung up into heaven, and for it Lucifer was cast out; by pride Nebuchadnezzar lost his throne. As he walked through Babylon he cried, "Is not this a great Babylon which I have built?" and he was hurled from his throne.

How many men who have become drunkards, who are all broken up – their will gone, health gone – and yet are just as full of pride as the sun is of light. It won't let them come to Christ and be saved. A great many live like this Pharisee – only in the form of religion; they don't want the wheat, only the husk; they don't want the kernel, only the shell. How many men are there in Chicago who are just living on empty form? They say their prayers, but they don't mean anything. Why, this Pharisee said plenty of prayers, but how did he pray? He prayed with himself. He might as well pray to this post. He didn't pray to God who knew his heart a thousand times better than he did himself. He thought he knew himself. He forgot that he was as a sepulcher, full of dead men's bones; forgot that his heart was rotten, corrupt, and vile, and he came and spread out his hands and looked up to heaven. Why, the very angels in heaven veil their faces before God as they cry, "Holy, holy, holy!"

But this Pharisee came into the temple and spread out his hands and said, "Lord, I thank You that I am not as other men are; I fast twice a week." He set before God what he had done in comparison with other men and was striking a balance and making out God to be his debtor, as thousands in Chicago are doing today. And then he said, "I give one-tenth of all I possess." I suppose if he were living in Chicago now, and we had gone to him and asked him for a donation to put up this Tabernacle, he would have said, "Well, I think it will do good; yes, I think it will – it may reach the vagabonds and outcasts – I don't need it, of course – but if it will reach that class it will do good. I will give $50, especially if you can get it in the morning papers, if you can have it announced, 'John Jones gave $50 to build the Tabernacle.'" That's the way some of the people give donations to God's cause; they give in a patronizing way, but in this manner, God won't accept it. If your heart doesn't go with your gift, God will not accept it.

This Pharisee said, "I give one-tenth of all I have, I keep up the services in the temple, I fast twice a week." He fasted twice a week, although only once was called for, and he thought because of this, he was far above other men. A great many people nowadays think because they don't eat meat, only fish, on Fridays, they deserve great credit, although they go on sinning all the week. Look at this prayer; there's no confession there. He had got so bad and the devil had so covered up his sins that he was above confession.

The first thing we have to do when we come to God is to confess. If there is any sin clustering around the heart, bear in mind we can have no communion with God. It is because we have sin about our hearts that our prayers don't go any higher than our head. We cannot get God's favor if we have any iniquity in our heart. People, like the Pharisee, have only been educated to pray. If they didn't pray every night, their conscience would trouble them, and they would get out of bed and say their prayers. But the moment they get off their knees, perhaps you may hear them swearing. A man may just as well get a string of beads and pray to them. It would do him as much good.

This Pharisee's prayer showed no spirit of contrition. There was no petition; he didn't ask anything from God. That is a queer kind of prayer. "Lord, I thank You that I am not as other men are, extortioners, unjust, adulterous, or even as the poor publican." Not a petition in his prayer. It was a prayerless prayer – it was downright mockery. But how many men have just got into that cradle and been rocked to sleep by the devil. A short time ago I said to a man: "Are you a Christian?" "Of course I am. I say my prayers every night." "But do you ever pray?" "Didn't I tell you I prayed?" he answered. "But do you ever pray?" "Why, of course I do; haven't I said so?" was his reply.

I found that he prayed, but he only went through the form, and after a little, I found that he had been in the habit of swearing! "How is this?" I asked. "Swearing and praying! Do your prayers ever go any higher than your head?" "Well," he replied. "I have sometimes thought that they didn't." My friends, if you are not in communion with God, your prayers are but forms. You are living in formalism, and your prayers will go no higher than your head. How many people in this assembly just go through the form? They cannot rest unless they say their prayers. How many are there with whom it is only a matter of education?

But this man trusted in his own righteousness; he ignored the mercy of God, the love of Jesus Christ. He was measuring himself by his own rule. Now, if you want to measure yourself, do it by God's law, by God's requirements. A great many people have a rule of their own by which they measure themselves and by that rule are perfectly ready and willing to forgive themselves. So it was with this Pharisee. The idea of coming to God and asking His forgiveness never enters his mind. While talking to a man – one of those Pharisees – some time ago about God and his need of Christ, he said, "I can do without Christ; I don't want Him. I'm ready to stand before God any time." That man was trusting in his own righteousness.

There are a good many in Chicago like this man. They think they can get on without Christ – without a mediator. Now take a good look at this man. You know I have an idea that the Bible is like an album. I go into a man's house, and while waiting for him, I take up an album from a table and open it. I look at a picture. "Why, that looks like a man I know." I turn over and look at another. "Well, I know that man." By and by I come upon another. "Why, that man looks like my brother." I am getting pretty near home. I keep turning over the leaves. "Well, I declare, there is a man who lives in the street I do – why, he is my next-door neighbor. And then I come upon another and I see myself. My friends, if you read your Bibles, you will find your own pictures there. It will just describe you.

Now it may be there is some Pharisee here tonight. If there is, let him turn to the 3rd chapter of John and see what Christ said to the Pharisee, "Except a man be born again he cannot enter the kingdom of God." Nicodemus, no doubt, was one of the fairest specimens of a man in Jerusalem in those days, yet he had to be born again else he couldn't see the kingdom of God. But you may say, "I am not a Pharisee. I am a poor, miserable sinner, too bad to come to Him." Well, turn to the woman of Samaria and see what He said to her.

See what a difference there was between that publican and that Pharisee. There was as great a distance between them as between the sun and the moon. One was in the very highest station, and the other occupied the very worst. One had only himself and his sins to bring to God, and the other was trying to bring in his position and his aristocracy. I tell you, when a man gets a true sight of himself, all his position and station and excellences drop. See this prayer: "I thank God," "I am not," "I fast," "I give," "I possess." Why, if he had delivered a long prayer, and it had been put into the printers' hands, they would have had to send out for some "I's." "I thank God," "I," "I," "I."

When a man prays, not with himself, but to God, he does not exalt himself. He doesn't pass a eulogy upon himself. He falls flat down in the dust before God. In that prayer you don't find him thanking God for what He had done for him. It was a heartless, prayerless prayer – merely a form. I hope the day will come when formal prayers will be a thing of the past. I think the reason why we cannot get more people out to the meetings is because we have too many formal prayers in the churches. These formal Christians get up like this Pharisee and thank God they are better than other men, but when a man gets a look at himself, he comes in the spirit of the publican. You see this man standing praying with himself, but God could not give him anything. He was too full of egotism – too full of himself. There was no religion in it. God could not bless him.

Now, for a moment, take a look at that poor publican. Just give his prayer your attention. There was no capital "I" there, no exalting of himself. "God be merciful to this Pharisee. God be merciful to the other people who have injured me. God be merciful to the church members who have not been true to their belief." Was that his prayer? Thank God he got to himself. "God be merciful to me, a sinner." It was very short. He had got his eye upon himself; he saw that his heart was vile. He could not lift his eyes to heaven, but thank God he could lift his heart to heaven. There is not a poor publican in the audience tonight but can send up this prayer. No matter what your past life has been – no matter if it has been as black as hell – if you but send up the prayer, it will be heard. He didn't buy his own righteousness, and God heard his prayer. Spurgeon, speaking of that publican, said he had the soundest theology of any man in all England. He came before God, struck his hand on his heart, and cried, "God, be merciful to me, a sinner!"

There was a man at one of our meetings in New York City who was moved by the Spirit of God. He said, "I am going home, and I am not going to sleep tonight till Christ takes away my sin; if I have to stay up all night and pray, I'll do it." He had a good distance to walk, and as he went along, he thought, "Why can't I pray now as I go along instead of waiting to go home?" But he did not know a prayer. His mother had taught him to pray, but it was so long since he had uttered a prayer that he had forgotten. However, the publican's prayer came to his mind. Everybody can say this prayer. That man in the gallery yonder, that young lady over there: "God be merciful to me, a sinner." May God write it on your hearts tonight. If you forget the sermon, don't forget that prayer. It is a very short prayer, and it has brought joy – salvation – to many a soul. Well, this prayer came to the man, and he began, "God be merciful to me a –," but before he got to sinner, God blessed him. He got up in the young converts' meeting and told us as he said those words, the light of eternal truth broke upon his soul – the light from the celestial regions of glory broke upon him – and when we left New York he was walking in the righteousness of God.

In a meeting recently, a man got up. I didn't know him at first. When I was here, he was a rum seller and broke up his business and went to the mountains. This is how it happened. When I was here before, he opened a saloon and a grand billiard hall. It was one of the most magnificent billiard halls on the West Side all elegantly gilded and frescoed. For the opening he sent me an invitation to be present, which I accepted, and went around before he opened it. I saw the partners and asked them if they would allow me to bring a friend. They asked me who it was. "Well, it isn't necessary to tell who it is, but I never go without him." They began to mistrust me. "Who is it?" they again inquired. "Well, I'll come with him and if I see anything wrong, I'll ask him to forgive you." "Come," said they, "we don't want any praying." "You've given me an invitation, and I am coming." "But if you come, you needn't pray."

"Well," said I, "I'll tell you what we'll do. We'll compromise the matter. If you don't want me to come and pray for you then, let me pray for both of you now," which they agreed to.

It turned out that one of them had a praying mother, and the prayer touched his heart, and the other had a mother in heaven. I asked God to bless their souls, and just to break their business to pieces. In a few months, their business did go all to pieces. The man who got up in the prayer meeting told me a story that touched my soul. He said with his business he hadn't prospered. He failed and went away to the Rocky Mountains. Life became a burden to him, and he made up his mind that he would go to some part of the mountains and put an end to his days. He took a knife with him which he proposed driving into his heart. He sought a part of the mountains to kill himself. He had the knife ready to plunge into his heart when he heard a voice – it was the voice of his mother. He remembered her words when she was dying even though he was a boy then. He heard her say "Johnny, if ever you get into trouble, pray to God." That knife dropped from his hand, and he asked God to be merciful to him.

He was accepted, and he came back to Chicago and lifted up his voice for Him. He may be in this Tabernacle tonight. Just the moment he cried for mercy, he got it. If you only cry, "God, be merciful to me a sinner," He will hear you. Is there anything to hinder you from doing this tonight? Is there anything to hinder any man, woman, or child in this hall tonight from sending up this prayer? What a glorious thing it would be if every soul in this hall would but lift up their hearts with the prayer, "God, be merciful to me a sinner."

Now, a man asked me the other day, "How is it that a man who has lived an ungodly life can come in here and be saved all at once?" Why, God so loves the sinner that He is willing to give them salvation instantly. He wants to save every one now in Chicago. The trouble is that we don't want God to be merciful; we don't want His forgiveness. God is full of compassion and love. It is the spirit of the devil that makes you believe the sins committed during the past twenty years cannot be forgiven tonight. My friends, won't you try Him? But I will take you who believe this way upon your own ground.

Here is a father down here. He is full of self-righteousness; he is a

Pharisee. He has a boy whom he has not seen for twenty years. Well, as he goes home tonight, his servants tell him, "Your absent son has returned." "What!" he exclaims, "my absent boy Johnny here – in this house?" "Yes, he is down in the kitchen. We wanted him to go into the parlor, but he wouldn't; he said the kitchen was good enough for him." He tells those servants to take him to his son, and for a moment the boy looks at him. "Father, father!" he cries. "I have been bad; I haven't done a good act in twenty years. I have been very unkind to you, but, father, won't you forgive me?" Say, father, wouldn't you forgive him? Wouldn't you? I would like to see a man in Chicago who would not.

I can give you a little experience of my own family. Before I was four years old the first thing I remember was the death of my father. He had been unfortunate in business and failed. Soon after his death, the creditors came in and took everything. My mother was left with a large family of children. One calamity after another swept over the entire household. Twins were added to the family, and my mother became ill. The eldest boy was fifteen years of age, and to him my mother looked as a stay in her calamity, but all at once that boy became a wanderer. He had been reading some of the trashy novels, and the belief had seized him that he had only to go away and make a fortune.

Away he went. I can remember how eagerly she used to look for tidings of that boy; how she used to send us to the post-office to see if there was a letter from him and recollect how we used to come back with the sad news, "No letter." I remember how in the evenings we would sit beside her in that New England home, and we would talk about our father; but the moment the name of that boy was mentioned she would hush us into silence. Some nights when the wind was very high, and the house, which was upon a hill, would tremble at every gush, the voice of my mother was raised in prayer for that wanderer who had treated her so unkindly. I used to think she loved him more than all the rest of us put together, and I believe she did.

On a Thanksgiving Day – you know that is a family day in New England – she used to set a chair for him thinking he would return home. Her family grew up and her boys left home. When I got so that I could write, I sent letters all over the country, but could find no trace of him. One day while in Boston the news reached me that he had returned. While in that city I remember how I used to look for him in every store – he had a mark on his face – but I never got any trace.

One day while my mother was sitting at the door, a stranger was seen coming toward the house, and when he came to the door he stopped. My mother didn't know her boy. He stood there with folded arms, and a great beard flowing down his breast, his tears trickling down his face. When my mother saw those tears, she cried, "Oh, it's my lost son!" and entreated him to come in. But he stood still. "No, mother," he said, "I will not come in till I hear first you have forgiven me." Do you believe she was not willing to forgive him? Do you think she was likely to keep him long standing there? She rushed to the threshold and threw her arms around him and breathed forgiveness. Ah, sinner, if you but ask God to be merciful to you, a sinner, ask Him for forgiveness. Although your life has been bad – ask Him for mercy, and He will not keep you long waiting for an answer.

May that be the cry of every lost soul in this Tabernacle tonight. "God be merciful to me, a sinner." Now, do you want to have mercy? Say, young man, will you ask Him tonight? Young lady, will this be your cry tonight, "God, be merciful to me, a sinner?" May the love of God break every obdurate heart here tonight and may this be the cry of every sinner. Don't have so much pride, don't have the spirit of the Pharisee – that's the spirit that keeps you from entering the inquiry room and coming to the God of love, the God of compassion, the God of mercy, of peace, of joy, of everlasting happiness. Let every man and woman in this assemblage out of Christ take the place of this publican and go into the inquiry room. Let us pray.

Address to Businessmen

I want to call your attention for a few minutes this evening to this man that the Savior has brought before us in this portion of Scripture. You will see by reading it that he was what we would call nowadays a successful businessman – a man that many parents would hold up to their sons as a model. I don't think he was a drinking man; there's nothing in the story that would lead us to suppose he was. He hadn't made his money in getting up corners on grain. He didn't get it by any acts of usury by which he drew twenty percent. He didn't get it by making a corner on gold or getting up a Black Friday. He didn't make his money by betting on elections or buying stocks, but he got it lawfully. No doubt he was a moralist; certainly, there is nothing in what we have read tonight against his character. That was not his fault. He didn't rent his property for billiard halls, for liquor saloons, or to harlots – he was a farmer.

I don't know of a more lawful occupation than that of a farmer. He was a successful man. I don't believe he ever compromised with his creditors by paying 50 cents on the dollar when he could pay 100. He didn't get his money that way. He didn't get it by shaving notes or by taking advantage of the widow and orphan, or those who were poor, but he got it lawfully. He was an upright man. I presume if he were here, we would send him to Congress, or if we could not send him to Congress we would make him Mayor. He was a thoroughly good businessman who paid all he promised to pay. He was what we would call a shrewd man – a long-headed man, just deluged with business, and undoubtedly, if you had spoken to him about his soul's welfare, he would have turned to Scripture and said, "Be not slothful in business." Business must be attended to first; that's what Scripture teaches.

And I think that Chicago men have got as far as that in Scripture, and there they stop. A man came out here from the East, and a minister asked him to preach in his pulpit, and he picked out the text, "not slothful in business," but went no further. "Why," said the minister to him, "don't you know that all Chicago have got that down in their soul? Why don't you preach upon the whole of the text and not a part?" "Not slothful in business." Chicago doesn't want that kind of preaching. He forgot the rest – "fervent in spirit, serving the Lord." This man was earnest with business. He had got off that part of the text. Undoubtedly, he moved in the best society of his time. He had the best carriage in that part of the country. He had the best farm in that section of the country and the best horses and cattle. If he had been living today, probably he would have had the best short-horn cattle and the very finest wool sheep. He had the very best undoubtedly, in his time and had been called a great success.

No doubt in those days they had revival meetings. Of course they had, because one of the greatest revivals that ever took place occurred in those days under John the Baptist. Perhaps it took place near his farm, but he could not leave his business to attend it. Great multitudes flocked past his house from early morn till late at night on their way to the banks of the Jordan to hear the greatest revivalist that ever lived, except Jesus Christ. But he didn't leave his business to go; he probably thought they were fanatics. The idea that a businessman would turn from his legitimate business, from his merchandise – to waste his time to hear that preacher. No doubt he belonged to the synagogue. He believed in set doctrines and walked accordingly. He would not hear of those innovations. The idea of spending his time in going to listen to a man who was clothed with a leather girdle and fed on locusts and wild honey! No, sir. He wouldn't hear him.

Undoubtedly Jesus and His apostles passed by that way, and he might have one night entertained Him. Perhaps he had heard about the dead being raised by this man as these drunkards are being raised in Chicago today – men who are being lifted from sin and degradation and a new song put into their mouth. Like a great many of these businessmen today, perhaps he said, "Oh, it's only a nine days' wonder, and the excitement will be gone soon." Christ came and went, but he was so pressed with business that he hadn't time to attend to what that heavenly preacher said. He hadn't time to go to those meetings on the banks of the Jordan. So it is with men today. They haven't time to look into this great question of Jesus Christ. They have heard of Him but can't stop to see how He came, why He came, or what He has done.

Business is so pressing. Undoubtedly, he had the very best wine there was in the land, and it was always on his table, although he wasn't a drunkard. He had the very best fruit, the very best fish and game upon his table. The very best material he wore – perhaps he sent all the way down to Egypt to buy clothing for his wife and daughters. His carriage was the most stylish – probably he was often seen with a four-in-hand on the highway. Everybody said he was getting along nicely. If a friend came to see him, he would take him all around and show him his land and his barns and point to this and that part that he was going to pull down and make larger; business was increasing. He would show him all through his grand house and tell how he was once a poor boy, how his father died, and how the creditors came and took everything – how he had commenced life with nothing and had made all his friend saw. Just like a great many men here. They will tell how they came to Chicago poor boys; how by hard work, by incessant toiling, they have gained what they have now, taking all the glory to themselves instead of giving it to God. Look at him! If a man cheated him out of $5 how he would resent it. Shrewd, practical, businessman; and yet, the devil was cheating him out of his soul. That is the way today. They are just living for time. The great trouble with this man was he was blind – he was just living from the cradle to the grave. He didn't want to take death into his plans. "In every man's garden there is a sepulcher." My friends, in every man's home there is a sepulcher. Death is inevitable, and is not a man mad who does not take it into his plans?

Look at him. One night, he is in the drawing room of this beautiful, palatial home, and he stands with an architect looking over plans. He is going to have a new barn built. It is going to be the best that money can erect. He doesn't want any of his neighbors to approach him. It is going to be the very best. The architect has gone away, and he stands there looking over the plans. His family have retired, and all the servants have gone to bed. The doors and windows are all double-locked, double-barred, sealed, chained – fastened securely, but a stranger comes in slowly and lays a cold hand upon him, and says, "Come! I must take you away." "Who are you, stranger?" "I am Death." He should not have been any stranger to him.

The idea of Death being a stranger to any of us. Why, death is all around us. No doubt he had attended many funerals, and perhaps acted as pallbearer. Perhaps he was like some people in Chicago; he never heard a sermon except when he attended a funeral. He had heard a sermon then and had seen the body laid in the ground, and now his time has come. He wants to bribe Death and offers him thousands of dollars to give him a little more time; but he cannot bribe Death. You can bribe politicians, you may bribe these businessmen, but there is an officer that never can be bought, never can be bribed, and when he comes, we have to obey his summons.

When Death says, "Come, you must go with me," we have to obey him. When Death entered that chamber and said, "Come, I want you," he might have cried, "Let me live a little longer; let me have these places finished, just a few years longer." "Come," says Death, "come." "Why, what are you going to do with me? Where are you going to take me?" "You have had time enough to see to that; you must come now." The man weeps and cries, "I've got a loving wife, I have loving children, I have got a perfect palace – a beautiful home, which I have been all my life preparing. I've just got it fixed up now; don't summon me away now! Oh Death, spare me a little longer." Like that queen he cries, "O for an inch of time!" But says Death, "Come!" and lays his cold hand upon that heart and it ceases to beat. Perhaps when the servants come in, they find him sitting at his desk dead.

The news spreads through the house, and that wife learns she is a widow. I see that widow and those children gathering around the body of that father. The family physician comes. He looks at that body and puts his hand on that pulse, but the pulse that told the man how fast he was traveling toward eternity had ceased to beat. There is a stir in that community next morning – "Squire so-and-so is dead; he was a shrewd man, a practical, successful man." Perhaps at the funeral the whole community turned out and probably got a minister, as they get them in our day, to come to the funeral and deliver a eulogy over him, who said he was very benevolent to the poor, he was very philanthropic, and held him up as an example.

It appears to me there is more lying at funerals than anywhere else. Men stand up and pronounce a eulogy over men who have lived a churchless, godless life – who have gone down to a Christless, godless grave, and say because they have been wise and good to the poor they have gone to a better world. God sees differently. You and I may try to make out this man as a shrewd man, a wise man, a man to be held up as an example, but just see what the Son of Man says about him. He says such a man is an abomination to God. The Son of Man says, "You fool." He wrote his epitaph, and it has been handed down to us as a warning – handed down for 1,800 years.

I can imagine some of you saying, "If I had known that he would have talked about death tonight, I would not have come. Why doesn't he talk about life, about happiness; why doesn't he tell us about how to get on in business – how to get through the battle of life? Why does he speak about death only?" I will tell you why it is. It is because nine out of every ten die unexpectedly; it is because nine out of every ten die wholly unprepared. They may have been warned; death may have come very near. It might have entered their house and taken away a loved wife, loved children, a loved father or mother – death may have come into their homes four, five, six, seven, ten times, and taken away relatives from their midst. Yet they are unprepared. Do you know that six million people die annually in the world?

Since I came here and began preaching in this Tabernacle, death has thrown its mantle around many a one. Do you remember that death in this cold, dark, bleak night is doing its work? I am speaking to some who may be in eternity tomorrow. I come to tell you to be prepared. Is not it downright folly to spend your lives in piling up wealth and to die as this man died, without hope, without Christ, without eternal life? Let me call your attention to this. The sin of this man was simply neglect. It is clear. We cannot condemn his business. It was honest, legitimate. But the thing we do condemn is that he neglected to secure his soul's salvation.

A great many say, "Am I not kind to the poor? Am I not honorable in all my transactions? Do I not pay a hundred cents on a dollar always?" But are you honest to your soul's salvation? You may fold your arms and depend upon your deeds, but if you do not seek salvation in this world you will be lost. You know that there are three steps down the hill, and they are to neglect, to refuse, and to despise. Now all in this audience are standing on some of the steps of this ladder. You can see how if a man neglects his salvation, he will be lost.

All you men, if you neglect your business, leave it to itself, you know you will soon become bankrupt. And if man wants to die, all he has to do is to call in a doctor. Look at a general of an army of 10,000 men. He knows that there is an army of 10,000 coming to meet him, but he goes and takes his glass and sees in the distance another army of 10,000 men who are coming up to reinforce his enemy. He knows he cannot delay; if he does, he will soon be overwhelmed by the 20,000 men ahead of him. A man who neglects his soul's salvation does not look at what is ahead of him, and the enemy comes up and overwhelms him. Death comes, as it probably came to this man, at the midnight hour, unexpectedly and unbidden. You know more men die at night than in the day – from midnight to three o'clock in the morning. How many men die unexpectedly.

Look at the millions and millions who die unexpectedly. Although we live an allotted time – three score and ten – when death comes, it comes unexpectedly. This man had provided for his family; he had built up a great business, had provided for his own wants, but he made no provision for his own soul. You might have gone to his house and taken up a pencil and written on everything he possessed "You fool." He spent all his life in accumulating money, and then he had to leave it all. A sailor was telling a man that his father and his grandfather and his great-grandfather were all drowned at sea, and the man said, "Why don't you get prepared to die, then, you may be drowned any day, too?" "Where did your father die?" inquired the sailor. "On land." "And your grandfather?" "On land." "And your great-grandfather?" "On land, too."

"Are you prepared to die?" "Well, no." "Why don't you get prepared?" asked the sailor. He didn't think he was in danger continually himself, but that the sailor was.

I think the greatest text that is given to us is, "Prepare to meet your God." Are you ready? Why do you neglect any longer to accept salvation? All the children of Israel had to do to be cured was to look on that brazen serpent; they were healed instantly. If they neglected to look upon that serpent, they died. All you have got to do is to look upon Christ and receive life. Look at the Indian who is in his canoe. He has gone to sleep. Perhaps he may be dreaming about hunting grounds, perhaps he may be dreaming of his friends in the Indian village. Yet he is in the rapids which are taking him over the cataract. He is not rowing toward it; he is sound asleep, the paddle lies in the bottom of that canoe. Without any effort of his own, the current is taking him toward the fall.

By and by the poor man wakes up, and he sees he is on the brink of the cataract. In a few moments he will plunge over. He gives an unearthly cry, and down he goes into the jaws of death. All here tonight are in the current that is carrying them to the cataract – rushing on to judgment. A great many things in this world are not sure. You may buy grain, you may buy land; you are not sure whether the value will go up or down, but there is one thing that you are sure of, and that is death. "For it is appointed unto men once to die, but after this the judgment." After that the judgment. You can be sure of that.

Now the question is, are you ready? I can imagine some of you saying, "I've got time enough. I don't propose to settle this question just yet: there's a good many years before me." Is there a man who can say this? Is there a man who can say, "Tomorrow is mine?" We are on the journey toward the judgment. Have you got a hope in the future, have you that which will take you over the grave? Have you that power which will carry you through death and judgment? You go to Graceland and summon up the dead. Bring them into this hall in the midst of this audience with their ghastly winding-sheets, and see how many of them died old. You will find that more of them died young than old. Why, whole populations are swept into eternity before they reach their allotted age. Instead of three score and ten the allotted age nowadays is about 30 years. My friends, we will soon be in eternity. What are you doing? Are you reflecting?

Some of you are on the second round of the ladder. You are refusing. I was talking to a lady last night, and she said calmly, coolly, and deliberately, "I don't want Him; I don't want Christ." "Do you really mean this?" I asked. "Yes, I don't want Him." I presume a few years ago she would not have said this, but she had got on the second round of the ladder, and some now despise it. If you get a tract upon the streets, you just tear it up. You mock and make light of the God of your father and your mother. You have got on the bottom round of the ladder, and you despise the gift of God. My friends, that is the last round. A man has sunk pretty low when he despises the gift of God – when he hurls it back to God and says, "I will not have it."

Now, I want to ask you this question. What are you going to do? Will you think a few minutes, young men? Will you stop for a few minutes and just think? I wish I could wake this audience up for five minutes. Just ask yourselves where you are, or to make it more personal, "What am I? Where am I going?" A dying man called a Hindu priest to his bedside and asked him where he was going. The priest said he was going into an animal. "Well after that, where am I going?" "Going into another animal." "Where next?" "Into another animal," and he went on telling the man he would enter into this and that animal until he stopped. Then the man asked, "Where shall I go after that?" The poor heathen priest could not tell him. Ah, won't you settle this question tonight? "What shall it profit a man if he gain the whole world and lose his own soul?" Suppose a man has the whole wealth of Chicago rolled at his feet, and then he dies. What has he gained?

A father was on his deathbed lately, and he called in his son. The boy was careless; he would not take death into account. He wanted to enjoy the pleasures of life, and he took no heed of the future. The old man said, "My son, I want to ask you one favor, and that is, when I am dead, promise me you will come into this room for five minutes every day for thirty days. You are to come alone, not to bring a book with you, and sit here." The thoughtless young man promised to do it. The father died.

The first thing when he went into that room that he thought of was his father's prayer – his father's words, and his father's God, and before the five minutes expired, he was crying out, "God be merciful to me!" It seems to me if I could get men to always ask themselves, "What is going to be my end? Where am I going to spend eternity?" it would not be long before they would come to Christ. You may be moralists, you may be proprietors of a successful business, you may be what the world calls successful businessmen, yet where are you going to spend eternity? Can you tell me where you will be next year? Can you tell me where you are going to be ten years hence? Can you tell me?

I want to read a little notice on a card which is headed: "I have missed it – at last." A few months ago in New York, a physician called upon a young man who was ill. He sat for a little by the bedside examining his patient, and then he honestly told him the sad intelligence that he had but a short time to live. The young man was astonished; he did not expect it would come to that so soon. He forgot that death comes "in such an hour as you think not." At length he looked up in the face of the doctor, and with a most despairing countenance repeated the expression, "I have missed it – at last." "What have you missed?" inquired the tenderhearted, sympathizing physician. "I have missed it – at last," again the young man replied. The doctor, not in the least comprehending what the poor young man meant said, "My dear young man, will you be so good as to tell me what you –?" He instantly interrupted saying, "O doctor, it is a sad story – a sad, sad story that I have to tell. But I have missed it!"

"Missed what?" "Doctor, I have missed the salvation of my soul." "Oh! say not so. It is not so. Do you remember the thief on the cross?" "Yes, I remember the thief on the cross. And I remember that *he* never said to the Holy Spirit – Go your way. But *I did*. And now He is saying to me, Go *your way*." He lay gasping awhile, and looking up with a vacant, staring eye he said, "I was awakened and was anxious about my soul a little time ago. But I did not want religion then. Something seemed to say to me, don't postpone it. I knew I ought not to do it. I knew I was a great sinner and needed a Savior. I resolved, however, to dismiss the subject for the present. Yet I could not get my own consent to do it, until I had promised that I would take it up again, at a time not remote and more favorable.

I bargained away, insulted, and grieved away the Holy Spirit. I never thought of coming to this. I meant to have religion and make my salvation sure. And now I have missed it – at last." "You remember," said the doctor, "that there were some who came at the eleventh hour." "My eleventh hour," he rejoined, "was when I had that call of the Spirit. I have had none since – I shall not have. I am given over to be lost." "Not lost," said the doctor, "you may yet be saved." "No – not saved – never. He tells me I may go my way now. I know it – I feel it, feel it here," laying his hand upon his heart. Then he burst out in despairing agony, "Oh, I have missed it! I have sold my soul for nothing – a feather – a straw – undone forever!" This was said with such unutterable, indescribable despondency that no words were said in reply. After lying a few moments, he raised his head, and looking all around the room as if for some desired object – turning his eyes in every direction – then burying his face in the pillow, he again exclaimed, in agony and horror, "Oh, I have missed it at last!" and he died.

Dear friends, you may not hear my voice again. I may be speaking to you for the last time. You may never come into this Tabernacle again, and I beg of you as a friend and as a brother, do not go out of this Tabernacle without salvation. Let this night be the night that you will accept everlasting life. Let this be the night on which you will cry from the depth of your heart, "Let me have Christ, let me have salvation." "Though it cost me my right hand or my right eye, I will have Christ tonight." May that be the cry of everyone here tonight, and salvation be accepted for time and eternity by every soul in this building. May God wake up every soul here tonight, and when that summons comes, may you go to triumph over the grave and so enter into a glorious immortality. Let us unite in prayer.

The Life and Character of Jacob

The key to all Jacob's difficulties will be found in the 20th chapter of Matthew. It is the story of the laborers in the vineyard. The thought is in the 2nd verse. The first men hired agreed to the bargain. The men would not go until the owner of the vineyard had made a bargain with them. He told them that he would pay them what was right. They got a penny. He gave them the lawful wages. "Is that all you're going to give me?" they probably said. Jacob was all the time making bargains. The Christians who are making bargains with the Lord do not get as much as those who trust Him. It does not pay to make bargains with the Lord. Jacob is a twin brother of most of us. Where you will find one Joseph or one Daniel you will find a hundred Jacobs. We are not willing, all of us, to take God at His word and trust Him.

There is a strong contrast between the character of Joseph and Jacob. The one trusted God implicitly, but Jacob wanted to trust Him no farther than he could see God. There would have been a great deal of murmuring if Jacob had been thrown into jail in Egypt. Jacob no doubt got a great deal of his weakness from his mother. There was a division in that home. Isaac favored Esau, and Rebekah favored Jacob. Such dissensions are just the thing to stir up the old Adam in the man. A mother and a father have no right to take this course. Rebekah planned continually to keep Jacob at home. The very thing that Rebekah tried to achieve, in that, she failed. By nature, Esau was the better of the two. If such a mean, contemptible nature as Jacob's could be saved, then there is hope for all of us.

The Lord promised to Jacob from the top of the ladder what he should have. Jacob gets up and says if God will be with me and keep and clothe me, then shall the Lord be my God. What a low, contemptible idea he had. God had promised him all from Dan to Beersheba. That's the difficulty with the people at the present time. If God will bless us in our basket and store, we shall have Him for our God. We find Jacob after this in Haran driving bargains all the time, and the worst of it is he gets beat every time. He had to work seven years for his wife and then gets another woman in her place. He gets paid back in his own coin. We must not think that God will allow us to deceive without punishing us for it. He forgot all the vows he had made at Bethel, but God did not forget His.

Some of God's promises are unconditional. The promise he made at Bethel was unconditional. God chose Jacob rather than Esau. Some people say that God hated Esau before he was born. This is not the teaching of Scripture, even though one of the minor prophets long years after mentioned it. God says to Jacob after he had been in Haran for so many years, "I am the God of Bethel; arise and dwell there." He ought to have been proud, but instead of leaving Haran like a prince, he steals away like a thief. He starts off, and his uncle and father-in-law pursue. God took care of him; God was going to keep His vows. There is no doubt that had not God interfered, Jacob would have been slain. We find that Jacob stays behind like a miserable coward after he had sent his effects away. A man out of communication with God is a coward always.

There was a man who wrestled with Jacob. It was Christ. When did he prevail? When his thigh was out of joint. All he could do was to hold on and get the blessing. The man who is the lowest down is the man that God lifts up the highest. The man that has the greatest humility will be the most exalted. A great many say that Jacob was a different man. Would to God his thigh had been left out of joint so that there was no more of the flesh in him. The next thing we find Jacob and Esau embracing, and we would suppose that he would be filled with gratitude. But no; he goes down to Shechem and builds an altar and calls it by a high-sounding name. Jacob in Shechem with this altar with a high-sounding name was no better than he was in Haran without an altar.

It would be a good day if we people in Chicago would bury our idols, rum bottles, tobacco, and cigars beneath an oak in Shechem. The trouble is that we have slipped down to Shechem. There his sons fell. It is when men go down to Haran and Shechem, instead of staying in Bethel, that they fall into sin. Let the church of God come out and stand before the world free from idols. There would be no need for idols. The only thing that keeps back the blessing of God are the church members. He built an altar finally at Bethel. He said that he would go to Bethel and build an altar to his God, as if the Shechem altar was no altar. He called it El-Bethel. Just the moment he came to Bethel, the Lord God met him, and just as soon as the church leaves Shechem and comes to Bethel, then the Lord God will meet it.

The next thing we hear is the saddest episode in Jacob's life – the death of Rachel, his favorite wife. His sons go back to Shechem and hunt up the old idols. His sons bring him back news from there that his beloved son was dead. Do you see how he begins to reap the sins of his own earlier days? For twenty long years he mourned that beloved boy. He deceived his own father, and his own sons deceived him. What a bitter life. What was Jacob's dying testimony to Pharaoh? It would take ten thousand Jacobs to get one convert like Pharaoh. "Few and evil," Jacob said, "had his days been." He started with a lie in his mouth. He died in exile. He died in Egypt, not in the land God promised him. He would not let God choose for him. He was saved by fire, or as Job said, by the skin of his teeth. We must walk less by sight and more by faith. It is safer for God to choose and to do the planning. It is for us to be satisfied with God's writ. Let us be satisfied and wait upon Him saying, "Your will be done and not ours."

Address to Parents

Second Address

I have had a little trouble to find a text for tonight. All last night and this morning I was trying to find one but could not. This morning, however, in coming out of Farwell Hall prayer meeting, a mother, whom I have known for a great many years, came to me with tears running down her cheeks, and with grief, nearly sinking to the floor. "O Mr. Moody," she said, "have these meetings to close and not one of my children saved?" and the thought flashed on my mind, "I have got a text, and it is in the 9th chapter of Mark," which we have read: *"Bring him unto me."*

The disciples had failed to cure this man's son. James and John and Peter had been with the Master upon the mount where they had seen the transfiguration, and when they came down from that scene they found a great company around His disciples, asking them questions. I suppose the skeptics were laughing and ridiculing the religion of Jesus Christ and its teachers. His disciples had failed – they had not been able to cast out the dumb spirit, and the father said, when asked a question, "I have brought my son to your disciples, and they cannot heal him," and He said, "Bring him to Me."

When he was brought, the devil threw him down. The moment the poor deaf and dumb man came into the presence of Christ, the spirit within began to tear at him. This is often the case now. Sometimes when there is a good deal of prayer going up for people, they become worse. When the Spirit begins with men, instead of getting better, they sometimes become worse, and it seems as if God did not answer prayer. But this is only a sign that God is at work.

A mother was praying for and giving good counsel to a loved son lately, and he said if ever she spoke to him about religion again, he would leave the house. Whenever the word was presented to him, he became worse. That mother did not take her son to the preachers, but thank God, she took him to Christ. She didn't take him to the church, she did not take him to her friends – she knew that if he was to be saved it was only by Jesus Christ. She took him to the Master, and the result was that within forty-eight hours after saying this to his mother, that wayward boy was brought to the feet of Jesus.

So if any have been praying earnestly and faithfully for their sons without success, my dear friends, get your eyes off the church, off friends, off everything else but Him, and let your prayer go up day and night, and it will be heard because we have God's word for it. An answer is sure. We are not sure whether the sun will rise tomorrow morning, but we are sure that He will answer our prayers. It is sure. If we hold on to God in prayer and find that we don't get our supplications answered in a month – in a year – we are to hold on till the blessing comes. Now, it may be that this mother, like a great many mothers, has been looking to the prayers here – looking to what has been going on in these meetings, and has been saying, "There are so many Christian people praying, and surely God will bless my boys owing to these prayers."

Now, we must get our eyes from off multitudes, from sermons, from others' prayers, and let all our expectations be only from Him, and a blessing will come. These meetings have been very profitable, and during the weeks past I have noticed that those fathers and mothers who have gone out after other people's children have had their own wonderfully blessed. Whatever good you do to other people's children, the reflex will come back upon yours. It may be that that mother was very selfish and wanted her sons blessed only; she hasn't, perhaps, been trying to bring others under the influence of the Lord Jesus Christ.

Everyday fathers and mothers come to me with tears in their eyes – fathers and mothers who have gone out after other people's children – testifying how their children have been blessed. A mother who has been working for Him here, told me that her five children – every one of them – had been blessed by these meetings, and I suppose that if I put it to the vote, many parents here would stand up and testify as to the answers received to prayers and personal efforts for their children. I was very much surprised lately to see an old citizen coming into our meetings with a wayward son by his side night after night. Every evening he was to be seen with him, and last Monday evening he got up and told what God had done for him in answer to personal effort. That father got woke up and did not rest till he was answered.

Now it seems to me, just as we are leaving this city, that a great many parents are beginning to wake up to the fact that these meetings are about to be closed and their children have not been blessed. When we were in Great Britain, in Manchester, a father woke up to the fact that we were going away from that town. Just as we were about closing, he got wonderfully interested in the meetings, and when we had gone to another town he said to his wife, "I have made a mistake: I should have taken you and the children and the servants to those meetings. Now I'm going to take my son from business and take you and the children and the servants to the town where they are being held now and take a house and have you all attend the meetings." He came and took a house and sat down determined to remain there till all had been blessed. I remember him coming to me one night soon after arriving and saying, "Mr. Moody, my wife has got converted. Thank God for that. If I get nothing else, I am well paid."

A few nights after, he came in and said his son had become converted and then told me one of the servants had been brought under the influence, and so he went on until the last day we were to be in that town arrived, and he came to me and said the last one of the family had yielded himself up to Christ, and he went back to his native city rejoicing. When we were in London, the father and son came up and assisted in the work, and I don't know a happier man in all Europe than that one. How many parents living almost within sight of this building have felt no interest in these meetings, yet they know their children are hastening down to death and ruin. Business must be attended to, time is very precious, and they have wasted the opportunity to bring their sons and daughters under religious influences, and the result will be that many and many a family in this city will see dark days and bitter hours, and many a parent will go down to their graves on account of wayward children. Now, why won't you, even in the closing hours of these meetings – why won't parents wake up and bring their children to Christ; just hold them up in the arms of their faith and pray, "Lord Jesus, save these children that God has given me. Grant, O God, that they may be with me in glory."

It may be that some father or mother is saying, "I have not been living right myself in God's sight, so how can I talk to my children of Him?" It seems to me the best thing to do under those circumstances is to make a confession. I knew a father who a few days ago told his children that he had not been living right. The tears rolled down his cheeks as he asked their forgiveness. "Why" said one child, "do you ask us for forgiveness? Why, father, you have always been kind to us." "I know I have, my child," he answered, "but I have not been doing my whole duty toward you. I've never had a family altar: I have paid more heed to your temporal welfare than to your spiritual, but I am going to have a family altar now." He took down his Bible and began there, and it wasn't long before his children were touched.

Suppose you haven't been living in accordance with the gospel. Why not make an open confession to your wife – to your children – set up a family altar and pray for your children, and it will not be long before you will be blessed. Let us come to Him. Let us look straight away from the churches; let us look from every influence to only the Master Himself, and let His words ring in the soul of every parent here tonight, "Bring him to Me." Have you got a wayward son? He may be in some distant state or foreign land and by the last news you received of him was rushing headlong down to ruin. My friend, you can reach him – you can reach him by intercession at the throne.

A short time after I got here, I received a letter from Scotland. I haven't time to read it. The letter was sent to a minister and he forwarded it to me. It was the gushing of a loving father. He asked us to look out for his boy, whose name was Willie. That name touched my heart, because it was the name of my own boy. I asked Mr. Sawyer to try and get on the track of that boy some weeks ago, but all his efforts were fruitless. But away off in Scotland that Christian father was holding that boy up to God in prayer, and last Friday, in yonder room, among those asking for prayer was that Willie, and he told me a story there that thrilled my heart and testified how the prayers of that father and mother in that far off land had been instrumental in affecting his salvation. Don't you think the heart of that father and mother will rejoice? He said he was rushing madly to destruction, but there was a power in those prayers that saved that boy. Don't you think, my friends, that God hears and answers prayers, and shall we not lift up our voices to Him in prayer that He will bless the children He has given us?

You know how Elisha was blessed by the Shunammite woman, and she was blessed in return by a child. You know how the child died, and how she resolved to go at once to the man of God. I can imagine Elisha sitting on Mount Carmel and seeing that woman afar off and saying to his servant, "Do you see that woman? I think I know her face – it is the Shunammite now that I see her face. Go run and ask her, 'Is it well with you?'" Off the servant runs, and when the servant came to her, she said, "It is well." Although her child was dead, she said, "It is well." She knew that the man who gave her the child could raise it up. She runs up to the master and falls down, putting her arms about his feet, and the servant tried to put her away. But Elisha wouldn't let him. He says to the servant, "Here, take this staff and go and lay it upon the face of the dead child," and tells the servant to go home with her, but she won't leave the man of God. She doesn't want to lean upon the staff or the servant.

It wasn't the servant or the staff that she wanted, but the man of God that she wanted with her. "You come with me," she says. "You can raise it up." She would not leave him till he came to her house. He went in and closed the door and prayed to God that the child would be restored, and then lay upon the child, mouth to mouth, eyes to eyes, hands to hands. The child began to sneeze, and there was the child of the Shunammite woman raised up. Bear in mind that it was not the servant nor the staff, but the Master Himself that saved the child. My friends, if we lean upon the Master, we shall not be disappointed. The moment that child was brought to the Master, the wish of that woman was granted, and if we as parents, bring our children to Him, we shall not be disappointed.

But there is another thing I want to call your attention to. We don't fast enough. This fasting doesn't mean fasting from food only, as many people think. It seems to me if I had a wayward boy I should put myself at the feet of Christ and fast a little, by keeping away from amusements, from theatres. I find a great many worldly Christians going off into the theatres. They say, "I only go for a little relaxation. Of course I could stop going whenever I like and needn't be influenced by them; I only go occasionally." A worldly Christian said to me, "I only go once a month." "Well," said I, "how about your boy? He may not have the willpower you have, and your example in going only once a month may only be the means of his going there all the time." A man, my friends, may have great willpower, yet his son may have very little. And therefore, fasting in this regard, would be good for our children. We should abstain from all pleasures that are liable to be hurtful to our children.

If you fathers and mothers want your children to keep from evil influences you ought to keep away from them yourselves. If they see you indulging in these pleasures, they think they are on the right side by doing the same thing. A young man says, "I don't want to be any better than my father, and he goes to the theaters." Now, there are young men who have come into the inquiry rooms one night and the next night have gone off to the theaters. I don't know if a man with the Spirit of God should go there. These men may one night be here and the next night may go off to some amusement where they hear as a waltz, "What Shall the Harvest Be," or "Almost Persuaded." How Christian men and women can go to such places as that, I cannot conceive. If it is not sacrilege, then nothing is. What can those worldly Christians expect from their children if they frequent such places? I think the time has come for fasting. When Christ died, it was to separate His church from the world, and how can a man who has consecrated himself as a child of God go back to the world without trampling that blood under his feet? When will the day come when a man of God shall make known by his conversation, by his actions, by his general appearance, that he has been freed from the curse of the world?

Then another thing. It seems to me that every man should have a family altar in his house. And if we cannot deliver prayers, let us take up each of our children by name. Let us ask that Johnny, while playing with his schoolmates, may be kept from temptation. Why, we forget that a little child's temptations are just as much to him as ours are to us. The boy at school has just as heavy trials as we have. And then pray for Mary. If she is in trouble, bring it out and pray that God may give her power to overcome any besetting sin that she may have in her heart. I believe the day has come when we should have more religion in our families, more family altars. I believe that the want of this is doing more injury to the growth of our children than anything else. Why, long before the church was in a building, it was in the homes of the people. We can make the family altar a source of happiness. By it, we can make the home the pleasantest place in the world.

Let us when we get up in the morning, bright and fresh, have some family devotions. If a man runs downtown immediately on getting up and doesn't get home until five o'clock and then has family devotions, the children will be tired and so go sound asleep. And it seems to me that we should give a little more time to our children and call them around the altar in the morning. Or suppose we ask them to recite a verse, to recite a portion of a hymn – it must not necessarily be a long one – and, after that, have some singing if the children can sing. Do not be in a hurry to get it out of the way, as if the service were a nuisance; take a little time. Let them sing some religious hymns. The singing need not be all psalms, but there should be a few simple religious hymns. Let the little children be free from all restraint. Then pray for each of them.

Another thing. It seems to me that we devote too little time to studying the Sunday school lesson. You know now we have a uniform lesson all over the country. That lesson should be taken up by parents and they should try to explain it to their children. But how many ever think of this? How many parents ever take the trouble to inquire even as to the kind of Sunday school teachers who instruct their children? And then we should take our children into the churches with us. It seems to me we are retrograding at the present day. A great many of our children are never seen in the churches at all. Even if the sermon doesn't touch them, they are getting into good habits. And then if the minister says a weak thing, don't take it up, don't pick it out or speak of it before the children, because you are bringing your minister into disrespect with your children.

If you have got a minister whom you cannot respect, you ought to get out of that church as soon as you can. Encourage them to bring the text home. Let the word be spoken to them at all times, in season and out of season. If the great Bible truths sink down into their hearts, the fruit will be precious; wisdom will blossom upon them, and they will become useful in the church and in the world. Now, how many parents will not take the trouble to explain to the children what the minister preaches. Take your children into the pews and let them hear the Word of God, and if they do not understand it, show it to them. You know the meat they require is the same as we feed on, but if the pieces are too large for them, we must cut it up for them – cut it finer. If the sermon is a hard one, cut it into thin slices so that they can take it.

There was a time when our little boy did not like to go to church and would get up in the morning and say to his mother, "What day is tomorrow?" "Tuesday." "Next day?" "Wednesday." "Next day?" "Thursday," and so on, till he came to the answer, "Sunday." "Dear me," he would moan. I said to his mother, "We cannot have our boy grow up to hate Sunday in that way; that will never do." That is the way I used to feel when I was a boy. I used to look upon Sunday with a certain amount of dread. Very few kind words were associated with that day. I don't know that the minister ever said a kind thing or ever even put his hand on my head. I don't know that the minister even noticed me unless it was when I was asleep in the gallery, and he woke me up. This kind of thing won't do. We must make Sunday the most attractive day of the week, not a day to be dreaded, but a day of pleasure.

Well, the mother took the work up with this boy. Bless those mothers in their work with the children. Sometimes I feel as if I would rather be the mother of John Wesley or Martin Luther or John Knox than have all the glories in the world. Those mothers who are faithful with the children God has given them will not go unrewarded. My wife went to work and took those Bible stories and put those blessed truths in a light that the child could comprehend, and soon the feeling of dread for the Sabbath with the boy was the other way. "What day's tomorrow?" he would ask. "Sunday." "I am glad." And if we make these Bible truths interesting – break them up in some shape so that these children can get at them, then they will begin to enjoy them.

Now, there's no influence like a mother's, and if the mothers will give a little time to the children in this way, and read them some Bible story, or tell them it in a simple way, it will not be long before the child knows the Bible from beginning to end. I know a little boy, eleven years of age, who got up last Monday in the meeting and told how he found Christ. His father began by telling him Bible stories, and now he knows them as well as I do. The little fellow of eleven years is quite a preacher. Let us pick out the stories that will interest them from Genesis to Revelation, and that is the way to bring our children to Christ. It will fill them with the gospel – fill them with Christ. They will soon be so full of Jesus that when an infidel comes to unseat their faith, he will find no room for infidelity.

Now, the New Year's Day is coming on. I haven't much time to speak about that now, but let me ask what are you going to do when the young men come to your homes on that day? Are you going to set wine before them? Are you going to tempt the sons of others to go astray? Don't offer them, I implore you, that hellish cup; don't be the instruments to lead the children of others away from the God of their fathers. I hope that in this city this infernal custom will soon be swept away. The idea of having some of our best young men reeling on the streets beastly drunk on the first day of the year is revolting, and yet there are Christians who, when young men visit them on New Year's Day, just urge the cup on them – press them to take it. They have got some new kind of wine, and they want them to taste it, and urge the young man just to take a little and the young man hasn't got will – hasn't got backbone enough to resist the temptation. He hasn't the power to say no. He goes to another house, and the same thing is repeated, and so on, until at night the poor fellow goes home intoxicated and breaks the heart of some mother.

Remember when you offer the cup, if it is not to your own boy, it is to somebody else's boy. I have a great respect for that old woman who with ribbons flying ran into a crowded thoroughfare and rescued a child from under a wagon. Someone asked her, "Is it your child?"

"No," she replied, "but it is someone's child." She had a mother's heart, and bear in mind when a young man comes to you, as you put the cup before him – remember he is some other one's child. God has given us a charge, not only in looking to the salvation of our own children, but we have to see to the salvation of the children of others.

Now, let me say a word to the unfaithful fathers. At the close of this meeting, if you have been unfaithful to the children God has given you, why not stay and then go home and make an honest confession to your children? If you have a boy who is a reckless young man – if he is a drunkard, ask yourselves, "Have I done all that I could; have I ever set before him the truth of Christ?"

Not long ago a young man went home late. He had been in the habit of going home late, and the father began to mistrust that he had gone astray. He told his wife to go to bed and dismissed the servants and said he would sit up till his son came home. The boy came home drunk, and the father in his anger gave him a push into the street and told him never to enter his house again and shut the door. He went into the parlor and sat down and began to think: "Well, I may be to blame for that boy's conduct, after all. I have never prayed with him; I have never warned him of the dangers of the world." And the result of his reflections was that he put on his overcoat and hat and started out to find his boy.

The first policeman he met he asked eagerly, "Have you seen my boy?" "No." On he went till he met another. "Have you seen anything of my son?" He ran from one to another all that night, but not until the morning did he find him. He took him by the arm and led him home and kept him till he was sober. Then he said, "My dear boy, I want you to forgive me. I've never prayed for you. I've never lifted my heart to God for you. I've been the means of leading you astray, and I want your forgiveness." The boy was touched, and what was the result? Within twenty-four hours that son became a convert and gave up that cup. It may be that some father has had a wayward son. Go to God and on your knees confess it. Let the voice of Jesus sink down in your heart tonight. "Bring him unto Me."

A father whom I have known for many years said to me this afternoon, with the tears trickling down his cheeks, "I want to tell you something that I have never told in public. Forty-three years ago, when I was five years old, I was sick with scarlet fever, and my mother knelt down and prayed to God if it was His will, that her boy might be spared. My father was a drinking man, and she also prayed that I might be kept safe from the cup. My mother died early, but my mother's prayer has followed me all those years, and I have never touched one drop of liquor." Last night a young man, the son of that man, got up and told his experiences. Yes, the mother's prayer for her little boy, five years old, was answered. That prayer was answered. Why shall we not lift up our hearts in prayer for our children? Let us plead day and night till God saves them – till He brings them into the ark of safety. May the God of Israel save our children.

I remember being in the camp and a man came to me and said, "Mr. Moody, when the Mexican war began, I wanted to enlist. My mother, seeing I was resolved, said if I became a Christian, I might go. She pleaded and prayed that I might become a Christian, but I wouldn't. I said when the war was over I would become a Christian, but not till then. All her pleading was in vain, and at last, when I was going away, she took out a watch and said, 'My son, your father left this to me when he died. Take it, and I want you to remember that every day at twelve o'clock your mother will be praying for you.' Then she gave me her Bible and marked out passages and put a few different references in the flyleaf. I took the watch, and it was twelve o'clock. I had been gone four months, but I remembered that my mother at that hour was praying for me.

Something prompted me to ask the officer to relieve me for a little, and I stepped behind a tree away out on those plains of Mexico and cried to the God of my mother to save me." My friends, God saved him, and he went through the Mexican war. "And now," he said, "I have enlisted again to see if I can do any good for my Master's cause," and the old man was down among the soldiers there preaching Christ. My friends, let us believe that God answers prayer, and let us not cease our supplication till salvation comes to our children and all our little ones are brought into the ark of safety. Let us all unite in prayer.

The Life of Peter

The first glimpse we had of him was when Andrew called him. He was first called as a disciple, not as an apostle. The second call was when he was called to the work of the ministry. The next glimpse we had was related in the 5th chapter of the gospel of Luke, when the Lord spoke to the people the words of God from the boat at the seaside. Then follows the miraculous catch of fish. Then it was that Peter said, "Depart from me, for I am a sinful man, O God." Then Jesus said that thereafter Peter would catch men. When Peter was called, he didn't leave his work until called twice.

There are too many unprepared men in the Lord's work; there are too many men made ministers in the world today. There are a good many young men, young converts, who are looking to the work of the ministry and thinking they are called to that. John Wesley used to say to young men, candidates for the ministry, when they preached, "Did you make any one mad?" "No." "Did you convert anybody?" "No." "Then," Wesley said, "that's a very good evidence you're not called." Men need to have souls before they begin this work.

The Lord first made these men to go to the lake and take a great haul of fish, and then when they were called, they had something to leave. They didn't have much to leave, but they left what they had. What had they to leave? A few broken nets and a haul of fish. And that's the way with a great many Christians of the present day. They don't want to leave their little draft of fishes and their broken nets.

The next time we get a glimpse of Peter is in the 14th chapter of Matthew where the Lord tells Peter to walk on the water. Here we find Peter in Doubting Castle. And that was when Peter got his eye off the Lord, and he saw the waves and heard the wind, then his eyes wandered away from Christ. But Peter's prayer was to the point. It didn't begin with a long preamble, which would have put him forty feet under water before the Lord heard it. But it was to the point, "Lord save me; I perish." Again, in the 16th chapter we find that Christ is asking, "Whom say men that I am?" and then He asked Peter, and Peter said, "You are the Christ, the Son of the Living God." There is power in confessing Christ.

Peter was a true Trinitarian; he got square on the rock. Again we find him indulging in man-worship, the first beginning of Rome. This was on the occasion of the Transfiguration, on the mountain. Peter said, "God, let us make three tabernacles," and as soon as he said this, why, God just snatched Moses and Elias away and left them only Jesus.

There is too much of this minister worship, of this church worship at the present day. Look in the 22nd chapter of Revelations, 9th verse, where the angel said, "Worship God." If Christ was not the Son of God, then Christians are the greatest idolaters that ever lived. Again, we find Peter in the 26th chapter of Matthew, at the 23rd verse, where Peter's fall was recited. He became self-confident and spiritually proud. The Lord couldn't use him until he had been humbled, and here he stood up among the Lord's disciples, just as though he was all-powerful. This lesson of humility must be learned by every man whom God uses. "Let him that stands take heed lest he fall."

The greatest Bible characters fell because they failed in their strongest points. Moses was not allowed to see the promised land, and there were Saul and David and Jacob who fell also, and Peter, too, at the very time when he was boasting of his own power. I am always sure that young converts who say they're safe are where the devil will trip them up. Again, Peter was asleep in the garden when the Lord told him to watch. When Satan has Christians in the churches asleep, then troubles come in the churches.

Then came the next step – "He followed Him afar off." And this was the gradual downward course. No one would find a Christian man in the theater; those Christians who are in such places are all asleep. Men of the world say they like "liberal Christians," but these men are never sent for by dying men. You will never find a card-playing, a smoking and chewing, a horse-racing and a dancing Christian who amounted to anything.

Then the next downward step was when Peter drew his sword and cut off the ear of the High Priest's servant. Afterwards, Peter denied the Lord, first to the young maid, and then to another servant. Here were two denials by the very man who but a few hours before had said he would never betray or forsake the Lord. Then, again, the third time the servant said, "Your speech betrays you," but Peter answered with oaths that he never knew Him. It's hard for a Christian to forget the speech of the Lord's people, even after he has long departed from the ways of God and Christ. But one look brought Peter back, one word undid all that Satan had been doing for hours, and he went out and wept bitterly. One of the first words that Christ said after the crucifixion and resurrection was "Tell the disciples and Peter," and Peter had a personal interview with the Lord. And then when Christ was leaving him, He asked him, "Do you love Me more than these?" But Peter didn't answer; he had learned humility. After the Lord had asked him again, Peter, now humble, already meet for the Master's use said, "Lord, You know."

Address to Young Men

Second Address

You will find my text this evening in the 6th chapter of Galatians, 7th, 8th, and 9th verses: *"Be not deceived; God is not mocked; for whatsoever a man sows, that shall he also reap. For he that sows to his flesh shall of the flesh reap corruption, but he that sows to the Spirit shall of the Spirit reap life everlasting. And let us not be weary in well doing, for in due season we shall reap, if we faint not."* You who were here last Wednesday night remember that we had for our text, "Their rock is not as our rock, even our enemies themselves being judges," and then we tried to find a text which everyone would admit was true. I think that we have one tonight that no infidel, no skeptic, or deist can attack.

There are some passages which we do not have to prove by the Word of God, but merely by our own experience. Your own lives will prove many passages in Scripture. You can take up the daily papers and see them fulfilled under your own eyes. This is one of them. Perhaps there has not been a text of Scripture run out in this Tabernacle as this one has. Night after night we have said something about it; night after night Mr. Sankey has sung out, "Whatsoever a man soweth that shall he also reap." My friends, we cannot quote it too often. We want to quote it and preach it till it gets down to the hearts of the people.

Now it is very natural to be deceived. I suppose there is not a man or woman here but who has been deceived by his or her most intimate friends. You have been deceived by your own friends, and you have been deceived by your enemies, and how many could rise up here and say they have not been deceived by themselves? How many of us have found our own heart more treacherous than anything else? How many of us have not found the truth of that passage, "The heart of man is deceitful above all things, and desperately wicked." We can be deceitful to each other, to our friends, and to ourselves, but bear in mind we cannot deceive God. How often does man find that Satan has deceived him? But has he ever found God deceiving him? I have never found a man who has said that he has been or that he has heard of anybody whom God has deceived. How many times has man said he has been deceived by his fellows – by his own treacherous heart; and our experience in this direction only shows that we cannot rely upon man, upon ourselves, but only upon God.

Now, it is a law of nature that if a man sows, he will reap what he sows. If a man sows watermelons, he doesn't look for cauliflowers. If a man sows potatoes, he doesn't look for cabbages. If he sows onions, he doesn't look for corn. If he plants potatoes, he expects potatoes; if he sows corn, he looks for corn; or wheat, he expects to reap wheat. So in the natural world, a man expects to reap what he sows. If a man learns a carpenter's or a builder's trade, he expects to put up buildings for a living. If a man toils and studies hard for a profession – if he is a lawyer, he expects to practice law. He doesn't expect to have to preach the gospel for a living. He has been sowing for years, and he expects to reap. As a man sows, so he expects to reap. This is the law in the natural world, and so it is with the spiritual: "Blessed are they that mourn, for they shall be comforted." "Blessed are the peacemakers, for they shall be called the children of God." "Blessed are they which hunger and thirst for righteousness' sake" – why? because they shall get rich? no – "for they shall be filled." Now, you will see that a certain result is the product of certain conditions.

This is the law, which you will find carried out all through the world, in natural and spiritual things. If a man is a thief, you expect to see him come to an ignominious end. If a man is drunken and dissipated, we look, as a natural consequence of his dissipation, to see him go to ruin. Yet men themselves don't see this; their eyes are closed to their folly. A friend who was coming down with me tonight said, "When I look back, I see that I started wrong when I came here. It seems as if I must have been blind. I did not see this till within the last two or three weeks." My friends, that's what Satan does with a man – he just blinds him, and when he has got a man blinded he does anything he wants with him. It is very hard to make men understand this simple truth, that they will have to reap what they sow, especially young men from seventeen to twenty-one. That, you know, is the ugly age. There is more trouble with them then than at any other stage.

I remember when I was at that age. I knew a good deal more than my mother or any of my friends. You take a young man at that age, and you'll find he knows a great deal more than his father, his grandfather, or even his great-grandfather all put together. "He is wise in his own conceit." It is during that ugly age that characters are forming for good or evil. And bear in mind, you young men, that "Whatsoever a man sows, that shall he also reap." If a man sows tares, he has got to reap them. It may not be tomorrow, or next week, or next year, but the time of reaping will assuredly come, and when the reaping time comes you will moan bitterly. Then you will want to change places with those Christians whom you despise now. When the reaping time comes, you will want to give a good deal if you could exchange places with the humblest looking Christian.

I suppose that Cain would give a good deal to exchange places with Abel tonight. Do you think Pilate would not like to change places with Elijah, with Obadiah, or Peter tonight? Don't you think the Emperor Nero would like to exchange places now with Paul? Paul is reaping what he sowed, and so is Nero. All through Scripture you can see the proof of this text. Don't you think that the rich man at whose door the beggar Lazarus lay would like to exchange places with that poor Christian now? Bear in mind that you may look upon Christians with contempt, but the time is coming when you will give anything to exchange places with the poorest Christian that walks the streets of Chicago.

I used to believe twenty years ago in this text, but I believe it more now than ever before. The longer I live the more I become convinced of its awful truth. You know I used to live in Chicago, and I used to go from house to house among the poor, and in going among the poor I gained no little experience of the rich people. In visiting the poor, I became acquainted with a good many rich families, and there is scarcely a week passes now but I hear of rich families who have gone down to ruin. Just this afternoon I heard of a family who, twenty years ago, occupied a position among the best. They had a beautiful daughter, who could have adorned any station, and a lovely home, and I heard today that they had gone down to ruin. They looked upon Christianity with scorn and contempt. The father brought the children up to treat all religion with contempt, and his sons have gone down to their graves drunkards, and his daughter has died of a broken heart. Yes, a man who sows tares must reap them, and sometimes the harvest is a whirlwind.

Now, just let us divide that text up – not that I want to preach under different heads, but just for the sake of greater clearness. When a man sows, he expects to reap. This truth must be admitted first. A farmer that planted grain and never reaped his fields you would say has gone clear mad. No man sows that doesn't expect to reap. That is just what he does expect to do.

The next point: A man always expects to reap more than he sowed. If he sows a handful of grain, he expects to get from that handful a bushel, and if he sows a bushel, he expects a harvest of five hundred bushels. And just so it is in spiritual matters.

If a man scatters handfuls of tares in spiritual things, his spiritual harvest will be bushels of tares and not wheat. Whatever he sows he shall reap; just that and nothing more. And if he sows the wind, he must reap the whirlwind. A man must expect a harvest of just the kind that his seed is, and this great law is even more true of spiritual growth than of natural growth. If a man is bad and corrupt in his thoughts, you can tell precisely what his deeds will be. If a man is profane and blasphemous, look to his children to be the same. If a father is a lying man, his children will grow up to deceive him just as he deceived others. A bad boy is too often the living penalty of the sins of his parents; they have sown and watered, and now he is reaping the punishment.

Another point: if a man sows, he must reap the fruit, no matter how ignorant he may claim to be, or really be, of the nature of the seed. A plea of ignorance won't do. You sow tares and think it wheat, but nothing but tares will spring up. You may call it wheat, or rye, or grain of whatever name you please, but you get nothing but weeds and tares. You must look to what kind of seed you are sowing, for neither ignorance nor any other excuse can make tares bring forth wheat.

And now, see how true that is, in regard not only to individuals but nations. Nations are only collections of individuals, and what is true of the part in regard to character is always true of the whole. In this country our forefathers planted slavery in the face of an open Bible, and didn't we have to reap? When the harvest came nearly half a million of your young men were buried, many of them in a nameless grave. Didn't God make this nation weep in the hour of gathering the harvest, when we had to give up our young men, both North and South, to death; and every household almost had an empty chair, and blood, blood, blood, flowed like water for four long years? Ah, our nation sowed, and how in tears and groans she had to reap!

Then look at that king in Egypt. He made a decree that all the male infants should be put to death and to death they were put with all the horrors that hatred and jealousy could invent. It was terrible. Well, now, I suppose some people think it strange that God didn't punish Egypt with swift destruction. But look, the punishment only tarried. The mill of God grinds slow, but it grinds exceedingly small. In eighty years cast your eye on that miserable land. God's vengeance at length came down and ruin along with it. In every house in Egypt the firstborn was slain, from the palace to the lowest hovel. There still lived a God, and this immutable law of His had still to be executed. They had to reap just what they had sown.

Then, sometimes the mill is not so slow. Sometimes the punishment comes rapidly – like lightning. No sooner did the voice ascend that Cain had killed his brother than God came down and put a mark upon his forehead. Scarcely had Judas betrayed his Master than he came back with his thirty pieces of silver, and torn with remorse, threw them down before the priests and went out and hung himself. You will find that very often judgment and destruction come very sudden – come like a flash from the throne of God.

I remember, in the north of England, a prominent citizen told me a sad case that happened there in the town of Newcastle-on-Tyne. It was about a young boy. He was very young, but he said he was too young to go to a Sunday school. He was an only child. The father and mother thought everything of him and did all they could for him. But he fell into bad ways. He took up with evil characters, and finally got to running with thieves. He didn't let his parents know about it.

One night they got him to break into a saloon – what the people there call a public house. They stood outside while he entered the house and broke into the till. He was caught, and in one short week he was tried, convicted, and sent for ten years to Van Dieman's Land. His term of servitude expired, and he returned to his native land. He came to the town where his mother and father used to live, and soon stood at the door of his old home. He had been gone ten years, and what a change he found there. My friends, ten years seem a short time, but look back over the period of ten years in your own lives and see how many changes have taken place. He went to his old home and knocked, but a stranger came to the door and stared him in the face. "No, there's no such person lives here, and where your parents are, I don't know," was the only welcome he received. Then he turned through the gate and went down the street, asking even the children that he met about his folks, where they were living, and if they were well. But everybody looked blank.

Ten years had rolled by, and though that seemed perhaps a short time, how many changes had taken place! There, where he was born and brought up, he was now an alien and unknown even in his old haunts. But at last, he found a couple of townsmen that remembered his father and mother, and they told him the old house had been deserted long years ago; that he had been gone but a few months before his father was confined to his house, and very soon after died brokenhearted, and that his mother had gone out of her mind. He went to the madhouse where his mother was and went up to her and said, "Mother, mother, don't you know me? I am your son!" But she raved and slapped him on the face and shrieked, "You are not my boy!" and then raved again and tore her hair. He left the asylum more dead than alive, so completely brokenhearted that he died in a few months. Yes, the fruit was long growing, but at last it ripened to the harvest like a whirlwind, and vengeance made quick work of it. The death harvest was reaped.

But bear in mind what I have said tonight, and be not doubters, even if the harvest is slow. Let me read you the passage: "Because sentence against their evil deeds is not executed speedily, therefore the hearts of the sons of men are fully set in to do them evil. Though a sinner do evil a hundred times and his days be prolonged, yet surely I know that it shall be well with them that fear God, which fear before Him; but it shall not be well with the wicked, neither shall He prolong his days, which are as a shadow, because he fears not before God."

My friends, if you sow in the flesh you will reap disappointment; you will reap gloom, despair, and remorse. The harvest will be death and hell – that will be the end, but if you sow of the Spirit, you will reap peace, joy, happiness, life everlasting, for God has said it. There are a great many things in this world that we are not sure of – we are sure of nothing, I may say. I am not sure that I will finish this sermon. I am not sure that I may go home tonight. We cannot say, positively, that the sun will rise tomorrow morning. Yes, my friends, there are a great many things that we are not sure of, but there is one thing we are sure of, for God has said it. You can be sure that your sins will find you out. If we don't judge ourselves and confess our sins, they will find us out. He that covers his sin shall not prosper." That is God's decree.

Now I have been censured by many for advising two men who had committed crime to go back and confess their sin. One man the other day was cursing me for doing so. "A pretty kind of religion this is," he said. But my friends, if a man has gone into a court and publicly perjured himself, he cannot serve God till he publicly confesses it. If he has sinned in public, he must confess his sin in public. These men have gone back and written letters full of encouragement. One of them says, "Perhaps I will go to the penitentiary for three years, but what is that in comparison to the burden I would have carried had I not confessed." Now bear in mind that if you cover your sin you shall not prosper; you may keep it secret, but it will eventually come out.

Look at the sons of Jacob! Look at them when they took away their brother, and after they had delivered him into slavery, see them coming back. How much they must have suffered with their secret during those twenty years. What misery they must have endured as they looked during all these years at their old father sorrowing for his son Joseph.

They knew the boy had not been killed – they knew he was in slavery. For twenty years the sin was covered up, but at last it came back upon them. God had in the meantime been doing everything for Joseph; he had raised him nearly to the throne of Egypt. A famine struck the land of the father, and the old man sent his sons down to Egypt to get corn. God was at work. He was making these men bring their own sin home to themselves. Their conscience smote them, and they confessed in the presence of Joseph that their sin had found them out. Twenty years after it was committed that sin was resurrected and with it, they were brought face to face. My friends, be sure at once that your sin will find you out. God has said it, and if He says a thing, He means it. "He that covers his sins shall not prosper,"

I can imagine someone saying to Absalom when he started out to fight his father, "You shouldn't do this; you are committing a sin, and it will find you out." I can see that young friend looking down upon that man with scorn and contempt. The idea of his sins ever finding him out, ever coming back upon him. He probably would have said "That man's talking for effect," like a good many say of me. You will hear some people say, "Well, now, any man who knows anything about education knows well enough that Moody is only preaching for effect." If a man tells me I am preaching for effect, I say, "Amen, Amen." That's what I am trying to do. What does a man preach for if it is not for effect? I am trying to create an effect and so wake you up to your condition, and if you don't wake up, the reaping time will come upon you, the whirlwind of troubles and sorrows will rush over your defenseless head and then you will reap what you have sown in years gone by.

But let me say that if you are willing to confess your sins – I don't care what the sin may be – God is willing and ready to take it away. As I have said, there has been a good deal of talk about my interfering with those prisoners lately. Someone has said in speaking about that man in Ohio, "Well, that is a queer kind of Christianity, to send a man away back to the penitentiary to suffer." Let me say here that that young man has said in his last letter, "I think I am happier than you are, Mr. Moody. God is helping me to bear the burden; God is answering my prayers." My friends, it was a great deal better for that man to confess his crime than to try to hide it away.

If a man commits a crime, he should suffer the penalty. I must suffer the penalty if I break my arm in fighting. The man with whom I fought may forgive me for fighting with him, but I have to suffer all the same with my arm. A man got into a quarrel and got crippled, and some time ago he became converted, but although God has forgiven him his sin, he has to remain a cripple all his life. So a man must reap what he sows. I heard of an illustration that just helps me out here. Suppose I have a field, and I say to a man, "I want you to sow that field with wheat." The man has become very angry – all out of sorts with me, and when he sows that wheat, he puts in a lot of tares. When the wheat has come up, I see among it a great many tares. I say to him, "Did you sow these tares?" "Well," he says, "I will confess. Yes, sir. I did it; I sowed these tares. I will confess it instead of covering it up, but, sir, I am very sorry," and I forgive him. But when the wheat has to be harvested, I make the man reap the tares also.

You know how David fell. No man rose so high and fell so far, I think. God took him from the sheepfold and put him upon a throne. He took him from obscurity and made him king of Israel and Judea. He gave him lands in abundance and would have given him more if he had wanted them. He was on the pinnacle of glory and honored among men. But one day, while looking out of a window, he saw a woman with whom he became enamored. He yielded to the temptation and ordered her to be brought into the palace and committed the terrible sin of adultery. After that, as is the case with all men who commit a sin, he had to commit another to cover it up, so he laid plans to kill her husband and ordered him to be put in a position in the ranks of his army so that he could be killed.

Months rolled away and one day Nathan came into the palace of the king. I can imagine that David was glad to see him. Nathan began to tell him about two men who dwelt in a certain city. The one was rich, the other poor; one had herds and flocks, and the other had only a little ewe lamb, and he went on to tell how this rich man seized this ewe lamb, all that the poor man had, and slew it. I can see the anger of David as it flashed from his eye when he heard the story, and he cried, "As the Lord lives, the man that has done this thing shall surely die!" He turned to Nathan, and in tones of thunder demanded who the man was. "You are the man," was the reply of Nathan. David had convicted himself. "The man who did this thing shall die."

Then the Lord said, "I will raise up evil against you out of your own house, because you have kept this thing secret." Soon after the hand of death was put upon that house; not only did death enter his house, but it wasn't long before his eldest son committed adultery with his sister, and another committed murder – murdered his own brothers and went off into a foreign land into exile. Then he got up a rebellion and drove the king from the throne and at last died and was buried like a dog, and they heaped stones upon his resting place. "Whatsoever a man sows, that shall he also reap."

David committed adultery, so did his son; David committed murder, his son did the same. He was paid back in his own coin. He learned the truth of this passage: "Whatsoever a man sows, that shall he also reap." Why, I hear things every day in this city of Chicago that make my ears tingle. I heard of three cases within the last six hours where men who have gone to the altar and sworn before God to love, cherish, and protect the women who became their wives – who have become, some of them, mothers of children – and because these men have seen other women they like better, they have cast off these women whom they have sworn before God to love.

Do you think there is a God in heaven? Do you think that God is not going to punish these men? They may go on in their career – punishment may not come for a little while, but the wheels of judgment are going on and retribution will come. Some of these heartbroken wives say it is hard. Wait a little while. His eyes cover all the earth, and man cannot deceive Him. He has said, "Whatsoever a man sows, that shall he also reap." High heaven has decreed it, and I beg of you, if you have committed this sin, go and cry to the God of mercy. Go, confess it; don't try to cover it up. Let every sin be brought out. If you don't, your own conscience will turn against you by and by.

When I was in London I went into a waxwork there – Madame Tussaud's – and I went into the chamber of horrors. There were wax figures of all kinds of murderers in that room. There was Booth, who killed Lincoln, and many of that class. But there was one figure that I got interested in who killed his wife because he loved another woman, and the law didn't find him out. He married this woman and had a family of seven children. Twenty years passed away and then his conscience began to trouble him. He had no rest; he would hear his murdered wife pleading continually for her life. His friends began to think he was going out of his mind. He became haggard and his conscience haunted him till at last he went to the officers of the law and told them that he was guilty of murder. He wanted to die; life was so much of an agony to him. His conscience turned against him. My friends, if you have done wrong, may your conscience be awakened, and may you testify against yourself. It is a great deal better to judge our own acts and confess them, than go through the world with a curse upon you. And if you tonight will judge your own sin and confess it, He is faithful to forgive. He will forgive every sinner here if you but come to Him in faith and will blot out all your iniquities.

I was telling of a young man who spoke up in the association one night. He got up at the close of the meeting and said, "Mr. Moody, may I say a few words?" Well, I thought I wouldn't, but then I thought perhaps he has a message from God, and I told him to speak. He went on and urged these young men to accept salvation. "If you have friends praying for you, if you have mothers praying for you, treat them kindly, for you will not always have them with you." Then he went on to tell how he had once a father and mother who loved him dearly and who prayed continually for him. He was an only child. His father died, and after the burial his mother became more anxious than ever for his salvation.

Sometimes she would come to him and put her arms around his neck and say with kindness, "O my boy, I would be so happy if you would only be a Christian and could pray with me." He would push her away, "No, mother. I'm not going to become a Christian yet; I am going to wait a little longer and see the world." He would try to banish the subject from his mind altogether. Sometimes he would wake up at the midnight hour and would hear the voice of that mother raised in supplication for her boy, "O God, save my boy; have mercy upon him." At last, this is the way he put it, "it got too hot for him." He saw he had either to become a Christian or run away. And away he ran and became a prodigal and a wanderer. He heard from her indirectly; he could not let his mother know where he was, because he knew she would have gone to the end of the world to find him.

One day he got word that his mother was very sick. He began to think, "Suppose mother should die, I would never forgive myself," and he said, "I will go home." But then he thought, "Well, if I go home, she will be praying at me again, and I can't stay under her roof and listen to her prayers," and his proud, stubborn heart would not let him go. Months went on, and again he heard indirectly that his mother was very sick. His conscience began to trouble him. He knew he would never forgive himself if he didn't go home, and he finally determined to go. There were no railroads, and he had to go in a stagecoach. At night he got into the town. The moon was shining, and he could see the little village before him. The mother's home was about a mile from where he landed, and on his way he had to pass the village grocery. And as he went along, he thought he would pass through the graveyard and see his father's grave. "What," he thought, "if my mother has been laid there?"

When he got up to the grave, he saw by the light of the moon, a new-made grave. He felt the turf, and the earth was fresh and soft. He knew who had been laid there, and for once in his life the thought flashed upon him, "Who will pray now for my lost soul? My mother and father lie there, and they are the only ones who ever prayed for me." "Young men," said he, "I spent that night at my mother's grave, and before the sun rose, my mother's God had become my God. But I can never forgive myself for murdering my mother, although Christ has forgiven me." My friends, that poor fellow had to reap what he sowed.

I may be speaking tonight to some young man whose mother perhaps just now is in her closet wrestling in prayer for you. Bless God, boy, for that mother. Do not treat that mother contemptuously; do not deny her prayer tonight. Do not make light of your mother's cries to God this night. God's best gift on earth to you is that praying mother. She is your dearest, most unselfish friend in all the world. Will you not heed her pleading prayer? Come out like a man, come to your mother's Savior, and take Him to be your God. May the God of heaven convict you of sin, and draw you to Himself, and this will be the best night you've had upon earth.

How many are there in this room tonight, who have moral courage to stand up right in this Tabernacle and say, "Pray for me?" How many in this room tonight would like to become Christians? How many are there in this room now who would like to have prayer for them, beseeching prayer that God will save them? I am going to lead in prayer and as many as would like to have prayer – personal prayer to God, will just rise. You can just stand right up one after another. Never mind if there is but one of you; just remain standing. There's another who's got moral courage to rise tonight. Just stand up, will you, and remain so while others join you. There, there, friends, don't get up as if you were ashamed or scared. Rise right up and show me and God that you are in earnest. I would like to see every man out of Christ rising right up here. There's another in the gallery and another. Well, keep rising; I would sit here all night and see you rise up in the galleries there and everywhere. Every man and woman in this assembly, every boy, who would like to be a Christian, will you just rise now, all of you.

The Sacrifice of Christ

You will find my text tonight in the 15th chapter of First Corinthians, and part of the 3rd verse: *"Christ died for our sins according to the Scriptures."* I was going to preach in the city of Dublin a few years ago and the town was placarded giving notice of the meeting. There was one passage of Scripture at the bottom of the bill that my eye rested upon: "Christ died for our sins." I had read it a great many times, but I seemed to see it now in a new light, and that light flashed into my soul as it never did before: "Christ died for *my* sins." That's the way to put it – "for *my* sins." And I wish I could get everyone here to take it that way, and just keep saying it while I preach to you tonight, "Christ died for me." My friends, will you only make this personal and remember that He died for you? Let that little boy and girl remember that He died for you just as much as for that gray-headed man and let those who came in to scoff at the meeting remember that the text is for them – that Christ died for you.

I have often thought that if I could only make people feel this really and could tell the story of His death as it ought to be told, I would only preach one sermon and go up and down the world and just tell this one story. I don't know anything that would break the heart of the world like this story if it could be brought before men and women and they would feel it. I know it broke my heart, and I have often thought if I could tell it as it ought to be told, I would be the happiest man in the world. I don't believe it has ever been told yet. I don't believe the man has been born who could tell it; I don't believe that the angels in heaven could tell it.

Sometimes people say we have overdrawn the pictures in the Bible, but there is one story that has never been overdrawn – the story of His death. No one ever did justice to that story; no one ever made that real. I believe the heart of every man in this audience would be broken if I could make that story real. I remember during the war how I would take up a paper and read about the great battles and loss of life, but I would lay down the paper and soon forget all about the thousands that had been slain. But I went into the war and was at the Battles of Fort Donelson and Pittsburg Landing. After I came home and began to read the papers and see the accounts of the great battles, the whole thing would come up before me. I could hear their dying groans; I could hear them crying for their mothers, their appeals for water. The whole thing was real, and the whole trouble is that the most people take up this story of the Bible and don't make it real. They look upon it as the old story of 1,800 years ago which they have heard from their cradle.

I remember I went 500 miles to Dublin to attend a meeting, and when I got there the preacher got up and began to talk about the death of Christ. "Well," I said, "he should give us something new." But when I went home to the house where I was staying there were two old pilgrims sitting, and they were talking about the sermon and the death of Christ. The tears were trickling down their cheeks, and they spoke about the event as if Christ had died in Dublin that afternoon. I felt rebuked, ashamed at myself that those old men should speak so lovingly about this event, while I had treated it so lightly. I believe, if we were living as we ought to, it would be fresh every night, every hour, of our lives.

Now tonight I propose to take up the last hours of Christ before He went to Calvary. You know we love to hear the last words of our friends. I remember a few weeks ago, when I went to look upon the dead face of my eldest brother and how earnestly I enquired, "What were his last words?" – how I went round the places where he had been, and how for days I tried to pick up what he had said to this and that man; how I treasured up his last words. And it seems to me every Christian ought to linger round the cross and pick up the loving words of our Savior and treasure them up. So tonight, I want you just to go back 1,900 years. Let us forget we are living here in Chicago. Let us go back and imagine we are living in the land of Palestine – at Jerusalem; and let us just think we are walking down the streets of Jerusalem.

It is on a Thursday afternoon, and we see thirteen men coming down the street. Every eye is upon them. The boys are opening their eyes at them. Men, women, and children are running out of their houses to see those men. Let us imagine we are strangers, and we ask who these men are, and they tell us, "Why, that's the Galilean prophet and His apostles from the city of Capernaum." We look upon them with amazement. We have heard how that man has given sight to the blind, how He has cured the lepers, given bread to the hungry, and raised the dead. The whole land has been full of Him, and out of curiosity we follow the little band. They go along the narrow streets and come to a common looking house and enter and ascend a flight of stairs.

Suppose we go up those stairs with them. We there find them in a guest chamber, the Great Prophet seated with His twelve apostles. We are told He became exceeding sorry. He was soon to taste the bitter cup, to taste death for every man, to lay down His innocent life for the guilty, the just for the unjust, and then He is exceeding sorry. His soul is troubled, and as He sat there at that table, He lets out the secret of His heart and tells them that that night He is going to be betrayed by one of them. They look at one another, and one says, "Lord, is it I?" "No." And another says, "Master, is it I?" "No," and they one after another put the question till it comes to Judas. And that black-hearted traitor, the devil who had already been at the high priest's, turned to Him and said, "Is it I?" And the Lord said, "You have said it; and what you do, do it quickly." That ought to have broken his black heart, but it didn't, and he arose and went out of that chamber. Hear him as he goes down those stairs and into that dark night – we are told that it was the darkest the world ever saw.

That night the Son of Man was to be betrayed by man. He went off to the Sanhedrim, to the chief priests, and he sold Him – sold Him very cheap, my friends – sold Him for some $15 or $20. How many men are today selling Him as cheaply – selling him for a song! They don't want Him. A woman told me last night, "I don't want Him; I wouldn't take Him as a gift." She told me with her own lips that she would rather go to hell than heaven. Oh, what a hard heart! I hope if there is a hard-hearted person in this building like her, their heart will be broken tonight. But while Judas is out selling his Master, Jesus is speaking tender words to His disciples. What a tender parting! For three years He had been associated with that holy band. They had walked with the blessed Master and heard those wonderful parables. They had seen Him raise people from the dead, had seen Him cure the deaf, the dumb, and the blind – they had been in His company for three years, and now they were about to be separated for a time, and it was on this occasion He uttered those memorable words, "Let not your heart be troubled."

They were now by themselves; the traitor had gone out. "You believe in God, believe also in Me. In My Father's house are many mansions; if it were not so, I would have told you. I go to prepare a place for you." There was the Master in that dark hour, in that bitter, supremely bitter, hour, trying to cheer and comfort the little band. And then He uttered that wonderful prayer recorded in the 17th chapter of John. He poured His heart out to God in prayer. He not only prayed for His disciples that had stood firmly by His side, but He also prayed for His enemies. And afterward He said, "The hour of My departure is at hand."

And then He gathered the eleven around Him and they started out of the house and went down through the streets of Jerusalem. They went out through the eastern gate, passed over through the outlying space down to the Valley of Jehoshaphat, and so to the garden of Gethsemane. And there he took Peter and James and John and went on with them a little way apart and then withdrew about a stone's throw off from them and fell on his knees and began to pray. You can hear him in that cold night in that garden; you can hear his piercing cry, "Father, let this cup pass from me if it be your will." It was the prayer of agony, and he sweat as it were great drops of blood. Oh, the agony the Son of God passed through that night, not only physical agony, but a greater mental agony, because the sins of the world lay on Him. He bore in his person the sin of the whole world, and God the Father turned His face away from Him.

The Father had to turn His face away from Him. He could not take away the cup, but He had to leave Him drink it to the very dregs for you and me. And Peter and James and John fell asleep; they could not watch one single hour with Him. And so while they thus slept and Christ was wrestling in prayer, a band of men came on the scene. They came on with lanterns and torches as if they were hunting for someone. Jesus well knew who they were seeking. He woke up his disciples and went to the band and said, "Whom do you seek?" And they said, "We seek Jesus of Nazareth." Then said Jesus, "I am He," and there was something so mysterious about his person, something so wonderful about his face, that they were struck with awe. They trembled and felt as dead men and could not touch Him.

And then Judas stepped out from the band. We don't know but he put his arm around the Savior's neck. Ah, what a lesson to professing Christians! Judas was near enough to the Lord to put his arms around his neck, and yet he went down to hell. Ah, you are not to know true men by their making the greatest professions; that kind doesn't always stand the highest but sometimes the very lowest. Then Judas went on and carried out his bargain. He may have put his arm around his neck, but at all events he kissed Him. Christ turned and said, "Judas, do you betray the Son of Man with a kiss?" He may have said, "Professing to be My follower, do you betray Me with a kiss?" He might have asked, "What have I done that you should betray Me? Was I ever unkind; have I ever been untrue; have I ever deceived you; have I ever betrayed you? Why, Judas, do I receive this treatment from you?" But He merely said, "Do you betray the Master with a kiss?" "What is it that you have done to agree to betray your Master with a kiss?"

And then the men seized on Him and took those innocent hands that had been raised to bless people; that had brought bread to the hungry; had touched the leprous and made them clean; touched those that were blind and made them see, touched the deaf ears and hearts and made them hear and feel – those innocent hands that had been raised only to bless people, they took and bound them. And He resisted not. He gave himself up a willing sacrifice and was obedient to their will. And after they had bound Him, they started back to the city with Him.

And they took Him to Annas, the father-in-law of Caiaphas, the high priest. And they brought Him in, and instead of waiting till the morning, the Sanhedrim was gathered hastily together. They were so thirsty for His blood they couldn't wait even a few hours. They hurried Him before the assembled Senate where the first men of the nation were gathered together. Seventy of the rulers of the Jews came into the council that night. One after another they took their seats, and Caiaphas took his place at the head of the table. There they sat in solemn state, the highest court of the nation. And now they sought for witnesses to come and testify against Jesus. The law required that two men should agree together to establish any testimony. And at last, they found two false witnesses that came and swore they heard Him talk against the holy temple, that He said they might destroy it and He could raise it up again in three days.

Then being questioned, He said, "Before Abraham was, I am." And being further questioned, He answered not a word. At last, Caiaphas raised his voice and said, "I adjure you by the living God, that you tell us whether you be the Christ the Son of God." And Jesus said unto him, "You have said; nevertheless I say unto you, Hereafter shall you see the Son of Man sitting at the right hand of power, and coming in the clouds of heaven." And the moment Jesus said that, Caiaphas rent his clothes and said, "He has spoken blasphemy: what further need have we of witnesses? Behold, now you have heard his blasphemy!" Then he hurriedly put the question, "What think you?" And they rendered as their verdict: "He is guilty of death." How the sentence rung out in that council chamber. It was Thursday night, it may have been midnight; many of the citizens had retired, and it was not known until morning.

The next day was a notable feast day. There were people from all parts of the country; the whole city was crowded. Perhaps Zacchaeus was there from Jericho, perhaps many from whom he had cast out devils. Perhaps blind Bartimaeus, no longer blind, was there and that Samaritan woman Christ had met by the well of Sychar. Undoubtedly hundreds were there, who, but for Jesus, could not have got there. Would they stand by Him? Would they cling to Him now, in this hour of His need? And Peter – of course, he was there – would he be staunch? Only a few days before, he had solemnly promised to stand by his Lord to the last. "Though others might deny Him, he would die with Him." Would not Peter, at least, have moral courage to come out before all the world and own him? Alas, no. Why, that very night as Jesus was in the judgment hall, impetuous Peter denied Him with a curse and swore he never knew Him. It seemed there was no hand to defend Him, no hand to help Him. There He was that night in the hands of His enemy.

Very early the next morning, at what hour we do not know, the officers of the governor came and bound Him and took Him away to Pilate to have Him put to death. The Romans had taken away the power of sentencing to death, and so the Jews could only put Him to death by gaining the Romans' consent. So now they brought Him to Pilate. Pilate never had such a person as that before him. He had sentenced many to death, but not like Him. He had heard often of this Galilean; His fame had long ago reached him. Strange rumors about Him had come up from Bethlehem. Perhaps Pilate had even seen Christ and talked with Him. Quite likely so, and his curiosity must have been excited by the many stories he heard about Him among his subjects. Pilate, this time, was with Christ two hours.

At last, he came out after examining Him and said, "I find no fault in this man." But the crowd cried out, "If you let this man go, you are not Caesar's friend." They knew this would touch his loyalty and ambition to be a successful politician. He could not, they argued, tolerate any rival to the Roman power, and his first duty would be to put down everything like rebellion. "If you don't condemn him, you are not Caesar's friend," rang in his ears, as the crowd insisted that Christ was a rebel and wanted to get up an insurrection in the land, and His friends wanted to make Him King. They raised their yells and ended by repeating, "You are no friend of Caesar's! We will report you at Rome, and you will lose your office." Poor Pilate! He hadn't moral courage to stand firm. And so he said, "This Jesus, is He a Galilean?" Yes, they said, He was brought up in Nazareth, but has been living out in Galilee. So, the next thing, Pilate sent him to Herod.

Now you can see that crowd moving through the city in their way to the Galilean governor. When he saw Him, he probably thought it was John, whom he had put to death, that had been raised from the grave, and because of curiosity, was excited to see. But when he found out who it really was, we are told he got out some cast-off garments, probably some that had belonged to one of their kings and dressed Him in them, and pointing their finger in scorn at Him cried, "Hail, King of the Jews!" Then they blindfolded Him, and struck Him on the head, saying in derision, "You are a prophet; tell us who struck you." Some would spit upon Him. Amid a torrent of scorn and contempt, yes, my friends, they spat upon Him.

Suppose the Prince of Wales would come to this country, and someone would go up and spit upon him – why, all Europe would be up about it. But when the Son of Man came down to this earth they spat upon Him, and no one raised his voice against it. But with all this ignominy, that bloodthirsty Herod, who took the life of John, refused to take His life and sent Him back to Pilate. And now the crowd had increased. The whole city is excited. Everyone is talking about how the Galilean prophet had been brought before the Sanhedrin and found guilty of blasphemy and was to die the terrible death of the cross. All the time He was on trial, not a single friend stood up for Him. All forsook Him then. The very men who a few days before cried as He entered Jerusalem, "Hosanna, to the Son of David!" now lifted up their voices and cried, "Away with Him!" "Crucify Him!" And they brought Him back to Pilate, and undoubtedly, around his house a crowd had gathered as great as that assembled here tonight.

It didn't take much to rouse these Jews. They were very easily fired up, and the whole city was aroused. They are clamoring – thirsty for His blood. Pilate is still anxious to release Him. His conscience told him to release Christ, and he also received a communication from his wife in which she said, "Have nothing to do with this just man, for I have suffered many things this day in a dream because of him." He tried to release Him, but he wanted to be on both sides. At last, he said, "I've got a plan that will work, I think." It was customary, you know, to release a prisoner upon the day of the governor's feast, and he say,: "I will get the vilest wretch I can, the blackest-hearted murderer and robber and bring up this pure man and ask them which of the two they will have." But the chief priests heard what he was going to do, and went around among the crowd and told them and got their feelings worked up.

And now Pilate thought he was going to get rid of the terrible responsibility of putting Him to death. Picture the crowd standing around that governor's house. See the soldiers bringing out one with his hands dripping with the blood of his fellow man and another who had all His life healed the sick, given life, and done good. "Which will

I release unto you?" And they lift up their voices – it is the cry of the whole mob – "Barabbas, Barabbas, Barabbas!" and the poor governor, disappointed, cried out, "What shall I do with Christ?" "Let Him be crucified!" That was the burden of the voice that rang through the streets of Jerusalem that day.

"Away with this pestilent fellow – we don't want him. Put him to death!" Pilate turned around and washed his hands with water and said, "I am innocent of the blood of this just person." Poor, blind, deceived man. He thought that he could wash his hands of this iniquitous decision, but what a mistake. When he had said this they cried, "His blood be upon us and on our children." Would to God they had cried out ,"Let His blood be upon us and our children to save them," but that wasn't the cry. "Let His blood be upon us and on our children." And look what a punishment has come upon that race – see how they've been scattered to the four winds of heaven because they neglected Him. Only about seventy years afterwards Titus came and besieged Jerusalem, and nearly 1,100,000 people perished, and 97,000 were sold to slavery. It fell, and the Jewish people have been wanderers for 1,800 years.

And then Pilate gave him up to be scourged. Now, I was a Christian many years before I knew what the Roman custom of scourging was, but when the truth dawned upon me, when I learned what it really was, I wept for days and got down on my knees and asked Him forgiveness for not loving Him more than I had. The custom of scourging consisted in taking the wrists and binding them tightly together and then fastening them to a post or pillar. The back is bared, and a lash, composed of sharp pieces of steel plaited together, is brought down upon the back.

O sinner, look at the prophet Isaiah. "He was wounded for our transgressions, he was bruised for our iniquities, the chastisement of our peace was upon him, and with his stripes we are healed." He was wounded for me. Yes, with his stripes am I healed. May this be a reality to everyone here tonight. Don't let us conceal it. It was the God of heaven they scourged for us. For fifteen minutes they brought down blow upon blow on that innocent body. Oh, you who cast Him away, you who see no reason why you should love Him, you who cannot see why you should take your stand on His side; why you should defend His cause, think of this! And after scourging Him, instead of binding up His wounds and bringing oil and ointment and pouring it upon those wounds, instead of doing this, they put upon Him some other cast-off garments and made Him a crown of thorns, and some wretch put it on His head.

You know, when Queen Victoria sits on her throne, they put a crown upon her head filled with diamonds and precious stones worth about $20,000,000, but here they crowned God's Son with a crown of thorns, the curse of the earth. And in mockery of a king, they put a stick in His hand. You know, when the Queen of England sits on her throne, she has a scepter in her hand. And here in the hands of the Prince of heaven they put a stick and scoffingly shouted, "Hail, King of the Jews!" They jeered and mocked that precious Christ. At last, one of the crowd took the rod out of Jesus's hand and brought it down over His defenseless head driving those thorns into His brow. Oh, what treatment the Son of God received! And those wounds were made for us. He bore His stripes for you and for me. You can see the blood trickle down that innocent head, down that dear face, and over His bosom. And all for us! Oh, divine, infinite compassion; "He bore our sins in His own body on the tree."

And now they take off the purple robe of scorn and put His own garment upon Him, and they lift up His cross and lay it upon Him. It is not a gilded cross such as you ladies wear about the neck. It is not a cross of polished wood thickly set with diamonds and precious stones, but a great, rugged, heavy cross made roughly out of a tree. Now, I see them lift and lay it on His shoulders. And they lay crosses on two thieves who are to be led away and executed with Him. The devil wanted to blacken the name of Christ and so he is placed between two thieves who are made to carry their own crosses. Why the cross of Jesus was taken from His shoulders after a few steps, we can easily imagine. He cannot stand up – the sins of the whole world are piled upon him – and He cannot stand up, much less walk under the accumulated load. See Him reel and stagger! See Him fall, almost fainting to the earth! The mountain weight crushes down even the Son of God! They take the cross from His shoulders and lay it upon Simon the Cyrenian.

And now look, sinners, and behold your Savior. Behold the Lamb of God going up to Mount Calvary like a sheep to the slaughter. Away to Calvary they are leading Him to crucify and put Him to death. I see them on the way climbing the toilsome ascent. Jesus is calling on God in prayer, praying even for His murderers. And now they have got Him to the summit of the hill. They've arrived. It is Golgotha, the place of the skull. And they take and lay Him down on the cross. Yonder come the soldiers with hammers and nails in their hands. You can see them take those pliant arms and stretch them out, and against those blessed, innocent hands they point the sharp spikes. You can hear that hammer come down on that nail – blow, blow – and the hands of Jesus are pierced through, fastened bleeding to the cross. Long spikes are driven through both feet, and God, the Son of the Father, lies quivering, nailed to the cross.

And now they mock at Him. See, they spit on Him, hooting and laughing and yelling, "Away with Him! He saved others, let Him save Himself if He be Christ, the chosen of God." Then the Roman soldiers lifted up the cross and placed it upright between heaven and earth with those arms of Jesus outstretched still in blessing. The love that He had in His bosom kept those dear hands extended; they didn't need the nails. He might have come down from the cross. With one stroke of His hand, He could have summoned all the angels of God against His murderers or called down fire out of heaven to consume every one of them. But no. He willed to hang there between heaven and earth; His strength fainted not. Even "as Moses lifted up the serpent in the wilderness, even so must the Son of Man be lifted up, that whosoever believes in Him should not perish but have everlasting life."

O sinner, go to Calvary tonight; look on that Savior. Gaze on Him between those two thieves. Hear that piercing cry – does He call down fire from heaven? No, no! "Father, Father," He cries, "forgive them, for they know not what they do." Yes, I think that Christ did forgive from His heart every soul there on Calvary, even those that drove the spikes, even those that wagged their heads and reviled Him. Even the two thieves railed on Him. But at last, one of them cried out, "Lord, remember me when you come into your kingdom." Oh, sinner, did Christ rebuke him, or did He keep silent? No. A benediction fell from his lips, "This day you shall be with me in Paradise." That malefactor had but to cry and he was snatched from the brink of hell. Oh, lost one, only cry tonight to Jesus and He will save you. Will you not let Him? Oh, hear

His gracious words to the vile malefactor, "This day shall you be with me in Paradise." At last, He cried out, "I thirst," and they gave Him gall mixed with vinegar and mocked Him again. "Hail, King of the Jews, come down from your cross." But He patiently endured. And again, He opens his lips and we hear that cry from that cross, "Father, into your hands I commit my spirit." And then the end approaches, and He cries out in a loud voice, "It is finished." "It is finished." "It is finished."

What a thrill of joy must have swept through the streets of heaven. "It is finished! It is finished!" the angels cry as they strike their golden harps, and the bells of heaven, if there's any there, ring out the peal of joy. "It is finished, the whole world can now be saved! The work of the God-man is finished today on Calvary. All that man has to do is to believe and they shall be saved!"

The Son of Man had triumphed; He had died to make atonement, and through Him all flesh might die and yet live eternally. The work was complete; the world was saved! Ah, I can just imagine how the black powers of hell gathered around that dying scene, and the waves of hell and death dashed upon that cross. Sometimes, down on the beach of Lake Michigan there, you see the waves coming dashing on the breakwater. They come dashing along as though they would break everything to pieces, but the waves themselves are dashed to pieces and the breakwater stands invincible. So the dark waves of death and hell came dashing up against the bosom of the Son of God. They roared and surged, but all in vain. They fell back shattered into fine spray against the Rock, Christ – Christ the destroyer of death, Christ the victor over hell. When He shouted, "It is finished," I think I see the fiend creeping back to hell and hear him whispering, "It is finished; all mankind can now be saved." They have led on the children to kill the Son of God, but they are outwitted, for God "makes even the wrath of man to praise him."

But my friends, we will not leave Him there on the cross. We are told that straightway when He yielded up the ghost even nature owned its God. The sun refused to look longer upon the scene; darkness came over the earth for three hours. The rocks were rent and the earth was shaken, and many that slept came forth from their graves. And when Jesus was now dead, we are told that Joseph of Arimathea, a rich man and a member of the Sanhedrin, went boldly to Pilate and begged the

Lord's body that he might bury it. He was a just man, he was an honorable counsellor, and let me mention right here a most remarkable thing: Matthew, Mark, Luke and John all join in telling of this pious act of Joseph's. It is not everything in this story of the last agony that all four of them bring out, but they all give this.

Joseph of Arimathea, the secret disciple, was left to ask for the Lord's body. All his open disciples had forsaken Him and fled. All had forsaken Him – some had disowned him, and Judas had betrayed him. It was left for Joseph of Arimathea to go to Pilate and himself alone perform the last offices for the dead Master. It was the death of Jesus that brought out Joseph of Arimathea, the secret disciple – Oh backward, secret Christians, shall it not touch you, too? My friends, if Christ died for you on Calvary, shall you not live for Him? Shall you not speak for Him? Is not this the least you can do? He went boldly into the presence of the governor and asked him for the body of Jesus.

When Pilate heard he was dead he marveled. He gave orders to see that Jesus was dead. And now you can see those Roman soldiers going towards Calvary and Joseph with some of his servants behind him. See them standing at the cross and a soldier just goes up and puts a spear into the side of the Son of God, and that prophecy was brought out. "In that day there shall be a fountain opened in the house of David for sin and for uncleanness." The soldier put it in, and His blood covered the spear. Yes, Christ's blood covered sin. Yes, God in mercy covered sin. That act was the crowning act of indignity of earth and hell, to drive that spear into the very heart of the God-man, and the crowning act of mercy and love and heaven that blood came out and covered the spear.

And now Joseph and Nicodemus take down that body. You can see them wash the blood from that head, you can see them draw those nails out carefully from His hands, from His feet, and they take that mangled and bruised body down and wash it.

But thank God, He did not rest very long. I have not time to speak about His resurrection now, but God willing, I will speak about it before I leave. But let me ask you, are you going out of this Tabernacle saying you don't want Christ – saying you would rather be without Him? Are you going out despising His love, His death, His offer of mercy? "Christ died for our sins." Will you have the benefit of His death or send the message back to the God of heaven that you despise His love, His offer of mercy, that you despise this blessed Redeemer that came down to seek and save that which was lost?

Sinners Called to Repentance

I want to call your attention tonight to a text which you will find in the 5th chapter of Luke and 32nd verse. The text is also recorded in Matthew and in Mark, and whenever you find a passage recorded by all three of the evangelists you may for sure know that it is one of those important truths which He wants to impress upon people. *"I came not to call the righteous but sinners to repentance."* It was when He first came down to Capernaum that He uttered these words. He had been cast out of Nazareth; they didn't want Him. They wouldn't have salvation. And He came down to Capernaum, and there He found Levi sitting at the receipt of customs, and He called him to become one of His disciples. Levi was so full of joy when he found Christ – as all young converts are – that he got up a great feast, and he invited all the publicans and sinners to it.

I suppose he wanted to get them all converted – that was the reason he prepared a sumptuous feast. It was not to hear Jesus, but just to partake of the feast that Levi had prepared for them. And Jesus was there, too, among these publicans and sinners. The Pharisees were there too, and they began to murmur against His disciples, saying, "Why do these men eat with publicans and sinners?" and it was on this occasion that Christ uttered this wonderful text, "I came not to call the righteous but the sinners to repentance." That is what He came into this world for; He came into the world just for the very purpose of saving sinners.

Now a good many men come to Chicago to do a certain work. Some come to practice law, that's their profession; others come to practice medicine, because that's their business. Some are businessmen and some are mechanics. And when Christ came into this world He came for a purpose. He had a profession, if you will allow me the expression – He came to call sinners to repentance. You know when He was going down to the Samaritan town His disciples went down to see whether they would let Him come there. We find Him on His way from Galilee to Jerusalem. You know there was such a hatred between the Jews and the Samaritans that they would have no dealings with each other, and He sent His disciples on to see if He would be allowed to enter. The Samaritans would not allow Him there, and His disciples were so incensed that James and John asked Jesus to, "Command fire to come down from Heaven and consume them, even as Elias did." "Why," said the Son of Man, "I didn't come to destroy men's lives, but to save them." That's what He came for. He came to bless men. He came to do men good, and there is not a sinner here tonight who cannot be saved but will be saved tonight if they wish.

You may call this world a great hospital, and all the people are born ill. A great many people imagine their souls are never diseased; they think they don't need a physician. But when people wake up to the fact that their souls are diseased, then they find the need of a physician. But there is no need for the physician unless you feel you are sick. You know you could not send a physician to a man who was well.

Suppose I go on the West Side and ask a celebrated physician to come over and see Mr. White. Suppose he comes around and finds Mr. White sitting in his drawing room perfectly well. "Why, how is this? Mr. Moody told me you were sick and bade me make a professional call." Not only is the physician disgusted, but the patient is too. The world doesn't send for a physician till sickness comes. When it feels sick then it sends for a doctor, and the doctor comes. And whenever a man feels his need of Christ and calls, that moment He comes and is healed. There is a Physician here tonight for every sinner. I don't care what your sins may be or how long you have been living in sin. I don't care if your life has been as black as hell, the Great Physician is here. What for? Just to heal every man and woman that wants to be healed.

Now, the great trouble is to make people believe they are sick, but the moment you believe that you are, then it is that you are willing to take the remedy. I remember some years ago a patent medicine came out and the whole of Chicago was placarded about it. I could not turn my head but I saw "Paine's Pain Killer." On the walls, on the curbstones, everywhere was "painkiller," "painkiller." I felt disgusted at the sight of these bills constantly telling me about this patent medicine. But one day I had a terrible headache, so bad that I could hardly see and was walking down the streets and saw the bills again and went and bought some. When I was well, I didn't care for it, but when I got sick, I found it was the very thing I wanted. If there is one here who feels the heed of a Savior, remember the greater the sin the greater the need of a Savior.

I remember when I was coming back from Europe on the steamer there was a young officer. I felt greatly drawn out toward him, because I could see he was dying. It didn't seem to him as if he were dying, but you know death is very deceitful. He seemed to be joyous and lighthearted. He would talk about his plans and take out his guns and tell how he intended to go hunting when he arrived, but it seemed to me that he would not live to see this country. By and by he was taken down on his bed, and then the truth came to him that death was upon him. He got a friend to write out a telegram, which this friend was to send to his mother when they arrived. It read: "Mother, I am real sick. – Charlie." As soon as the boat touched the shore, he was to send it. "But" said someone, "why not tell her in the telegram to come?" "Ah," he replied, "she will come." He knew when she read it and saw that he wanted help, she would come. It was the knowledge of his need that would bring her.

So Christ is waiting to hear our need, and man's need brings out the help of God. As I said before, the real trouble is that men don't think they need Him. You know that in one place – in the 15th chapter of Luke – they brought this charge against Him: "This man receives sinners and eats with them." This charge was brought against Him again and again. I am told by Hebrew scholars that instead of "receives," it should be rendered, "He is looking out for them." And that's what He was doing. He was looking out for them. He didn't care how black in sin they might be; He was ready to take them.

Now, a great many say, "I am too great a sinner to be saved." That is like a hungry man saying he is too hungry to eat, or a sick man saying he is too sick to send for a doctor, or a beggar saying, "I am too poor to beg; I'll wait till I get some money first." If a man is hungry and perishing you must relieve him.

Now there is not a sinner in Chicago but has his representative in the Bible. Take for instance, the publicans. You know the Jews thought this class about the lowest in the world. They put them lower than any other kind of sinner. They placed them along with the sinners – "publicans and sinners." The publicans were the tax collectors, and they defrauded the people at every turn. For instance, a man in South Chicago will pay over, perhaps, a hundred thousand dollars for the privilege of just collecting the taxes, and then he goes to work and twists the people out of a hundred and fifty thousand dollars. He doesn't care a straw for justice or appearances. He comes into the cottage of the widow and taxes half she has. At every house the tax collector puts the blocks to his victims, and famine often comes in when he goes out. The people detest him; they hate him with a perfect hatred. They always find him a drag on them and feel he hasn't a bit of sympathy for them. Their money, they find, is taken without warrant; their homes are broken up, and trouble and starvation come on them.

And so the publican was hated wherever he turned. He was the agent of the Roman tyrant, and the people were brought up to shun him. He deserved all of it, and even more, by his heartless exactions, yet Christ forgave even him. And just so rumsellers can be saved. And another class that Christ had mercy on was the thieves. When on the cross, he saved a thief. There may be some thief here tonight. I tell you, my friend, you may be saved if you only will. There may be someone here who is persecuting a good wife and making her home a perfect hell on earth. But you, too, may be saved. There may be some here persecuting the Church, but there's salvation for you. When Saul was persecuting the Christians from city to city, he was stopped short by the voice of God; he was converted. And those high-headed Pharisees, so well versed in the law of Moses, even they were converted. Joseph of Arimathea was a Pharisee, and so was Nicodemus.

But tonight, I want to talk about another class that Jesus dealt with and led to a higher life. I want to talk about fallen women. There are some people who believe that these have fallen so low that Christ will pass them by. But my friends, that thought comes from the Evil One. In all this blessed book there is not one, not a solitary one of this class mentioned that ever came to Him but that He received them. Yes, He even went out of His way and sought her out.

Now I want to take three representative cases where these women had to do with Christ. One is the case of an awakened one. The Spirit of God has dealt with her anxious, wakened soul. The Lord was one day at Jerusalem and a banquet was given Him by Simeon. There was a banquet table in the house, arranged according to the fashion of that day. Instead of chairs for the guests, as was customary the guests sat reclining on lounges. Well, it was just one of these repasts that our Lord sat down to along with the wealthy Simeon and his many guests. But no sooner had He entered than this woman followed Him into the house and fell down at His feet and began to wash them with her tears.

It was the custom in those days to wash one's feet on entering a house. Sandals were worn and the practice was necessary. Well, this woman had got into the house by some means and once inside, had quietly stolen up to the feet of Jesus. And in her hands she brought a box, but her heart, too, was just as full of ointment as the box she carried. And there was the sweetest perfume as she stole to His feet. And her tears started to fall down on those sacred feet – hot, scalding tears that gushed out like water. She said nothing while the tears fell, and then she took down her long black hair and wiped His feet with the hair of her head. And after that she poured out the ointment on His feet. Then straightway the Pharisees began talking together. How all through the New Testament these Pharisees kept whispering and talking together. They said, shaking their heads, "This Man receives sinners," and then, "This Man, if He were a prophet, would have known who and what manner of woman this is that touches Him, for she is a sinner." No prophet, they insisted, would allow that kind of a woman near him but would push her away.

And then the Savior read these thoughts and quickly rebuked them. He said, "Simeon, I have something to say to you." And he said, "Master, say on." And He said, "Do you see this woman? I entered into your house, you gave me no water to wash my feet; but she has washed my feet with tears, and wiped them with the hairs of her head. You gave me no kiss, but this woman since I came in has not ceased to kiss my feet. My head with oil you did not anoint, but this woman has anointed my feet with ointment." Simeon was like a great many Pharisees nowadays who say, "Oh, well, we will entertain that minister if we must. We don't want to. He's a dreadful nuisance, but we will have to put up with him. It's our duty to be patronizing."

Well, the Master said more to His entertainer. "There was a certain creditor," He said, "which had two debtors; the one owed five hundred pence, and the other fifty, and when he had nothing to pay" – mark that, sinner; the debtor had nothing to pay. There is no sinner in the world that can pay anything to cancel his debt to God. The great trouble is that sinners think they can pay, some of them 75 cents on the dollar, some even feel able to pay 99 cents on the dollar, and the one cent that they are short, they think they can make that up some way. That is not the way; it is all wrong. You must throw all the debt on God. Some few, perhaps, will only claim to pay 25 cents on the dollar, but they are not humble enough either. They can't begin to carry out their bargain. Why, sinner, you couldn't pay one-tenth part of a single mill of the debt you are under to Almighty God.

Now it says in this parable that they could not pay him anything – they had nothing to give and the creditor frankly forgave them both. "Now, Simeon," the Master asked, "which should love that man the most?" "I suppose," was the reply, "he that was forgiven the most." "You have rightly judged; this woman loves much because she has been forgiven much," and went on to tell Simeon all about her. I suppose He wanted to make it plainer to Simeon and He turned to the poor woman and said, "Your sins are forgiven" – all forgiven; not part of them – not half of them, but every sin from the cradle up. Every impure desire or thought is blotted out for time and eternity, and He said, "Go in peace." Yes, truly, she went out in peace, for she went out in the light of heaven. With what brightness the light must have come down to her from those eternal hills – with what beauty it must have flashed on her soul. Yes, she came to the feet of the Master for a blessing, and she got it, and if there is a poor woman here tonight who wants a blessing, she will get it.

I want to call your attention to a thought right here. You have not got the name of one of those poor women. The three women who had fallen, who had been guilty of adultery and had been blessed by Him, not one of them has been named. It seems to me as if it had been intended that when they got to heaven, we should not know them – they will just mingle with the rest. Their names have not been handed down for 1,800 years. They have called Mary Magdalene a fallen woman but bear in mind there is nothing in Scripture to make us understand that she was a poor, fallen woman, and I believe if she had been, her name would not have been handed down.

Now the next woman was altogether different from the woman in Luke. She didn't come with an alabaster box seeking a blessing. She was perfectly indifferent; she was a careless sinner. Perhaps there are some poor, fallen women who have come tonight in a careless spirit – only out of curiosity. They don't want a Savior, they don't want their sins blotted out. They don't want any forgiveness. Perhaps she has heard that at Moody and Sankey's they were going to preach repentance and that a great many fallen women are likely to be here and thought she would just come down to see how they took it. Now you have a representative here.

After Christ had that interview with Nicodemus, we are told He went up to Galilee by Samaria. He could have gone up to Galilee without going to Samaria, but He knew there was a fallen woman there. He got to the well and sent off His disciples to get bread. Why did He not keep one with Him? Because He knew the woman was coming that way, and she would not probably like to see so many people.

While He is sitting on the curbstone of the well, a poor, fallen woman of Samaria comes along for water. You know the people in those days used to come out in the morning and evening to get their water, not in the blaze of the noonday sun. No doubt she was ashamed to come out there to meet the pure and virtuous at the well and that was the reason why she stole out at the hour. She brought her water pot to get water, and when she came up the Master stopped her and asked her for a drink, just to draw her out. She saw He was a Jew. We can always tell a Jew: God has put a mark upon them. "How is this? You a Jew and ask a Samaritan for a drink? The Jews have no dealings with the Samaritans." "Ah, you don't know Me," He replied. "If you would have asked Me for drink, I would have given you living water." "How could you give me living water? You have no vessel to draw water with." "Whosoever drinks of this water shall thirst again, but whosoever shall drink of the water that I shall give him will have a well springing up in his heart into everlasting life." "Well," probably she thought, "that is a good thing. One draught of water will give me a well – one draught of water for the rest of my days." She asked Him for this living water, and He told her, "Go, bring your husband." He was just drawing her out, just got her up to the point of confession. "I have no husband," she said. "For you have had five husbands, and he whom you now have is not your husband; what you said is true." I can see that woman's astonishment. She looks all around to see who had told Him all about her. Like a man who came up from Michigan lately, who came into the Tabernacle and listened to the sermon which as he told me, seemed all to be preached at him. He wondered who had told me all about him. He got Christ and is going back to Michigan to preach the gospel of Jesus Christ.

The word of God reached her, and she saw she was detected. "Sir, I perceive you are a prophet." Then she went on the old religious discussion, but the Lord turned her from that and told her that the hour had come when the people must worship the Father in spirit and in truth, not in this or that particular mountain, nor yet at Jerusalem. And she said, "When the Messiah comes He will tell us all things," and when she had said this, she was ready for the truth. Then Jesus said, "I am the Messiah." Just then she saw His disciples coming and probably she thought these men might know who she was. She got up her pot, and away she went to the city. The moment she got within the gates she shouted, "Come see this man I have met at the well. Is not this the Messiah? Why, He has told me all that ever I did." And you can see all the men, women, and children running out of that city up to the well. As He stands in the midst of His disciples and He sees the multitudes coming running toward them, He says, "Look yonder; look at the fields, for they are already white with the harvest. Look what that poor fallen woman has done." And He went into that town as an invited guest, and many believed on account of the woman's testimony, and many more believed on account of His own.

Now, my friends, He did not condemn the poor adulteress. The

Son of God was not ashamed to talk with her and tell her of that living water, and that those who drank of which would never die. He did not condemn her. He came to save her, came to tell how to be blessed here and blessed hereafter.

The next case is still much worse. You may say it is like black, blacker, blackest, compared with the other two. I want to speak about this one, that in the 8th chapter of John. One woman I have spoken of was at a dinner party in the house of a Pharisee, the other by the well of Sychar, and now we come to the Temple porch. They had taken a woman in adultery, had caught her in the very act. They had not got the man; they had held only the poor woman. While He is speaking, the Pharisees are driving this poor fallen woman right into the Temple. What a commotion there would be here tonight if such a scene should take place in the Tabernacle! She had broken the law of Moses, by which a woman caught in the act of adultery was to be put to death. The woman is brought toward Him and now they are about to put the question of her life or death before Him. He had said that He hadn't come to condemn the world but to save the world, and they are just going to try and condemn Him by His own words. They say to Him, "The law of Moses says stone her, what do you say?" But not a word did He speak.

Jesus stooped down and wrote on the ground as though he hadn't heard them. We don't know what He wrote. Perhaps, "Grace and truth come by Jesus Christ." Perhaps He wrote that, but while He thus busied Himself, they cried out the louder, demanding an answer to their question. So at length He lifted Himself up and said, "He that is without sin among you, let first him cast a stone at her." Never did an answer so completely serve its purpose; you who never were guilty of an offence, just you cast the first stone. And amid the strangest silence, He again stooped and wrought with His finger on the ground. This time perhaps He wrote, "I am not come to call the righteous, but sinners to repentance." And soon He rose again, but ere He did so, He heard the patter of retreating feet on the pavement, and when now He glanced up, He saw none but the woman.

One by one they had been convicted by their own conscience and slunk away; not one of them there could throw the stone. And the Savior looked at the woman. I can imagine the tears come trickling down her cheeks as Jesus Christ, in kindest tones, asked her, "Woman, where are your accusers? Has no man condemned you?" And for an instant she could not answer. Who knows how that poor soul had reached her sad plight! One of those very Pharisees who had left her, perhaps had led her astray.

The very man who had clamored loudest to condemn her was likely the guilty one. And there she stood alone. The betrayer was left untouched, as too often he is today – a miserable, unjust, untrue sentiment by which the man, who is equally guilty, is received in society and the woman is condemned. But at last, she gained her voice and said, "No man, my Lord," and then, perhaps, told how her parents had died when she was very young. A stepmother, perhaps, had taken her and treated her harshly and then had turned her adrift on the world. Or perhaps a drunken father had turned home into darkness, and she had been driven from it almost brokenhearted. And so in her helplessness, her innocent affections were gained, and then she had been led astray. The Master knew it all, and when He heard her reply He said, "Neither do I condemn you; go, and sin no more." She had been dragged into the Temple to be stoned, but now Christ had delivered her. She came to be put to death, but she received life everlasting.

My friends, the Son of God will not now condemn any poor fallen woman that leaves off her sins and just casts herself down at His feet. He will take you up just as you are. When in Philadelphia, a fallen woman came into the inquiry room and threw herself down on the floor. The Christian helpers talked and talked to her but couldn't get a word out of her; they couldn't do a thing with her. The Hon. George H. Stewart came to me and said, "We wish you would come, we don't know what to make of her." She was weeping bitterly, and as far off as I was, I could hear her sobs all over the room. So I went and said, "What is the trouble?" At last she spoke, and the bitterness of her despairing voice went to my heart. "I have fallen from everything pure, and God cannot save me; there is no hope."

I told her tenderly that God could still lift her up and save her. I said, "Are you only just willing to be forgiven? A merciful Father is waiting and longing to pardon." She said at last she could not abandon her course, as no one would give her a home. But that difficulty was got around by my assuring her kind friends would provide for her. And then she yielded, and that same day was given a pleasant place in the home of a Presbyterian minister. But for forty-eight hours after entering her new home, that poor reclaimed woman cried, day and night. We went for her mother, and on hearing our story the mother clasped her hands and cried, "Has my daughter really repented? Thank God for His mercy; my heart has just been breaking. I've prayed so long for her without result; take me to her." And that reformed daughter of sin has lived consistently ever since, and when I was last in Philadelphia, she was one of the most esteemed members in that Presbyterian Church.

And so every one of you can begin anew, and God will help and man will help you. Oh turn, and do not die. Seven short years is the allotted life of a fallen woman. Oh, escape your early doom, escape your infamy, and hear God's voice calling you to repent. Your resolution to amend will be borne up by hosts of friends; never fear for that. Just take the decided step, and you will be helped by every good man and woman in the community. Oh, I beseech you to act right now, and settle this great question for time and eternity.

I heard of a mother whose daughter was led astray, and the poor daughter tried to hide herself, thinking her mother would not forgive her. The mother went to the town where she supposed her child had gone, but she hunted and hunted unsuccessfully. The trouble is with most of those girls who go astray, they go under assumed names; this daughter had done the same thing and that mother couldn't find her. At last she found a place where fallen women resorted to, and the mother went to the keeper of that place and begged her to let her hang up her picture in the room, and consent was granted. Hundreds of fallen women came into that room and carelessly glanced at the picture and went out.

Weeks and months rolled on, until at length one night, a poor fallen girl came into the room. She was going out as careless as she had entered, when her eye caught the picture, and gazing at it for a moment, she burst into a flood of tears. "Where did you get it?" she sobbed. They told her how her mother came there, heartbroken, and asked to have her picture hung up in that room in the hope of finding her daughter. The girl's memory went back to her days of peace and purity, recalling the acts of kindness of that loved mother, and she then and there resolved to return. See how that mother sought for her and forgave her. Oh, poor fallen ones, the Son of God is seeking for you tonight. If you haven't got a mother to pray for you, the Son of God wants to be everything to you. He wants to receive you to Himself. Let me hold Him up to you as your best friend. He wants to take you to His loving bosom and this very night and very hour you can be raised if you will.

There was a woman who was trying to get a poor girl to go back to her home. She said, "Neither my mother, my father, nor my brothers will forgive me. They won't permit me to go back." "Will you give me your address?" the lady asked. The address was obtained, and the very next post brought a letter marked, "Immediately," and it seemed as if the whole hearts of her father and mother and brothers were poured out in that letter. It was filled with kindness and urged her to come home and all would be forgotten. There is many a poor fallen girl in Chicago whose mother is praying for her and whose heart is aching because she won't go back. Your mother will forgive you, and all your friends, if you will only show true signs of repentance. They will take you home.

O my friends, let this be the last night you will live in sin – in shame. Let this be your last night in which you will live in sin. Take those sins you have to Him, and He will forgive you. He has said, "Let the wicked forsake his ways," and pardon is ready. That is what our Lord will do. He will pardon you and make you pure. Will you let Him pardon you tonight?

Just before coming down this evening, I received a letter from a fallen woman. I've received a number during the past few days. Thank God the Spirit is at work among that class! And let me say right here, if there is any person here who keeps a brothel, if you will allow Christian ladies admittance, they will go gladly and hold meetings. This idea that Christian ladies do not care for your class is false – as false as the blackest lie that ever came out of hell. Why, some of the first ladies of the city have lately been visiting these houses personally and have been trying to save their erring sisters. A few days ago, several came to me and asked if I couldn't get a list of all the brothels of the city. I went to police headquarters and got the names of the keepers and addresses and gave it to these Christian women, and since then, many houses have been visited. These charges that Christian women will not have them in their homes are equally false.

The other night a lady of culture was on her knees with a poor one who told the lady that she was a fallen girl and did not know where to go if she didn't go back to her brothel. "Come and stay at my house," said the lady, "I will take care of you." That good Christian kept her till she got her a good situation. Another one not long ago received the truth, and one of our ministers wrote to her parents, got a pass, and sent her home to her forgiving parents. Let me ask you not to believe that we are cruel, that we are hard-hearted, that we do not care for the fallen women, but only for the abandoned men. We have a place to shelter you, and if that is not large enough, the businessmen will put up another. They will do everything for you if you are only repentant; they will not try to keep you down and cast you off. If you are sincere, there are hundreds and thousands of people in this city whose hearts will go out to you.

But I want to read this letter:

"Chicago, Dec. 14.

"Mr. Moody, Many fallen women in this city would, in these days, gladly change their mode of life and seek Christ and restoration to the homes and hearts of parents and friends whom they, weakly left many, many bitter years and months ago, if only they could see some way to have honorable living and friendly recognition and help when they should seek these."

Now, let me say here that any young woman who wants reclamation ought not to look into the future. Say to yourselves, "I will be saved tonight, come what will."

"You say, 'Seek first the kingdom of Christ; but, my dear brother (for such you seem even to me), why do this if only returning shame awaits us?"

I wish every fallen woman would think as this one does; why, I would be a brother to you all. Thank God, I've got a brother's heart for all of you. I wish every one of you would feel that I want to do you good – that I only want to lift you up.

"Suppose a hundred fallen women of this city were at the Tabernacle tonight – no doubt more than this number will be there – and that these should seek Christ and find forgiveness, for you assure us there is full forgiveness for even us, so that these scarlet stains should be 'whiter than snow – where, I ask, shall we live? What shall we do?

"We must return ere the echo of the last prayer in that Tabernacle has died away to the apartments which have only known our bitter shame and again meet the devil in his chosen home."

Let me say, again, that no woman in this audience need do that. There will be homes open for you. God will provide for you if you will trust Him. I hope there will be hundreds here tonight who will say, "I will never return to that place. I will never go back to that house of shame. I will never meet the devil in those houses more; I will rather die in the poorhouse than do it. I turn my back for ever upon death and hell."

"No home of parent or friend or praying Christian who joined in your prayer at the Tabernacle for us would offer our weary bodies shelter there or our willing hands labor wherewith honest bread might be earned. No Christian's purse affords tomorrow's bread."

Dear friends, let the morrow take care of itself. Don't be looking at the future. Just walk by faith. That's what every Christian must do.

"The very ones who came here to pray for us go away scorning us; and while with the virtuous wife and mother and the pure maiden we would plead a common Savior, they would thrust us from them. What can we do? Who will help us?

"There remains only a life of shame and an unwept death, physical and eternal, for us. Hopelessly, "One of Them."

Come

We have for our subject this afternoon the precious little word, "Come." I want to call your attention first to the "come" in the 53rd chapter of the prophecies of Isaiah. "Incline your ear, and come unto Me. Hear, and your souls shall live; and I will make an everlasting covenant with you, even the sure mercies of David."

"Incline your ear and come unto Me; hear and your soul shall live." Now, I find if we get people to listen – to pause and hear the voice of God, it isn't long before they are willing to follow that voice, but it is so hard to get people to stop and listen for a moment. The din of the world makes such a noise that the people don't hear the voice – that still small voice. He says, "Incline your ear and come unto Me." Now, if we could only get all the friends in this audience to incline their ears this afternoon – not only your natural ears but the ears of your soul, you could be saved today. But Satan does not want you to do this; he does all he can to keep your ears from hearing. He makes you think about yourself, about your sons, your homes, but, my friends, let us forget all those things today. Let us forget all our surroundings and close our eyes to the world and just try and listen to the Word of God and come and hear what He has to say.

"Incline your ear and come unto Me; hear and your soul shall live." Now, let us turn to the 10th chapter of Romans where we see, "Faith comes by hearing, and hearing by the word of God." Now, it is not my words I want to have you to listen to – it is not my words I want you to hear this afternoon, but I want you to hear the words of this loving King who calls you to Himself. What does He say? In another place He says, "Behold, I stand at the door and knock; if any man hear My voice and open the door, I will come in to him and sup with him and he with Me," or "if any woman," or any one – that's what it means, my friends – "hear My voice and open the door, I will come in to her, and will sup with her and she with Me."

I heard of a little child some time ago who was burned. The mother had gone out and left her three children at home. The eldest left the room, and the remaining two began to play with the fire and set the place in a blaze. When the youngest of the two saw what she had done she went into a little cupboard and fastened herself in. The remaining child went to the door and knocked and knocked, crying to her to open the door and let her take her out of the burning building, but she was too frightened to do it. It seems to me as if this is the way with hundreds and thousands in this city. He stands and knocks, but they've got their hearts barred and bolted, because they don't know that He has come only to bless them. May God help you to hear, and if you listen to Him and bring your burdens to Him, He will bless you. He is able to open the ears of everyone here if you let Him in. I was up here at the hotel the other night, and I had the door locked and bolted, and someone came and rapped. I shouted, "Come in!" The man tried to come in, but he couldn't. I had to get up and unlock the door before he could enter. That's the way with many people today. They've got the door bolted and barred; but if you only open it to Him, He will come in.

"If any man hears my voice and open the door I will come in and sup with him and he with Me." Now, my friends, can you hear it? Can you hear God's voice speaking through His own Word? "Incline your ear and come unto Me." Just listen. You know sometimes when you hear a man speaking whose voice you don't hear very well, and you want to hear every word the man says, you put your hand up to your ear to catch the sound clearer. Now listen. God says, "Incline your ear and come unto Me; hear and your souls shall live; and I will make an everlasting covenant with you." Now, is it not true? Can't you hear that loving voice speaking to you, and won't you obey that voice and let Him save you? But I can imagine some of you saying, "I can't hear anything." Take your ears to Him and He will make you hear.

Now let me take you to another course. While John and his disciples were standing, Jesus came along and John said, "Behold the Lamb of God!" and Jesus said, "What do you seek?" "Where do You dwell?" he asked. Jesus replied, "Come and see," and they just obeyed Him and never left Him. My friends, if I could introduce you to Christ – could just get you to catch one glimpse of Him, if you could but see the King in all His beauty, if you could but see Him in all His loveliness, you would never forsake Him, for we "shall grow up before Him as a tender plant and as a root out of a dry ground; He hath no form nor comeliness, and when we shall see Him there is no beauty that we should desire Him." Follow Him as your Savior.

In order to appreciate Him you have to be brought to Him, but if sin has come between you and Him, I cannot tell you anything about Him. It is just like telling a blind man about the beauties of nature, the loveliness of the flowers, or of the world. That is the way, if sin stands between you and Him, and when Christians try to tell you about the beauties of Christianity they fail, but if you come and have an interview with Him, you will see that you cannot help but love Him; you will see that you cannot but forsake all and follow Him.

I remember once hearing of a child who was born blind. He grew up to be almost a man when a skillful physician thought he could give the man his sight. He was put under the doctor's treatment, and for a long time he worked till at last he succeeded. But he wouldn't let the man see the light of the sun all at once, lest it would strike him blind. It had to be done gradually. So he put a lot of bandages upon his eyes and removed one after another until the last one was reached, and when it was taken off the young man began to see. When he saw the beauties of the world, he upbraided his friends for not telling him of the beauties of nature. "Why, we tried to tell you about the beauties of the world, but we could not," they said. And so it is with us. All that we can do is to tell you to come and see, come and see the loveliness of Christ.

I can imagine some of you saying, "I am blind, I cannot see any beauty in Him." Bring your blindness to Him as you bring your deafness and He will give you sight, as He did with the blind Bartimaeus – as He did with all the blind men on earth. There was never a blind man who came to Him requesting his sight whose request was not granted, and there is not a blind soul in this assembly but will be healed if you come to Him. He says that's what He came for, to give sight to the blind. If you cannot see any beauty in Him, pray to God to give you sight.

The next "come" is in the prophecies of Isaiah. "Come, now, and let us reason together," says the Lord: "though your sins be as scarlet, they shall be as white as snow; though they be red like crimson, they shall be as wool." I find a great many people say their reason stands between them and God. Now, let me say here, the religion of Jesus is a matter of revelation, not of investigation. No one ever found out Christ by reason. It is a matter of revelation. Now see what he says, "Come now" – that means this afternoon – "though your sins be as scarlet, they shall be white as snow." Now He puts a pardon in the sinner's face. "Your sins may be as scarlet, they shall be white as snow."

Take the scarlet in that lady's shawl. It is a fast color. You cannot wash it out and make it white. If you tried you would only destroy the shawl. But He will make your sins white as snow, though they be as scarlet, if you come to Him. Just come to Him as you are and instead of reasoning, ask Him to take them away. Then He will reason it out with you. The natural man does not understand spiritual things, but when a man is born of the Spirit, then it is that the spiritual things are brought out to him.

A great many people want to investigate – want to reason out the Bible from front to back, but He wants us first to take a pardon. That's God's method of reasoning. He puts a pardon in the face of the sinner. "Come now." Do you think there is not reason in this? Suppose the whole plan of salvation was reasoned out to you, why, death might step in before the end of the reasoning was reached. So God puts a pardon first. If you will be influenced today you will just bring your reason to Him and ask Him to give you wisdom to see divine things, and He will do it. "If any of you lack wisdom, let him ask of God that gives to all men liberally and up-braids not, and it shall be given liberally." The idea that this reason that God has given man should keep him from Christ.

A number of years ago as I was coming out of a daily prayer meeting in one of our western cities, a lady came up to me and said, "I want to have you see my husband and ask him to come to Christ." She said, "I want to have you go and see him." She told me his name, and it was of a man I had heard of before. "Why," said I, "I can't go and see your husband. He is a booked infidel. I can't argue with him. He is a good deal older than I am, and it would be out of place. Then I am not much for infidel argument." "Well, Mr. Moody," she says, "that isn't what he wants. He's got enough of that. Just ask him to come to the Savior." She urged me so hard and so strong that I consented to go. I went to the office where the judge was doing business and told him what I had come for. He laughed at me. "You are very foolish," he said, and began to argue with me. I said, "I don't think it will be profitable for me to hold an argument with you. I have just one favor I want to ask of you, and that is, that when you are converted you will let me know." "Yes," said he, "I will do that. When I am converted, I will let you know" – with a good deal of sarcasm.

I went off, and requests for prayer were sent here and to Fulton Street, New York, and I thought the prayer there and of that wife would be answered if mine were not. A year and a half after, I was in that city, and a servant came to the door and said, "There is a man in the front parlor who wishes to see you." I found the judge there. He said, "I promised I would let you know when I was converted. I've been converted." "Well," said I, "I'm glad to hear it! Tell me all about it." I had heard it from other lips, but I wanted to hear it from his own. He said his wife had gone out to a meeting one night and he was home alone, and while he was sitting there by the fire he thought, "Supposing my wife is right, and my children are right; suppose there is a heaven and hell, and I shall be separated from them."

His first thought was, "I don't believe a word of it." The second thought came, "You believe in the God that created you, and that the God that created you is able to teach you. You believe that God can give your life." "Yes, the God that created me can give me life. I was too proud to get down on my knees by the fire, and I said, 'O God, teach me.' And as I prayed, I don't understand it, but it began to get very dark, and my heart got very heavy. I was afraid to tell my wife when she came to bed and I pretended to be asleep. She kneeled down beside that bed and I knew she was praying for me. I kept crying, 'O God, save me; O God, take away this burden,' but it grew darker, and the load grew heavier and heavier. All the way to my office I kept crying, 'O God, take away this load of guilt.' I gave my clerks a holiday and just closed my office and locked the door. I fell down on my face. I cried in agony to the Lord, 'O Lord, for Christ's sake, take away this guilt.' I don't know how it was, but it began to grow very light. I said, 'I wonder if this isn't what they call conversion. I think I will go and ask the minister if I am not converted.' I met my wife at the door and said, 'My dear, I've been converted.' She looked in amazement. 'Oh, it's a fact. I've been converted!' We went into that drawing room and knelt down by the sofa and prayed to God to bless us."

The old judge said to me, the tears trickling down his cheeks, "Mr. Moody, I've enjoyed life more in the last three months than in all the years of my life put together." If there is an infidel here – if there is a skeptical one here, ask God to give wisdom to come now. Let us reason together, and if you become acquainted with God the day will not go before you receive light from Him.

The next "come" I want to call your attention to is a very sweet one. He says, "Come and reason," "Come and see," and now we have, "Come and rest." What this world wants is rest. Every man, every woman is in pursuit of it, and how many of us have found? How many are bearing burdens about our hearts always – how many have come into this hall today with a great burden on their hearts? What does He say? "Come unto Me, all you that labor and are heavy laden, and I will give you rest." Now a great many people have an idea that they get rid of their burdens themselves, but they must come to Him if they want to be relieved. That's what Christ came for.

Come to Him. "He has borne our griefs and carried our sorrows." There could not be a sweeter "come" than this. How many mothers are bearing burdens for their children – how many because of their sons, or perhaps you have husbands who have proved unfaithful, or maybe you are widows who have been without support. The future may look dark to you, but hear the loving voice of the Savior, "Come unto me, all you that labor and are heavy laden, and I will give you rest." There is not a soul here – I don't care what the burden may be – in this vast audience, but can lay their burden on the Lord Jesus Christ, and He will bear it for you. We can be released. We have found a resting place, and that is in the loving bosom of the Lord Jesus Christ. There is a hymn written by Dr. Andrew Bonar which can express this much better than I can. Let me read it:

> I heard the voice of Jesus say:
> "Come unto me and rest;
> Lay down, thou weary one, lay down
> Thy head upon my breast."
>
> I came to Jesus as I was,
> Weary and worn and sad;
> I found in Him a resting-place,
> And He has made me glad.
>
> I heard the voice of Jesus say:
> "Behold I freely give
> The living water – thirsty one,
> Stoop down and drink and live!"
>
> I came to Jesus and I drank
> Of that life-giving stream;
> My thirst was quenched, my soul revived
> And now I live in Him.
>
> I heard the voice of Jesus say:
> "I am this dark world's light;
> Look unto Me, thy morn shall rise,
> And all thy day be bright."
>
> I looked at Jesus and I found
> In Him my Star, my Sun.
> And in that light of Life I'll walk
> Till travelling days are done.

Oh, my friends, if you want rest today, come to Him. He stands with

His arms outstretched and says, "Come to Me and rest." Does the world satisfy you? Are not the griefs of this world crushing many a heart here? Hear the voice of Jesus, "Come and rest." The world cannot take it from you. The world's crosses and trials will not tear it from you; He will give you peace and comfort and rest if you but come.

The next "come" is "Come and drink and eat." You don't have to pay anything. You know it is hard for a man to get a tax on water unless when it has to be brought into the city. But this water is always without price, and salvation is like a river, flowing at the feet of everyone. All you have to do is to stoop down and drink of this living water and never die. The world cannot give you comfort – cannot give you water to satisfy your thirst, and every man and woman in this world is thirsty. That's the way our places of amusement are filled. People are constantly thirsting for something. But how are they filled with those amusements? They are as thirsty as ever. But if they drink the waters that He offers they will have a fountain in them springing up into everlasting life.

I remember coming down a river with some wounded soldiers. The water was very muddy, and as we had no filters, they had to drink the dirty water which did not satisfy their thirst. I remember a soldier saying, "Oh that I had a draught of water from my father's well." If you drink of the living water your soul will never thirst again. Not only does He say, "Come and drink of that living water," but He says, "Come and eat." In the 55th chapter of Isaiah, you are invited to come and eat. You know all that the children of Israel had to do in the wilderness was just to pick up the manna and eat. They didn't have to make it. And people had just to stoop down and pick up the manna and eat and drink from the flinty rock when the water flowed. And today the provision is brought to the door of your hearts. You haven't to go down to the earth for it or to go up to the skies for it. It is here, and all you've got to do is to eat.

You know almost the last words of Christ after his resurrection, when having a little fish, He said to his disciples, "Come and dine." Oh, what a sweet invitation – the invitation of the Master to his disciples, "Come and dine." I invite you now to come and dine with Him; He will quench that thirst. He will satisfy your hunger, and all you've got to do is to take Him at His word.

Is there a poor, thirsty one here today? I bid you come and drink of the fountain of living water. I bid you come and eat of the heavenly bread, yes, the bread made in heaven, the bread that angels feed on – Christ Himself is the bread of life.

Now, many people make a great mistake about accepting Christ. They think they've got something to do, think they've got to do some work, or that they've got to pray and wrestle before taking Him. They think it is a question of performances whether they are saved or not. Now, it is a question of simply taking what God offers you. I remember when I was out on the Pacific coast, a man took me through his house, out on his lands, and showed me his orchards, and then said, "Mr. Moody, you are a guest of mine, and I want you to feel perfectly at home; do what you like." Well, after this man said this, you don't suppose if I wanted an orange, I was going under the tree to pray that it would fall into my pocket? I just went up boldly and plucked what I wanted. And so the bread of heaven is offered to us, and all we've got to do is to go boldly up and take it. This is what God wants you to do. Everything is prepared for you.

There is a class, too, who say, "But I'm afraid I'll not hold out." How many people are stumbling over this! Now, if you come boldly up to the throne, you'll get all the support you need – "Let us therefore come boldly unto the throne of grace, that we may obtain mercy and find grace to help in time of need." There is a passage for you; that ought to be sufficient. And there is not a woman here today but can be kept, from this very day and this very hour, from evil – "For I the Lord your God will keep you, without spot or wrinkle, and without blemish." Some of the vilest men who have ever trodden this earth have been saved with the grace of God. Some have been kept sixty or seventy years merely by the grace of God and never wavered. "Come boldly to the throne of grace" and you will get power. That is sufficient. Won't you take Him at His word? It seems to me that it is madness not to take the gift offered us by God.

Let me call attention to another "come." My friends, the Bible is full of them, and you can't say if you don't come there have been no invitations. He says, "Come to the marriage." Now, you young ladies like marriages pretty well. Let a marriage come off in a church and hundreds will be there. And probably next night, at the prayer meeting, there will scarcely be a dozen of you present. Now here is a marriage and there is not a lady here whom God does not want to be present at the marriage feast. There is an invitation.

And here is another "come": "Come and inherit the kingdom prepared for you from the foundation of the world." God has got an inheritance for every one of you. The time will soon come, if you accept Christ and become as His bride, when you shall hear the voice of Him saying to you, "Come and inherit the kingdom prepared for you from the foundation of the world." What a mistake it will be, my friends, if you will not hear that invitation given to you! There is an inheritance incorruptible in the heavens, a building not made with hands, and He wants everyone to enter into this inheritance. So it is your privilege to be present at the marriage feast and receive the inheritance if you will.

You know the first "come" in the Bible is in regard to salvation. It was given to Noah. God said, "Come and all your house into the ark," not a part of them, but "all your house." That is the first "come," in the Bible and all through that blessed book it is repeated. And now we come to the last one. It seems as if the Bible was created by this word "come." "The spirit and the bride say come, and let him that is athirst come, and whosoever will, let him taste the water of life freely." There is our invitation, as broad as the world itself. And if God says you are to come in there, no power in heaven, or earth, or hell can stop you! He bids you come. Now bear in mind it is your sins God wants and not your faith. You have nothing about you that He wants except your sins. People are continually trying to come to Him by their faith, by their feelings, by their tears, by their good deeds, by their works. But you have to come to Him just as you are. There is not a woman present but can roll off every sin and leave them in this Tabernacle.

Now the question comes, "What right have you to come?" Why, because the King invites you. Suppose Queen Victoria had sent me an invitation to be present at Windsor at a feast given in honor of the marriage of one of her sons to a princess of Russia. I take the cars to New York, then the boat to Liverpool, then I would run down to London where I would get the train to Windsor Castle. There is a sentry walking up and down in front of the gate. If I hadn't my invitation, he would refuse me admittance, but there is not a soldier in the British army can keep me out because I've got the Queen's invitation. But suppose the man looks at me and says, "You can't go into the presence of the Queen with those clothes; you are not fit to stand before the Queen." That is none of his business; that's hers. So the invitation comes from Him, and He wants you to come and He will clothe you in garments fit for His presence You will be stripped of every rag of self-righteousness and a robe of spotlessness will be put upon you.

A great many people say, "I want to become clean before I come to Christ." Now, my friends, that is the devil's work. He tries to get people to believe that they can't come without getting rid of their sins, but as I've said, all through the Scriptures He bids you come as you are. We cannot take away our sins; come to Him and He will blot them out.

A few years ago, in London, there used to be a good many little children stolen to act as chimney sweeps. A child was stolen from a wealthy family and a great reward was offered, but it couldn't be found. This child had been kidnapped. One day he was sent up a chimney and came down on the other side and into a beautiful room. The little fellow was bewildered. A lady was sitting there and recognized him as her son, and although the little fellow was covered with smut, she ran to him and drew him to her bosom, and that is the way Christ will receive you. You needn't try to get rid of one particle of sin. He wants to save you as you are. "Whosoever will, let him come and drink of the waters of life freely." Will you come today? The spirit and the bride invite you this afternoon.

Now I want to ask you what are you going to do with these ten loving invitations today – "Come and hear," "Come and see," "Come and reason," "Come and rest," "Come and eat and drink," "Come and dine," "Come and find grace," "Come unto the marriage," "Come and inherit the kingdom prepared for you from the foundation of the world," "Whosoever will, let him come." Ask God to help you to come today. If I were in your place, I would settle this question before I left this building; I would just press up to the kingdom of God and take Him at His word. Now would you just all lift up your hearts in prayer. Let every Christian pray for every soul here today out of Christ. Let us now just unite in this one petition that every soul in this building may come to Christ today.

Work

I want to speak this morning about work. You know that was the keynote of the meeting when we first commenced here, and we want to have it the keynote of our message as we leave. Faith is an act of the mind, and work is the outward sign of faith. If a man has true faith in Christ, he cannot help working for Christ. You cannot have fire without heat; no more can you have faith without works. "Faith without works," the apostle tells us, "is dead." It is dead, and the quicker buried the better; get it out of the way. The moment that faith fails in works, that moment it dies. "Show me your faith without your works, and I will show you my faith by my works." If a man has faith in Christ, he cannot help working; it is second nature to him.

Those men who are trying to serve Christ without works are having a pretty hard time of it. They neither enjoy the world nor the church and have a great deal of contempt for themselves. Now when a man gets outside of himself and goes to work for others, he is blessed – he has floods of love and peace and joy the whole of the time. People may get to heaven without works perhaps, but as Job says, it will be by the "skin of their teeth." It'll not be an abundant entrance that will be administered unto them. And what they did do, if not with a right motive, will be swept away in that hour when God comes and tries men's faith.

Faithful Christians are those heeding Christ's words in the gospel according to John, 15th chapter and 4th and 5th verses: "Abide in Me and

I in you. As the branch cannot bear fruit of itself, except it abide in the vine; no more can you, except you abide in Me. I am the vine, you are the branches. He that abides in Me and I in him, the same brings forth much fruit; for without Me you can do nothing." There in that chapter it says in the 2nd verse, "And every branch that bears fruit, he purges it that it may bring forth more fruit." So it is abiding in Christ that brings forth much fruit. I think you will find in all the churches those who bring forth scarcely anything. I was going to say nothing. I don't know how you can call them Christians.

Again there are others who bring forth, some thirty-fold, some sixty, and some a hundred, and it is those Christians that abide in Christ that bring forth an hundred-fold: they can't help it. When a branch abides in the vine it produces good fruit. You have a good apple tree, and it can't help bearing apples; it can't help bringing forth good fruit. So every Christian is to abide continually in Christ, not through four or five weeks when there are special services, but through the 365 days in the year. These special meetings here, are about drawing to a close, and some here this morning are perhaps asking, "What is going to become of us, what are we going to do?" Some perhaps tremble lest they shall go back to their old lukewarmness.

Now my friends, if you are going to truly work for Christ, you must carry this revival spirit in your bosoms throughout the 365 days, throughout all the year. If a man cannot be used of God, what does he want to live for? It is the privilege of every child of God to be revived all the time. That is what we want to do. Why, in the primitive days, there were added daily to the Lord such as should be saved. If we abide in the Lord, there will be just such results now. The trouble lies in our going away from the Lord, so that the Lord cannot use us and we cannot bring forth fruit. How are we to abide in Christ? Study the Word of God. It is the only book that tells about Christ. The Bible is God's Word, and if you want to know about Christ, study in its pages about His life, His character, and His acts. Find out who He is and what He is. The man that is abiding with Christ would rather be with Him than with the world; he would far rather be an hour with the Word of God, than a year in worldly society.

Look at the 3rd chapter of the 2 epistle to Timothy, 15th, 16th, and

17th verses: "And that from a child you have known the Holy Scriptures which are able to make you wise unto salvation through faith which is in Christ Jesus. All Scripture is given by inspiration of God, and is profitable for doctrine, for reproof, for correction, for instruction in righteousness, that the man of God may be perfect, thoroughly furnished unto all good works." Just listen: "That the man of God may be perfect, thoroughly furnished unto all good works." And with this, let me read those words from the 1st chapter of James, 22nd verse: "But be doers of the word, and not hearers only, deceiving your own selves."

If we had as many doers of the word as we have hearers in Chicago, what a mighty work could be done. You have been pretty good, yes, very good hearers, but I have a pretty serious charge to bring against nine out of every ten of you. You have come here, but when the benediction was through, you have just got on your hats and gathered up your shawls and got out as quick as you could. You haven't liked to talk to inquirers. Some of you are Christians of thirty or forty years standing. You have listened to sermons all these years and gone Sunday after Sunday to the regular services of the sanctuary, but what have you been personally doing? That's the question. Oh, be not only hearers, but doers; that is just the working spirit we want in Chicago now. We have had eleven weeks of these special meetings, and many of you have listened remarkably well. For eleven weeks you've been listening, and now's the time for action. Now's the time to be doers of the word; you've been hearers long enough. Let everyone put a shoulder to the work and push it on. These past three months have been spent in getting the army ready and equipped; now let it move ahead. Let all take up and carry on the work. Let Christians wake up and go to work. More conversions may be made in the next three months than in the last three if you Christians will do your duty.

I have heard some say, "Yes, but I haven't got the ability." God will strengthen you, my friends. God is with you, and all you have to do is to ask of Him wisdom, power, and strength. The God of all power and might is at your side if you call on Him. Don't you see if each one of you does but a little how much you will accomplish. Mr. Spurgeon said to some discouraged students, as they were going out to preach, "Well, just go ahead, there's a good many of you; you go into the churches and you find a great many Christians there, and when all are gathered together, there's a great deal of strength." Then he illustrated by telling about Moses and the frogs. "I'll bring great frogs on you," said Moses to Pharaoh. "Frogs," said Pharaoh, "what do I care for frogs!" "But" said Moses, "there's a good many of them," and the old king found it out. They swarmed into his bedchamber and jumped into the kneading trough. They sprawled out upon the throne so he could not sit down; they got on to the royal table, and into the royal lap – frogs, frogs, frogs, everywhere. He couldn't step without squashing one.

Yes, there were a good many of them, and there are a good many Christians. Let them just take a look at the frogs of Egypt; let them just go into every room, corner, and attic in Chicago and bring men the blessed gospel. Don't you see how much, if you are only united, may be done in the next three months. Oh, be doers, and not hearers only. "If any be a hearer of the word," says James, "and not a doer, he is like unto a man beholding his natural face in a glass; for he beholds himself and goes his way and straightway forgets what manner of man he was. But whosoever looks into the perfect law of liberty and continues therein, he being not a forgetful hearer, but a doer of the work, this man shall be blessed in his deed."

Now what we want, my friends, is to get to work. A great many people are called pillars of the church because they pay their pew rents. They never go out to Wednesday night meetings; you never think of seeing them there. They will get out every fine Sunday morning, but no one expects they will turn out on Sunday night. But they say they've "the root of the matter in them." Suppose you have a flower garden and take a friend out to see the flowers, but there isn't one to be seen. Will you say, "Well, it's just all full of roots." You might say so just as properly of the fruitless Christian. The root of the matter is down there, sure enough, but there's never anything crops out. These "do-less" Christians, these drones, doing nothing, are too numerous; there's too many of these "pillars" in the church. We want workers. We want these men to come out, and then help bring others out. The time is coming when, if people will not come and hear the gospel, the churches must go to them. Let workers go and seek them out and hold cottage prayer meetings at their houses and talk with them about Christ and Heaven. Be ye doers.

A great many people would be workers, but they are afraid of being called "odd." They want just enough Christianity to make them respectable, but enough of the world to keep them from being considered odd or peculiar. The result is they're wretched people in the world. They have no spiritual power. They never take a class in Sunday school, or if they do, there are no conversions in it. They forget those words in Titus, 2nd chapter, 14th verse, "Who gave Himself for us that He might redeem us from all iniquity and purify unto Himself, a peculiar people, zealous of good works." Now, I am a poor sailor; I never go on the sea but I get sick, yet I think I would be willing to sail around the whole world to find an entire church – minister, deacons, stewards, all the church officers and members – a "peculiar" people of this sort.

I would find a church that would make the world tremble. I don't believe the world ever saw a church all of them peculiar. You find in every age when God wants any work done, He always brings out a peculiar man. I suppose Elijah was the most peculiar man perhaps that ever lived. He was the oddest genius that people ever hit upon. Daniel was the most peculiar man in all Babylon. The courtiers of Nebuchadnezzar undoubtedly called him puritanical and a bigot. Yes, in the midst of idolaters, this old Hebrew was a praying man, but how God blessed him. Moses was the most peculiar man in Egypt, but how God blessed him. Always, the men and women most used of God have been peculiar, and Christian workers must be peculiar. But that is just what many don't want; they're afraid people will say they are peculiar. Now let me say no man or woman is fit to work for God until they become peculiar in this biblical sense – until they give up sinful, worldly pleasures, and separate themselves to live and work for God. Then see how God will bless them. God grant that all may become chosen vessels and meet for the Master's use.

Then in Titus, 3rd chapter, 1st verse: "Put them in mind to be subject to principalities and powers, to obey magistrates, to be ready for every good work." "Ready for all good works;" if all heeded this, what could not be done! How many times I have been down at these meetings night after night and have spoken to Christian people who have been here – some of them professing His name for forty years – and asked them to speak to some poor inquiring soul, but the answer's come,

"Oh, Mr. Moody, don't ask me, don't you ask me." They've been in the church these long years and can't say a word to dying souls! Shame on the Christianity of the nineteenth century! May God have mercy on each one of us and forgive us our shortcomings! These people want to have you talk about their souls and tell them the way of life. If it is not a good work to talk to a soul burdened with sin, what is a good work? What have these church members been about all these years? What have they been doing, that they are not ready now, after fifteen, thirty and forty years of professedly Christian life, to talk with anxious souls? When will you be ready?

Oh, my friends, will you not get ready at once? What power is there in the greatest army in the world if it doesn't know how to use its weapons? An army of five hundred real soldiers could rout them and send them all flying. What each child of God wants is to get ready. If there is one Christian in this place this morning that has not had the joy of bringing a soul to God, I would not go out of this Tabernacle until I had gone into one of the inquiry rooms and asked some Christian brother or sister, "Won't you pray for my unprofitable life, my barren life, my life so fruitless with nothing to show but leaves?" Oh, friends, is it not our highest privilege and joy as well as duty to bring souls to Jesus? Let us go to work! Let us bring converts to the Savior! Let us bring all men to Christ!

Will you look at the 8th verse of the same chapter: "This is a faithful saying, and these things I will affirm constantly that they which have believed in God might be careful to maintain good works." Now, you know the charge is sometimes made that Evangelical Christians preach salvation by faith alone – that we are justified by faith and as soon as we believe we are saved. Now that is not the entire New Testament teaching. To be sure we are saved by faith, but it is only by a faith that manifests itself in good works. If we believe otherwise, we are staking our faith on some creed, some church, some particular minister, and not on Christ, who said, even at twelve years of age, "Don't you know that I must be about my father's business." The life of Jesus was one succession of good works, and if we would follow His example we cannot help working.

"Be careful to maintain good works." I suppose that means you are to carefully maintain the church. Let me say to all, maintain the church.

Let me say this especially to all young converts. I have heard that of these some say they can be Christians and not unite with the church, and I was told last night that one of them said I didn't belong to the church. That is a mistake. I tried as soon as I was converted to enter the church, but at first they would not let me; some doubted whether I was converted. But I have been in the bosom of the church ever since and have never seen the day or the hour that I would be out of it. I believe it is the dearest institution on earth and that there is no institution to be compared with it. It was the church that Christ died for because He loved it so dearly.

If a man is born of God he should take shelter in the Church, that it may be to him a nursing mother. To do so ought to be held not only the duty which it is, but also a glorious privilege. I have no sympathy with those people who stay out of the Church and simply throw stones at it and proclaim what it ought to be. If we can make it better, let us go in. Don't expect the Church of God upon earth to be without failings. If the Church is cold, go in and warm it up. Let us each do what we can to make it better. And then the Sunday school – let us make that better. Go out on the streets and get those children and teach them the words of life; that is the way to maintain good works. Bible societies should be maintained. Bible readings should be maintained – whatever the good work is, carefully maintain it.

If you have wealth, send that money around – use the Lord's money for the Lord. I hope to see the day when men will seek investments for the Lord, as they now seek them out for themselves. If a man has a few thousand dollars to invest for himself, how he seeks out the best investment! On this very ground why should not Christian men seek out investments for the Lord? I don't believe any other investments will bring in better dividends. Yes, I hope the time is coming more and more, when rich men will "carefully maintain good works." And to all I say, see that everything that is good is maintained. Cheer these young converts, do not be complaining, and be just as careful – every one of you, new converts and all – be just as careful to maintain good works as to accept Christ.

Now, look at the 2nd epistle to the Thessalonians, 2nd chapter and 17th verse: "Comfort your hearts and stablish you in every good word and work." Now, what we want is to get "stablished," to have a settled plan or method of doing good works. I have been a superintendent of Sunday schools for some years and noticed this: that teachers who swung around from place to place, who took in Dr. Kittredge's church, then the First Methodist, and then this, and then that have always proved failures. Now, I like these men that take hold of classes and don't give them up, who are in their regular pews every Sunday and are not drawn away by some eloquent preacher – some preacher from abroad who happens to be filling a Southside or Northside pulpit. Fifty-two Sundays in the year they are there. You know where to find them; they're right there at the accustomed post of duty. All the while their influence increases. But these teachers and others that are all the time running here and there never accomplish much.

A good many people are like a bundle of shavings – a spark falls, and quickly the shavings are all gone, and there's left scarcely any ashes even. My friends, ten thousand such Christians are not worth one that makes constancy his motto. We don't want any revival Christians – got enough of them; we don't want any Sunday Christians – got enough of them. What's wanted are these men "stablished" in good works, these men that hold on. A man that does one thing and one thing only is a terrible man. But the man who tries a hundred things fails at everything. If it is the Sunday school, if God calls me there, I will stand by my post. If God calls me to lead a cottage prayer meeting or read the Bible, I must win success there – I must hold on, and it won't be long before God will bring me success, for God has promised it: "You shall reap if you faint not." God will try you; you will have some things to discourage you, but you must hold on.

Next, please look at the 17th verse of the 3rd chapter of Colossians: "Whatsoever you do in word or deed, do all in the name of the Lord Jesus, giving thanks to God and the Father by Him." Don't work, as your highest motive, to advance the Centenary Methodist Church. Don't work for the Third Presbyterian Church, nor for the First Congregational Church. If a man goes to work to exclusively build up the Congregational, the Presbyterian, the Baptist, or the Episcopal Church, to build up exclusively any of the denominations, he is on the wrong path. It is not in the name of the church, but in the name of the Lord Jesus, that we are to do all things. If we do and suffer for Him, God will bless us. When we come to God and ask a blessing for Christ's sake, don't you see what a power we've secured? For Christ's sake! Jesus as our advocate!

In Detroit, at an international convention of the Young Men's Christian Association, Judge Olds was present as a delegate from Columbus. One evening he was telling about the mighty power that Christians summon to their aid in this petition, "For Christ's sake!" "In Jesus's name!" He told a story that made a great impression on me. When the war came on, he said, his only son left for the army, and he became suddenly interested in soldiers. Every soldier that passed by brought his son to remembrance; he could see his son in him. He went to work for soldiers.

When a sick soldier came there to Columbus one day, so weak he couldn't walk, the judge took him in a carriage and got him into the Soldiers' Home. Soon he became President of the Soldiers' Home in Columbus and used to go down every day and spend hours in looking after those soldiers, and seeing that they had every comfort. He spent on them a great deal of time and a great deal of money. One day he said to his wife, "I'm giving too much time to these soldiers. I've got to stop it. There's an important case coming on in court, and I've got to attend to my own business." He said he went down to the office that morning resolved in future to let the soldiers alone. He went to his desk and then to writing. Pretty soon the door opened, and he saw a soldier hobble slowly in. He started at sight of him. The man was fumbling at something in his breast, and pretty soon he got out an old, soiled paper. The father saw it was his own son's writing.

"Dear Father, This young man belongs to my company. He has lost his leg and his health in defense of his country, and he is going home to his mother to die. If he calls on you, treat him kindly,

"For Charlie's Sake."

"For Charlie's sake." The moment he saw that, a pang went to his heart. He got up for a carriage, lifted the maimed soldier in, drove home, put him into Charlie's room, sent for the family physician, kept him in the family, and treated him like his own son. When the young soldier got well enough to go to the train to go home to his mother, he took him to the railway station, put him in the nicest, most comfortable place in the carriage, and sent him on his way home to his mother. "I did it," said the old judge, "for Charlie's sake." Now, whatsoever you do, my friends, do it for the Lord Jesus's sake. Do and ask everything in His name, in the name of Him "who loved us and gave himself for us."

And then again, lastly, be united. It is the greatest force of all to be of "one mind and one spirit." The boast of infidels has been, "Christianity has been all divided up." "Be," I beseech you, "of one mind and one spirit." If jealousy comes in among you, you cannot do great things. If one minister is used more than others, let us praise God for that; let us thank Him that He has given divers gifts to men, all contributing to the glory of His name. This work, then, won't stop, but will go on. How many battles in the last war were lost just through jealousy in the officers?

When I was in the South, they told me that they lost many and many a battle because jealousy got in among the generals. Just so, many battles are lost to God's people. All must be willing to do anything that God's work may go on. When Grant's army lay in front of Richmond after the Battle of the Wilderness, when he was first repulsed, one dark night he called his four leading commanders to consult with him. All advised him to retreat.

The next morning early, an orderly came dashing to the four commanders bringing word to advance in solid column without delay. That attack defeated the Southern column and what did it was the steady, irresistible advance in solid column. So let the advance be made in the army of Jesus. Be not hearers of the word any longer, but doers. Let everyone do what he can to carry on this work; gird on your armor for the fight.

I am told that after Napoleon's great wars, medals were struck off with a scene of battle on one side, and on the other the simple words, "I was there." And after Napoleon had died and years had gone by, those old veterans would bring out their medals, and talking about the battle, or the prowess of the great general, they would proudly tell how they were in the thickest of the fight – "I was there."

Oh, my friends, rush forward to the thickest of the fight, and by and by it will be your boast, "I was there, I had a hand in that fight." And by and by – still keeping up the warfare even in your gray hairs and tottering age – shall someone say of you, "He was a true soldier of the cross and fell from the walls of Zion with the trump of God in his hand and a shout of victory on his lips." May that be the end of every child of God here in this Tabernacle, in this city. May we die – not in the wilderness – may we die with the trump of God in our hands and with shouts of victory on our lips.

Farwell Hall, Chicago

Prayer Meeting Talks

Mr. Moody's First Public Prayer in the Chicago Tabernacle:

"Our Heavenly Father, we thank Thee for bringing us back to Chicago. We thank Thee for the privilege of again meeting friends, with many of whom we have labored these past twenty years. O God, the Holy Spirit, descend upon such as are still out of Thy fold, that yet they may come to the higher and better life; that yet they may come to themselves and come to Christ. And to such as are Thy children, O God, do Thou draw very near, that they may be revived by Thy work in our midst. Forgive our lukewarmness, forgive our coldness of heart, forgive our backsliding, forgive our want of faith. Oh, help us on this morning to take away this dreadful stone of unbelief; help us to roll it away, so that the dead may come forth.

May we be prejudiced against Thy work no longer. May we no more view Thee with narrow, sectarian vision, Thou God of all souls. Bless all Thy people of every name and strengthen them to work today for Thee as they have never worked before. And those men of God who stand in the pulpit and proclaim a precious Savior, may there be riches opened up to them abundantly, beyond what we can ask; may they preach with an unction from on high, and with a God-the-Holy-Ghost power – not with intellectual power so much as with Holy Spirit power, and may they be endued everywhere and always with power from on high. And pour out Thy grace upon those in the Sunday schools and pews as well as pulpit, and may the work of Christ be blessed today in all churches, and tomorrow at 12 o'clock, when we again come together to pray. Do Thou, O Christ, look down upon us, and may we know that a mighty work of Thine is now beginning. O Son of God, hear our cry and save our souls and to Thy name shall be the praise and the glory forever. Amen.

The Right Spirit.

When Abraham came into God's presence, it was on his face; and in all the other instances where the patriarchs and prophets came to God, they came to Him in the same way. David was on his face in the psalm. He'd been away from God. Here he was getting back again; they had at first to get back to God, and the blessing would come. Then the right spirit would come into them. They must have just a clean heart, then the blessing was theirs. Had they a right spirit? Had they got to where they could say, as the Psalmist did, that they had sinned against God and were waiting for forgiveness? They must be able to teach transgressors God's way. How could they teach the wicked God's way? They had to get the Holy Spirit, and then came the joy of God's salvation. If they would convert sinners, they must have this spirit. How should the world know God? The world wouldn't read the Bible, but what did the apostles say of Christians? They were known and read of all men. This was the way the world read God in them, read Christ in them. If he knew his own heart, it was to have God's Spirit. With it they could do all things; without it their work was as sounding brass and as a tinkling cymbal.

Over in the book of Nehemiah it was said that there was joy in the hearts and lives of God's children. There were too many long-faced Christians. They always seemed to him to be under the lash. They'd never got away from the law. They wanted more joy. They needed greater gladness in their lives. "Then will I teach transgressors the way, and sinners shall be converted unto thee." "Then." This is when God had restored to them the joy of His salvation. They didn't place enough stress on the word "then." It was the turning point in their work. This was what Chicago wanted.

A few hundred live Christians that had this spirit could do a mighty work. The king could have given a good many sheep if God had wanted them, but He didn't. The Lord didn't want his money. What does He say?

Why, to obey was better than sacrifice. This is what was wanted – obedience. The human heart didn't want to obey. They must have a broken and a contrite heart. An incident of an Illinois minister whose labors had been unblessed for a time was recited, and it was related how his heart had been broken by love through a little three-year-old daughter of his, and a revival in the church followed. So, here in Chicago, said Mr. Moody, before we can have any great blessing, or any blessing at all, the hearts of the people have got to be broken, and then the blessings will come.

Prayer.

We have for our subject this afternoon the wonderful prayer of the prophet Daniel. There is an impression abroad now that it has always been women and a few weak men who have prayed, but you can scarcely find a bolder or a wiser man than Daniel. He was Prime Minister of that great nation for a long while. He was a wiser ruler and had more influence than any other man living on earth, and yet he was a man of prayer and was not afraid to pray publicly. We are told that when Daniel was taken down to Babylon, the great king had a dream, and no man in his realm could interpret it. The king thought of his captive Daniel and brought him and asked him what it meant. The young man, if he had not believed in God's power, might have turned away. But he didn't. He boldly told Nebuchadnezzar what God had written there.

But not only was Daniel a praying man, but he had faith that God would answer his prayers. Some people pray enough, but do not have faith that the Lord will hear them. They are lukewarm. There are a good many people of this sort here today. Daniel spoke to God with every confidence of being answered. Look at him when he went down into the den of lions. Look how he prayed. Prayer was with everything he did. I think we would have a good deal better government in this country if our rulers prayed more. There would be a good many sneers at first, but the result would be a good government and a wise one.

This man believed in prophecies, too, and I can fancy how the old man's eyes opened on turning away back to Jeremiah's writing, seventy years before, and reading: "I will punish them; the young men shall die by the sword, their sons and their daughters shall die by famine," and then looking around him and seeing how all the words pronounced had been fulfilled. They disobeyed the Lord. When they were in Palestine, He said to His people that they must rest on the Sabbath day, but for 490 years they disobeyed God's command, and the Lord said, "If they won't do what I want them, I will make them." So he sent Nebuchadnezzar out after them, and he captured them and held them for 70 years. If they would not give the Lord this, He said He would take it. And so if we do not give up what God wants us to, He will not forgive us our sins, but keep us in bondage, and we will never hang our harps upon the willow or sing the songs of Zion.

I will just read: "We have sinned, and have committed iniquity, and have done wickedly, and have rebelled even by departing from Your precepts and from Your judgments.

"And now, O Lord our God, You have brought Your people forth out of the land of Egypt with a mighty hand, and have gotten renown as at this day, we have sinned; we have done wickedly.

"O Lord, according to all Your righteousness, I beseech You let Your anger and Your fury be turned away from the city of Jerusalem, your holy mountain, because for our sins and the iniquities of our fathers, Jerusalem and your people are become a reproach to all that are about us.

"Now, therefore, O, our God, hear the prayer of your servant and his supplications, and cause Your face to shine upon Your sanctuary that is desolate for the Lord's sake."

He had not Christ to pray to like us. Daniel asks, "for the Lord's sake." He lived on the other side of Christ and could not, like us, say, "for Christ's sake. Oh, what a power we have in prayer in Jesus. And he goes on:

"Oh Lord, incline Your ear and hear; open Your eyes and behold our desolation and the city which is called by Your name, for we do not present our supplication before You for our righteousness, but for Your great mercies.

"O Lord, hear; O Lord, forgive; hearken and do; defer not, for Your own sake, O my God; for Your city and Your people are called by Your name.

"And while I was speaking, and praying, and confessing my sin" –

Mark that – "And confessing my sin" –

– "And the sin of my people Israel, and presenting my supplication before the Lord my God for the holy mountain of my God.

"Yea, while I was speaking in prayer, even the man Gabriel, whom I had seen in the vision at the beginning, being caused to fly swiftly, touched me about the time of the evening oblation.

"And he informed me, and talked with me, and said, O Daniel, I am now come forth to give you skill and understanding."

Before he got off his knees, Daniel's message was answered. I don't know how far off heaven is, but the angel Gabriel, the messenger of God, came to him while he was praying. Think of that. Here was a man who could not look at God for the sins of his people, who only prayed earnestly, and before he was through his prayer was answered, and Gabriel appeared. We know of only three visits that Gabriel ever made. This one, when he came to bring God's people to the Promised Land. Daniel was told that God was able to do everything, and the messenger not only told him that the children of Israel were going to the Promised Land, but he let Daniel into the secret of the Messiah's coming. The second time he came to Zacharias. At first Zacharias doubted him, but he said, "I am he who sits in the presence of God." And then he came to the young maiden who bore the Christ, and that was the third visit.

There are a great many young Christians in Chicago who have got into the way of the world, who are falling into the way of thinking and believing that God has given over answering prayer. God answers prayers today as readily as He did of old. Infidels and scoffers and scientists may tell us that the world must move along in a certain way and a Divine answer to a prayer is absurd – the affairs of the world are and always have gone along in a regular way. There were infidels and scoffers, doubtless, in Babylon, who very likely laughed at this answer to the prayer of Daniel.

But we have in this book a long list of promises to answer prayer. Let us unite in asking God's blessing on our meetings in Farwell Hall and that the harvest of converts will be abundant. Ask it sincerely and earnestly, and you will see how quick the Lord will come and revive His work in this city.

Heart-Searching.

I want to speak to you about the two verses – 23rd and 24th – of the 109th Psalm. *"Search me, O God, and know my heart; try me and know my thoughts: and see if there be any wicked way in me, and lead me in the way ever lasting."* "Search me" – not my neighbor, nor my brother, nor my sister, but "search me." You who have been here during the week will have seen that I have been trying to instill into all the system of heart-searching; that everyone will go down to the bottom of his own heart. Try to get all to say, "O Lord, know my heart." If God searches us through He will make quick work of Chicago. The great trouble is that people search themselves and do not ask God's aid. We want to ask God to come to us with His searching power, that our hearts may be bared. What is it that keeps away from us this searching of our hearts? It is not the world, it is not the devil, for he has not the power. The only thing that keeps it from us is our own will, and the only thing that keeps the blessing of God back from Chicago is the people.

A great many of us wonder how it is that our prayers have done no good – how it is that they have gone no higher than our heads. The truth would be discovered, if we examined, that we are not living in communion with God. Some of us think we are in communion with God, but it is a false thought. A false hope is worse than no hope at all, because in it a man is at rest and happy, and cannot do any work. If we get that heart-searching, truly we will know just where we stand. We must not look at what people think of us, but what we look like in God's sight. Therefore, we must beware that we have only a false hope and ask God to give us the true searching power. If we falsely believe that we have it, may God take it from us today so that the work may be deep in Chicago. I have been praying all along that the work might be deeper here than anywhere else, but unless we get this searching power, we won't do much good.

I was out on my brother's farm a short time ago, and he was plowing. He could not go very deep, owing to the roots in the ground. So it is in Chicago – the roots have got to be taken out before our work can go on. Let the prayer of David, "Teach me, O Lord, and know my heart," sink deep into us. Let us pray that this hour may be a heart-searching time, and if our hope is a false one, let us be willing to give it up.

I have heard of a lady who would not attend our meetings when everything was pleasant. If I was ill with an incurable disease and called a doctor in, and he was to say, "Well, you are all right, you will soon be around again," although he knew I should die in thirty days, I shouldn't like him. But there are a great many people whom this would suit. Those people do not like to come here and listen to us telling them that their souls are sick and diseased and prescribing just what will cure them. It is better to know the truth, that unless we search those hearts of ours and take out the disease there is no hope for us. So let us pray, and let it be an honest prayer from us. "O God, search our hearts." And if, when you go home, you feel troubled, don't say that you won't come back to the meetings, but ask God for more searching power, and then you will be ready to work.

A doctor comes to a man who has broken his arm. The doctor feels around at first and he says, "Does that hurt you?" The man answers, "No." The physician goes a little higher and says, "Does that hurt you?" "No, it doesn't." But by and by he touches the broken part, and the man cries out, "Oh, that hurts me!" And so it is with God. He touches our broken spot and we don't like it.

Now, I have been thinking that there is a passage in Christ's sermon on the mount that might point out our hindrances in Chicago – "Therefore, if you bring your gift to the altar, and there remember that your brother has something against you, leave there your gift before the altar and go your way; first be reconciled to your brother, and then come and offer your gift." Now, I don't want you to think me personal, but I hope the Spirit of God may be present today to carry the truth to everyone who has a quarrel going on. I believe the difficulty with us is the trouble in the church: the strife, the dissension going on among the brethren. If you have come to the altar with a quarrel between you and your brother, leave there your gift and go out and be reconciled to him. If you have any malice or hatred against anyone, your prayers will go for nothing – they will go no higher than your head. I believe this is the reason there is so much work lost among us – that you have something against someone, or someone has something against you.

I knew of two brothers who had a quarrel – a regular Cain and Abel over again. The mother could not get them reconciled. She could not sleep. Her prayers went up night after night. One of the brothers saw how his mother felt and was sorry for her. To please her, he bought a very costly gift and took it to her. "I don't want any gift," she said. "I want you to be reconciled to your brother." If he had been reconciled first and then brought the gift to his mother, it would have been all right. So it is with God. You take your gifts to the altar and keep in your heart hatred toward your brother. God doesn't want your gift until you are reconciled.

Now think for a moment. Think of anyone who believes you are a hypocrite, anyone who says you are black-hearted, and anyone who does not believe in anything you say in the meetings. Go and seek him out and be reconciled to him. That is the gospel of the New Testament. "Oh!" you say, "he will not believe me – he with whom I have a quarrel will not forgive me." Go and speak kindly to him, show him a forgiving spirit yourself, and be reconciled to God. Tell him that you want his forgiveness – that you do not want him to stumble in the way of his salvation over you. I do not think of anything that would lift Chicago more than the fact of everyone here taking this truth to their hearts. We would make quick work with it.

There is a passage in the 11th chapter of Mark if I know it correctly. I hear it quoted very often in the prayers at the meetings, "Whatsoever you desire, when you pray, believe that you shall receive them and you shall have them." But they stop there and do not go on to the next verse, and they say, "God has not answered my prayer," when nothing comes from their supplication. They should read the next verse for the reason: "When you stand praying, forgive, if you have something against any, that your Father which is in heaven may forgive your trespasses. But if you do not forgive, neither will your Father which is in heaven forgive your trespasses."

When they pray, they want God to forgive them, but they are not willing to forgive others. Suppose I was a minister, and I had trouble with a brother, and some pretty hard words arose from the quarrel. Well, I get up and go to a man and pray with him. I find he has a great deal of trouble, and I say to him, "Won't you just cast your troubles on the Lord?" He says, "Well, the fact is, I have had a quarrel with a man, and I feel bitter toward him." Then I say, "Go and forgive the man and be reconciled toward him." But he asks me, "You had a quarrel with a man, did you go to him and forgive him?" So we cannot go to men and preach Christ if we have hard feelings ourselves for anybody. If there is any worker here today who has a quarrel with his brother, let him go at once and seek a reconciliation.

Let us have a heart-searching here today. Let us ask God's and our own efforts, so that the car of salvation will rush along in the city. I tried to reconcile two men who stood very high in the community who had a quarrel, and in their churches the wheels of the salvation car were clogged.

I said to one of them, "Don't you know that God is not going to bless your church as long as this quarrel is going on? Now I would like you to go that other man and say, 'If you think I have done you an injustice, I want you to forgive me.'" "Well," said he, "I don't know that I can put it in that way. I fear that I am a little to blame, and I don't think he would receive me." The other man said the same thing, but I just reasoned with them and got them together, and they were soon down on their knees, asking God to bless the church. It was pride that kept these two men separate and hindered the work of their churches, and whenever that was reached and cut out everything went on smoothly.

There are a great many things that have to be rooted out in Chicago before the work goes on prosperously. If there is any secret sin clustering around our hearth, we must draw that sin out before our work will be blessed by fruit.

Getting Ready

When I left the ministers yesterday, I turned to the 30th chapter of Chronicles. I had thought I had read it pretty thoroughly already but began to think about it and that circular, (the call for a Fast Day) and I found that there was just the same scene enacted 2,500 years ago in Jerusalem that was being gone over in Chicago today. Hezekiah had cleared the temple and invited all to come and worship. His father was one of the worst kings Jerusalem ever had. Not only did he set up images for worship in place of the Lord, but he closed the gates of the temple of Jerusalem to all religious services, burned the young children, and through his cruelty was a terror to all. And he was the descendant of David – Jerusalem's king.

When he died after reigning nearly sixteen years, his son Hezekiah took the throne. The very first thing he did, in the very first year, in the very first month, was to open the temple. It took him eight days to clean it from all its filth and uncleanness, and to thoroughly purge it. It would be a good thing to clean out a few of the churches of Chicago in the same way. Clean out the fairs, the shows, the lyceums, the concerts that are held there. "Ah!" some of you will say, "how are we going to pay our debts, set ourselves on our feet? It will be pretty hard to do this if we put out all our fairs." If there is going to be a revival, we must do this, and if there is a revival your debts will soon be paid. I think we have been working in the wrong way. We need more earnestness and fewer fairs.

It is said in the 36th verse of the 29th chapter of 2nd Chronicles that, "Hezekiah rejoiced, and all the people, that God had prepared the people, for the thing was done suddenly." God will work mightily when we get ready, but we must be completely ready. We are not all of one mind yet. Some say, "Why don't you open the inquiry room?" We are not ready. Let us wait for a month if necessary, but let us be ready. God can do more in a day than we can do in all time. And we must bear in mind that more attention must be given to getting ready. It goes on:

"And Hezekiah sent to all Israel and Judah, and wrote letters also to Ephraim and Manasseh that they should come to the house of the Lord at Jerusalem, to keep the passover unto the Lord God of Israel. For the King had taken counsel, and his princes, and all the congregation in Jerusalem, to keep the passover in the second month.

"For they could not keep it at that time, because the priests had not sanctified themselves…"

The ministers were not ready, neither were the people, for we read: "Neither had the people gathered themselves together to Jerusalem."

So it is with us. We don't see eye to eye, toe to toe, heart to heart; we don't run together like drops of water. But when we do, the Lord will come suddenly.

"And the thing pleased the King and all the congregation.

"So they established a decree to make proclamation throughout all Israel, from Beersheba even to Dan, that they should come to keep the passover unto the Lord God of Israel at Jerusalem: for they had not done it of a long time in such sort as it was written."

They had not kept the Word of the Lord. It was commanded – given in the law of Moses – that they should keep the passover. It had been neglected for a long time, and so posts were sent out to tell the people to come into the temple now:

"So the post went with the letters from the King and his princes throughout all Israel and Judah, and according to the commandment of the King, saying: You children of Israel, turn again unto the Lord God of Abraham, Isaac, and Israel, and he will return to the remnant of you that are escaped out of the hand of the kings of Assyria."

When the faith of this king was seen by the Lord, He turned His judgment from His people, and the sons and daughters of those who had been held in Assyria by reason of their transgression were invited to the sanctuary. And I thought when I read this chapter how the judgment of God for the last sixteen years had been turned against Chicago. Do you remember, about sixteen years ago, how the spirit seemed to be stirred within us? How when the war came, we gathered together and how earnestly we learned to pray? It seemed as if the war had done more in teaching us to pray than anything else.

But see how we have been afflicted since then. You know how after that, people – Sunday school teachers and all – got a few straws and dollars together, and then they became careless. They went out riding on Sunday, enjoyed the world after their fashion, and forgot God: how the fire came, swept away what they had, and then they said, "We have no time to think of Christ; we must go in and make what we have lost." And then the panic came and made us more worldly, and so we see how we have been turned off the path. No city has had such an experience, and yet it seems to me no city has had such blessings. We had great advantages.

Ten years ago, you had your theatres shut on Sundays. There was a law against this thing then. Ten years ago, the people used to go to church, but now they have their Sunday newspapers and their printed sermons, and they keep out of church. They read the polished sermons and criticize them. When people look for the qualification of a minister now, they say, "Oh, he's an orator." They don't look at his faith at all – don't ask if he has the Spirit of God. What we want is earnestness and faith in the sermons, and then their power will sweep through the whole North-west.

In the 9th verse we read: "For if you turn again unto the Lord, your brethren and your children shall find compassion before them that lead them captive, so that they shall come again into this land: for the Lord your God is gracious and merciful, and will not turn away his face from you, if you return unto him."

They were ground down by their captivity, but if they turned unto the Lord, they would find compassion. There may be fathers and mothers in this audience who have sons, now spending their time in the billiard saloons and drinking halls, who have been swept into this captivity by the letting down of our principles and morals. Oh, my God! Show us the way to come down to days of peace and purity and forgive our sins.

The posts were sent out all over the country with the proclamation to the people: "So the posts passed from city to city through the country of Ephraim and Manasseh, even unto Zebulon: but they laughed them to scorn, and mocked them."

And the people who saw the proclamation laughed at it. Ah, how many men in the Northwest, when they see our circular, will take it up and say, "What! A day of fasting and prayer; that kind of thing has gone by," and will treat it with scorn. Why, my friends, we don't need to go back 2,500 years to find people who will scoff at a proclamation of this kind. But thank God, they did not all mock. People came in crowds to Jerusalem to attend the services. Jerusalem was the center of that country, as Chicago is the center of the Northwest. All through Judea the hand of God was seen, and they assembled through its influence at Jerusalem to keep the feast of unleavened bread.

"And they arose and took away the altars that were in Jerusalem and all the altars for incense took they away and cast them into the brook Kidron."

By the king's faith they gathered there and smote the altars and broke the idols. Let us act like Hezekiah here. Let us lead the people by our faith into true worship. Let us be of one mind and spirit – eye to eye and heart to heart for God and see how quick the blessing will come.

Give God the Glory

They had been at these noon meetings for four days now, and it didn't often happen that they had such an opportunity for self-examination. They hadn't often had such a heart-moving and such an overturning of themselves. It should trouble them, this question should, why God didn't use Christians more. They'd had this thought before them all the week. Now, what was the motive they had? Was it God's glory or their own they were working for? Was it Christ's name or their own? The longer he lived the more he was convinced that the greatest enemy he had was spiritual pride. The soul that wasn't renewed had enough of pride, God knew. But when it came to the Christian, he had it too. It was spiritual pride. He wanted all this rubbish in the heart cleared away. They'd got to live in the power of God, and feel the truth of the hymn, "Oh, to be nothing!"

The subject he'd read, he said, was in the 10th chapter of 1st Corinthians, and at the 31st verse: *"Do all to the glory of God."* They'd got to get self out of the way. They'd got to feel just as the apostle did when he wrote this. Whatever they did had to be done to the glory of God. How quick God would come into their hearts when they got self out of the way. In another place Paul says that Christians are not to give this glory to men. They had got to empty themselves of self and come to Him. They weren't fountains, they're only channels the streams flowed through; they weren't light, but merely the pipes the gas came through.

John the Baptist was only "a voice" in the wilderness. And when Elijah was under the juniper tree he got to be jealous and wanted to die and said he wasn't any better than his father. It was the same with Jonah. He couldn't do anything until he let God use him just as He wanted to. It wasn't the glory of God he was seeking. They had got to get out of self, then it would be easy enough for God to use them. It seems strange that twelve men had been with Jesus for three whole years and yet hadn't got out of self. But they hadn't.

In the 9th chapter of Mark at the 31st verse we read that He told

His disciples that He'd have to be delivered into the hands of sinful men and be killed and then rise again on the third day. They could not understand Him and were afraid to ask Him. But a little further on, Mark says, when they got to Capernaum, Jesus asked His disciples why they disputed on the way. When they were silent, He told them that they'd been talking about who'd be the greatest. Then Jesus taught them humility. They were ashamed of themselves. This was why they did not speak when He asked them. He prayed God would make each one ashamed of himself. They might have an unholy ambition. It was their own glory, not Christ's, they were looking after and thinking of. "Who should be the greatest?" He put a little child where they could see it in their midst. Jesus wanted to show them their sin and folly. John wasn't humble enough and yet was the most loving. They might be jealous because they didn't belong to some clique or party. They shouldn't have any such feeling.

Then again, in the 10th chapter of Mark, at the 33rd verse, He had to reprove the same thing. He was on His way up to Jerusalem, Jesus was, now coming to the cross, and His heart was sorrowful. James and John came to Him in the midst of all this, and after He had been talking about His suffering – how He'd be killed and cast out – these two disciples nearest to him wanted to sit, the one on His right hand, the other on His left in the kingdom. This is what comes in the churches when there is strife among the brethren. And even at His death, in the 22nd chapter of Luke, 19th verse, when He was at the last supper, the disciples were again discussing who should be greatest.

Here we had it in a Baptist minister going across the way to see how a Methodist minister was getting on. He didn't thank God for the work; until they were ready to do that they wouldn't be vessels fit for the Master's use. They hadn't got deep enough yet. They must be emptied of self. God must show them the sins that clustered around their hearts. Could they rejoice when God blessed someone else? Then they had got down where God wanted them. If it was God's glory they were after, all will be willing to be nothing.

The Disciples' Prayer.

"After this manner therefore pray: Our Father which art in heaven, Hallowed be your name, Your kingdom come, Your will be done in earth, as it is in heaven. Give us this day our daily bread. And forgive us our debts, as we forgive our debtors. And lead us not into temptation, but deliver us from evil: For yours is the kingdom, and the power, and the glory, for ever. Amen." Each of you should ask yourself the question, "Can I pray this prayer?" This prayer has been called by a good many, "the Lord's prayer," but it wasn't; it was the disciples' prayer. The disciples had been with Jesus, and He was praying. And when He finished, they said to Him, "Teach us, Lord, how to pray." They didn't ask Him to teach them how to preach. Man knows how to do that, but they wanted to know how to pray. They'd all soon know how to preach if they only knew how to pray. I believe I speak the feelings of thousands of Christians who don't know what it is to pray.

"Teach us" should be the prayer of every Christian heart. If the disciples nearest Jesus needed to be taught how to pray, how much more do Christians today, as lukewarm as the church is now, need this spirit and teaching. What we need is heartfelt, heart-searching prayer. I have never been more impressed with the lesson than in the morning when I was reading over the chapter before the meeting.

In the 20th chapter of Matthew, at the 20th verse, it was said that the mother of James and John came to Jesus and asked Him that her two sons, Zebedee's children, might sit, the one on Christ's right hand, the other on His left, in His kingdom. And Jesus answered, "You know not what you ask. Are you able to drink of the cup that I shall drink of, and to be baptized with the baptism that I am baptized?" They say unto Him, "We are able. And He said unto them, You shall drink indeed of my cup, and be baptized with the baptism that I am baptized with; but to sit on My right hand and on My left, is not Mine to give, but it shall be given to them for whom it is prepared of My Father. And when the ten heard it they were moved with indignation against the two brethren." John was nearest Jesus, and yet, like the others, though he knew how to preach, he did not know how to pray. These words were uttered by Jesus in the evening of his ministry.

The mother of James and John came to Him with this prayer, but because it was prompted by a desire to be great in His kingdom, the Holy Spirit didn't put into her heart, and Jesus didn't answer it. The ten disciples when they heard it were indignant and jealous. There would have been trouble if Christ hadn't been there. Jesus then went on to speak about humility in Matthew 20:25 and said to His disciples that whosoever would be chief among them, let him be the servant. "Even," said Jesus, "as the Son of Man came not to be ministered unto, but to minister, and to give His life a ransom for many." In other words, Christ taught His disciples not to be ambitious in the ways of the world. Probably the mother of James and John wanted her sons to be made prime minister or chief secretary, or to be appointed to some high office in Christ's kingdom when it was established, as many thought it would be.

Christians today ought to pray and ask to be taught how to pray. In the 9th chapter of Luke it is related that when Jesus steadfastly set His face to go to Jerusalem, He sent on some of His disciples to a village of the Samaritans to make ready for Him. The people wouldn't receive Him because His face was as though He would go to Jerusalem. And when these same disciples saw it, they wanted Jesus to send down fire from heaven and destroy the village. But Christ rebuked them, and told them they didn't know of what manner of spirit they were, "For the Son of Man came not to destroy men's lives, but to save them." These disciples were closest to Christ, had been with Him all through His ministry, and yet even when it was about to close, they hadn't learned how to pray.

The Lord's prayer to His Father was given in the 17th chapter of John, but what was commonly called the Lord's prayer was the disciples' prayer, the one Jesus taught them. There was no difference between a disciple's prayer and a sinner's prayer. One spoke to God as, "Our Father," the other as the great God who ruled this world and all the worlds. The 1,800 years since Jesus taught His disciples how to pray had rolled away, but it hadn't been changed; it hadn't been improved. "Thy will be done." The ungodly man couldn't say that. The sinner's stumbling block is that he isn't willing to give up his will for God's. The ungodly man cannot forgive others, and so he can't ask God to forgive him. God's grace only can make man do this. Many men stumble over this prayer into perdition. Many say their prayers like the man who counts his beads – there's no soul in it.

Unanimity

At a meeting in Glasgow where a man said to him, "I have been at work in the inquiry room lately, but the work got into me last night, and there is a good deal of difference." So among those ministers who have come up here, in whom the work has entered. We will hear from them, whereas with those who are in the work only – well, we may never hear of them again. He rejoiced at the spirit of unanimity which he noticed during this session of the convention. He declared that he had not seen a Methodist, a Presbyterian, or an Episcopalian – they all seemed to be children of God. Oh, those miserable sectarian walls! May the great God knock them down.

Dwight L. Moody – A Brief Biography

Dwight Lyman Moody was born on February 5, 1837, in Northfield, Massachusetts. His father died when Dwight was only four years old, leaving his mother with nine children to care for. When Dwight was seventeen years old, he left for Boston to work as a salesman. A year later, he was led to Jesus Christ by Edward Kimball, Moody's Sunday school teacher. Moody soon left for Chicago and began teaching a Sunday school class of his own. By the time he was twenty-three, he had become a successful shoe salesman, earning $5,000 in only eight months, which was a lot of money for the middle of the nineteenth century. Having decided to follow Jesus, though, he left his career to engage in Christian work for only $300 a year.

D. L. Moody was not an ordained minister, but was an effective evangelist. He was once told by Henry Varley, a British evangelist, "Moody, the world has yet to see what God will do with a man fully consecrated to Him."

Moody later said, "By God's help, I aim to be that man."

It is estimated that during his lifetime, without the help of television or radio, Moody traveled more than one million miles, preached to more than one million people, and personally dealt with over seven hundred and fifty thousand individuals.

D. L. Moody died on December 22, 1899.

Moody once said, "Some day you will read in the papers that D. L. Moody, of East Northfield, is dead. Don't you believe a word of it! At that moment I shall be more alive than I am now. I shall have gone up higher, that is all – out of this old clay tenement into a house that is immortal; a body that death cannot touch, that sin cannot taint, a body fashioned like unto His glorious body. I was born of the flesh in 1837. I was born of the Spirit in 1856. That which is born of the flesh may die. That which is born of the Spirit will live forever."

Similar Updated Classics

The Way to God, by Dwight L. Moody

There is life in Christ. Rich, joyous, wonderful life. It is true that the Lord disciplines those whom He loves and that we are often tempted by the world and our enemy, the devil. But if we know how to go beyond that temptation to cling to the cross of Jesus Christ and keep our eyes on our Lord, our reward both here on earth and in heaven will be 100 times better than what this world has to offer.

This book is thorough. It brings to life the love of God, examines the state of the unsaved individual's soul, and analyzes what took place on the cross for our sins. *The Way to God* takes an honest look at our need to repent and follow Jesus, and gives hope for unending, joyous eternity in heaven.

Available where books are sold.

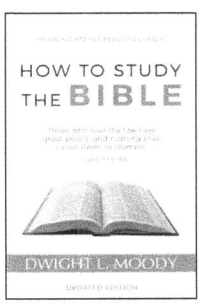

How to Study the Bible,
by Dwight L. Moody

There is no situation in life for which you cannot find some word of consolation in Scripture. If you are in affliction, if you are in adversity and trial, there is a promise for you. In joy and sorrow, in health and in sickness, in poverty and in riches, in every condition of life, God has a promise stored up in His Word for you.

This classic book by Dwight L. Moody brings to light the necessity of studying the Scriptures, presents methods which help stimulate excitement for the Scriptures, and offers tools to help you comprehend the difficult passages in the Scriptures. To live a victorious Christian life, you must read and understand what God is saying to you. Moody is a master of using stories to illustrate what he is saying, and you will be both inspired and convicted to pursue truth from the pages of God's Word.

Available where books are sold.

The Overcoming Life, **by Dwight L. Moody**

Are you an overcomer? Or, are you plagued by little sins that easily beset you? Even worse, are you failing in your Christian walk, but refuse to admit and address it? No Christian can afford to dismiss the call to be an overcomer. The earthly cost is minor; the eternal reward is beyond measure.

Dwight L. Moody is a master at unearthing what ails us. He uses stories and humor to bring to light the essential principles of successful Christian living. Each aspect of overcoming is looked at from a practical and understandable angle. The solution Moody presents for our problems is not religion, rules, or other outward corrections. Instead, he takes us to the heart of the matter and prescribes biblical, God-given remedies for every Christian's life. Get ready to embrace genuine victory for today, and joy for eternity.

Available where books are sold.

***A Life for Christ*, by Dwight L. Moody**

In the church today, we have everything buttoned up perfectly. The music is flawless, the sermon well-prepared and smoothly delivered, and the grounds meticulously kept. People come on time and go home on time. But a fundamental element is missing. The business of church has undermined the individual's need to truly live for Christ, so much so, that only a limited few are seeing their life impact the world.

Dwight L. Moody takes us deep into Scripture and paints a clear picture of what ought to be an individual's life for Christ. The call for each Christian is to become an active member in the body of Christ. The motive is love for the Lord and our neighbor. The result will be the salvation of men, women, and children everywhere.

Available where books are sold.

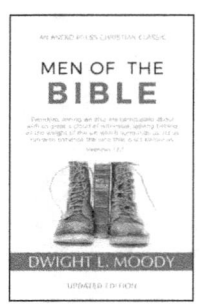

Men of the Bible, by Dwight L. Moody

When you wish to know something about godly living, where do you look? Is there a better place to look than to the men of the Bible? The Lord, in all His wisdom, left us with a wonderful textbook – the Holy Scriptures.

Some make the mistake of worshiping these heroes of the faith. Others make the mistake of only highlighting these men's weaknesses. Somewhere in the middle, though, is what God intended, and if our heart is right, we can learn all we need to know about healthy, rewarding Christian living from these incredible men of the Lord.

Available where books are sold.

The Ten Commandments,
by Dwight L. Moody

The ten commandments are not popular today. Atheists want them nowhere in sight. Many Christians say they are outdated. But Dwight L. Moody challenges us to take a closer look. Which of the ten commandments can we honestly say are not good? Which of the ten commandments can we break and not suffer the consequences, both here and in eternity?

This book will challenge you to examine God's rules for life. God doesn't ask anything of us that is difficult or unreasonable, and this is certainly true with Jesus Christ as our strength and the Holy Spirit to guide us. This book is a challenging yet refreshing look at some of the oldest, most well-known words of God.

Available where books are sold.

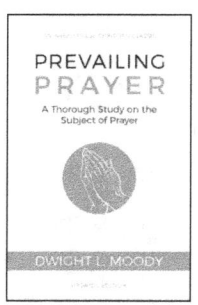

Prevailing Prayer, by Dwight L. Moody

This book is a comprehensive study on the subject of prayer, and will show you that there are nine elements which are essential to true prayer. These elements are as follows:

> Adoration, confession, restitution, thanksgiving, forgiveness, unity, faith, petition, and submission.

Dwight Moody expounds on these nine attributes in this volume, using illustrations and stories to validate what he is saying and to help make the truths in this book stick.

Available where books are sold.

Faithful to Christ, **by Charles H. Spurgeon**

I believe that many Christians get into a lot of trouble by not being honest in their convictions. For instance, if a person goes into a workshop, or a soldier into a barracks, and if he does not fly his flag from the beginning, it will be very difficult for him to run it up afterwards. But if he immediately and boldly lets them know, "I am a Christian, and there are certain things that I cannot do to please you, and certain other things that I cannot help doing even though they might displease you" – when that is clearly understood, after a while the peculiarity of the thing will be gone, and the person will be let alone.

– Charles H. Spurgeon

Available where books are sold.

www.ingramcontent.com/pod-product-compliance
Lightning Source LLC
Chambersburg PA
CBHW070123080526
44586CB00015B/1538